Rethinking Violence

States and Non-State Actors in Conflict

Erica Chenoweth and Adria Lawrence, editors

Belfer Center Studies in International Security

The MIT Press
Cambridge, Massachusetts
London, England

Library of Congress Cataloging-in-Publication Data

Rethinking violence : states and non-state actors in conflict /
edited by Erica Chenoweth and Adria Lawrence.
p. cm. — (Belfer Center studies in international security)
Includes bibliographical references and index.
ISBN 978-0-262-01420-5 (hardcover : alk. paper) — ISBN 978-0-262-51428-6 (pbk. : alk. paper) 1. Conflict management. 2. Ethnic conflict—Prevention. 3. Political violence—Prevention. 4. Forced migration. 5. War—Moral and ethical aspects. I. Chenoweth, Erica, 1980– II. Lawrence, Adria, 1973– III. Belfer Center for Science and International Affairs.
JZ6374.R48 2010
303.6—dc22   2010003877

10 9 8 7 6 5 4 3 2 1

Rethinking Violence

The Belfer Center Studies in International Security book series is edited at the Belfer Center for Science and International Affairs at the Harvard Kennedy School of Government and is published by The MIT Press. The series publishes books on contemporary issues in international security policy, as well as their conceptual and historical foundations. Topics of particular interest to the series include the spread of weapons of mass destruction, internal conflict, the international effects of democracy and democratization, and U.S. defense policy.

A complete list of Belfer Center Studies appears at the back of this volume.

To our parents, to Allison and Matt, and to William Ian Chenoweth and Audrey Elena Kocher, in the hopes that they will know a less violent world.

Contents

Acknowledgments

This project would have been impossible without the help and support of numerous friends and colleagues. At the Belfer Center for Science and International Affairs at the Harvard Kennedy School, we are grateful to Steven Miller, Stephen Walt, Robert Rotberg, and Sean Lynn-Jones for their support of this project, as well as their incisive comments and their mentorship. The essays contained in this book were the product of a workshop called "Paths to Violence," hosted by the International Security Program and held at the Harvard Kennedy School in April 2008. Special thanks are due to Matthew Fuhrmann and Matthew Adam Kocher, both of whom attended the entire workshop and painstakingly reviewed the papers. Karen Motley has been a stellar editor. Without her, this book would not have been possible. We thank her for her efforts, efficiency, and good cheer. We also thank Nicholas Quah for assistance in preparing the index. Our cohort at the Belfer Center from 2007–2008 was an especially vibrant and engaging collection of scholars, and we are particularly grateful to Boaz Atzili, Emma Belcher, Jonathan Caverley, Erik Dahl, Ehud Eiran, Michal Ben-Josef Hirsch, Sarah Kreps, Matthew Kroenig, and Phil Potter for their encouragement throughout the project. And, of course, without Susan Lynch, all of us would have been lost.

In addition, Chenoweth gratefully acknowledges her colleagues in the Government Department at Wesleyan University, whose friendship and support make life at Wesleyan a true joy. The International Center on Nonviolent Conflict has been a constant source of new ideas and opportunities, and she especially thanks Jack DuVall, Peter Ackerman, Hardy Merriman, and Stephen Zunes for their continued support of her work. She is especially grateful to Maria Stephan for their collaboration, and for giving her so many opportunities and so much encouragement to pursue interesting new questions. Chenoweth also thanks her mentors and colleagues at the University of Colorado. Jessica Teets, Orion Lewis, Michael Touchton, Helga Sverrisdottir, and Marilyn Averill remain great friends and colleagues, and Colin Dueck, Susan Clarke, Steve Chan, David Leblang, and Jennifer Fitzgerald all gave invaluable mentorship and advice that have carried her through all stages of her career. Chenoweth also gratefully acknowledges the University of California at Berkeley's Institute of International Studies, which provided resources and support for her research from 2007–2009, while she was a visiting fellow there. Finally, she has benefited from intellectual inspiration and motivation from the University of Maryland's National Consortium for the Study of Terrorism and Responses to Terrorism (START), and gratefully acknowledges the continued support of outstanding colleagues like Laura Dugan, Victor Asal, Kathie Smarick, Gary Ackerman, Gary LaFree, John Horgan, and Mia Bloom.

Lawrence wishes to thank her supportive colleagues at Yale University, particularly Thad Dunning, William Foltz, Stathis Kalyvas, Ellen Lust, Ana L. De La O, Ian Shapiro, Susan Stokes, and Elisabeth Wood for their excellent advice and comments on this project. Her research on nationalism and violence got its start in the stimulating intellectual environment at the University of Chicago. She would like to thank her cohort and advisers there for their ideas, feedback, and support, especially Bethany Albertson, H. Zeynep Bulutgil, Anne Holthoefer, Jenna Jordan, Charles Lipson, John Mearsheimer, Michelle Murray, Emily Nacol, Robert Pape, Keven Ruby, John Schuessler, Frank Smith, and Lisa Wedeen. Lawrence also gratefully acknowledges her colleagues at the Olin Institute for Strategic Studies, which provided support for this project from 2006–2007. She would also like to thank participants in workshops at Harvard University, Yale University, and MIT, particularly David Cunningham, Harris Mylonas, Roger Petersen, and Jonah Schulhofer-Wohl.

Last, but certainly not least, we wish to express our gratitude to our families. Lawrence thanks her family for their friendship, love, and support. Chenoweth's family, all of whom are musicians, have given her an appreciation for the qualities of discipline, a striving for excellence, artistic expression, and the willingness to "think big." Their contributions have made the world a more beautiful place to live, and their loving and unconditional support has made it easier for her to pursue her own professional aspirations. Chenoweth also acknowledges her other family—Kathe, Angi, Jon, Joyanna, Melody, Kathy and George, Tommy, Sarah, Scott, Rachel, Vic, and on and on—for showing her how to keep things in perspective and use her gifts for a better purpose. And finally, she thanks Allison for always believing in her and loving her no matter what.

Foreword

Internal Conflict and Political Violence: New Developments in Research

Stathis N. Kalyvas

It is no exaggeration to say that the study of internal conflict and political violence has undergone a remarkable boom during the past twenty years. This area of study—how order, conflict, and violence interact—has grown from a peripheral topic to a central concern for scholars of both comparative politics and international relations. What is more, economists, anthropologists, psychologists, historians, and sociologists have joined in the quest to better understand this set of political and social phenomena. While each of these disciplines and subfields continues to be characterized by its own methodological preferences, some of the best emerging work is characterized by questions and methods that cross traditional disciplinary and subdisciplinary divides and synthesize insights from multiple fields. It is worth taking a step back and asking about the explosion of interest in civil conflict. I believe that it reflects the convergence of three distinct political developments.

The first one is a rather delayed effect of the realization that interstate conflict has become an increasingly uncommon occurrence—and is likely to remain so. The end of World War II and the institutionalization of territorial nationalism into a fundamental component of international politics spelled the end of wars of conquest, even where ethnic minority issues remained unresolved and, thus, a source of intra- and inter-state friction. At the same time, the invention of nuclear weapons has made Great Power war obsolete. As a result, a previously residual type of war turned into the main, if not the only, war actually fought: civil war. Studying war now calls for taking internal conflict seriously—a hard lesson for scholars hardwired to assume state unity and dismiss non-state actors as secondary.

The second development is associated with the end of the Cold War. By disconnecting internal conflict from superpower competition, this momentous political development persuaded scholars of comparative politics that civil wars were fully legitimate domestic phenomena and, therefore, worth incorporating into the study of comparative politics. The difficulty here consisted in engaging the messy world of militarized conflict, in which the rules of the game were both less familiar to scholars of comparative politics and harder to discern compared to those of peaceful internal political processes, whether democratic or autocratic.

The third development consisted of the realization by political economists that internal conflict was a major impediment to economic development. This realization, also greatly conditioned by the end of the Cold War, convinced economists that they had to take internal political conflict seriously if they were to understand and tackle the obstacles to economic development.

In sum, the decline of interstate war led international relations scholars to focus their attention much more on civil wars, just when the end of the Cold War convinced both comparative politics researchers and development economists that civil wars were domestic processes with important political and economic repercussions. The advent of the wars in Afghanistan and Iraq, on the eve of the twenty-first century, reinforced this development by injecting into it a higher dose of political salience.

Naturally, this development has not occurred without growing pains. International relations scholars often conceptualize non-state political factions involved in civil wars as monolithic actors akin to states writ small. In the process, ethnic groups have been reified as political actors at the expense of a reality characterized by political organizations making more or less credible claims in the name of ethnic groups. Comparative politics scholars have tended to downgrade transnational and international factors affecting domestic political conflict, and have generally ignored the military dimension of these conflicts. Finally, economists have been prone to the temptation of caricaturing political institutions and dismissing the political dimensions of civil wars in favor of facile characterizations based on criminality.

Fortunately, an emerging generation of scholars is moving beyond these shortcomings. While building on existing research, they are able to overcome the divide between interstate and domestic politics, combine methods from several disciplines, and pay close attention to context and history. Overall, recent research is characterized by a key step: theoretical and empirical disaggregation on several dimensions:

• The disaggregation of space so as to focus on subnational and subregional variation, thus making possible a better understanding of the complexity inherent in these processes and generating data of higher quality.

• The disaggregation, or sequencing, of the temporal processes that precede, accompany, and follow violent conflict. In turn, this allows exploration of the sequence of polarization and violence, all too often assumed to causally precede each other.

• The disaggregation of levels of analysis and the recognition of the empirical interconnectedness of action at the micro, meso, and macro levels, as opposed to the unreflective imputation of motives and choices from one level onto the others.

• The disaggregation of the actors involved in the process, and especially the recognition that actors and dynamics internal to ethnic groups often drive the process of conflict between ethnic groups. This also makes it possible to recognize processes of interaction between local, national, and international actors.

- The disaggregation of violent conflict and the replacement of the dichotomous conceptualization of nonviolence/violence by one that recognizes a much wider space of strategic options available to actors.

Empirical and theoretical disaggregation has led us to a point where we are able to ask more clearly defined questions about the dynamics of conflict and to use more appropriate techniques to address them. For example, we have moved away from largely sterile debates about the primordial versus constructed nature of ethnic identities, or the greedy versus aggrieved motivations of rebel actors. Instead, we are moving toward formulating research questions that investigate the precise ways in which ethnicity is configured as political action and explore how exactly motivations interact with context.

Clearly, this is a research agenda that requires considerable methodological versatility, a commitment to problem-based rather than method-based research, a dedication to careful and in-depth empirical inquiry, and the ability to conceptualize categories in ways that are simultaneously theoretically sophisticated and empirically realistic. In many ways, this research bridges traditional area-studies research with new methods, and as such it is also moving us beyond obsolete methodological debates about qualitative versus quantitative methods. Seen from this perspective, *Rethinking Violence* is testament to the maturity of both the field and the disciplines within which this field is embedded.

Chapter 1

Introduction

Adria Lawrence and Erica Chenoweth

Recent years have seen the emergence of a growing subfield within political science that brings together scholars of international security, warfare, civil war, area studies, and comparative politics: the study of political violence. The increasing attention and resources devoted to studies of conflict and violence reflect, at least in part, profound changes in the international system. For much of the twentieth century, scholars of international security have focused on the behavior of states in the international system, and particularly on the eruption of wars between advanced states. Yet a decline in major wars, especially among industrialized democracies, has meant that the type of violence that predominates in the world today has altered.[1]

Modern interstate warfare differs from other kinds of political violence in many ways, not least because its practitioners at least purport to abide by certain conventions. One of these is the distinction between combatants and non-combatants. As Stathis Kalyvas writes, "modernity is inextricably linked with the attempt, however imperfect, to draw a line between combatants and civilians, thus limiting violence to the battlefield."[2] The task of warfare was delegated to professional armies who represent-

---

1.   For more on the decline of major war, see John Mueller, *The Remnants of War* (Ithaca, N.Y.: Cornell University Press, 2004); Meredith Reid Sarkees, Frank Wayman, and J. David Singer, "Inter-State, Intra-State, and Extra-State Wars: A Comprehensive Look at Their Distribution over Time, 1816–1997," *International Studies Quarterly*, Vol. 47, No. 1 (March 2003): pp. 49–70; Steve Chan, "In Search of a Democratic Peace: Problems and Promise," *Mershon International Studies Review*, Vol. 41, No. 1 (May 1997), pp. 59–91; Bruce Russett and Harvey Starr, "From Democratic Peace to Kantian Peace: Democracy and Conflict in the International System," in Manus Midlarsky, ed., *Handbook of War Studies II*, 2nd ed. (Ann Arbor: University of Michigan Press, 2000), pp. 93–128; Bruce Russett and John Oneal, *Triangulating Peace: Democracy, Interdependence, and International Organizations* (New York: W.W. Norton, 2001); and James Lee Ray, "A Lakatosian View of the Democratic Peace Research Program," in Colin Elman and Miriam Fendius Elman, eds., *Progress in International Relations Theory: Appraising the Field* (Cambridge, Mass.: MIT Press, 2003), pp. 205–243.

2.   Stathis N. Kalyvas, *The Logic of Violence in Civil War* (Cambridge: Cambridge University Press, 2006), p. 54.

ed populations that generally remained on the sidelines. Historians have suggested that attitudes about the use of violence changed between 1700 and the twenty-first century, "with a growing antipathy toward cruelty of all kinds" and attempts to limit the ubiquity of warfare in everyday life.[3]

This image of interstate warfare as a contest between states carried out via rival armies was never entirely accurate; civilian populations have been targeted with violence in interstate wars and have fought in irregular campaigns that accompanied conventional wars.[4] But conventional interstate war is characterized by the presence of armed forces attacking one another across established front lines.[5] And violence in conventional war is primarily the duty of disciplined, uniformed professionals acting on behalf of the state.

In the twenty-first century, much of the political violence that we witness looks quite different from conventional war. Collective violence no longer primarily concerns contests between the armies of major states, in which soldiers are the main violent actors. Instead, civilians are often the targets of violence, its practitioners, or both. Episodes of political violence pit the state against segments of the citizenry, often defined in religious, ethnic, and national terms. Non-state actors within states have in turn launched violent challenges to the state, attacking representatives of state power, state symbols, and state institutions, but typically seeking to avoid direct combat with state armies. Insurgents, terrorists, and rioters are thus unlike the trained, regimented forces of major wars, not simply because they are different kinds of actors, but because the very nature of warfare they employ differs. These types of violent conflicts are hardly new, but the reduction in the incidence of major, interstate warfare has served to turn scholars' attention to conflict among domestic actors and prompted a renewed interest in the study of unconventional conflict.[6]

Despite increasing scholarly attention, violence between states and non-state actors remains puzzling in several regards. First, states' ostensible *raison d'être* is to provide security and govern populations; it is star-

---

3.   See David Garland, *Punishment and Modern Society: A Study in Social Theory* (Chicago: University of Chicago Press, 1990), p. 232.

4.   On civilian targeting, see Alexander B. Downes, *Targeting Civilians in War* (Ithaca, N.Y.: Cornell University Press, 2008). For an example of civilian involvement in irregular warfare during wartime occupation, see Karma Nabulsi, *Traditions of War: Occupation, Resistance, and the Law* (Oxford: Oxford University Press, 1999).

5.   Kalyvas, *The Logic of Violence*, p. 67.

6.   See Stathis N. Kalyvas, Ian Shapiro, and Tarek Masoud, eds., *Order, Conflict, and Violence* (Cambridge: Cambridge University Press, 2008). This volume brings together scholars from different disciplines and sub-fields to address problems of global conflict, and Shapiro has suggested that the study of order, conflict, and violence constitutes a field in its own right.

tling if they instead choose to target civilian populations with violence.[7] Likewise, domestic actors who seek concessions from the state typically do not resort to violence; attacking the state is an extreme form of conflict. Yet, as many of our authors note, relatively little attention has been paid to understanding why erstwhile non-violent actors sometimes suddenly turn violent. Given that violence can drag on for years, be immensely destructive, and impose costs on the actors involved and on society in general, the move to abandon non-violent ways of resolving conflict in favor of violence is difficult to explain. Violence sometimes seems ineffective, raising the question of why actors would act violently even when violence does not appear to work. We need theories that elucidate the conditions under which violence in particular becomes the form that conflict takes.

This volume takes on these puzzles. Specifically, we investigate state violence against civilians and the use of violence by non-state actors against the state. Our contributors address two central questions. First, how, why, and when do states and non-state actors come to use violent strategies against one another? Second, how effective is this use of violence?

Rethinking Violence: Two Conceptual Moves

The scholarly literature on political violence has sought and proposed answers to these questions, but further progress, we argue, requires rethinking the way we study violence. To do so, this volume revisits some fundamental questions about violence: is violence a distinctive kind of conflict, or does it grow out of unresolved non-violent conflict? Under what conditions are peaceful strategies such as negotiation, popular protest, and accommodation replaced with violence?

In considering these questions, we make two conceptual innovations. The first is to disaggregate. Violence is often coded dichotomously, as either present or absent.[8] But treating violence as binary neglects the diver-

---

7. This understanding of the benign purpose of the state reflects one view of state behavior; for an alternative way to think about the state, see, among others, Charles Tilly, "War Making and State Making as Organized Crime," in Peter B. Evans, Dietrich Rueschemeyer, and Theda Skocpol, eds, *Bringing the State Back In* (Cambridge: Cambridge University Press, 1985), pp. 169–191.

8. The large-N literature on civil war, for instance, often codes a civil war as either present or absent, thereby failing to capture lower levels of violence that do not reach the threshold of civil war or alternative non-violent strategies of opposition. See, for instance, Paul Collier and Anke Hoeffler, "Greed and Grievance in Civil War," *World Bank Report* (2001); James D. Fearon and David D. Laitin, "Ethnicity, Insurgency, and Civil War," *American Political Science Review*, Vol. 97, No. 1 (2003), pp. 75–90; Lars-Erik Cederman and Luc Girardin, "Beyond Fractionalization: Mapping Ethnicity onto Nationalist Insurgencies," *American Political Science Review*, Vol. 101, No. 1 (2007), pp. 173–185. Some studies use a threshold of 1,000 battle deaths; see, for instance, Kristian Gleditsch, "A Revised List of Wars Between and Within Independent States, 1816–2002," *International Interactions*, Vol. 30, No. 3 (2004), pp. 231–262; Faten Ghosn, Glenn Palmer, and Stuart Bremer, "The MID3 Data Set, 1993–2001: Procedures, Coding Rules,

sity of options available to actors. The absence of violence, for instance, can characterize several different situations: it may indicate a complete absence of conflict, or it may mean that actors in conflict are utilizing any of a number of non-violent strategies to attain their objectives. Combining these situations into a single category (i.e., no violence) is problematic because they have different implications for our understanding of how violence begins; violence may replace non-violent strategies under particular conditions, or violence may erupt suddenly where conflict had previously been dormant. Although Charles Tilly has called for studies that examine both violent and non-violent action, in practice the study of violence is often separated from the study of non-violent strategies.[9] Overlooking the non-violent options that actors have at their disposal, however, results in a failure to consider how violence becomes appealing in the first place and why violence sometimes replaces non-violent strategies of contestation.

Just as the non-violent category can be unpacked, so too can violence itself be disaggregated. States can vary in the amount and kind of violence they use against civilian populations: they can deploy police forces to arrest or fire at demonstrators; they can indiscriminately attack population centers; they can ethnically cleanse populations through population exchanges; they can even commit genocide. Non-state actors can also employ different forms of violence to challenge the state, such as terrorism,

---

and Description," *Conflict Management and Peace Science*, Vol. 21 (2004), pp. 133–154; and Meredith Reid Sarkees, "The Correlates of War Data on War: An Update to 1997," *Conflict Management and Peace Science*, Vol. 18, No. 1 (2000), pp. 123–144. For a critique of the high battle death threshold for inclusion into the Correlates of War dataset, see Nils Petter Gledistch, Peter Wallensteen, Mikael Eriksson, Margareta Sollenberg, and Håvard Strand, "Armed Conflict 1946–2001: A New Dataset," *Journal of Peace Research*, Vol. 39, No. 5 (2002), Also, few statistical studies of terrorist attacks or terrorist group emergence nest terrorist activity within broader non-violent social movements. For an exception, see Erica Chenoweth, "Why Democracy Inadvertently Encourages Terrorism," unpublished manuscript.

9.   Charles Tilly, "Large-Scale Violence as Contentious Politics," in William Heitmeyer and John Hagan, eds., *Handbook of Research on Violence* (Boulder, Colo.: Westview, 2000). For an example of work that examines only violent action, see Michael E. Brown, ed., *The International Dimensions of Internal Conflict* (Cambridge: MIT Press, 1996), p. 2. This volume explicitly sets aside political disputes of a non-violent nature, although the authors indicate their interest in studying those that have the potential to escalate and generate sustained violence. Other scholars have collected data that codes protests without distinguishing between violent and non-violent events. See, for instance, Charles Lewis Taylor and Michael C. Hudson, *World Handbook of Political and Social Indicators II, 1948–1967: Annual Event Data*, Yale University, World Data Analysis Program. 2nd ICPSR ed., Ann Arbor, Mich: Inter-university Consortium for Political and Social Research, 1975. Exceptions include the Minorities at Risk Project (2005), College Park, Md.: Center for International Development and Conflict Management. Retrieved from http://www.cidcm.umd.edu/mar/ on September 15, 2008; Douglas Bond (2002), Integrated Data for Event Analysis. Retrieved from http://vranet.com/ IDEA/ on September 15, 2008; Doug Bond, J. Craig Jenkins, Charles L. Taylor, and Kurt Schock, "Mapping Mass Political Conflict and Civil Society: The Automated Development of Event Data," *Journal of Conflict Resolution*, Vol. 41, No. 4 (1997), pp. 553–579; Ronald A. Francisco, European Protest and Coercion Data, retrieved from http://web .ku.edu/ronfran/data/index.html on September 15, 2008.

suicide bombing, insurgency, and rioting. Scholars have studied these different types of violence, but often without considering why one type gets employed rather than another.[10] To take one example, in his influential study of suicide bombing, Robert Pape argues that organizations employ this strategy because it is effective. He supports this claim by suggesting that suicide terrorism works more often than it fails.[11] But he does not consider whether suicide terrorism is more or less effective than other violent or non-violent strategies that opposition groups might employ. Without an understanding of the relative effectiveness of suicide bombing compared with other strategies, it is difficult to sustain the argument that the strategy is chosen for its effectiveness. To fully grasp the causes of a turn to suicide bombing, we need to ask what other options were available and why suicide bombing became the tactic of choice.

The practice of treating violence as dichotomous hinders our understanding of its emergence, appeal, and effects. To develop compelling explanations for why particular contexts are conducive to violence, we need to consider the range of non-violent and violent options available to actors. The chapters in this volume begin to address this challenge by studying the alternatives available to actors and asking how they come to embrace specific strategies.

The second conceptual move we make in this volume is to consider the dynamic nature of violent conflicts and reflect on the conditions that lead to the eruption of violence at particular moments in time. The tendency in the literature is to compare non-violent and violent places, and identify differences between them.[12] Variables commonly used, such as

---

10.   For examples of recent work on terrorism, see Martha Crenshaw, "The Causes of Terrorism," in Catherine Besteman, ed., *Violence: A Reader* (New York: New York University Press, 2002); Bruce Hoffman, *Inside Terrorism*, 2nd ed. (New York: Columbia University Press, 2006); Walter Enders and Todd Sandler, *The Political Economy of Terrorism* (New York: Cambridge University Press, 2006); Andrew Kydd and Barbara F. Walter, "The Strategies of Terrorism," *International Security*, Vol. 31, No. 1 (Summer 2006), pp. 49–80; Max Abrahms, "Why Terrorism Does Not Work," *International Security*, Vol. 31, No. 2 (Fall 2006), pp. 42–78; and Max Abrahms, "What Terrorists Really Want: Terrorist Motives and Counterterrorist Strategy," *International Security*, Vol. 32, No. 4 (Spring 2008), pp. 78–105. For examples on insurgency, see Fearon and Laitin, "Ethnicity and Insurgency"; Nicholas Sambanis, "A Review of Recent Advances and Future Directions in the Literature on Civil War," *Defense and Peace Economics*, Vol. 13, No. 2 (June 2002), pp. 215–243; Kalyvas, *The Logic of Violence*; and Jeremy M. Weinstein, *Inside Rebellion: The Politics of Insurgent Violence* (New York: Cambridge University Press, 2007). For examples of studies of riots, see Donald L. Horowitz, *The Deadly Ethnic Riot* (Berkeley: University of California Press, 2001); Ashutosh Varshney, *Ethnic Conflict and Civil Life: Hindus and Muslims in India* (New Haven, Conn.: Yale University Press, 2003); and Steven I. Wilkinson, *Votes and Violence: Electoral Competition and Ethnic Riots in India* (Cambridge: Cambridge University Press, 2004).

11.   Robert A. Pape, *Dying to Win: The Strategic Logic of Suicide Terrorism* (New York: Random House, 2005). For alternative explanations of suicide bombing, see Mia Bloom, *Dying to Kill: The Allure of Suicide Terror* (New York: Columbia University Press, 2005); Diego Gambetta, ed., *Making Sense of Suicide Missions* (Oxford: Oxford University Press, 2006).

12.   Even studies of civil war onset that employ panel datasets, such as Fearon and

regime type and mountainous terrain, are often relatively static and therefore unable to account for changes over time.[13]   As a result, we know less about the triggers of violence than we know about the broad structural factors that make a place more likely in general to experience violence.[14] As James Rule put it, "we know a lot of things that are true about civil violence, but we do not know when they are going to be true."[15]

Any explanation for the eruption of violence requires consideration of what preceded violence. Case studies and histories of particular conflicts are far better at discussing the events that lead up to an outbreak of violence, but they can be subject to inferential biases if the method of identifying triggers is to look backward from a particular episode of violence and seize upon preceding events as the likely causes of violence. Investigating variation over both time *and* place is essential for understanding why violence begins. The chapters in this volume examine the conditions that trigger the onset of violence.

Studies of Violence

The scholarly literature on collective violence includes studies of contentious action, riots, repression, civil wars, ethnic conflict, revolutions, rebellion, interstate war, and genocide carried out by scholars in diverse fields, such as history, political science, sociology, anthropology, and policy analysis. Attempting to characterize all the relevant arguments that have been made to explain violence here would surely result in an incomplete and unsatisfying summary of an extensive body of knowledge. This section instead aims to identify some of the most prominent explanations in circulation—those that influence policymakers and ongoing scholarship—and point to some of their explanatory strengths and weaknesses. Specifically, we focus on explanations centered on state weakness, ethnic and national differences, state authoritarianism, and the role of elite manipulation.

Laitin, "Ethnicity, Insurgency, and Civil War," or Collier and Hoeffler, "Greed and Grievance," have little to say about when violence will begin, focusing instead on variables more suitable for explaining cross-sectional variation than temporal variation.

13. Theories based on changes in regime type are not static; here we are referring to theories that see a particular type of regime as generally more prone to violence.

14. On the importance of developing explanations that account for the timing of violence, See Michael E. Brown, "Introduction," in Brown, ed., *The International Dimensions of Internal Conflict*, p. 22; and Rui J.P. de Figueiredo, Jr. and Barry R. Weingast, "The Rationality of Fear: Political Opportunism and Ethnic Conflict" in Barbara F. Walter and Jack Snyder, eds., *Civil Wars, Insecurity, and Intervention* (New York: Columbia University Press, 1999), pp. 261–302.

15. Rule is quoted in Brown, "Introduction," p. 22.

STATE WEAKNESS

A number of leading studies have linked state weakness to a rise in intra-state violence.[16] The empirical finding appears fairly robust: weak, poor, underdeveloped states are far more likely to experience violence than wealthier states.[17] The causal logic underpinning the finding is, however, less clear. Fearon and Laitin argue that weakened state capacity facilitates insurgency in a number of different ways, but specifying just what aspects of state capacity prompt a turn to violence is quite difficult.[18] Rotberg notes that no single indicator of weakness can explain a state's descent into failure and violent conflict.[19]

Several scholars have suggested mechanisms to link state weakness to the onset of violence. Lake and Rothchild argue that when state weakness leads states to lose their ability to arbitrate between groups or provide guarantees of protection, collective fears of the future prompt ethnic violence.[20] Fearon posits a similar logic, but using a rationalist calculus; he argues that when groups find themselves without a third party—the state, which can credibly guarantee agreements—their commitment to peace is less credible and violence ensues.[21] Posen argues that when the state is weakened and conditions akin to anarchy exist, ethnic groups face a security dilemma: the actions they take to ensure their own security threaten others, and ethnic violence results.[22] These arguments serve to connect state weakness to the very specific outcome of violence, particularly ethnic violence, and suggest how the state affects domestic actors within it.

But there is a mismatch between these arguments and the empirical record. The state, rather than being absent and unable to serve as a secu-

---

16. See Fearon and Laitin, "Ethnicity, Insurgency, and Civil War"; and Rogers Brubaker and David D. Laitin, "Ethnic and Nationalist Violence," *Annual Review of Sociology*, Vol. 24 (August 1998), as well as the essays in I. William Zartman, ed. *Collapsed States: The Disintegration and Restoration of Legitimate Authority* (Boulder, Colo.: Lynne Rienner, 1995); and Robert I. Rotberg, ed., *When States Fail: Causes and Consequences* (Princeton, N.J.: Princeton University Press, 2004).

17. For a review of the quantitative findings in the civil war literature, see Nicholas Sambanis, "A Review of Recent Advances and Future Directions in the Literature on Civil War."

18. For an empirical and theoretical critique of the state capacity argument, see Matthew Adam Kocher, "Insurgency, State Capacity, and the Rural Basis of Civil War," paper presented at the Program on Order, Conflict, and Violence, Yale University, October 31, 2007. He argues that by defining state capacity in terms of the factors thought to hamper violence, the argument ends up with little explanatory power.

19. Robert I. Rotberg, "The Failure and Collapse of Nation-States: Breakdown, Prevention, and Repair," in Rotberg, ed., *When States Fail*, p. 25.

20. David A. Lake and Donald Rothchild, "Spreading Fear: The Genesis of Transnational Ethnic Conflict," in Lake and Rothchild, eds., *The International Spread of Ethnic Conflict* (Princeton, N.J.: Princeton University Press, 1998), p. 4.

21. James D. Fearon, "Commitment Problems and the Spread of Ethnic Conflict," in Lake and Rothchild, eds., *The International Spread of Ethnic Conflict*, pp. 108–109.

22. Barry R. Posen, "The Security Dilemma and Ethnic Conflict," *Survival*, Vol. 35, No. 1 (Spring 1993), pp. 27–47.

rity guarantor, is often an active participant in violence. The state may not serve as a referee between ethnic groups even when it is capable of doing so, but may take sides or even initiate ethnic violence. The essays in the first half of this volume investigate state violence against civilians and minority groups. These essays do not depict a neutral state, but one that under certain circumstances attacks civilians and combatants inside and outside its borders.

The relationship between state weakness and violence needs to be taken seriously; it is one of the few empirical regularities that has been documented through a variety of different kinds of evidence and tests. Yet the correlation between state weakness and violence does not constitute a causal story. State weakness is an incomplete explanation for two reasons. First, state weakness, measured in a variety of ways, is not a sufficient explanation for violence, because many weak states do not slip into state failure and violence.[23] State weakness is also not necessary for violence, because strong states do occasionally experience violence, albeit at lower rates. Second, state weakness is often an enduring condition, while violence may erupt sporadically or only at a certain point in time. It is difficult to rely on state weakness to explain why violence erupts at particular times.[24] Where the state experiences a sudden shock and descends into weakness, the argument may hold, but currently it is difficult to map changes in weakness to episodes of violence.[25] As Rotberg puts it:

Research on failed states is insufficiently advanced for precise tipping points to be provided. It is not yet correct to suggest that if GDP falls by X amount in a single year, if rulers dismiss judges, torture reporters, or abuse the human rights of their subjects by X, if soldiers occupy the state houses, or if civilian deaths rise by more than X per year, that the state in question will tip for sure from weak to failing to failed.[26]

Further work is needed to address just when and how state weakness produces violence.

ETHNIC AND NATIONAL DIFFERENCES

Explanations for violence based on ancient hatreds and immutable identities have been widely criticized in the literature on ethnic and nationalist violence. Yet, while primordial arguments have fallen out of scholarly favor, the view that ethnicity and nationalism play a role in violence

---

23. Rotberg, "The Failure and Collapse of Nation-States," p. 11.

24. See Adria Lawrence, "The Competitive Origins of Nationalist Violence," *International Security*, forthcoming.

25. See, for instance, the literature that links state crises to revolution by scholars such as Theda Skocpol, *States and Social Revolutions: A Comparative Analysis of France, Russia, and China* (Cambridge: Cambridge University Press, 1979); and Jeff Goodwin, *No Other Way Out: States and Revolutionary Moments, 1945–1991* (Cambridge: Cambridge University Press, 2001).

26. Rotberg, "The Failure and Collapse of Nation-States," p. 25. Note that Rotberg considers intrastate violence as a key factor distinguishing weak from failed states.

persists; something about ethnic and national identities seems, to many scholars and observers, to matter in the turn to violence.[27] Several of the authors cited above suggest that ethnicity plays a role in violence, as ethnic fears and violence are activated when the state stops regulating relations between groups.[28] The logic underpinning these arguments is that ethnic groups are prone to fighting, but they are typically constrained by the presence of a strong state.

Others have suggested alternative mechanisms linking ethnicity and nationalism to violence. Some have found that ethnic heterogeneity produces violence,[29] but the finding has come under critique from those who question the measurement used.[30] Ethnic and national differences alone may not produce violence, but where there are exclusionary policies based on these differences, violence may ensue.[31] Cederman and Girardin find that violence is more likely when the ruling ethnic group is a demographic minority.[32] Toft argues that violence occurs when an ethnic group is geographically concentrated and seeks sovereignty.[33] Alternatively, ethnicity and nationalism may simply generate more passion than other kinds of motivations, thus facilitating mobilization and violence.[34]

The sense that ethnic and national differences are linked to violence is fairly intuitive in an age in which ethnic and national cleavages are manifest in many conflicts. But the existing causal logics linking ethnicity and nationalism to violence face three potential challenges. First, existing explanations cannot explain why inter-communal relations are so often peaceful and cooperative; accounts that see ethnic and national differences as prone to prompting fear, resentment, and exclusion tend to over-predict

---

27. For a thoughtful discussion of what makes ethnic identities in particular distinctive, see Kanchan Chandra, "What is Ethnic Identity and Does it Matter?" *Annual Review of Political Science*, Vol. 9 (June 2006), pp. 397–424.

28. See particularly Lake and Rothchild, "Spreading Fear," and Posen, "The Security Dilemma."

29. Nicholas Sambanis, "Do Ethnic and Nonethnic Civil Wars Have the Same Causes?" *Journal of Conflict Resolution*, Vol. 45, No. 3 (June 2001), pp. 259–282.

30. Cederman and Girardin, "Beyond Fractionalization."

31. See Donald L. Horowitz, *Ethnic Groups in Conflict* (Berkeley: University of California Press, 1985). He distinguishes between groups that are hierarchically ranked and those that are not. See also Roger D. Petersen, *Understanding Ethnic Violence: Fear, Hatred, and Resentment in Twentieth-Century Eastern Europe* (Cambridge: Cambridge University Press, 2002), in which he argues that resentment of ethnic others can produce violence; and Ted Robert Gurr, *Minorities at Risk: A Global View of Ethnopolitical Conflicts* (Washington, D.C.: United States Institute of Peace, 1993).

32. Cederman and Girardin, "Beyond Fractionalization."

33. Monica Duffy Toft, *The Geography of Ethnic Violence* (Princeton, N.J.: Princeton University Press, 2003).

34. Stuart J. Kaufman, *Modern Hatreds: The Symbolic Politics of Ethnic War* (Ithaca, N.Y.: Cornell University Press, 2001); and Ashutosh Varshney, "Nationalism, Ethnic Conflict, and Rationality," *Perspectives on Politics*, Vol. 1, No. 1 (2003), p. 89.

the occurrence of violence.[35] Even where an ethnic group faces discrimination and domination, these conditions do not always produce violence and can be enduring features of the political landscape. Cederman and Girardin, for instance, qualify their finding that violence is more likely where the dominant group is a demographic minority by noting that this increased probability does not mean that all or even most such contexts experience violence. They suggest the need to go beyond their model "by separating those cases that feature actual ethnonationalist escalation from structural situations that are conducive to conflict."[36]

A second, related challenge is the inability of many of these arguments to account for temporal variation. Like regime type and geographical features, ethnic heterogeneity, settlement patterns, and historical conditions of inequality and discrimination are often fairly stable over time, and therefore tell us little about when we are likely to see violence begin. The only arguments able to provide predictions about timing are those that see violence following state collapse, but those arguments do not account for ethnic and nationalist violence that occurs when the state is intact.

A third challenge to these arguments can be developed from the literature that sees ethnic and national identities as constructed and malleable.[37] Accounts that link ethnic and national identities to violence may fail to consider that such identities are not always foremost in people's minds; people may identify themselves in other ways, and ethnicity and nationalism are not always salient. Ethnicity and nationalism may only become important as a result of conflict, not prior to it. For example, in this volume, Bulutgil investigates the role of ethnicity in producing ethnic cleansing, and argues that ethnic cleavages are not fully exogenous to violence, but are heightened in situations of war and conflict. In addition, Mylonas shows that states often seek to diminish internal ethnic differences by implementing policies of assimilation and accommodation, while enemy states often try to politicize such differences. Studies like these suggest the need to consider how ethnic and national differences come to be emphasized in the first place.

STATE AUTHORITARIANISM

The nature of state rule has been posited to affect the probability of violence in several different ways. First, regime type may matter for violence. Numerous studies have pointed to a relationship between semi-democra-

---

35. James D. Fearon and David D. Laitin, "Explaining Interethnic Cooperation," *American Political Science Review*, Vol. 90, No. 4 (December 1996), pp. 715–735. They find that ethnic groups very rarely engage in violent conflict.

36. Cederman and Girardin, "Beyond Fractionalization," p. 182.

37. For examples, see Benedict Anderson, *Imagined Communities: Reflections on the Origin and Spread of Nationalism* (London: Verso, 1983); Ronald Grigor Suny, *The Revenge of the Past: Nationalism, Revolution, and the Collapse of the Soviet Union* (Stanford: Stanford University Press, 1993); and Rogers Brubaker, *Nationalism Reframed: Nationhood and the National Question in the New Europe* (Cambridge: Cambridge University Press, 1996).

cies, dubbed "anocracies," and violence.[38] The logic is that in fully authoritarian regimes, political dissent is stifled, while in democracies, peaceful collective action is possible. It is thus in semi-democratic regimes, those caught between authoritarianism and democracy, that we see the most violence. In anocracies, peaceful collective action may be ineffective or restricted, leaving violence as the only way to demand change. Several large-N studies have shown a correlation between anocracies and civil war violence.[39] A 2008 study, however, has overturned this finding after correcting for problems in the measurement of anocracy used in prior studies; this study suggests that the anocracy finding may be due to the conflation of anocracy with already-existing political violence.[40]

A second possibility is that it may not be the type of regime that affects violence, but specifically its use of repression. There is no existing scholarly consensus on the relationship between repression and violence. State repression may quell violent consent, provoke it, or it may have a non-linear relationship with violence, meaning that violence is likely at intermediate levels of repression.[41]

---

38.   James DeNardo, *Power in Numbers* (Princeton, N.J.: Princeton University Press, 1985); Edward N. Muller, "Income Inequality, Regime Repressiveness, and Political Violence," *American Sociological Review*, Vol. 50, No. 1 (1985), pp. 47–61; Edward N. Muller and Mitchell A. Seligson, "Inequality and Insurgency," *American Political Science Review*, Vol. 81, No. 2 (June 1987), pp. 425–452; Edward N. Muller and Erich Weede, "Cross-National Variation in Political Violence," *Journal of Conflict Resolution*, Vol. 34, No. 4 (1990), pp. 624–651; Karl-Dieter Opp, "Repression and Revolutionary Action," *Rationality and Society*, Vol. 6, No. 1 (1994), pp. 101–138; and Patrick M. Regan and Errol A. Henderson, "Democracy, Threats and Political Repression in Developing Countries: Are Democracies Internally Less Violent?" *Third World Quarterly*, Vol. 23, No. 1 (February 2002), pp. 119–136.

39.   Fearon and Laitin, "Ethnicity, Insurgency, and Civil War," and Håvard Hegre, Tanja Ellingsen, Scott Gates, and Nils Petter Gleditsch, "Toward a Democratic Civil Peace? Democracy, Political Change, and Civil War, 1816–1992," *American Political Science Review*, Vol. 95, No 1 (March 2001), pp. 33–48.

40.   James Raymond Vreeland, "The Effect of Political Regime on Civil War: Unpacking Anocracy," *Journal of Conflict Resolution*, Vol. 52, No. 3 (June 2008), pp. 401–425.

41.   On repression and violence see, among many others: Stathis N. Kalyvas and Matthew Adam Kocher, "How Free is 'Free Riding' in Civil Wars? Violence, Insurgency, and the Collective Action Problem," *World Politics*, Vol. 59, No. 2 (January 2007), pp. 177–216; Douglas A. Hibbs, *Mass Political Violence: A Cross-national Causal Analysis* (New York: Wiley, 1973); Charles Tilly, *From Mobilization to Revolution* (New York: McGraw-Hill, 1978); Mark Irving Lichbach and Ted Robert Gurr, "The Conflict Process: A Formal Model," *Journal of Conflict Resolution*, Vol. 25, No. 1 (March 1981), pp. 3–29; Muller and Weede, "Cross-National Variation in Political Violence"; Will H. Moore, "Repression and Dissent: Substitution, Context, and Timing," *American Journal of Political Science*, Vol. 42, No. 3 (July 1998), pp. 851–873; and Jeff Goodwin, *No Other Way Out: States and Revolutionary Moments, 1945–1991* (Cambridge: Cambridge University Press, 2001). In this volume, Cunningham and Beaulieu consider how non-state actors respond to state repression, and argue that it is the consistency with which repression is used that affects non-state actors' choices to employ violent or non-violent tactics. Lawrence, however, cautions that repression may be too ubiquitous in some states to explain episodes of violence.

A third way that the nature of the state may affect violence stems from the quality of state rule. Particular kinds of states and state leaders may be more prone to using violence against civilians. Additionally, predatory states may provoke violent responses. For instance, states with a ruling elite that has historically dominated particular ethnic groups or classes may invite violent uprisings, a hypothesis that Lawrence and Pearlman consider in this volume. Hechter argues that states that rule directly over different nations within their borders may prompt nationalist rebellion, while indirect rule is more conducive to ruling diverse populations.[42] States themselves may initiate civil violence when it is in their interest to do so.[43] For example, in this volume, Bulutgil and Mylonas demonstrate that state policies toward ethnic groups depend upon the international environment, while Bakke suggests that relationships between elites within a state may affect the adoption of violence. These studies point to the need to consider the nature of the state and the quality of its rule as a variable, rather than a fixed state characteristic. Changes in state behavior, rather than particular classes of states, may better explain episodes of political violence.

ELITE MANIPULATION

A final set of important explanations for violence focuses on the role that elites play in instigating violence. A number of studies have suggested that elites may stir up mass sentiment, serve as first movers, and incite others to act violently.[44] According to Brown, for example, bad leaders are responsible for internal violence.[45] These kinds of explanations raise questions about just why masses are willing to follow elites and engage in violence. Fearon and Laitin consider a number of reasons why masses might be influenced by elite manipulation: masses might have limited access to other sources of information; they might discount elite roles and blame

---

42. Michael Hecter, *Containing Nationalism* (Oxford: Oxford University Press, 2000).

43. For example, see Steven I. Wilkinson, *Votes and Violence;* he argues that political parties sometimes seek to instigate riots to gain an electoral advantage. To take another example, in V.P. Gagnon, "Ethnic Nationalism and International Conflict: The Case of Serbia," *International Security*, Vol. 19, No. 3 (Winter 1994/1995), pp. 130–166, the author suggests that leaders in Serbia initiated violence to detract attention from other domestic problems.

44. Gagnon, "Ethnic Nationalism;" Lake and Rothchild, "Spreading Fear," p. 19; Varshney, "Nationalism, Ethnic Conflict, and Rationality," pp. 88–89; Wilkinson, *Votes and Violence;* Russell Hardin, *One for All: The Logic of Group Conflict* (Princeton, N.J.: Princeton University Press, 1995), chap. 6; James D. Fearon and David D. Laitin, "Violence and the Social Construction of Ethnic Identity," *International Organization*, Vol. 54, No. 4 (Autumn 2000), pp. 845–877.

45. Brown, *The International Dimensions of Internal Conflict*, p. 23. Mueller suggests an alternative logic; he maintains that ethnic violence is often carried out by thugs, not community leaders. These thugs then intimidate and coerce the population. John Mueller, "The Banality of Ethnic War," *International Security*, Vol. 25, No. 1 (Summer 2000), pp. 42–70.

ethnic and national others; or they might be convinced by elites that there is a security threat.[46]

Others maintain that elite manipulation cannot be the entire story. Varshney argues that while elites may be motivated by the desire for power, the masses must have good reasons to follow them, particularly when violent action entails risk. "For something to be manipulated by a leader when death, injury, or incarceration is a clear possibility, it must be valued as a good by a critical mass of people."[47] He once again comes back to the power of identity to mobilize, suggesting that elite manipulation can only work in combination with other commitments.

The argument that violence occurs when elites incite it appears capable of providing only a partial explanation for episodes of violence. Scholars have to consider why elite messages resonate, how elites are affected by other actors, and why elites seek to inflame their followers in particular times and places. Elites may continually wish for more power, but they may not always see violence as an effective means to gain it. Elite explanations thus work best in combination with other kinds of explanations.

This section has grouped explanations for violence into four major categories: state weakness, ethnic and national differences, state authoritarianism, and elite manipulation. Each set of explanations contributes toward our overall understanding of the kinds of places likely to see violence, but also raises further questions about how violence works. Drawing on these literatures, the studies in this volume posit new explanations for violence that challenge conventional wisdoms. The next section discusses the substantive contributions this volume makes to understanding violence.

Understanding Violence: A Balance of Power Approach

The chapters in this volume draw on empirical evidence from a variety of places and time periods: Northern Ireland, Palestine, the French Empire, Chechnya, Punjab, Eastern Europe, the Balkans, World War I and II, and the break-up of the Ottoman Empire, to name a few. The chapters are also methodologically diverse; our authors use field work, archival research, systematic quantitative tests, and case studies. Additionally, the authors approach the study of violence in analytically different ways; some see violence as a strategic choice made by actors rationally weighing their options; some suggest that violence is carried out by actors with a wide range of motivations and incentives; while others suggest that violence is a byproduct of other conflicts and processes. Surprisingly, despite these diverging approaches, methods, and evidence, there is a good deal of substantive consensus about how violence does and does not work. Specifically, the pieces in this volume challenge the conventional wisdom in the existing literature in three ways.

---

46.   Fearon and Laitin, "Violence and the Social Construction of Ethnic Identity."

47.   Varshney, "Nationalism, Ethnic Conflict, and Rationality," p. 89.

First, our contributors call into question the relationship between ethnicity, nationalism, and violence. The majority of the chapters deal with violent conflicts that have been defined in ethnic or national terms, meaning that ethnicity or nationality constitutes the main, most visible cleavage in the conflict. Many of the contributions address either the desire of ethnic and national groups for their own nation-states or state decisions to embrace or reject particular minority groups. This focus makes considerable sense for investigations of violence, since the establishment of new national states is a notoriously bloody process.[48] Despite the attention paid to conflicts that are explicitly ethnic and nationalist in nature, however, our contributors find little evidence that ethnic and national cleavages play a direct causal role in violence. Polarization along ethnic and national lines may be causally related to conflict in general, but does not explain the adoption of violence in particular.

Second, instead of finding support for explanations that link group-level attributes to violence, our contributors generally find that violence is a function of uncertainty and threat, either from outside the state or within it. For instance, a number of our contributors link states' decisions to employ violence to regional instability and interstate war.[49] For non-state actors, our contributors point to competition and uncertainty among elites at the domestic level as triggers of violence.[50] Taken together, these pieces suggest an alternative set of explanations for violence, which might be termed a *balance of power approach* to political violence. Scholars of the international system have long studied shifts in the international balance of power and the consequences of these for interstate war. The essays in this volume point to the importance that the international and domestic balance of power can have for domestic conflict.

Shifts in the balance of power can create conditions of uncertainty and affect the use of violence by civilians and against civilians. This approach resembles Posen's "Ethnic Security Dilemma," because he too considers the balance of power among ethnic groups, but there is an important difference: for Posen, the threat of violence always exists; in times of peace,

---

48.   Andreas Wimmer and Brian Min, "From Empire to Nation-State: Explaining Wars in the Modern World, 1816–2001," *American Sociological Review*, Vol. 71, No. 6 (December 2006), pp. 867–897.

49.   Bulutgil and Mylonas, for example, find that states seek to ethnically cleanse minority populations when those populations ally with rival states. Jenne argues that regional instability and states' geostrategic goals can lead to renewed conflict among ethnic groups and their respective kin states, even after ethnic populations have been partitioned. Downes and Cochran suggest that states at war turn to violent strategies against civilians because they fear defeat; they may wish to terrorize civilians and compel surrender in long wars of attrition, or they fear that civilians in conquered lands will turn against them.

50.   Specifically, Lawrence and Pearlman suggest that the interactions among non-state actors, and particularly competition among them, produces violence, while Bakke argues that deteriorating relationships among elites leads to violence. Cunningham and Beaulieu find that uncertainty about state responses leads minority groups to abandon peaceful strategies in favor of violence.

groups are just constrained from using violence by the state. The authors here suggest that the demand for ethnic violence is not pre-existing, but emerges endogenously from conflict. Changes in the international climate can affect states' perceptions of the loyalty of their own citizens, as Mylonas, Bulutgil, and Jenne show. Domestic power shifts among elite actors, such as the emergence of new leaders or the removal or repression of others, can produce uncertainty within groups that challenge the state and lead to the adoption of violence, as Lawrence, Bakke, Cunningham and Beaulieu, and Pearlman suggest. One of the primary conclusions from the authors in this volume is that intrastate political violence is often a function of interstate politics.[51] Interstate and domestic turmoil can disrupt the domestic balance of power and prompt intrastate violence.

This focus on power shifts reflects the authors' desire to build dynamic theories of violence that account for the eruption of violence at particular points in time. Studying moments at which existing power-holders change and domestic politics are disrupted can also help account for changes in the kinds of strategies actors employ; peaceful strategies make more sense in stable contexts than they do in highly uncertain ones. Additionally, uncertainty may prevent actors from coordinating their actions and lead to a proliferation of both violent and non-violent acts.

The third way that this volume challenges the conventional wisdom is by disputing the effectiveness of violence.[52] As Stephan and Chenoweth note, scholarly theories often implicitly assume that the most effective means of waging political struggle entail violence.[53] Kydd and Walter explicitly state that if actors choose to attack, "it must be because this improves their welfare."[54] The effectiveness of violence is often seen as a potential cause of violence; actors make estimates about how well violence will work in attaining their goals before adopting it. Yet the effectiveness of violence is a separate research question that cannot be assumed solely from observing actors' use of it.

---

51.   Gourevitch has likewise suggested that international factors can have significant effects on domestic political outcomes. Peter Gourevitch, "The Second Image Reversed: The International Sources of Domestic Politics," *International Organization*, Vol. 32, No. 4 (Autumn 1978), pp. 881–912.

52.   For example, Downes and Cochran provide reasons to be skeptical that attacking civilians helps states win wars. While they find that states who victimize civilians win at higher rates than those that do not, they point to other evidence that undermines the hypothesis and suggests that the effectiveness of civilian targeting is limited. Jenne argues that the violent policy of displacing and partitioning ethnic groups does little to prevent future conflict. Pearlman shows that Palestinians employed violence even when it was ineffective, and Chenoweth and Stephan lay out some potential advantages of peaceful strategies.

53.   Maria J. Stephan and Erica Chenoweth, "Why Civil Resistance Works: The Strategic Logic of Non-violent Political Conflict," *International Security*, Vol. 33, No. 1 (Summer 2008), p. 7.

54.   Andrew Kydd and Barbara F. Walter, "Sabotaging the Peace: The Politics of Extremist Violence," *International Organization*, Vol. 56, No. 2 (Spring 2002), p. 278.

Our study thus calls into question the argument that perceptions of the efficacy of violence contribute to its adoption. When violent strategies are sub-optimal, and other strategies would work better, there must be other reasons why actors embrace violence, unless we are to assume that actors typically misperceive the effectiveness of violence. Violence is often described as costly[55] (and therefore a sign of strong commitment), but it may be that other kinds of coercive strategies are even more costly. Non-violent protest, for example, may require resources that violent strategies do not. Actors may therefore turn to violence not out of effectiveness, but because they lack such support.

Understanding the effectiveness of particular uses of violence requires thinking through the relative effectiveness of alternatives. Actors can use a variety of methods to coerce their opponents, including both non-violent and violent methods. This volume thus suggests again the necessity of comparing different kinds of strategies, rather than conceptualizing violence as dichotomous. Theorizing violence as a choice to use violence or do nothing distorts both the ways that actors come to use violence and our understanding of how well violence works.

Organization of the Book

This volume is organized into two parts. Both parts consider the causes and effectiveness of violence. Part I studies state violence. The chapters in this section probe the use of violence against civilians; many of the chapters consider how states manage minority groups within their own borders. Part II investigates the use of violence by non-state actors. The chapters in this section largely focus on groups and organizations seeking greater autonomy; separatism and nationalism are a primary motivation for many of the non-state actors considered.

In Chapter 2, Alexander B. Downes and Kathryn McNabb Cochran examine the efficacy of state violence against civilians in the context of interstate war. Downes and Cochran take on a controversial and provocative topic—whether inflicting mass civilian casualties helps states win wars. Downes and Cochran find that states that inflict civilian casualties are more likely to be victorious. This correlation does not necessarily imply causation, however, and they argue that civilian victimization is often an outcome of victory rather than a cause.

In Chapters 3–5, H. Zeynep Bulutgil, Harris Mylonas, and Erin K. Jenne look closely at the micro-dynamics of state violence against civilians. Each of these chapters investigates state policies toward minorities by carefully examining ethnic dynamics in a particular region: the Balkans and Eastern Europe. In Chapter 3, Bulutgil argues that ethnic cleavages are not the main causes of state policies of ethnic cleansing, but rather that interstate relations determine how states will react to various ethnicities within their territories. Specifically, Bulutgil contends that ethnic cleans-

---

55. Lake and Rothchild, "Spreading Fear," p. 11.

ing is most likely to occur when interstate relations break down. She uses historical evidence to develop a theory that accounts for the rarity of ethnic cleansing in history.

In Chapter 4, Mylonas examines more peaceable alternatives to ethnic cleansing, and argues that states typically accommodate or assimilate minority groups. Using archival research, Mylonas concludes that a state's nation-building policy toward non-core groups is driven by both its foreign policy goals and its relations with other states. Exclusionary policies are therefore driven by geostrategic factors.

In Chapter 5, Jenne asks whether population transfers and the subsequent partitioning of ethnically different populations produces peaceful relationships between groups emerging from civil conflict. Jenne's findings echo those of Bulutgil and Mylonas: ethnic partition is not a determinant of stability; rather, ethnic conflict recurs when alignments between states and ethnic groups in other states shift due to geostrategic developments. Jenne's work calls into question the validity of partition theory, and suggests that interstate relations are most important in preventing recurring conflict.

In Chapter 6, Adria Lawrence considers whether violence should be understood as a degree of conflict or a specific form of conflict. Drawing on cases from the French Empire, she examines the claim that violence grows out of unresolved conflict and argues against the view that nationalist violence is a last resort against repressive occupying forces. She suggests instead that violence arises from competitive dynamics within nationalist movements.

Kathleen Gallagher Cunningham and Emily Beaulieu evaluate the effects of uncertainty on non-violent and violent protest in Chapter 7. Using empirical data on minority protests in Europe, Cunningham and Beaulieu argue that states send mixed signals to protestors by inconsistently applying repression and accommodation. Such mixed signals intensify uncertainty among protestors, who are likelier to take greater risks and adopt violence as a protest strategy in response to uncertainty about the state's resolve.

In Chapter 8, Wendy Pearlman explores the use of violent and non-violent action in the context of Arab anti-occupation activity in Palestine. She argues that the Palestinian case demonstrates a feature common to many movements: actors are rarely unitary, but are made up of entities that often fail to act in concert with one another. She critiques the unitary actor assumption that characterizes many studies of violent action.

In Chapter 9, Kristin M. Bakke explains the onset of violence by comparing center-periphery relationships in federal states. Specifically, Bakke argues that the outbreak of violence is a response to souring relations between central and regional politicians. In this respect, Bakke addresses the timing and location of violence.

Taken together, Chapters 6 through 9 assert that violence often arises out of conditions of uncertainty and political competition among actors struggling for power within their states. Conflicts are often not unitary, and involve major factions who pursue their own interests. Intra-ethnic conflict is ubiquitous even in conflicts that are explicitly inter-ethnic. Like the authors in Part I, these studies suggest that the balance of power among actors, rather than ethnic antagonisms, matters for the eruption of violence.

The volume concludes with a chapter by Erica Chenoweth and Maria J. Stephan, which lays out a research agenda for future work. Chenoweth and Stephan question the utility of violence in the context of resistance campaigns. They argue that non-violent resistance is often more effective than violent resistance in obtaining strategic goals because non-violent campaigns are better able to galvanize mass participation, which provides multiple strategic advantages throughout the course of the conflict. They identify a number of hypotheses that call into question the utility of violence for non-state actors.

Conclusion

The way we think about violence matters for the kinds of explanations we build and the kinds of policies that we recommend to contain it. This volume advocates three critical ways of rethinking violence to advance our understanding of the causes and consequences of political violence. First, rather than conceptualizing violence as dichotomous, either present or absent, we point to the need to unpack the concept and consider the variety of actions that are all too often subsumed under "0" or "1" categorizations of violence. In so doing, we can develop better explanations for why we see particular kinds of opposition. Moreover, by considering both peaceful and violent strategies in the same analytic field, we can better understand the conditions that make non-violence appealing and provide policymakers with ways to encourage non-violent over violent opposition.

Second, we highlight the importance of considering the dynamic nature of violent action: its eruption at particular moments in time. By thinking through the temporal variation in violence, we move closer to developing theories of the proximate causes of violence. A focus on the triggers of violence rather than the broad structural factors that make some places more susceptible to violence is helpful not only because it moves us closer to uncovering the factors that prompt particular forms of violent and non-violent action, but also because proximate causes may be easier to for policymakers to recognize and address. It is very difficult to act upon structural factors such as poverty and state weakness, which are sadly ubiquitous in much of the world. A better understanding of how violence emerges over time may suggest recognizable trigger points that serve as warnings of imminent violence.

Finally, the works in this volume stress once more the importance of considering multiple levels of analysis when exploring the causes and effects of violence and its alternatives. Our authors find that interstate relations have major consequences for intrastate stability. Thus we point to linkages between work in comparative politics and international relations, and advocate considering the interaction between domestic and international conditions in predicting and preventing political violence.

Part I
Rethinking State Violence

Chapter 2

Targeting Civilians to Win? Assessing the Military Effectiveness of Civilian Victimization in Interstate War

Alexander B. Downes and
Kathryn McNabb Cochran

War, as Clausewitz argued long ago, is an act of violence in which actors attempt to impose their will on each other. Although Clausewitz depicted war as a duel on a larger scale that is most frequently won when one side or the other captures the enemy's capital or destroys its army in battle, the impact of war is rarely confined to the military sphere. Civilians sometimes suffer in wartime even when combatants do not intend to harm them. Epidemics of typhus and cholera have often followed in the wake of marching armies, and civilians fleeing from the battle area are subject to hunger and privation. Moreover, in many cases munitions meant for enemy combatants hit civilians instead, resulting in what we now euphemistically call "collateral damage." Finally, in certain instances belligerents set their sights on civilians on purpose, targeting them as a means to achieving their military or political goals in the war.

Unfortunately, this third type of violence against noncombatants is not uncommon. Various studies have found that states adopt strategies that target civilians or inflict mass killing on noncombatants (50,000 or more dead) in one-fifth to one-third of all wars.[1] Despite a fruitful literature that has arisen in the last decade to explain the causes of civilian targeting, the effectiveness of civilian victimization for achieving belligerents' war objectives remains an open question. Much of this new literature on the

Earlier versions of this chapter were presented at the International Studies Association annual meeting, San Francisco, Calif., March 26–29, 2008, and the Association for the Study of Nationalities annual meeting, New York, N.Y., April 10–12, 2008. For helpful comments and suggestions, the authors would like to thank Ana Arjona, Charli Carpenter, Erica Chenoweth, Matthew Fuhrmann, Matthew Kocher, Adria Lawrence, and Jason Lyall.

1. Ivan Arreguín-Toft, "How the Weak Win Wars: A Theory of Asymmetric Conflict," *International Security*, Vol. 26, No. 1 (Summer 2001), pp. 93–128, and Ivan Arreguín-Toft, *How the Weak Win Wars: A Theory of Asymmetric Conflict* (Cambridge: Cambridge University Press, 2005); Benjamin Valentino, Paul Huth, and Dylan Balch-Lindsay, "'Draining the Sea': Mass Killing and Guerrilla Warfare," *International Organization*, Vol. 58, No. 2 (April 2004), pp. 375–407; and Alexander B. Downes, "Desperate Times, Desperate Measures: The Causes of Civilian Victimization in War," *International Security*, Vol. 30, No. 4 (Spring 2006), pp. 152–195.

causes of civilian victimization suggests that war participants implement these strategies because they believe that targeting civilians will help them accomplish their military or political goals.[2] In some wars, for instance, national leaders adopt strategies of civilian victimization because they believe that targeting civilians will terrorize the enemy population into pressuring its government to concede. In other wars, leaders target civilians to enhance the likelihood of military victory by preventing the emergence of fifth columns that could aid their enemy on the battlefield. The logic of civilian victimization is different for each type of war, but each type of logic assumes that belligerents make a strategic choice to target civilians because leaders believe that doing so increases the likelihood that they will achieve their objectives. This begs the question: does killing civilians enable leaders to achieve their wartime goals? Is targeting noncombatants an effective military strategy?

The answer to this question is both policy-relevant and normatively important. Although war is never something to be undertaken lightly, and it has many other ill effects besides killing civilians, the death and destruction visited upon noncombatants is one of the worst consequences of armed conflict. Efforts to minimize the harm inflicted on non-participants in armed conflict have a long (if not always successful) pedigree, dating back to the Peace of God in the tenth century and culminating in today's formal international treaties. Furthermore, modern public opinion—not just in the United States, but in many countries around the world—opposes the targeting of civilians, and agrees that belligerents should go to great lengths to protect noncombatants from harm.[3] If civilian victimization rarely delivers tangible benefits in wartime, then there is not a conflict between strategy and morality because doing the morally correct thing—that is, avoiding harm to noncombatants—is also the strategically wise course of action. The "problem of dirty hands"—in which political leaders engage in immoral activity (such as torture) to prevent an even greater

2. See, for example, Stathis N. Kalyvas, "Wanton and Senseless? The Logic of Violence in Civil Wars," *Rationality and Society*, Vol. 11, No. 3 (August 1999), pp. 243–285; Stathis N. Kalyvas, "The Logic of Terrorism in Civil War," *Journal of Ethics*, Vol. 8, No. 1 (2004), pp. 98–137; Stathis N. Kalyvas, *The Logic of Violence in Civil War* (Cambridge: Cambridge University Press, 2006); Benjamin A. Valentino, *Final Solutions: Mass Killing and Genocide in the Twentieth Century* (Ithaca, N.Y.: Cornell University Press, 2004); Valentino, Huth, and Balch-Lindsay, "'Draining the Sea,'" and Benjamin Valentino, Paul Huth, and Sarah Croco, "Covenants without the Sword: International Law and the Protection of Civilians in Times of War," *World Politics*, Vol. 58, No. 3 (April 2006), pp. 339–377; Michael Mann, *The Dark Side of Democracy: Explaining Ethnic Cleansing* (Cambridge: Cambridge University Press, 2005); Jeremy Weinstein, *Inside Rebellion: The Politics of Insurgent Violence* (Cambridge: Cambridge University Press, 2006); and Downes, "Desperate Times, Desperate Measures"; Alexander B. Downes, "Restraint or Propellant? Democracy and Civilian Fatalities in Interstate Wars," *Journal of Conflict Resolution*, Vol. 51, No. 6 (December 2007), pp. 872–904, and Alexander B. Downes, *Targeting Civilians in War* (Ithaca, N.Y.: Cornell University Press, 2008).

3. Greenberg Research, *The People on War Report: ICRC Worldwide Consultation on the Rules of War* (Geneva: ICRC, 1999), p. 13, http://www.icrc.org/web/eng/siteeng0 .nsf/html/p0758.

evil (like a terrorist attack)—assumes that the immoral act can success-fully stop the evil from occurring.[4] If it cannot, then the problem of dirty hands washes away because dirtying them serves no purpose. Research that demonstrates the failure of civilian victimization to achieve military or political objectives could possibly persuade leaders who target civilians to forgo this strategy.

If, on the other hand, killing civilians is a war-winning strategy, the situation is far more difficult because morality and efficacy conflict. Even statesmen who would like to do the morally right thing and leave civil-ians alone will have incentives to target them because doing so increases the likelihood of victory. Killing noncombatants might also further oth-er goals that leaders have, such as reducing their own military losses or making territorial gains. The task for opponents of civilian victimization would similarly be harder: to convince leaders to abandon this strategy despite its military effectiveness. Scholars would need to focus their at-tention on why civilian victimization has not been even more common historically given its war-winning potential. Manipulating these factors might give policymakers better tools to convince warring states to eschew this strategy even if it is effective militarily.

The goal of this chapter is to explore whether civilian victimization in war helps or hinders the achievement of wartime objectives. We focus specifically on the impact that civilian targeting has on the likelihood of victory. We therefore define effectiveness as achieving a positive outcome in the war.[5] A second goal of the paper is to propose and investigate hy-potheses regarding the conditions under which targeting noncombatants might be more or less effective.[6] Effectiveness may vary depending on the type of war in which these strategies are employed. One might expect, for example, that a strategy of targeting civilians would be relatively ineffec-tive in protracted wars of attrition when both sides are fully mobilized, compared to wars intended to conquer and annex a slice of an adversary's territory. Effectiveness may also vary according to target characteristics such as regime type and state size. We use ordinal logit models to estimate the effect of civilian victimization on interstate war outcomes (win, lose, or draw) between 1816 and 2003. We follow up the statistical analysis by examining cases of civilian victimization to determine whether the cor-relations identified are in fact causal.

Our statistical analysis produces several interesting results. First, in the aggregate, and controlling for other determinants of victory in war,

---

4. Michael Walzer, "Political Action: The Problem of Dirty Hands," *Philosophy and Public Affairs*, Vol. 2, No. 2 (Winter 1973), pp. 160–180.

5. Other potential indicators of effectiveness that could be investigated include whether civilian victimization lowers a state's military casualties relative to those of its adversary (its loss-exchange ratio) or its civilian fatalities, or leads to shorter wars.

6. Many of these conditional hypotheses were originally outlined in Alexander B. Downes, "Hypotheses on the Effectiveness of Civilian Victimization in War," paper presented at the International Studies Association annual meeting, March 22–25, 2006, San Diego, Calif.

such as initiation, regime type, and relative capabilities, states that inflict civilian victimization on their opponents are significantly more likely to win the wars they fight. This positive correlation persists in both wars of attrition and wars of territorial annexation. Second, civilian victimization appears to have become much less effective as time has passed. In the more distant past, targeting civilians may have produced results, but in more recent times civilian victimization has not contributed to victory. Third, smaller states are more vulnerable to civilian victimization, as they are more likely to lose wars when their opponent employs a strategy of civilian targeting. Finally, contrary to expectations, civilian victimization does not work better against democracies.

A preliminary examination of the cases, however, suggests that the effect of civilian victimization on war outcomes is more ambiguous. In wars of territorial annexation, for example, we argue that inferring that civilian victimization is a cause of victory may be problematic because states have to be "winning"—advancing and taking enemy territory—in order to target civilians. In wars of attrition, on the other hand, an examination of the cases strongly suggests that civilian victimization is effective only against small targets in particular campaigns—such as sieges of cities—already facing dire military circumstances. When employed against entire states from the outside-in, the strategy appears to have a poor record. Despite the statistical finding, in other words, case evidence indicates that the relationship between civilian victimization and victory is endogenous (in the case of territorial annexation) or contingent upon the effect of another variable (in wars of attrition).

The chapter unfolds as follows. In the first two sections, we survey the literature on the effect of civilian victimization on war outcomes. Much of the literature posits an unconditional effect: civilian victimization is uniformly effective or ineffective. Some studies, however, suggest that civilian victimization is more effective in some circumstances than others, and thus we also develop hypotheses regarding conditional effects. In the third section, we describe the data, variables, and methods used, while in the fourth section we present the results of the analysis. The fifth section then takes a closer look at the data to investigate the causal effect of civilian victimization on war outcomes. We conclude by summarizing our findings and offering some suggestions for further research.

Targeting Civilians to Win or to Lose? Unconditional Arguments

Few studies attempt to evaluate systematically the effectiveness for winning wars—or otherwise achieving belligerents' objectives—of military strategies that target and kill noncombatants.[7] Although large-scale violence against civilians occurs frequently, our knowledge about how well it

---

7.   Throughout this paper, we use the terms "civilian" and "noncombatant" interchangeably to indicate individuals who "do not participate in armed conflict by fighting, carrying weapons, serving in the uniformed military or security services, or building weapons." Downes, *Targeting Civilians in War*, p. 14.

works tends to be compartmentalized into observations about particular wars or types of military campaigns (strategic bombing, counterinsurgency, etc.). Although military and political leaders have often maintained that civilian victimization works, the scholarly literature almost unanimously argues otherwise.

TARGETING CIVILIANS: IT WORKS

A glance at a few historical cases reveals that policymakers and military officers have frequently argued that targeting civilians can achieve important wartime objectives. British leaders during the Second Anglo-Boer War (1899–1902) certainly subscribed to this view. Lord Frederick Roberts, the British commander, justified his practice of retaliating for insurgent attacks on British lines of communication by burning nearby Boer farms with the comment, "The more difficulty the people experience about food … the sooner the war will be ended." Prime Minister Lord Salisbury approved of his military commander's policy, writing, "You will not conquer these people until you have starved them out."[8] Early airpower theorists also believed that targeting noncombatants could end wars quickly with less overall suffering. As Giulio Douhet put it in his book *Command of the Air*, "A complete breakdown of the social structure cannot but take place in a country subjected to this kind of merciless pounding from the air. The time would soon come when, to put an end to horror and suffering, the people themselves, driven by the instinct of self-preservation, would rise up and demand an end to the war."[9] Former British Prime Minister Stanley Baldwin argued in 1932 that punishment bombing would be the key to victory in future wars: "the bomber will always get through. The only defense is in offense, which means that you have to kill more women and children more quickly than the enemy if you want to save yourselves."[10] During World War II, President Franklin D. Roosevelt viewed the British destruction of Hamburg in July 1943 as "'an impressive demonstration' of what America might achieve against Japan," and believed that firebombing could shorten the war in the Pacific.[11] These statements suggest the following hypothesis:

---

8. Quoted in S. B. Spies, *Methods of Barbarism? Roberts and Kitchener and Civilians in the Boer Republics, January 1900–May 1902* (Cape Town: Human & Rousseau, 1977), pp. 122, 175.

9. Quoted in Robert A. Pape, *Bombing to Win: Air Power and Coercion in War* (Ithaca, N.Y.: Cornell University Press, 1996), p. 60.

10. Quoted in Max Hastings, *Bomber Command* (New York: Dial Press, 1979), p. 43.

11. Michael S. Sherry, *The Rise of American Airpower: The Creation of Armageddon* (New Haven, Conn.: Yale University Press, 1987), pp. 102, 156. Some historians have suggested that civilian victimization can contribute to victory indirectly by forcing a target state to transfer scarce resources away from combat to population defense, thereby weakening its overall war effort. One possible case of this phenomenon was the bombing of Germany in World War II. See Richard Overy, *The Air War, 1939–1945* (New York: Stein and Day, 1980), p. 123.

- *Hypothesis 1*: States that employ civilian victimization are more likely to prevail in war.

TARGETING CIVILIANS: IT'S FUTILE

Contrary to the beliefs of these political and military officials, most social scientists have found little support for the view that punishing civilians leads to victory.[12] The case against the efficacy of targeting civilians has been made most powerfully and systematically by Robert Pape in his work on strategic bombing.[13] In *Bombing to Win*, Pape argues that modern nation-states hardly ever make significant concessions in response to bombing campaigns directed at noncombatants. According to Pape, the reason that such punishment strategies fail is that "states involved in coercive disputes are often willing to accept high costs" and that making substantial concessions offends the nationalism of a state's population.[14] Since most coercive disputes that escalate to war are about important issues of national interest, nationalism makes it unlikely that states will forfeit the issue or object being contested. Moreover, Pape contends, "conventional munitions can inflict only limited damage on civilians" and "modern states can minimize their vulnerability to counter-civilian attacks by defense, evacuation of threatened areas, and rapid adjustment to economic dislocations."[15] In short, modern states are resistant to coercion by punishment owing to nationalism, on the one hand, and because the combination of strong bureaucratic state structures and the size and wealth of states allows them to lower their vulnerability to punishment by building shelters, evacuating cities, rationing food, substituting one good for another, or cultivating more land to increase food production.[16]

Even the use of atomic weapons against Japan in 1945, according to Pape, was not the decisive factor causing Japan's capitulation; he credits the U.S. naval blockade, which crippled Japanese industry, and the Soviet invasion of Manchuria, which he argues invalidated Japan's military strategy for defending the home islands.[17] Similarly, the severe aerial bludgeoning inflicted upon Germany between 1942 and 1945 by British Bomber Command (with help from the U.S. Eighth and Fifteenth Air Forces),

---

12. Studies aimed at a more popular audience reach similar conclusions. See, for example, Caleb Carr, *The Lessons of Terror: A History of Warfare against Civilians* (New York: Random House, 2002).

13. Ironically, Pape is also one of the few scholars to argue that civilian victimization—in the form of suicide terrorism—can be effective. See Robert A. Pape, *Dying to Win: The Strategic Logic of Suicide Terrorism* (New York: Random House, 2005).

14. Pape, *Bombing to Win*, p. 21.

15. Ibid., pp. 22, 23.

16. See also Mancur Olson, *The Economics of the Wartime Shortage: A History of British Food Supplies in the Napoleonic War and in World Wars I and II* (Durham, N.C.: Duke University Press, 1963). Reinforcing the stubbornness of states is the possibility that leaders who make concessions to adversaries could face removal or punishment after the fact by their constituents.

17. Pape, *Bombing to Win*, pp. 108–136.

induce the enemy regime to renounce its war aims, or alternatively that the suffering meted out to noncombatants will cause them to rise up and demand an end to the war.[25] In wars of attrition, however, both sides are likely to be highly resolved. In these conflicts, states have experienced the initial costs of combat and chosen to continue fighting rather than nego-tiate a settlement. Civilian victimization thus tends to occur only in the most demanding set of circumstances, when the adversary is most primed to resist. Indeed, studies of coercion consistently find that coercion of any kind rarely succeeds.[26] A major reason for this lack of success is that the process of escalation to war—and then escalation in war—weeds out the unresolved types and leaves only those that care deeply about the out-come, and are willing to suffer significant costs to achieve their aims. This observation suggests our first conditional hypothesis.

- *Hypothesis 3*: States that employ civilian victimization in wars of attrition are not more likely to prevail.

A second circumstance in which states victimize noncombatants is when they intend to seize and annex territory from a neighboring state.[27] These annexation cases are invariably conventional wars, but violence against civilians perpetrated in such conflicts is not usually intended to lower their morale. Rather, states target civilians—namely those who share the ethnicity, nationality, or political sympathies of the adversary—to eliminate them from the territory they wish to seize, thereby removing an actual or potential fifth column and reducing the risk of future resistance to their rule.[28] In the First Balkan War (1912–1913), for example, Bulgaria, Serbia, and Greece attacked the Ottoman Empire's remaining European territories and cleansed Turkish Muslims to facilitate their annexation of these lands. When the victors then fell to quarreling over the spoils, ethnic Bulgarians were evicted as the Serb and Greek armies defeated the Bul-garian Army and seized tracts of Bulgarian-inhabited land.[29] Moreover, it appears that civilian victimization as a tool of territorial expansion and consolidation has been successful in a good share of cases. The Balkan

---

25. Pape, *Bombing to Win*, p. 59; and Downes, *Targeting Civilians in War*, pp. 4, 30, 84–86.

26. Pape, *Bombing to Win*; Pape, "Why Economic Sanctions Do Not Work"; Gary Clyde Hufbauer, Jeffrey J. Schott, and Kimberly Ann Elliott, *Economic Sanctions Reconsidered*, 2nd ed. (Washington, D.C.: Institute for International Economics, 1990); and Robert J. Art and Patrick M. Cronin, eds., *The United States and Coercive Diplomacy* (Washington, D.C.: United States Institute of Peace Press, 2003).

27. Downes, "Desperate Times, Desperate Measures"; "Restraint or Propellant?" and *Targeting Civilians in War*.

28. This implies that an additional metric for "success" in annexation cases is wheth-er ethnic cleansing in fact leads to lower rates of rebellion or war-recurrence. We intend to pursue this question in future research.

29. International Commission to Inquire into the Causes and Conduct of the Balkan Wars, *The Other Balkan Wars* (Washington, D.C.: Carnegie Endowment for International Peace, 1993).

states' expansion at the expense of the Ottoman Empire in 1912–1913, for instance, was a great success because the Ottomans were weak and no Great Powers were willing to come to their rescue. Other examples include Israel's seizure of Arab land and expulsion of its inhabitants in the War of Independence, which eliminated the main threat to the viability of a Jewish state, and Turkey's intervention in Cyprus in 1974, which carved out a Turkish enclave in the northern part of the island by ejecting 200,000 Greek Cypriots from their homes. This leads to the following hypothesis about the effectiveness of civilian victimization in wars of territorial annexation.

- *Hypothesis 4*: States that employ civilian victimization in wars to seize and annex territory are more likely to prevail.

TARGET SIZE

Much of the evidence for the ineffectiveness of civilian victimization in coercive wars stems from the resilience of the modern nation-state. Pape, as noted above, argues that modern states can reduce their vulnerability to punishment by, for example, constructing bomb shelters, evacuating citizens from targeted areas, or providing emergency economic relief to those affected. In addition, these states are willing and able to tolerate high costs to achieve important goals. Targets of coercion, however, have not always been so resilient, and this helps explain why punishment in earlier historical epochs appears to have been more successful than in the age of nation-states.

Coercion by starvation or bombardment in ancient, medieval, and early modern siege warfare, for example, was often effective because the targets were towns or cities, not countries. Cities are simply smaller, more vulnerable, and less resistant targets than states. The inhabitants of cities or towns typically do not raise or produce their own food, but rather rely on the surrounding countryside to provide them with sustenance. Townspeople can easily be cut off from this source of supply by even relatively small armies surrounding their town. Cities may also be separated from their hinterlands by walls of circumvallation, which prevent the inhabitants from sortieing out to forage. Furthermore, an army encamped outside of a town may consume or destroy all the available foodstuffs in the area, making such sorties pointless. Moreover, the small size of cities compared to states enables the whole town to be struck easily by artillery and vulnerable to fire, and thus more susceptible to damage and civilian casualties from bombing. Finally, cities are densely populated, which allows disease to spread quickly with devastating consequences. When belligerents have been able to surround population centers in modern wars, starvation and bombardment have often produced results, as in the Siege of Vicksburg in the U.S. Civil War, and the Siege of Paris in the Franco-Prussian War.

Although we are limited by the temporal span of our data to wars of the last two centuries, the foregoing discussion implies that civilian victimization might be more effective against small states and states with small populations because they have fewer resources to mitigate the effects of civilian suffering.

- *Hypothesis 5*: The smaller the geographic area or population of the target, the more likely that civilian victimization will contribute to victory.

CHANGE OVER TIME

This discussion also implies that civilian victimization may have become less effective in more recent wars. There are several potential arguments to support this hypothesis. As discussed above, the emergence of the modern state and the advent of nationalism have rendered states exceptionally cohesive and relatively resistant to punishment. States are almost always larger and more resilient targets than towns or cities. Sieges are nowadays more likely to be conducted against entire countries rather than individual cities. One might expect, then, that civilian victimization in the era of modern states—roughly after 1648, but even more so after the French Revolution—is less likely to deliver results than in previous eras.

- *Hypothesis 6*: Civilian victimization in war should decrease in effectiveness over time.

TARGET REGIME TYPE

Finally, the regime type of the target may also influence the effectiveness of civilian victimization. Because citizens have a say in governance in democracies, and obviously prefer not to be killed by enemy attacks, civilian victimization should be more effective when the target is a democracy than when it is an autocracy. As Pape has written in the context of suicide terrorism, "Domestic critics and international rivals, as well as terrorists, often view democracies as 'soft,' usually on the grounds that their publics have low thresholds of cost tolerance and high ability to affect state policy."[30] Some dictatorial opponents of democracies have held this view, notably Saddam Hussein when he argued before the First Persian Gulf War that the United States could not stomach ten thousand dead in one battle. A variety of commentators have argued that advanced industrial democracies have entered an age of "post-heroic warfare" in which the highest priority of military operations is to minimize casualties among one's troops.[31] If democracies are averse to casualties among their armed forces, it follows that deaths among the civilian population would be even more unpopular. Indeed, some democracies have believed this about themselves. The British Air Staff, for example, argued in 1937 that Britain was at a disadvantage if a war against Nazi Germany devolved into a

---

30.   Pape, "Strategic Logic of Suicide Terrorism," p. 349.

31.   Edward N. Luttwak, "Toward Post-Heroic Warfare," *Foreign Affairs*, Vol. 74, No. 3 (May/June 1995), pp. 109–122; and Luttwak, "A Post-Heroic Military Policy," *Foreign Affairs*, Vol. 75, No. 4 (July/August 1996), pp. 33–44.

counter-city slugging match because "a military dictatorship is likely to be less susceptible to popular outcry than a democratic Government. It is, consequently, unsafe to assume that ... [Britain and France] will be able, by attacking the morale of the German people, to produce an effect in any way comparable with that which would result from German air attack against our own."[32] This logic leads to our final conditional hypothesis:

- *Hypothesis 7*: If the target state is a democracy, civilian victimization is more likely to contribute to victory.

Evaluating the Effectiveness of Civilian Targeting: Data, Variables, and Method

In this chapter, we propose a simple metric for evaluating the effectiveness of civilian victimization: war outcome. If targeting noncombatants is as ineffective as the majority view in the literature believes, then civilian victimization or large numbers of civilian casualties should be uncorrelated (or negatively correlated) with victory for the state that inflicts these casualties. War outcome is an imperfect measure, of course, and finding a correlation between civilian victimization and winning or losing is not the same as finding that targeting civilians caused the outcome. Statistical analysis is merely the starting point for more in-depth investigation. The basic question of the association between civilian victimization and war outcome is still unknown, and thus discovering the nature of that association is worthwhile. We measure war outcomes using a trichotomous indicator: losses are coded as zero, draws as one, and wins as two. Our analysis includes the war outcomes for the major combatants for all interstate wars between 1816 and 2003.[33]

We employ two types of statistical tests to assess the effectiveness of targeting civilians in war. First, we use simple cross-tabulations to com-

---

32.   Quoted in George H. Quester, *Deterrence before Hiroshima: The Airpower Background of Modern Strategy* (New York: John Wiley and Sons, 1966), p. 94.

33.   The list of interstate wars is taken from Correlates of War Interstate War Data, 1816–1997, version 3, http://correlatesofwar.org. The dataset has been modified to update it through the 2003 Iraq War and several multi-phase wars (World Wars I and II, for example) have been divided into separate conflicts. For detailed descriptions of these and other changes, see Dan Reiter and Allan C. Stam, *Democracies at War* (Princeton, N.J.: Princeton University Press, 2002), pp. 38–39; Downes, "Desperate Times, Desperate Measures," pp. 193–194; and Downes, *Targeting Civilians in War*, pp. 57–58. COW defines interstate wars as armed conflicts between two or more recognized states that exceeded 1,000 total battle deaths. Data on war outcomes are taken from the Correlates of War Project, supplemented in some cases by Reiter and Stam's codings from *Democracies at War* as well as our own judgments for some recent conflicts. In several wars, COW includes many states that made only minor contributions to the conflict. Our judgment is that such minor allies rarely possess independent decision-making ability on military strategy. To avoid counting such non-entities as "winners" or "losers" when they hardly participated in the conflict, we drop them from the analysis. Doing so does not affect our core results.

pare war outcomes for combatants that employed strategies of civilian victimization and those that did not. Combatants are considered to have used *civilian targeting* if they adopted a military strategy that targeted civilians on purpose or if they used force so indiscriminately that tens of thousands of civilians died.[34] In order to assess whether the effect of civilian victimization is conditional on the type of war being fought, we created dummy variables for wars of attrition and wars of territorial annexation and compared the cross-tabulations of civilian targeting and war outcome for each type of war. Wars of attrition are defined as "conflicts generally lacking in maneuver or movement, which are instead dominated by linear, static, or trench operations."[35] Wars of territorial annexation consist of wars in which at least one belligerent went to war intending to annex some or all of an opponent's territory.

In our second set of statistical tests, we attempt to isolate the effect of civilian victimization while controlling for other determinants of victory using ordered logit analysis with our war outcome variable as the dependent variable of interest. Our key explanatory variable is the *civilian targeting* variable discussed above, although we also look at two other indicators of civilian victimization. *Mass Killing* is a dummy variable coded one when a state killed more than 50,000 noncombatants. The variable *civilian fatalities* consists of the log of the total number of civilians killed by each state during the war.[36] Owing to spotty data availability, analyses using civilian fatalities exclude nineteenth-century wars. In order to assess the conditional hypotheses, we interact civilian targeting with the two war-type dummy variables discussed above, the log of the enemy's population, a year-counter variable to measure the passing of time, and two measures of the adversary's regime type: a dichotomous variable indicating whether the enemy was a democracy, and the Polity score of the enemy's regime.[37] In addition to our explanatory variables and interactive terms, we control for several other factors identified by previous research that influence war outcomes: relative material capabilities, the regime type of the state, whether the state initiated the conflict, an interactive term for

---

34. This variable is described in detail in Downes, *Targeting Civilians in War*, pp. 14–21; for a list of cases, see ibid., pp. 45–47. It consists of artillery or aerial bombardment of urban areas, as employed in World War II, for example; starvation blockades and sieges, such as the blockade of the Central Powers in World War I; and counterinsurgency or cleansing campaigns that kill civilians intentionally or treat noncombatants in ways that will foreseeably result in serious mortality among them.

35. Downes, "Restraint or Propellant?" p. 884.

36. On mass killing, see Valentino, *Final Solutions*, and Valentino, Huth, and Balch-Lindsay, "'Draining the Sea'." On civilian fatalities, see Downes, "Restraint or Propellant?" and *Targeting Civilians in War*. We also use a variable for intentional civilian casualties: the number of civilians killed during a campaign of civilian targeting. This is similar to the measure employed in Valentino, Huth, and Croco, "Covenants without the Sword."

37. The year-counter variable starts in the year of the first war in the dataset (1823) and thus captures the number of years that have passed since that time.

regime type and war initiator, and a dummy variable for conflicts occurring after 1945.[38]

Statistical Results

UNCONDITIONAL HYPOTHESES

We begin by discussing the unconditional effect of civilian targeting on war outcomes. On average, does targeting civilians pay? Table 2.1 shows a bivariate cross-tabulation of civilian targeting in all wars and our trichotomous war outcome variable: win, lose, or draw. The table yields a surprising result: states that employ civilian targeting as a war strategy are significantly more likely to win. According to Table 2.1, states that targeted noncombatants won 62 percent of the wars they fought, compared to 41 percent of states that did not target civilians. In addition, states that targeted civilians were about half as likely to lose as states that left civilians alone, while there is not much difference in the percentage of draws (13 versus 12 percent, respectively). The bivariate evidence thus suggests that targeting civilians increases the likelihood of victory and reduces the probability of defeat.

Table 2.1. Cross Tabulation of Civilian Targeting and Interstate War Outcomes, 1816–2003.

	Civilian Targeting		
War Outcome	Yes	No	Total
Win	33	80	113
	62.3%	41.0%	45.6%
Draw	7	23	30
	13.2%	11.8%	12.1%
Lose	13	92	105
	24.5%	47.2%	42.3%
Total	53	195	248
	100%	100%	100%

NOTE: Pearson $Chi^2(2) = 9.244$ $p = 0.010$

---

38. Emphasizing democracy and war initiation are Reiter and Stam, *Democracies at War*; emphasizing power is Michael C. Desch, *Power and Military Effectiveness: The Fallacy of Democratic Triumphalism* (Baltimore, Md.: Johns Hopkins University Press, 2008). On the decline in the number of victories in wars after World War II, see Page Fortna, "Where Have All the Victories Gone: War Outcomes in Historical Perspective," paper presented at the American Political Science Association annual meeting, September 2–5, 2004, Chicago, Ill.

Table 2.2. Ordinal Logit Estimates of Civilian Victimization and Interstate War Outcomes (Lose, Draw, Win): Unconditional Hypotheses.

	1	2	3
Civilian Targeting	0.78*** (0.28)	-	-
Mass Killing	-	0.47 (0.50)	-
Civilian Casualties (Log)	-	-	0.37*** (0.10)
Material Capabilities	1.81*** (0.60)	1.81*** (0.58)	1.53* (0.78)
Democracy (Dummy)	1.19* (0.68)	1.20* (0.71)	1.21* (0.66)
War Initiator	0.64 (0.44)	0.65 (0.43)	0.62 (0.56)
Democracy (Dummy) × Initiator	-0.15 (0.84)	-0.23 (0.85)	-0.16 (0.89)
Post-1945	-0.83*** (0.20)	-0.74*** (0.21)	-0.80*** (0.27)
N	246	253	155
Log Pseudo-LL	-211.42	-222.11	-130.76
Wald Chi²	37.90***	33.01***	33.64***

NOTES: Robust standard errors clustered on each war in parentheses; * = $p < 0.10$; ** = $p < 0.05$; *** = $p < 0.01$.
Civilian Targeting and Mass Killing, 1816–2003; Civilian Casualties, 1900–2003.

The results of the ordinal logit analysis support this conclusion. As shown in Table 2.2, civilian targeting, mass killing, and the number of civilian fatalities are each positively associated with winning, even after controlling for other determinants of victory. Civilian targeting and the number of civilian fatalities are statistically significant and substantively important. Figure 2.1 shows the changes in states' probability of victory associated with changes in the values of different independent variables.[39]

39. These changes in probability were generated by setting all other dichotomous measures to their modes and continuous measures to their means. Changes are thus calculated from the baseline case of autocratic states that did not initiate wars or target civilians in wars prior to 1945. Changes in probability are calculated by shifting binary variables from zero to one and continuous variables from one standard deviation below the mean to one standard deviation above the mean. Because democracy and initiator are included with an interactive term, assessing their marginal effects is nonsensical. The effect of democracy shown in Figure 2.1 is the change in probability of victory that results from moving from an autocratic non-initiator to a democratic non-initiator; the effect of initiator is that of changing from an autocratic non-initiator to an autocratic initiator. Although these effects are not significant individually, the joint effect of democracy and initiation (i.e., changing from an autocratic non-initiator to a

The solid bars indicate change in probability; the lines inside each bar show the 95 percent confidence intervals surrounding the estimates.

Figure 2.1. Effect of Relevant Variables on Probability of Victory.

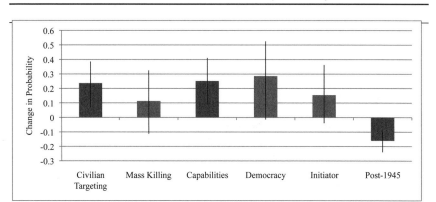

Substantively, a policy of targeting civilians increases the probability of winning by 23 percent. This is only slightly less than the 25 percent increase that results from increasing a state's share of total military capabilities from 6 percent to 68 percent (one standard deviation below the mean to one standard deviation above the mean). Mass killing has a smaller substantive impact (an 11 percent increase), but it is not statistically significant. Figure 2.2 shows a belligerent's probability of winning as a function of the number of civilian fatalities it inflicts. The scale is logarithmic, but it shows a clear trend: the more civilians killed, the higher the probability of winning. This is true whether we include all civilian fatalities or only those inflicted during campaigns of civilian targeting. The data thus provide support for Hypothesis 1 and disconfirm Hypothesis 2: civilian victimization appears to be an effective strategy.

CONDITIONAL EFFECTS

Our second set of hypotheses suggests that the effectiveness of civilian targeting depends on the situations in which it is employed. In order to assess these conditional effects, we compare sets of cross tabs and employ interactive terms in our regression analysis. Table 2.3 breaks down the relationship between civilian victimization and victory by war type. Civilian victimization is positively associated with victory in both types of wars. In wars of attrition and wars of territorial annexation, civilian victimizers are over 50 percent more likely to win than states that do not target civilians.

---

democratic initiator) is. Since this is not the subject of this chapter we do not present results here, but they are available from the authors upon request.

Figure 2.2. Effect of Number of Civilians Killed on Probability of Victory.

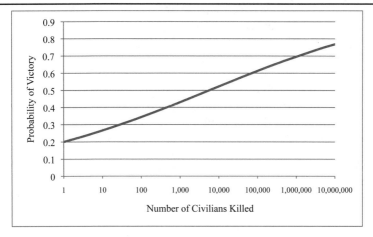

Table 2.3. Cross Tabulation of Civilian Targeting and Interstate War Outcomes in Wars of Attrition and Wars of Territorial Annexation, 1816–2003.

War Outcome	Wars of Attrition				Territorial Annexation		
	Target Civilians	No Targeting	Total		Target Civilians	No Targeting	Total
Win	24	23	47		20	27	47
	63.2%	41.8%	50.5%		58.8%	35.5%	42.7%
Draw	7	5	12		7	7	14
	18.4%	9.1%	12.9%		20.6%	9.2%	12.7%
Lose	7	27	34		7	42	49
	18.4%	49.1%	36.6%		20.6%	55.3%	44.5%
Total	38	55	93		34	76	110
	100%	100%	100%		100%	100%	100%

NOTE: Pearson Chi^2(2) = 9.3233 p = 0.009   NOTE: Pearson Chi^2(2) = 11.7130 p = 0.003

The results from our multivariate regression analyses, which employ interactive terms to isolate the effect of civilian victimization in different scenarios, lend partial support to these hypotheses. Table 2.4 shows the regression output; because the coefficients for the interaction terms are difficult to interpret, we rely primarily on graphs to display the substantive effects and statistical significance of the interactions.[40] Targeting civilians

40.   Thomas Brambor, William Roberts Clark, and Matt Golder, "Understanding Interaction Terms: Improving Empirical Analysis," *Political Analysis*, Vol. 14, No. 1 (Winter 2006), pp. 63–82.

increases the probability of winning in both types of wars, and the effect is statistically significant at the 95 percent level of confidence for territorial wars and at 90 percent for wars of attrition. Substantively, as shown in Figure 2.3, the impact is larger for wars of annexation, where targeting civilians increases the probability of winning by 34 percent. In wars of attrition, civilian victimization increases the probability of victory by 17 percent. Thus, the evidence seems to contradict Hypothesis 3 and confirm Hypothesis 4: civilian victimization is an effective strategy in both wars of attrition and territorial annexation, although the larger substantive effect for the latter indicates that targeting civilians is more effective in annexationist than in attrition wars.

Figure 2.3. Effect of Civilian Targeting on Probability of Victory for Different War Types.

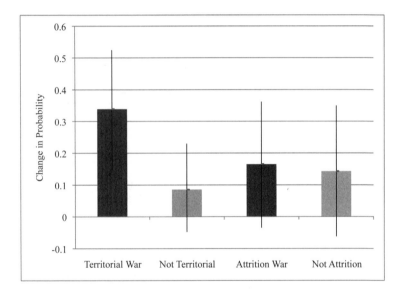

The evidence we have on the conditioning effects of the size of the enemy population is mixed, but generally supportive of Hypothesis 5. Figure 2.4 shows the change in probability of winning for states that target civilians for different sizes of the enemy's population. The solid line charts the change in probability; the dotted lines track the 95 percent confidence intervals. Variables are statistically significant when this interval does not straddle zero. The downward trend is evident. States that use civilian victimization against very small populations—less than 500,000—increase their probability of winning by more than 25 percent. States that target very large populations, on the other hand—more than 500 million—increase their chance of winning by less than 13 percent. This effect is statistically significant (at the .05 level) for enemy populations between 5

Table 2.4. Ordinal Logit Estimates of Civilian Victimization and Interstate War Outcomes (Lose, Draw, Win): Conditional Hypotheses.

	1 Attrition	2 Annexation	3 Enemy Population	4 Enemy Democracy (Dummy)	5 Enemy Polity Score	6 Time
Civilian Targeting	0.63 (0.46)	0.36 (0.31)	1.90 (2.18)	1.02** (0.45)	0.72 (0.69)	3.86*** (1.06)
War of Attrition	0.26 (0.32)	-	-	-	-	-
Civilian Targeting × War of Attrition	0.05 (0.64)	-	-	-	-	-
War of Annexation	-	-0.46** (0.21)	-	-	-	-
Civilian Targeting × War of Annexation	-	1.08** (0.48)	-	-	-	-
Enemy Population (Log)	-	-	-0.18 (0.19)	-	-	-
Civilian Targeting × Enemy Population (Log)	-	-	-0.23 (0.46)	-	-	-
Enemy Democracy (Dummy)	-	-	-	-1.27*** (0.47)	-	-
Civilian Targeting × Enemy Democracy (Dummy)	-	-	-	-0.78 (1.17)	-	-
Enemy Polity Score	-	-	-	-	-0.06* (0.03)	-
Civilian Targeting × Enemy Polity Score	-	-	-	-	0.01 (0.06)	-
Year Counter	-	-	-	-	-	-0.009** (0.003)
Civilian Targeting × Year Counter	-	-	-	-	-	-0.03*** (0.01)
Material Capabilities	1.88*** (0.61)	1.83*** (0.61)	1.66*** (0.60)	1.47** (0.64)	1.72*** (0.63)	1.93*** (0.60)
Democracy (Dummy)	1.16* (0.66)	1.11 (0.71)	1.29* (0.70)	0.82 (0.64)	1.05 (0.71)	1.25* (0.64)
War Initiator	0.59 (0.45)	0.57 (0.45)	0.66 (0.45)	0.72 (0.44)	0.71 (0.44)	0.62 (0.45)
Democracy (Dummy) × Initiator	-0.05 (0.84)	0.08 (0.87)	-0.16 (0.85)	-0.11 (0.82)	-0.18 (0.86)	-0.22 (0.83)
Post-1945	-0.83*** (0.20)	-0.77*** (0.21)	-0.86*** (0.23)	-0.45*** (0.16)	-0.65*** (0.18)	-
N	244	246	245	246	243	246
Log Pseudo-LL	-209.56	-209.47	-210.22	-203.97	-204.71	-207.22
Wald Chi²	41.07***	38.46***	37.77***	43.54***	42.64***	58.51***

NOTE: Robust standard errors clustered on each war in parentheses; * = p < 0.10; ** = p < 0.05; *** = p < 0.01.

million and 175 million, which comprise the majority of the observations.[41] Thus, it appears that targeting civilians increases the probability of winning regardless of the size of the enemy population, although it becomes less effective as the enemy population gets larger.

Figure 2.4. Effect of Civilian Targeting on Probability of Victory by Size of Enemy Population.

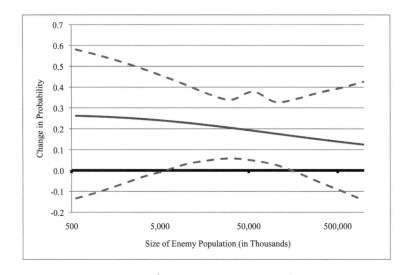

Our results regarding whether civilian victimization is a function of the regime type of the enemy are also mixed. Ordinal logit analysis using an interaction between civilian targeting and a dummy variable for adversary democracy suggests that contrary to Hypothesis 7, civilian victimization is effective against non-democracies but not against democratic regimes. Targeting the civilians of a non-democracy, for example, increases the probability of winning by a statistically significant 24 percent. When democracies are targeted, by contrast, the impact of civilian victimization increases the probability of winning by a mere 5 percent and the effect is not statistically significant.

This pattern does not hold when we use a continuous measure of democracy, however. Figure 2.5 shows the impact of civilian targeting on the probability of winning as a function of the enemy regime's Polity score, with 1 representing the most autocratic and 21 representing the most democratic states. The effect of civilian targeting is always positive, causing roughly a 20 percent increase in the probability of winning. This effect does not vary by Polity score. Given the differential effects found

41. For large populations, statistical insignificance is probably driven by a scarcity of data: fewer than 10 percent of the states in the dataset face opponents that have populations larger than 175 million. Data scarcity cannot explain insignificance at the lower end of the range, given that we have more observations and a larger substantive effect for this part of the range.

when a dichotomous indicator was used, this is a surprising result. It is possible that the relationship between the two variables is not linear: civilian targeting could be more effective against anocracies or mixed regimes because of the fragility of those regime types than against either democracies or autocracies, which tend to be more consolidated.[42] If the increased efficacy of civilian targeting in non-democracies is driven by its effectiveness against anocracies rather than its effectiveness against autocracies, there would not necessarily be evidence of a linear relationship—which our ordinal logit analysis assumes—between civilian targeting and the Polity score of the enemy regime. We tested this hypothesis in two ways: creating a trichotomous indicator of regime type (autocracy, anocracy, and democracy); and generating a squared term of states' scores on the Polity index. Each was interacted with civilian targeting. The results mirror those in Figure 2.5: targeting noncombatants of any regime type increases the probability of victory by about 18 percent but is statistically significant only for anocracies, providing little support for the non-linear hypothesis. Although further investigation is warranted, we tentatively conclude that contrary to Hypothesis 7, the regime type of the target state does not strongly condition the effect of civilian victimization on the probability of victory.

Figure 2.5. Effect of Civilian Targeting on Probability of Victory by Enemy Regime Type.

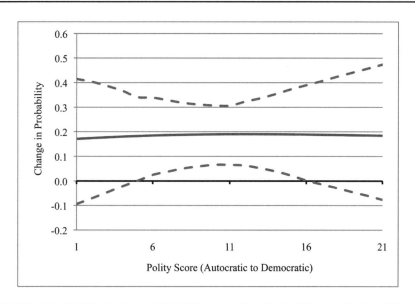

One of the most striking findings of our analysis is the decrease in the efficacy of civilian targeting over time. Figure 2.6 plots how the probability of winning changes when a state targets civilians as a function of time.

42.   See H. E. Goemans, *War and Punishment: The Causes of War Termination and the First World War* (Princeton, N.J.: Princeton University Press, 2000).

The figure demonstrates a clear decrease in the effectiveness of this strategy over time. Civilian victimization increased the probability of victory by a statistically significant (but ever dwindling) amount prior to 1950; after about 1975, however, targeting civilians began to decrease the probability of winning, although the effect is not statistically significant.

In addition to decreasing the likelihood of victory, civilian victimization has also influenced the probability of draws and losses over time. In the nineteenth century, for example, civilian victimization increased the probability of winning and lowered the likelihood of both losing and ending up in a draw (see Figures 2.7 and 2.8). As time has passed, civilian victimization has become a less important driver of all three outcomes. After roughly 1975, the strategy does not have a statistically significant impact on the probability of winning, losing, or tying. However, the trend lines suggest that civilian victimization may become counterproductive in the future by decreasing the probability of victory and increasing the probability of losing. The trend line for the probability of a draw is less clear.

Figure 2.6. Effect of Civilian Targeting on Probability of Victory over Time.

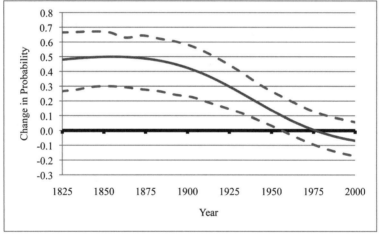

The apparent decreasing effectiveness of civilian victimization over time is a remarkable finding. The problem, of course, is that time can be a proxy for a plethora of factors, such as technology, industrialization, nationalism, norms and laws against civilian targeting, and the spread of global media, to name a few. Earlier we suggested that the spread of nationalism has made modern states exceptionally cohesive and difficult to coerce. Another potential explanation for the decreasing effectiveness of civilian victimization over time is that massive depredations against noncombatants have become more likely to spark intervention in wars by third parties, leading to the victimizer's defeat. Beginning in the nineteenth century, states began to negotiate treaties that limited the amount and type of force they could employ in wartime. Although early iterations of these agreements—the Hague Conventions, as well as attempts to limit the practice of aerial bombing—exerted little effect on the conduct of war, the horrors of World War II spurred further codification of the laws of armed conflict, including the Geneva Conventions and Additional Protocols, as well as the Genocide Convention. As more states have adhered to these agreements and the norms contained in them have disseminated across the international system, one could argue that the likelihood that states will intervene to put a stop to civilian victimization has increased.

Figure 2.7. Effect of Civilian Targeting on Probability of a Draw over Time.

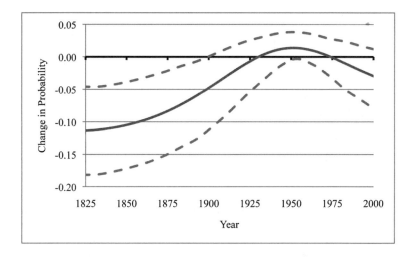

Figure 2.8. Effect of Civilian Targeting on Probability of Defeat over Time.

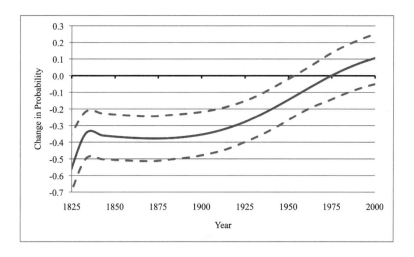

NATO's air campaign to coerce Slobodan Milošević to stop expelling Kosovo Albanians and accept some form of autonomy for Kosovo—although it took place in the context of an internal conflict rather than a conflict between states—is a possible recent example of third-party intervention to halt civilian victimization. According to this interpretation, Milošević's refusal to grant autonomy to Kosovo and the brutal nature of the Serbian counterinsurgency campaign in the province brought about NATO intervention to end the violence.[43] Civilian victimization was counterproductive in this case because it led to intervention and loss of Serbian control (and now sovereignty) over Kosovo.[44] Another possible example is the massacre of Bosnian Muslims at Srebrenica in July 1995 by the Bosnian Serb Army, which played a key role in bringing about U.S. air strikes and coercive diplomacy to end the war.[45] Such intervention, of course, remains highly variable and inconsistent. NATO intervened in Bosnia and Kosovo, for example, but not in Rwanda or Darfur.[46] Still, one could argue that even with the uneven spatial application of intervention to oppose civilian victimization, it has become more common over time.

A third possible explanation is that any decrease in the effectiveness of civilian victimization could be a function of deterrence. During the Cold War, several conflicts were waged between a superpower and a country supported by the other superpower. In conflicts like these, the infliction of more severe violence on noncombatants may have been restrained by the threat that the other major power would enter the war or retaliate in some fashion. In Vietnam, for example, the Lyndon B. Johnson administration exerted careful control over the bombing of North Vietnam because the president and his close advisers feared that a more aggressive campaign against urban areas (with larger numbers of civilian casualties) would trigger overt Chinese or Soviet intervention in the war.[47] Deterrence, how-

---

43. This is a separate issue from the question of whether NATO intervention prompted Milošević to employ even greater brutality against the Kosovar Albanians. See Kelly Greenhill, "The Use of Refugees as Political and Military Weapons in the Kosovo Conflict," in Raju G. C. Thomas, ed., *Yugoslavia Unraveled: Sovereignty, Self-Determination, and Intervention* (Lanham, Md.: Lexington Books/Rowman and Littlefield, 2003), pp. 205–242.

44. It is plausible that violence on a smaller scale in this case might have avoided such intervention and succeeded in weakening the Kosovo rebels.

45. This is not to say that U.S. air strikes alone brought the war to a halt. The Croatian and Bosnian government ground offensive in western Bosnia—which significantly reduced the portion of the country under Serb control—probably played an even greater role.

46. A suggestion for future research is thus to examine whether civilian victimization (or genocide) in fact triggers third party intervention; where in the world is such intervention likely to occur; and who intervenes?

47. To give but one example, in August 1967 President Lyndon B. Johnson rejected proposed air strikes on the port of Haiphong and the Red River dikes because he feared they might prompt China or Russia to enter the war. See Lyndon Baines Johnson, *The Vantage Point: Perspectives of the Presidency, 1963–1969* (New York: Holt, Rinehart, and Winston, 1971), p. 369. Many of Johnson's advisers shared this view. See, for instance, Robert McNamara, "Evaluation of the Program of Bombing North Vietnam," July 30,

ever, cannot explain the failure of the relatively unrestrained civilian victimization undertaken against some countries in which the United States or the Soviet Union intervened, such as South Vietnam or Afghanistan.[48] We can only speculate as to the reasons behind the decreasing effectiveness of civilian victimization in recent times. This question is clearly one that begs further investigation.

The statistical results in this section demonstrate that indicators of civilian victimization are positively, and often significantly, correlated with victory in interstate wars. These relationships persist in both wars of attrition and wars of territorial annexation. Notably, however, these findings are contingent on time, as the efficacy of civilian targeting has decreased over the past two hundred years. Consistent with our expectations, victimization of noncombatants seems to work better against states with smaller populations. Contrary to the literature, however, the regime type of the target state does not seem to influence the effectiveness of civilian targeting.

Civilian Victimization and War Outcomes: A Closer Look

States that target civilians appear to win more often than they lose. This is an interesting and provocative finding, but what remains unclear is whether the relationship is causal. This section argues that in fact the correlation between civilian victimization and victory may be only partially causal. Some of the cases of civilian victimization by war winners in interstate wars—for reasons explained below—do not bear on the reasons these states prevailed. In the cases that remain—which must be examined in detail for evidence regarding the causal force of civilian victimization—targeting noncombatants contributed to victory in between one-quarter and one-half of them. This success rate, however, is not much different from the rate at which states that did not target civilians win wars, calling into question the conclusion that civilian victimization significantly increases a state's chances of winning.

WARS OF ANNEXATION AND ETHNIC CLEANSING

As we have seen, states that inflict civilian victimization in the midst of wars to seize and annex territory from neighboring states prevail near-

---

1965, in Senator Mike Gravel, ed., *The Pentagon Papers*, Vol. 3 (Boston: Beacon Press, 1972), pp. 386–387; and John McNaughton, "Some Observations about the Bombing," January 18, 1966, in *Pentagon Papers*, Vol. 4, (Boston: Beacon Press, 1972), p. 43.

48.   The United States employed bombing with far fewer restraints in South Vietnam than in the North. See Matthew Adam Kocher, Thomas B. Pepinsky, and Stathis N. Kalyvas, "Aerial Bombardment, Indiscriminate Violence, and Territorial Control in Unconventional Wars: Evidence from Vietnam," paper presented at the American Political Science Association annual meeting, Boston, Mass., August 28–31, 2008. The civilian death toll in Afghanistan in the 1980s exceeded one million. Marek Sliwinski, "Afghanistan: The Decimation of a People," *Orbis*, Vol. 33, No. 1 (Winter 1989), p. 39.

ly 60 percent of the time. Yet it is unclear what contribution civilian victimization makes to these victories. There is no question that targeting noncombatants in these types of cases possesses some military utility: aggressor states typically view "foreign" civilian populations as actual or potential fifth columns that could assist the enemy. In some cases, actual resistance by members of a population prompts the invader to take action, but in other cases it is simply the potential for resistance and the location of a group in the rear of the battle area that leads groups to be targeted. Moreover, allowing a substantial number of the adversary's population to remain could prompt a rescue attempt and also form an impediment to achieving cohesive nation-states. For all of these reasons, groups that are not believed to be easily assimilated are often the object of massacres, expulsions, and ethnic cleansing campaigns designed to eliminate them from the conquered territory.

The violent removal of a population perceived to be hostile, however, is not always the key to victory in wars of territorial annexation. In order to be able to expel potentially problematic groups, the aggressor state must advance militarily on the ground. There are a few exceptions to this rule, such as when war breaks out among populations that are closely intermingled, as in Palestine in 1947 or Bosnia in 1992. Still, in many cases cleansing is a consequence of military victory, not the cause of it. This fact is demonstrated by the Greek advance into and retreat from Anatolia between 1919 and 1922. Shortly after Greek troops landed in Smyrna in 1919, they massacred 200–300 Turks.[49] This was only the beginning. According to Justin McCarthy, "More than a million Turkish refugees fled the advancing Greeks. They had good reason to flee: slaughter of Turkish civilians had begun on the day the Greeks landed. Turkish shops and factories were looted of all their goods. More than 700 Turks were killed."[50] As the Greeks moved inland from the coast, the violence continued and spread: "The mayhem continued wherever the Greeks occupied. In the cities of Aydin, Tire, Menemen, Kasaba, Manisa, Nazilli and others, Ottoman gendarmes (police) were disarmed, their guns given to local Greeks, and the towns pillaged, with attendant murders of civilians. Ottoman officials were singled out for imprisonment and murder. Organized massacres took place in cities and all over the countryside. Greek civilians were given Greek Army weapons and organized as armed bands."[51]

The Greeks capitalized on the disintegration of the Ottoman Empire in the wake of World War I to move into western Anatolia and realize the "Megali Idea" of a Greece spanning both sides of the Aegean Sea. The cleansing of ethnic Turks from western Anatolia may have stabilized Greek control over the area, but it did not prevent the Greek Army from being defeated in the summer of 1922 by the resurgent Turks under Mus-

---

49. Marjorie Housepian, *The Smyrna Affair* (New York: Harcourt Brace Jovanovich, 1966), p. 50.

50. Justin McCarthy, *The Ottoman Peoples and the End of Empire* (London: Arnold, 2001), p. 132.

51. Ibid., p. 134.

tafa Kemal. The Greeks had advanced almost all the way to Ankara, the new Turkish capital, in 1921, but the war bogged down into a stalemate after the Greeks were repulsed in the Battle of the Sakarya River. The Turkish counter-offensive, which began in August 1922, routed the Greeks and within two weeks led to the evacuation of what remained of the Greek Army from Smyrna. The retreating Greeks left a trail of scorched earth behind them as they torched Turkish towns and villages along their line of retreat, killing thousands in the process. Christian civilians (Greeks and Armenians) fled before the advancing Turks, but thousands died in massacres and the burning of Smyrna. Hundreds of thousands of refugees were evacuated from Smyrna on Greek, British, and U.S. warships, and the remaining Greek population in Turkey—minus the 150,000 or so men who were deported to the Anatolian interior in labor battalions—were exchanged for Turks living in Greece in the Treaty of Lausanne.[52]

This tragic episode highlights the fact that in some wars of territorial annexation, civilian victimization is made possible by conquest, which it may then help to solidify. Civilian victimization in these cases is less a cause of victory than a consequence of it. Furthermore, targeting civilians cannot always prevent defeat later in the war: no matter how homogeneous and peaceful ethnic cleansing renders the conquered territory, if the military cannot defend it against a strengthened adversary, it will be lost. In extreme cases, such as that of Nazi Germany, civilian victimization may be pursued so zealously for non-security reasons that it contributes to the aggressor's defeat by reducing its military ability to defend the captured territory. In more recent cases, such as Bosnia, repeated atrocities may eventually prompt third-party intervention in the war for humanitarian reasons and lead to the reversal of an aggressor's gains.

In sum, the Greek case suggests that the positive correlation between civilian victimization and victory in wars of territorial annexation may not be causal. In many of these cases civilian victimization occurs only because military victory has provided states access to territory inhabited by enemy noncombatants. The expulsion or murder of these people solidifies the attacker's grip on the territory, but this grip only lasts if the state is able to defeat enemy counterattacks and win the war. Victory appears to prompt civilian victimization rather than the other way around. Endogeneity, in other words, may plague the relationship between civilian victimization and victory in wars of annexation. Future research should attempt to address this issue. The case, however, also implies different metrics for measuring success in cases of territorial annexation that should be investigated in future research: does civilian victimization lower the likelihood of future armed rebellion by the targeted group? Does the expulsion of people raise or lower the probability of conflict recurrence between the aggressor state and its victim? And does ethnic cleansing provoke third parties to intervene and defeat the victimizer?

---

52. On these events, see Howard M. Sachar, *The Emergence of the Modern Middle East: 1914–1924* (New York: Alfred A. Knopf, 1969), pp. 424–425, 433–436, and 446–448; and Norman M. Naimark, *Fires of Hatred: Ethnic Cleansing in Twentieth-Century Europe* (Cambridge, Mass.: Harvard University Press, 2001), pp. 44–56.

WARS OF ATTRITION AND CIVILIAN VICTIMIZATION

Civilian victimization is more likely to be chosen when states become desperate to win or to conserve on casualties. These cases tend to be stalemated wars of attrition. In our data set, battle deaths for belligerents in such conflicts are more than thirty times higher than for other wars. Moreover, wars of attrition last about five times longer than other wars. In conflicts like these—a partial list includes Crimean, Franco-Prussian, Russo-Japanese, World War I, Chaco, Sino-Japanese, World War II, Korean, Vietnam, and Ethiopian-Eritrean—the stakes are likely to be high and both sides highly resolved. We thus tend to observe civilian victimization in cases in which it is least likely to work, and not observe it in easier cases where the adversary might be less determined.

Still, the statistical evidence showed that states which targeted noncombatants or killed more civilians won more often than states that did not. But was civilian victimization responsible for these victories? Table 2.5 divides states that targeted noncombatants in wars of attrition by whether they won, lost, or drew the war. Among the six losses, it seems clear that civilian victimization by two of the losers made things worse and contributed to their defeat. First, Boxer attacks on Western missionaries and their besieging of the foreign legations in the capital prompted Great-Power intervention, against which the Boxers and Chinese soldiers were no match.[53] Second, Germany's U-boat blockade of Britain starting in February 1917 brought the United States into the war against Germany. In three of the other four cases (Germany, World War II West and World War II East; Azerbaijan), civilian targeting simply did not work: the Blitz on Britain (1940–1941) failed to knock the British out of the war; the Wehrmacht's brutal policy of reprisal massacres on the Eastern Front fed the partisan cause and its siege of Leningrad (1941–1943) killed over 600,000 people but the city never fell; and indiscriminate Azerbaijani rocket and artillery barrages on Stepanakert did not break the will of the Karabakh capital's population.[54] The Greco-Turkish case is not relevant because the targeting actually resulted from annexationist motives.[55] Among the draws, it is possible to make judgments regarding particular campaigns of civilian

---

53. The vast majority of the civilians killed by the Boxers, however, were fellow Chinese. Nat Brandt, *Massacre in Shansi* (Syracuse, N.Y.: Syracuse University Press, 1994), pp. xiii, 270.

54. On these cases, see, respectively, Matthew Cooper, *The German Air Force, 1933–1945: An Anatomy of Failure* (London: Jane's, 1981), pp. 165–166, 171, and 173–174; Harrison E. Salisbury, *The 900 Days: The Siege of Leningrad* (London: Pan Books, 2000); Michael P. Croissant, *The Armenia-Azerbaijan Conflict: Causes and Implications* (Westport, Conn.: Praeger, 1998), p. 78; and Thomas de Waal, *Black Garden: Armenia and Azerbaijan through Peace and War* (New York: New York University Press, 2003), p. 175.

55. Nazi Germany's extermination of Soviet Jewry on the Eastern Front and general indifference to the welfare of the occupied population was counterproductive and also resulted in a diversion of resources to killing operations, to the neglect of fighting the Red Army. This killing was largely driven by ideological and annexationist motives, however, rather than coercive ones. The same can be said of Romania's targeting of Jews in the East.

victimization even though the overall war outcome was indecisive. For example, the North Vietnamese and Viet Cong assassination campaign in the South should be considered a partial success, as these killings helped Communist forces gain control over large tracts of South Vietnam.[56] Four other cases, however, are clear failures. Japan's terror bombing of Chinese cities and other atrocities failed to cause China to surrender, as did U.S. strategic bombing in Korea.[57] The Rolling Thunder campaign of strategic bombing by the United States against North Vietnam exerted little effect on Hanoi's determination to continue the war; the relatively small amount of bombing of Iraqi cities by Iranian air forces did not cause Saddam Hussein to negotiate peace. We are unable to judge the case of Iraqi bombing of Iran in the 1980s: it is clear that Saddam Hussein tended to launch Scud missiles at Iranian cities when his forces were under severe military pressure at the front; what is less clear is whether these Scud barrages had any effect on the prosecution of Iranian offensives.[58] The final two cases—North and South Korea—consisted of attempts by the two sides to eliminate ideological enemies and thus are not relevant to evaluating the effect of civilian victimization for coercive goals.

The most important cases, however, are the war winners. Did civilian victimization help them achieve victory? Six cases should be dismissed because civilian victimization was not relevant to victory or defeat: the Boxer Rebellion, ethnic cleansing in the First Balkan War, Turkey in World War I, the Greco-Turkish War, the Soviet Union in World War II, and Armenia-Azerbaijan. The reason is that the civilian targeting in these cases occurred after the outcome of the war was already decided by strictly military means or sprang from a source other than coercing the enemy government.[59] Among the coercive cases, the Russo-Finnish War is a clear failure: the Red Air Force bombed Finnish cities to no effect, forcing the Soviet High Command to expend tens of thousands of Russian soldiers to

---

56.   Communist control slipped in the war's later years, however, owing to improved U.S. counterinsurgency techniques that relied at least in part on violence against noncombatants. See, for example, Mark Moyar, *Phoenix and the Birds of Prey: The CIA's Secret Campaign to Destroy the Viet Cong* (Annapolis, Md.: Naval Institute Press, 1997); and Stathis N. Kalyvas and Matthew Adam Kocher, "How 'Free' is Free-Riding in Civil War? Violence, Insurgency, and the Collective Action Problem," *World Politics*, Vol. 59, No. 2 (January 2007), pp. 177–216.

57.   The main U.S. bombing campaign of urban areas in North Korea occurred in the winter of 1950–1951, first to deter Chinese entry into the war and later to hinder the Chinese advance down the peninsula. It failed in both instances.

58.   Efraim Karsh, *The Iran-Iraq War: A Military Analysis* (London: International Institute for Strategic Studies, 1987), p. 31; and Efraim Karsh, "Lessons of the Iran-Iraq War," *Orbis*, Vol. 33, No. 2 (Spring 1989), p. 217.

59.   The Boxer cases consist of reprisal massacres. The Turkish case in World War I is ethnic cleansing of Armenians during the Turkish invasion of the Caucasus in 1918, whereas the Turks in the Greco-Turkish war expelled and massacred Greeks and Armenians in the wake of the defeat of the Greek Army in 1922. The Soviet case is reprisals for German barbarities in Russia as well as calculated ethnic cleansing to drive Germans out of what was to become Poland. Ethnic cleansing in the First Balkan and Armenian-Azerbaijani Wars stemmed from annexationist motives.

wear down the outmanned and outgunned Finns. At most, the bombing of Germany from 1942 to 1945 by Britain and the United States forced the Germans to transfer resources into air defense that were needed elsewhere and put a lid on the expansion of German war production; it certainly did not cause a popular revolt or influence the Nazi leadership to give up the fight. We lack sufficient data to judge whether the Japanese bombing of Shanghai in 1932 contributed to victory in Japan's war with China.

In the other eight cases, however, civilian victimization may have contributed to victory in smaller or larger ways. Our own back-of-the-envelope coding would categorize the sieges of Paris in the Franco-Prussian War, Plevna in the Russo-Turkish War, Adrianople in the First Balkan War, and Beirut in the Lebanon War as possible successes, along with the bombing of Warsaw in 1939 and Israeli expulsions in the Palestine War. Several analysts, for example, conclude that although Prussian bombardment had little impact on Parisian morale, hunger and the prospect of large-scale starvation contributed to the French decision to surrender.[60] Others argue that German air attacks on Warsaw—particularly the massive raids of September 25, 1939—triggered the capitulation of Polish forces in the city.[61] Similarly, the Israeli bombardment of Beirut in 1982 succeeded in obtaining the ouster of the Palestine Liberation Organization from Lebanon. As Benny Morris puts it, "Over the long haul, [Defense Minister Ariel] Sharon's brutal measures worked: They persuaded Arafat that the PLO no longer had a choice."[62] In two other cases, civilian victimization arguably played a partial role in causing the loser's defeat. The Allied starvation blockade of Germany and Austria-Hungary in World War I may have contributed to the swift collapse of the Central Powers in 1918, but only after it became clear that the tide on the battlefield had turned.[63] The firebombing of Japan seems like a clear failure—the population did not rise up and the naval blockade had already curtailed the war production that bombing was meant to destroy—but some argue that the

---

60.   On the effect of hunger, see Robert Baldick, *The Siege of Paris* (London: History Book Club, 1964), p. 222; and Melvin Kranzberg, *The Siege of Paris: A Political and Social History* (Ithaca, N.Y.: Cornell University Press, 1950), p. 164. On the ineffectiveness of bombardment, see Alistair Horne, *The Fall of Paris: The Siege and the Commune 1870–71* (New York: St. Martin's Press, 1965), p. 217; and Kranzberg, *Siege of Paris*, p. 133.

61.   Robin Neillands, *The Bomber War: The Allied Air Offensive against Nazi Germany* (New York: Barnes and Noble, 2001), p. 35; and Cajus Bekker, *The Luftwaffe War Diaries: The German Air Force in World War II*, trans. and ed. Frank Ziegler (Garden City, N.Y.: Doubleday, 1968), p. 59.

62.   Benny Morris, *Righteous Victims: A History of the Zionist-Arab Conflict, 1881–1999* (New York: Knopf, 1999), p. 537. On Plevna and Adrianople, see Rupert Furneaux, *The Siege of Plevna* (London: Anthony Blond, 1958), pp. 186–187; and Richard C. Hall, *The Balkan Wars, 1912–1913: Prelude to the First World War* (London: Routledge, 2000), pp. 86–90. On the success of Israeli civilian victimization directed against the Palestinian Arab population in 1948–1949, see Downes, *Targeting Civilians in War*, chap. 6.

63.   As Avner Offer has put it, "The Allied offensive was the hammer, the home front provided the anvil." Avner Offer, *The First World War: An Agrarian Interpretation* (Oxford: Clarendon Press, 1989), p. 72.

Table 2.5. Wins, Losses, and Draws by States that Targeted Civilians in Wars of Attrition.

	WIN	LOSE	DRAW
1	Franco-Prussian (1870–1871) • Prussia: Siege of Paris	Boxer (1900) • China: Massacres	Sino-Japanese (1937–1945) • Japan: Terror bombing, germ warfare, etc.
2	Russo-Turkish (1877–1878) • Russia: Siege of Plevna	WW1 West (1914–1918) • Germany: Bombing of cities, blockade of UK	Korea (1950–1953) • DPRK: Massacre of anti-Communists
3	Boxer (1900) • Russia, UK, France, U.S.: Reprisal massacres	Greco-Turkish (1919–1922) • Greece: Massacres, ethnic cleansing of Turks	Korea (1950–1953) • ROK: Massacre of Communist sympathizers • U.S.: Bombing of DPRK
4	First Balkan (1912–1913) • Bulgaria, Serbia: Siege of Adrianople • Bulgaria, Serbia, Greece: Ethnic cleansing of Turks	WW2 West (1940–1945) • Germany: Blitz of UK	Vietnam (1965–1973) • DRV: Assassinations in RVN
5	WW1 West (1914–1918) • UK, France, U.S.: Blockade	WW2 East (1941–1945) • Germany: Anti-partisan war, siege of Leningrad • Romania: Massacres of Jews	Vietnam (1965–1973) • U.S.: Rolling Thunder
6	WW1 East (1914–1918) • Turkey: Massacres of Armenians in Caucasus, 1918	Armenia-Azerbaijan (1992–1994) • Azerbaijan: Bombing of Stepanakert	Iran-Iraq (1980–1988) • Iraq: Bombing of cities
7	Greco-Turkish (1919–1922) • Turkey: Cleansing of Greeks and Armenians		Iran-Iraq (1980–1988) • Iran: Bombing of cities

Table 2.5. *continued*

8	Sino-Japanese (1931–1933) • Japan: Bombing of Shanghai		
9	Germany-Poland (1939) • Germany: Siege of Warsaw		
10	Russo-Finnish (1939–1940) • Russia: Bombing of Finnish cities		
11	WW2 West (1940–1945) • UK, U.S.: Bombing of Germany		
12	WW2 East (1941–1945) • Russia: Cleansing of Germans		
13	Pacific War (1941–1945) • U.S.: Bombing of Japan		
14	Palestine War (1948–1949) • Israel: Expulsion of Palestinians		
15	Lebanon War (1982) • Israel: Siege of Beirut		
16	Armenia-Azerbaijan (1992–1994) • Armenia: Cleansing of Azeris	Contribute to defeat: 2 (2 states) Simple failure: 3 (3 states) Not relevant: 1 (2 states)	Partial success: 1 (1 state) Failure: 4 (4 states) Unable to judge: 1 (1 state) Not relevant: 2 (2 states)
	Possible success: 6 (7 states) Partial success: 2 (4 states) Failure: 2 (3 states) Unable to judge: 1 (1 state) Not relevant: 6 (11 states)		
	WARS: Possible Success Rate: 30% (6/20) Possible + Partial Success Rate: 45% (9/20) STATES: Possible Success Rate: 29% (7/24) Possible + Partial Success Rate: 50% (12/24)		

atomic bombings hastened the Japanese surrender, so this case might be a partial success.[64]

In short, an examination of the relevant cases of civilian targeting by states that won coercive contests suggests that this strategy played some role in defeating the enemy in eight out of the ten wars in which judgment is possible, and played a major role in six out of the ten. A substantial number of cases, however, are false positives: there are six wars (totaling eleven winning states) in which civilian victimization was not relevant to victory or defeat for various reasons. The earlier statistical findings are thus probably inflated by these false positives. Overall, the record of civilian victimization is not quite as successful as a cursory glance at Table 2.5 would suggest. Eleven cases were clear failures, two of which also contributed to the defeat of the state that employed civilian victimization. These failures involved twelve states. Six cases involving seven states were probable successes—civilian victimization played a significant role in defeating the enemy—and three other cases involving five states could be considered partial successes. Civilian victimization was probably an important component of victory in 30 percent of the wars of attrition (29 percent of states) and at least partially contributed to victory in 45 percent of such wars (50 percent of states). This analysis is preliminary and subject to further investigation, but relative to the rates of victory for states or sides that did not target noncombatants in wars of attrition—40 percent—civilian targeting is not radically less (or more) effective than fighting more conventionally.

Three final points are worth noting. First, even in the cases in which civilian victimization arguably affected the outcome, the target's level of military vulnerability was also high. It may therefore be the case that civilian victimization works only in situations when the targeted state would have lost anyway or when it was combined with strategies that target military assets. Second, it is interesting to note that of the six successes for civilian targeting, five of them occurred in sieges when the enemy army was holed up in a city, supporting the argument that civilian victimization is more effective against smaller targets. Finally, with the exception of the siege of Beirut in 1982, each of the successes occurred sixty or more years ago, which supports the view that civilian victimization has decreased in effectiveness over time.

Conclusion

In this chapter, we set out to determine whether or not civilian victimization helps states win wars. Statistical analysis of civilian targeting, mass killing, and numbers of civilian casualties inflicted showed a positive and in some instances significant correlation between these variables and vic-

---

64. The relative importance of the atomic bombs and Russia's entry into the war in causing Japan to surrender are hotly debated. See Tsuyoshi Hasegawa, ed., *The End of the Pacific War: Reappraisals* (Stanford: Stanford University Press, 2007), for example.

tory in all interstate wars, wars of attrition, and wars of territorial annexation. Civilian victimization also appears to work better against smaller targets. Moreover, the efficacy of civilian victimization has clearly decreased over time, a finding that merits further investigation.

The relatively simple statistical analysis performed in this paper does not yield sufficient information to render a final judgment on the efficacy of civilian victimization, because states choose strategically whether or not to use this method. When states target civilians in wars of territorial annexation, civilian victimization may be a product of victory rather than a cause, and thus these cases are of questionable relevance for judging the effectiveness of the strategy. Further analysis is required to deal with this endogeneity problem.

In costly, protracted wars of attrition, the deck is stacked against civilian victimization because states are highly resolved. More sophisticated statistical analysis may help untangle this selection effect, but in this chapter we have supplemented the statistics with a close look at civilian targeting in wars of attrition. We found several cases that were false positives—civilian victimization that occurred for other reasons or which was unrelated to the war's outcome. Of the relevant cases, civilian victimization arguably played a role in producing the successful outcome a majority of the time. Overall, civilian victimization yielded positive results in 30 to 50 percent of wars of attrition. This is not so different from the rate at which states prevailed when they refrained from targeting civilians. If this finding holds up to further analysis, it would indicate that civilian victimization sometimes succeeds even when the deck is stacked against it, in costly wars of attrition. This result is qualified, though, by the fact that clear successes tend to occur only when the outcome of the war hinges on the siege of a city and when military vulnerability as well as civilian vulnerability is high. Furthermore, most of these successes occurred in the relatively distant past.

This chapter represents a first cut at answering some of the difficult questions surrounding the effectiveness of civilian victimization in war. It points to many interesting questions for further research. Future research should grapple with the problem of selection effects in wars of attrition and the problem of endogeneity in wars of territorial annexation. Careful case studies will also be needed to assess the role that civilian victimization played in contributing to war outcomes that we only sketched out above. It would also be useful to expand the definition of effectiveness in wars to annex territory in order to test the effect of civilian targeting on rebellion, war recurrence, and third-party intervention. More needs to be done to explain why this strategy has become less effective over time. We have posited some potential hypotheses; future research should isolate and test these (and other) hypotheses.

Chapter 3

War, Collaboration, and Endogenous Ethnic Polarization: The Path to Ethnic Cleansing

H. Zeynep Bulutgil

To what extent does the depth of ethnic cleavages play a role in the process that leads to ethnic cleansing? The question is important, as the conventional explanation for ethnic cleansing takes deep ethnic cleavages as the main exogenous variable that explains this phenomenon.[1] The idea is that in societies where ethnic cleavages are deep, relations between different ethnic groups are more strained, and issues that have to do with ethnicity dominate over other politically relevant questions. This leads to the emergence of "organic" nationalism, which views ethnic minorities as inherently different and deserving of exclusion, rather than "civic" nationalism, which aims to incorporate ethnic minorities.[2] In contexts where organic nationalism predominates, ethnic cleansing follows whenever events such as state collapse, war, or geopolitical instability eliminate the constraints against this policy.

This chapter argues that relations between ethnic groups and organic nationalism are to a large extent functions of relations between states rather than of deep ethnic cleavages. In particular, interethnic relations deteriorate and ethnic cleavages trump other cleavages when competing sides in an interstate conflict ally themselves with different ethnic groups in a given society. Such a situation typically emerges when states form

I would like to thank Carles Boix, Stathis Kalyvas, and Lisa Wedeen, as well as the editors of this volume, Adria Lawrence and Erica Chenoweth, for their comments on earlier versions of this chapter.

1. The depth of ethnic cleavages refers to the significance of the differences between ethnic groups in a given context. This significance is determined by a combination of the cultural characteristics of the groups (such as whether or not they speak similar languages or whether or not they practice the same religion) and the historical experience that filters these cultural characteristics (such as whether or not the minority group has had access to a separate education system or an autonomous religious organization).

2. See Michael Mann, *The Dark Side of Democracy: Explaining Ethnic Cleansing* (New York.: Cambridge University Press, 2005); Norman M. Naimark, *Fires of Hatred: Ethnic Cleansing in Twentieth-Century Europe* (Cambridge, Mass.: Harvard University Press, 2001); and Rogers Brubaker, *Citizenship and Nationhood in France and Germany* (Cambridge. Mass.: Harvard University Press, 1992).

alliances with the minority groups in their rival's territory and use these alliances to control the rest of the population during wars and occupations. This situation not only poisons the relations between ethnic groups and radicalizes the politicians that represent the majority ethnic group, but also puts the issue of minority treatment on top of the political agenda once the occupation or war is over. According to this argument, polarized relations between ethnic groups and organic nationalism are not permanent traits that characterize societies with deep ethnic divisions, but variables endogenous to interstate interactions. Put differently, tense relations between ethnic groups are proximate rather than structural or exogenous causes of ethnic cleansing.

To develop this argument, the chapter studies the evolution of the relationship between the majority and minority ethnic groups in the following cases: the Germans in inter-war Czechoslovakia and the Greeks in Ottoman Turkey. These cases were selected for two reasons. First, in both cases the differences between minority and majority groups were historically quite deep. Hence, these are precisely the kind of contexts in which one would expect to observe polarized interethnic relations and organic nationalism as exogenous conditions. Second, the cases cover different historical backgrounds: the Austro-Hungarian Empire in the case of the Germans in Czechoslovakia, and the Ottoman Empire in the case of the Greeks in Ottoman Turkey. Thus, the conclusions do not depend on a specific historical experience associated with the policies of a single empire.

The chapter has three parts. First, I outline the observable implications of the argument. Second, I present the case studies. Finally, I summarize and discuss the findings of the chapter.

The Argument and Observable Implications

What types of observations would support the contention that interethnic relations and ethnic cleansing are endogenous to interstate relations? The logic of the argument suggests that during times of peace, ethnic cleavages do not trump non-ethnic ones, and the politicians representing the majority ethnic groups prefer inclusionary policies rather than ethnic cleansing. Once the minority group is allied with a rival during a war, ethnic cleavages gain relative importance and majority politicians turn to more hostile policies.[3]

---

3.   At the individual level, multiple motivations, including resentment and fear, might lead to this shift in the priorities and opinions of the majority leaders. Hence the argument here is not incompatible with the literature that argues that these motivations lead to mass ethnic violence. On resentment, see Roger Petersen, *Understanding Ethnic Violence. Fear, Hatred, and Resentment in 20th Century Eastern Europe*, (Cambridge: Cambridge University Press, 2002); on fear, or, as more commonly known, the "security dilemma," see Russell Hardin, *One for All: The Logic of Group Conflict* (Princeton, N.J.: Princeton University Press, 1995); and Barry R. Posen, "The Security Dilemma and Ethnic Conflict," *Survival*, Vol. 35, No. 1 (Spring 1993), pp. 27–47. This paper, however, is different in that it provides a theory of the process that paves the way to these motivations.

A number of observable implications follow. To start with, even in societies with deep ethnic cleavages, non-ethnic political divisions, such as those between social classes or center and periphery, should frequently take precedence over ethnicity. To see if this is the case, one needs to focus on the political organization of minority and majority ethnic groups and the relations between them. If ethnic groups are represented by several competing political parties that reflect class or other non-ethnic cleavages and these parties cooperate with each other across ethnic divisions, this would support the argument that ethnicity is not the main cleavage in a given society.

The argument also has implications for the policies that majority politicians follow *vis-à-vis* ethnic minorities. At the very least, in the absence of alliances between outside states and minority groups, majority political leaders should follow inclusive policies, such as assimilating the minority or providing autonomy. These politicians should then become more antagonistic toward minorities when an outside state forms wartime alliances with the minorities.

The potential problem with these implications is that the policies that majority politicians follow during times of peace might not reflect their true preferences. Majority politicians might be avoiding ethnic cleansing because of constraints, such as lack of a location to which minorities could be deported. Given this constraint, they might be using other policies such as forced assimilation to pressure the minority group to leave of its own accord.

There are two solutions to this problem. First, one can ask what type of policy is clearly *not* a substitute for ethnic cleansing in a given context. For example, if the majority politicians spend resources on policies that are aimed at improving the cultural rights or economic conditions of a given ethnic group, this would suggest that their main preference is not permanent exclusion of the group from the territory of the state. Similarly, if majority politicians encourage immigration by the members of the minority group from outside the state, one can also assume that they do not desire to use ethnic cleansing. Second, one can also ask whether majority politicians within or across political parties disagree with each other on how to treat minority ethnic groups. Majority politicians who advocate more pro-minority policies are not more likely to hide their true intentions than politicians who advocate ethnic cleansing or repressive policies that might be designed to substitute for ethnic cleansing. Hence it is reasonable to assume that the politicians who oppose ethnic cleansing or potential substitutes for it are genuinely more favorable toward inclusionary policies. This argument would gain particular support if those politicians who consistently support inclusionary policies during times of peace change their minds after a wartime alliance between the minority group and an occupying state.

Finally, the argument also has implications for the formation of alliances between outside states and minority groups. I argue that ethnic polarization and ethnic cleansing are outcomes of international factors, rather than of deep ethnic divisions. Hence, the argument also implies that the willingness of minority groups to form an alliance with an outside state is primarily exogenous to ethnic divisions between the minority and majority groups.

There are basically two ways in which these alliances can be formed. The first possibility is that in contexts where the differences between majority and minority groups run deep, the minority leadership is a coherent group of individuals who favor independence or joining another state and who are ready to enter into alliances with expansionist states to achieve these ends. If this is how ethnic differences influence alliance formation between minorities and outside states, then ethnic differences do play an important, though indirect, role in the process that leads to ethnic cleansing.

The second possibility starts from the premise that the minority leadership is composed of a variety of types with different preferences on whether to collaborate with outside states or not. In this context, the outside state can play a crucial role by selecting out those minority leaders who favor collaboration while undermining those who oppose it. During peacetime, the outside state can achieve this end by providing financial assistance or strategic aid to those factions that are sympathetic to its goals. During occupations, the outside state might use more direct means, such as providing weapons and other strategic aid to sympathetic factions while eliminating the opposing factions by incarceration or killing. If this "selection story" depicts the formation of alliances more accurately, then the argument of this chapter would receive support.

I have laid out a theory of ethnic cleansing that has implications for the way in which minority and majority ethnic groups interact. During times of peace, the argument predicts the existence of notable non-ethnic cleavages that cut across ethnic ones, as well as cooperation across ethnic cleavages. This type of interaction ceases to exist and majority politicians switch to ethnic cleansing when an outside state tries to annex the territory of the state and forms an alliance with an ethnic minority in the process. The theory also has implications for the formation of the alliances between outside states and minority ethnic groups: the policies of the outside states should play a major role in this process. The case studies below provide a qualitative test of the theory by focusing on the evolution of the historical processes that relate to these implications.

Czechoslovakia: From the Switzerland of the East to Ethnic Cleansing

The Czechoslovak Republic was officially recognized in 1919 at the Paris Peace Conference. It had a highly ethnically heterogeneous population, with about 48 percent Czechs, 23 percent Germans, 16 percent Slovaks, and smaller numbers of Ukrainians, Hungarians, and Poles. In addition to being the second largest group, the Germans constituted one-third of the population of Bohemia, the most economically developed region in Czechoslovakia. Most of the German population lived in a strip of territory on the Czechoslovak-German border, called the Sudetenland, where they formed the majority of the population. Smaller numbers of Germans also lived in Slovakia and Carpatho-Ukraine.

The initial takeover of German areas by Czech forces was relatively smooth, without much resistance from the German population. However, there were several instances in which the Germans expressed their disappointment in being included in the Czechoslovak Republic. For example, the German leadership organized a demonstration in March 1919, during which the Czech police forces panicked and opened fire on the demonstrators. There were also more symbolic acts of protest. German deputies in the newly elected Czech Parliament initially refused to participate in parliamentary proceedings and issued a declaration proclaiming that they would not recognize the Czechoslovak state's right to Sudetenland.

Despite these early signs of protest, German opinion was from the beginning very much divided on the question of which country they should be located in. Many favored incorporation into Austria, which was not unexpected, as they had previously been part of the Austro-Hungarian Empire. Small but significant factions preferred incorporation into Germany or Czechoslovakia. One group that favored incorporation into Czechoslovakia was the industrialists, who thought that they would be at an advantage within Czechoslovakia rather than within Germany, where they would face substantial competition from indigenous firms.

From the early 1920s, the German leadership showed two important characteristics. First, it was divided among several political parties that fit on a typical left-right spectrum. The dominant party on the left was the German Social Democratic Party, which proved to be the largest German party in the 1925 and 1929 elections. The major center-right parties included the German Christian Democrats and German Agrarians. The parties on the left and right were truly at odds with each other, especially on issues that related to socioeconomic policies. In the words of an expert at the time, "the most striking thing about the Sudeten Germans, politically, was the number of parties into which they had redivided, and the squabbles between these groups."[4]

Second, all major German parties, regardless of their ideological orientation, decided to take the "activist" path.[5] In other words, they declared loyalty to the Czechoslovak State and displayed a willingness to collaborate with the Czech parties that shared their ideological orientations. The combined vote of these parties, which included the Social Democrats, Christian Democrats, and the Agrarians, was about 70 percent of the German vote in Czechoslovakia until the 1935 elections. The only exceptions to this trend were the German Nationalist Party and the German National Socialists (DNSAP). These were the only parties which stuck to an irre-

---

4. Elizabeth Wiskemann, *Czechs and Germans: A Study of the Struggles in the Historic Provinces of Bohemia and Moravia* (New York: Oxford University Press, 1938), p. 131.

5. In the context of interwar Czechoslovakia, the term "activist" referred to parties that were open to cooperation with the Czechoslovak state. I also use this word to refer to these parties.

dentist agenda and denied loyalty to the Czechoslovak State; their vote share among the Germans was considerably smaller than the "activist" parties.

The Czechs for their part also had a number of political parties located on the left-right spectrum. The Agrarian Party was the largest party on the right, and the Social Democratic Party dominated on the left. Notably, there was substantial cooperation between the German and Czech parties with similar socioeconomic agendas. The center-right parties, the German Agrarians, Czech Agrarians, and German Christian Democrats, formed a coalition in 1925 as a reaction to the increasingly "strong performance of communists."[6] In 1929, this right-wing coalition was replaced by a coalition of Czech and German Social Democratic parties.

The Czechoslovak policies toward the Germans were quite liberal under both right-wing and left-wing governments. In fact, one could argue that they not only fulfilled the requirements of the minority treaties but also at times went beyond them. For example, during World War I, a good number of Sudeten Germans had bought war bonds from Germany, but at the end of the war Germany was unable to fulfill these loans. This situation left many Czechoslovak Germans under economic distress; hence the Czechoslovak state fulfilled these loans, albeit at a reduced rate.[7] On more conventional issues such as education, the Czechoslovaks treated Germans fairly. Germans enjoyed a system of public and private schools that taught in German, as well as a German university. In fact, the number of schools per student in the German areas of Czechoslovakia exceeded the number of schools per student in Prussia at the time.[8] The area where the Germans clearly lost was their share in the bureaucracy. The decline in the number of Germans in public service was mostly due to the new requirement that all civil servants should be able to speak Czech.

All in all, in the 1920s and mid-1930s, neither the Czech nor the German populations displayed a radical, organic form of nationalism. Both groups were divided between right- and left-leaning factions that regularly cooperated with their ideological counterparts in the other group, and the German parties that favored irredentism were confined to the margins of politics. In fact, to an observer in the early 1930s, Eduard Benes's depiction of Czechoslovakia as "the Switzerland of the East" was not a far-fetched analogy. Yet an observer looking back from the 1950s would find the analogy rather ill-fitting, for in less than a decade the Sudeten Germans had turned almost uniformly pro–Third Reich, collaborated with the occupying German forces, and were deported to Germany. How did the German leaders in Czechoslovakia shift towards Nazi Germany within a couple of years?[9] How did the Czech leaders, who had adopted

---

6. Joseph Rothschild, *East Central Europe Between Two World Wars* (Seattle: University of Washington Press, 1974), p. 112.

7. Radomir Luza, *The Transfer of the Sudeten Germans: A Study of Czech-German Relations, 1933–1962* (New York: New York University Press, 1964), p. 45.

8. Ibid, p. 41.

9. Also see Erin K. Jenne, *Ethnic Bargaining: The Paradox of Minority Empowerment*

quite liberal policies toward the Germans throughout the 1920s and 1930s, decide to deport them from their territory?

Economic factors undoubtedly played a role. An important aspect of the Czechoslovak economic structure was that the Germans tended to dominate in the export-oriented light industries, whereas the Czechs dominated in heavy industry geared toward domestic consumption. The Great Depression and tightening international trade restrictions therefore took a higher toll on the German industries than the Czech ones. In the immediate aftermath of the Great Depression, rates of unemployment were higher in German areas than in Czech areas, and economic recovery arrived more quickly to the Czech regions due to an increase in the demand for military equipment. The government introduced social insurance measures to alleviate the effects of the Depression in Czech as well as German areas. In fact, the Germans received more than their national share of the benefits that the government provided to the unemployed. But high unemployment rates still urged some Germans to look beyond the mainstream parties.[10]

Yet the Sudeten German shift toward a more nationalist and pro-German attitude cannot be attributed to just domestic economic factors, as this trend continued and accelerated even after the German areas of Czechoslovakia recovered economically. The key driving force for the German population's shift toward a radical platform was intervention from Germany. Organizations that aimed at preserving the identity of Germans in central Europe existed long before Hitler's accession to power. Their main function was to ensure that the Germans located in central Europe remained culturally distinct, which in the future could help justify Germany's claim to these territories. Among these, the main organization was the VDA (Society for Germandom Abroad), an association that professed to have cultural rather than political goals and busied itself with founding cultural societies in Czechoslovakia as well as elsewhere. After the Nazis came to power, they increased the funding for the VDA and created other organizations with more aggressive platforms such as the VoMi (*Volksdeutsche Mittelstelle*).[11] Germany also influenced the German minority in Czechoslovakia by channeling funds through its consulates in various cities of Czechoslovakia. Intervention from Germany led to two notable changes in the structure of the German minority and its leadership. The first was a general shift away from political parties that concentrated on socioeconomic issues to parties with a nationalist platform; the second

---

(Ithaca, N.Y.: Cornell University Press, 2007) on this question. The analysis below diverges from Jenne's work in that it focuses on the political cleavages within the Czech as well as the German community in interwar Czechoslovakia and, given that it is primarily interested in ethnic cleansing rather than ethnic bargaining, it pays specific attention to the formation of the wartime alliance between the German minority in Czechoslovakia and Germany and the impact of this alliance on the decision to deport the Germans after the war.

10.   Ibid, p. 17.

11.   Lumans O. Valdis, *Himmler's Auxiliaries: The Volksdeutsche Mittelstelle and the German National Minorities of Europe, 1933–1945* (Chapel Hill: University of North Carolina Press, 1993).

was an internal shift within the nationalist party from a moderately nationalist, autonomy-seeking platform to a radical, irredentist platform.

Reflecting these two changes, three important events shaped the future of German politics within Czechoslovakia. First, the German Nazi Party in Czechoslovakia disbanded itself in autumn of 1933, around the same time the German Nationalist Party was banned by the Czechoslovak government. Second, a new German party with a nationalist platform, the Sudeten Home Front (SHF), later named the Sudeten German Party (SdP), was formed in October 1933 under the leadership of Konrad Henlein. Third, the Nazi regime in Germany, which took over in 1933, decided to put its weight behind this new party, as opposed to other German parties. Through organizations such as the VDA and the German consulates in Czechoslovakia, the SHF was given substantial financial assistance on several occasions. For example, before the 1935 elections, the SHF received a large amount of financial assistance from the German Foreign Ministry.[12]

The assistance from Berlin also took more indirect forms. The German cultural associations that received financial aid from Berlin were encouraged to unite under an umbrella organization and were instructed to follow the SHF. These interventions from Germany bore fruit in the 1935 elections when the SHF, then renamed SdP, received 63.17 percent of the German votes in Bohemia and 56.12 percent of the German votes in Moravia and Silesia.[13]

Why was the German turn from a moderate to a nationalist platform so sudden? The answer is that despite the shift to the SdP in 1935, the change in German public opinion was not so sudden after all. In fact, it is unlikely that when the Sudeten Germans voted for the SdP in 1935, they were actually voting for a radical, irredentist platform. Many non-German observers of the SHF-SdP did not consider it a radical and dangerous threat to the state. Among these was the party with the largest vote share in Czechoslovakia, the center-right Czech Agrarian Party. The Agrarians considered the socialist and communist movements within the German community as more dangerous than the nationalist platform of the SHF, and provided financial and political assistance to the SHF on several critical occasions. In 1933 and 1934, Henlein met with one of the prominent leaders of the Czech Agrarian Party, Viktor Stoupal, and received large amounts of money to help the SHF overcome the left-leaning German parties in the elections.[14] In addition, when the cabinet was considering whether to dissolve the SHF, the Agrarians strongly objected to such a policy. The decision was eventually left to the President of Czechoslovakia, Jan Masaryk, who decided to let the SHF participate in the elections. The SHF-SdP also had other unlikely allies. For example, Henlein traveled to Britain several times and was considered by the British a sensible

---

12.   Ibid, p. 74.

13.   Ibid, p. 80.

14.   Ronald M. Smelser, *The Sudeten Problem, 1933–1938: Volkstumspolitik and the Formulation of Nazi Foreign Policy* (Middletown, Conn: Wesleyan University Press, 1975), p. 102.

politician who could be an important counter-weight to "the Communist threat" in Czechoslovakia.

Furthermore, it is questionable whether the leadership of the SHF-SdP was initially planning to turn into a pro-Nazi party. From before the 1935 elections to 1937, Henlein professed loyalty to the Czechoslovak State and followed a cooperative line toward the Czech parties. In 1934, the SHF issued a decision to fight against fascism, including fascism in the form of National Socialism. In October 1934, Henlein gave a speech in front of 20,000 spectators, proclaiming his loyalty to democracy and the Czechoslovak Republic and condemning pan-Germanism as well as pan-Slavism.[15] Henlein also went a step further and entered into negotiations with the Czech Agrarians on a potential election coalition, but the two parties failed to reach an agreement.[16]

One can dismiss the importance of these acts by arguing that they were mere tactics designed to calm the Czech leadership, rather than actions that reflected the true intentions of the SHF leader. It is important to note, however, that Henlein's conciliatory attitude toward the Czechs was controversial within his own party and within the German nationalist leadership in general. As a matter of fact, he was heavily criticized by the more radical members of the SHF, as well as by the National Socialists in Czechoslovakia, for his willingness to cooperate with the Czech government.

The second important change in the leadership of the German minority in Czechoslovakia was the shift within the SHF-SdP toward a radical and pro-Reich nationalism. The core of the SHF leadership came from an organization called the Kameradschaftsbund (KB), formed by a small number of young Germans after the independence of Czechoslovakia. The KB was an exclusionary organization whose membership did not exceed 200–500 persons, but it provided the leadership cadre of the SHF, including important figures such as Walter Brand and Heinz Rutha.[17] Most of these individuals had studied in Austria under Othmar Spann, who espoused an elitist, conservative, and anti-Marxist ideology, and they considered themselves Spann's disciples.[18] While not one of the leading members, Henlein also had strong ties with the KB.[19]

The KB and the leadership of the SHF-SdP initially differed in important respects from the adamantly anti-Czechoslovak political parties, the National Socialists and German Nationalists. The KB members were traditionalist and pro-Church, and, more importantly, they were "interested in the unity of the Sudeten Germans within the context of the Czechoslo-

---

15. Smelser, *The Sudeten Problem*, p. 101. Also see Keith Robbins, "Konrad Henlein and the Sudeten Question and British Foreign Policy," *Historical Journal*, Vol. 12, No. 4 (December 1969), pp. 674–697.

16. Smelser, *The Sudeten Problem*, p. 132.

17. John Haag, "'Knights of the Spirit': Kameradschaftsbund," *Journal of Contemporary History*, Vol. 8, No. 3 (July 1973), pp. 133–153.

18. Haag, "Knights of the Spirit."

19. Robbins, "Konrad Henlein."

vak State."[20] The National Socialists, by contrast, were anti-Church and favored unification with Germany from the beginning. In the words of a German minister in Prague, "the National Socialists looked to Germany, whereas the KB wanted to create a Sudeten German man analogous to an Austrian."[21] Geographically, the strengths of the National Socialists and the KB lay in different regions. The KB had its stronghold in Northern Bohemia, where the professional German classes had close ties with Prague, whereas the National Socialists were stronger in western parts of Bohemia, particularly in the city of Asch, which had close ties with Germany.[22]

The differences between the KB and the National Socialists were not lost on the Nazi regime. In a meeting in December 1933 held to determine how funds should be channeled to the members of the defunct German National Socialists, they decided that KB must be "ruled out in advance as unreliable" and should not receive subsidies from the Reich.[23] Funds from Germany must have been quite important, because Konrad Henlein and Walter Brand travelled to Berlin, met with the director of the VDA, and convinced him to provide funds to the SHF-SdP. Meanwhile, the Berlin government started to consider SHF-SdP useful because its relatively moderate line made it more palatable for the Sudeten Germans and the Czechoslovak government.

Moreover, after the dissolution of the German National Party and the German National Socialists, some members of these parties joined the SHF-SdP. As a result, two factions, one KB and the other National Socialist, emerged within the SHF-SdP. These factions had important disagreements. For example, it was the KB-oriented members of the SHF-SdP who drafted the conciliatory speech that Henlein gave in 1934, a speech heavily criticized by the leaders with a National Socialist background, as well as by the more radical members of SHF-SdP such as K. B. Frank.[24] The KB and National Socialist factions came into conflict on several other occasions.[25] In the beginning, the KB side of the party, backed by Henlein, seemed to have the upper hand in these conflicts. This must have worried the Reich officials about the true nature of Henlein's aims, as they demanded a declaration of solidarity with Germany. Henlein complied on June 21 in the Nazi stronghold of Asch, declaring, "it is essential that Prague should create a new, decent relationship to the entire German race, particularly to the German Reich…I prefer to be hated in the company of Germany than to draw advantages out of hatred of Germany."[26]

The friction within the SdP continued until the end of 1937. By then, the political context was completely different. Within Germany itself, for-

---

20.   Smelser, *The Sudeten Problem*, p. 57.

21.   Ibid, pp. 61, 62.

22.   Ibid, pp. 62–64.

23.   Haag, "Knights of the Spirit," p. 143.

24.   Robbins, "Konrad Henlein," p. 681.

25.   Ibid., p. 684.

26.   Ibid., p. 685.

mer allies of the KB leaders had lost their positions, and the VDA was replaced by VoMi under the leadership of Heinrich Himmler. In March 1938, the situation changed even further when Germany invaded Austria and declared the Anschluss. After these developments, the KB leaders and Henlein expressed their allegiance to National Socialism increasingly more vocally. Both opportunism and fear seems have played a role in this shift. The invasion of Austria made it clear that Hitler would soon move on Sudeten Germany, and those who wanted a career under the new regime were well-advised to follow a pro-Nazi line. At the same time, the mentor to many KB members, Othmar Spann, and his son were taken to a concentration camp after the invasion of Austria. Their harsh treatment signaled to the KB leaders the potential harm that might come from not fully complying with the Berlin line.[27] The former KB members were not alone in these assessments. After the Anschluss, several formerly "activist" conservative political parties such as the German Agrarians and German Christian Democrats disbanded their parties and joined the SdP.

In sum, after the independence of Czechoslovakia, the Germans had highly diverse political leanings and organizations, most of which did not adhere to an extreme nationalist platform that favored unification with Germany. Even among nationalist Germans there was an important distinction between those that were for unification with Germany and those that sought to achieve complete autonomy within the Czechoslovak state. The intervention from Berlin—especially in the form of financial aid—fundamentally changed the structure of the German leadership by gradually unifying it on a radical platform that was ready to act as the ally of Germany within Czechoslovakia.

The Czech response to the growing radicalization of the German community was for a long time highly restrained. On the one hand, parties that adamantly refused to cooperate with the system, such as the National Socialists and German National Party, were banned after the Nazi accession to power in Germany. On the other hand, Czech politicians tried to turn the tide of German nationalism by letting the SdP function as a legitimate political party. Czech politicians also tried to appease the Germans in other ways. For example, in 1936, the Czechoslovak President Eduard Benes toured the German areas of Bohemia, attending cultural events such as the opening of a German theater and giving conciliatory speeches. In 1937, the Czech government also accepted a program outlined by the "activist" German parties, which expanded Germans' rights within Czechoslovakia by increasing their representation in the public sector and securing government contracts for German-owned companies. However, the SdP rejected the plan.[28]

In 1938, the relations between the SdP and the Czech government grew tenser. By then, Henlein was aware of the impending German invasion and was instructed from Germany to demand more until the Czech side could not accept the proposed reforms. Unable to reach an agree-

27. Haag, "Knights of the Spirit," p. 152.
28. Luza, *The Transfer of the Sudeten Germans*, pp. 96, 97.

ment with the SdP and faced with a German revolt, on September 13 the Czech Army took control of the Sudetenland and declared martial law. In the aftermath of the takeover, the leading figures of the SdP, including Henlein, escaped to Germany, and the rest of the SdP members defected to a compromising position with the Czech government. These developments, however, were rendered insignificant with Germany's invasion of the Sudetenland in November 1938 and then the rest of Czechoslovakia in March 1939.

The occupation of Czechoslovakia fundamentally changed the relationship between the Czechs and Germans and the Czech leadership's approach to the German problem. From the beginning, the members of the German minority in Czechoslovakia were visibly involved in the occupation regime. K. B. Frank, a prominent SdP leader with close ties to Himmler, was chosen to be the State Secretary of the Protectorate of Bohemia and Moravia. The Sudeten Germans also played an important role in the lower echelons of the occupation administration. For example, the commissars running the cities were mostly Sudeten Germans.

Among Frank's first actions were closing down Czech universities, theaters, and most Czech publications. After mass demonstrations in the summer of 1939, about 8,000 public figures were arrested. In response to student protests that took place in November 1939, nine leading student activists were shot and about 1,200 students were sent to concentration camps.[29] Reinhard Heydrich's appointment as the Reich Commissar to Bohemia and Moravia further increased the level of repression. The Czech Prime Minister and five other leading figures were killed in September 1941, and the number of executions and deportations to concentration camps increased. An important turning point was the assassination of Heydrich on May 27, 1942, carried out by parachutists who were sent from Britain. In a response that came to symbolize the brutality of the occupation for the Czechs, the Germans carried out 1,148 arrests, 657 summary executions, and razed a village named Lidice, killing all of its male inhabitants.

The policies of the German occupiers and Sudeten Germans' visible connection to them had a profound impact on the Czech leadership. After the occupation, two groups of Czechoslovak leaders emerged. One was the resistance movement within Czechoslovakia, known as "the Central Committee of Home Resistance" (UVOD), dominated mostly by Social Democrats.[30] The other was the government-in-exile in Britain, led by Eduard Benes, the Czechoslovak President at the time of the German invasion. Given that the experience of the UVOD members with the German occupation was more direct, it is not surprising that they were the first ones to advocate a complete deportation of the German population once the occupation was over. As early as 1940, UVOD incorporated the idea of the transfer of Sudeten Germans in its program. In September 1941, the

---

29. Ibid.
30. Ibid., p. 220.

UVOD newspaper declared, "the third republic will be a national state—it cannot tolerate any more the old conception of the minority policy." [31]

The leaders of the government-in-exile changed their opinions more slowly, but they also eventually converged on the deportation of the Germans. For example, in the winter of 1940–1941, they discussed several potential solutions for the German minority problem in Czechoslovakia. Among the proposals considered were the transfer of Czechs to German regions; the cession of some German territories, such as Asch and its surrounding area, to Germany; the forced assimilation of Germans, the deportation of Germans to Germany; and combinations of these policies. By the end of 1941, however, there was general agreement that any plan at the end of the war would involve a comprehensive deportation of Germans. In September 1941, Benes declared that he "accepted the principle of the transfer of populations"; in January 1942, he argued that "it will be necessary to rid our country of all German bourgeoisie, the pan-German intelligentsia, and the workers who have gone over to fascism."[32]

The gradual radicalization of the Czech opinion in exile can also be observed in their interactions with the Sudeten Germans, mainly German Social Democrats, who had also escaped the Nazi invasion of Czechoslovakia. Between 1940 and 1942, the leader of the German Social Democrats, Wenzel Jaksch, and Eduard Benes met at least four times. At the first meeting in August 1939, Jaksch offered to join the liberation movement in return for guarantees for a federal Czechoslovakia after the war, and Benes rejected the offer. The negotiations in July 1940 had more positive results: Jaksch declared solidarity with Benes, and Benes responded by inviting the German Social Democrats to join the State Council. By the end of 1941, however, Benes had to adjust this decision. At a meeting in September, he told Jaksch that they would need to postpone the joining of the Germans in the State Council because of the rising levels of repression in Czechoslovakia. Finally, by January 1942, cooperation with German Social Democrats was completely out of the question. In their last meeting, Benes told Jaksch that the events in Czechoslovakia and the demands of the underground movement made it impossible for the Germans to participate in any liberation movement.[33]

Given the gradual radicalization of the Czech leadership throughout the war, it was not surprising that once the German armies pulled out, the Czech leaders proceeded to implement ethnic cleansing against the Czechoslovak Germans. The deportation of the German population of Czechoslovakia took place in two episodes. The first episode started immediately after the Soviet forces entered Czechoslovakia and lasted until the Potsdam Conference in August 1945, which sanctioned the orderly transfer of Germans from Czechoslovakia as well as from Poland and Hungary. The deportations in this period were sporadic and carried out

---

31. Ibid., pp. 220, 221.

32. Ibid., p. 233.

33. Edvard Beneš, *Memoirs of Dr. Eduard Beneš: From Munich to New War and New Victory* (Boston: Houghton Mifflin, 1954).

by the members of the Czech resistance with the aid of the Red Army. The second episode started after the Potsdam Conference and lasted until the end of 1947. During this period, orderly convoys of Czechoslovak Germans were organized and sent to Soviet- or U.S.-occupied German territory. By the end of 1947, a total of 3,200,000 Germans had been forced to leave Czechoslovakia, leaving Bohemia with virtually no Germans.[34]

The Ottoman State: From Multinational Empire to Ethnic Cleansing

At the beginning of the twentieth century, the Greek population of the Ottoman Empire lived in several areas. The largest concentrations were in the capital city of Istanbul, where 300,000–400,000 Greeks lived; the western regions of Anatolia, including the city of Izmir, where 300,000–500,000 Greeks lived; and Thrace and Macedonia, where about 600,000 Greeks lived.[35] There were also significant Greek populations in the province of Trabzon in Northeastern Anatolia, in Central Anatolia, and in the area around the city of Bursa. In total, the Greeks constituted about 14 percent of the Ottoman population in the early twentieth century.

The main factor that historically held the Greek community together was the practice of Orthodox Christianity and its place in the Ottoman system. As part of the millet system, the Greek Orthodox Church had extensive privileges, which basically allowed it to organize the internal affairs of the Orthodox population. These privileges included a court system responsible for resolving intra-communal disputes, authority over the education of the Orthodox population of the Empire, and the right to collect taxes from this group. Historically, the entire Orthodox population of the Ottoman Empire, including Bulgarian and Serbian speakers, had been under the jurisdiction of the Orthodox Patriarch. By the 1900s, however, the picture had changed; the Serbs had gained their independence and, to curb the power of the Orthodox Patriarch in the face of territorial demands from the Greek state, the Ottomans had allowed the Bulgarians to form their own Exarchist Church with similar rights to the Orthodox Patriarchy. Hence, by the beginning of twentieth century, the overlap between the Greek national identity and membership in the Orthodox Patriarchy was tighter than it had ever been.

The Ottoman Greeks had historically played an important role in both the Ottoman administration and the economy. Immediately after Greek independence in 1821, there was a certain decline in Greek predominance

---

34.   Joseph B. Schechtman, *European Population Transfers 1945–1955* (Philadelphia: University of Pennsylvania Press, 1962).

35.   For Anatolia and Istanbul, see Alexis Alexandris, "The Greek Census of Anatolia and Thrace (1910–1912): A Contribution to Ottoman Historical Demography," in Dimitri Gondicas and Charles Issawi, eds., *Ottoman Greeks in the Age of Nationalism* (Princeton, N.J.: Darwin Press, 1999). For Macedonia and Thrace, see A. A. Pallis, "Racial Migrations in the Balkans during the Years 1912–1924," *Geographical Journal*, Vol 66, No. 4 (October 1925), pp. 315–331.

in the Ottoman administration.[36] But in the 1850s, the Greeks still had highly significant positions in the Ottoman administration, especially in the diplomatic corps, and represented the Ottoman Empire against foreign countries, including Greece. Economically, the Greeks were the most active segment of the Ottoman middle class; they dominated sectors such as shipping, mining, commercial agriculture, and banking. They played a substantial role in the economy of the wealthiest regions of the empire, such as the Aydin Province and Istanbul.

In the second half of the nineteenth century, the Ottomans made a halfhearted attempt to "Ottomanize" the Greek population, along with the other minorities of the empire. The first steps toward this direction were taken with the declaration of the Edict of Tanzimat in 1839 and the Gulhane Hatti Humayun in 1856. Both documents declared the Greeks and other Christian communities to be equal citizens of the empire and gave them the right to serve in the army. The latter policy was potentially important because the Christian population had previously been excluded from serving in the army and had been forced to pay an additional tax instead. In the following years, other laws were passed, including ones extending state control over education and controlling brigandage in the countryside. However, most of these reforms remained on paper, and the communal structure of the Ottoman society survived more or less intact until the twentieth century.

Demographic changes in the empire also reflected the Ottoman attitude toward the Greeks at the time. During the period between 1831 and 1881, the Greek population grew by 2 percent per year, whereas during the same period the Muslim population remained roughly the same.[37] The growth in the Greek population was especially significant in the Western regions, particularly in the Aydin Province. For example, in the city of Izmir, the Greek population grew from 20,000 in 1830 to 200,000 in 1910.[38] What is noteworthy is that in addition to the natural population increase, the rise in the Greek population resulted from emigration from mainland Greece. Remarkably, the Ottoman Empire encouraged such immigration to attract occupants for unused land in western Anatolia.[39] Hence, if the demographic policies of the empire are a guide, in the second half of the nineteenth century, the Ottoman State did not consider the existence of a substantial Greek population on its territory to be a problem.

With the exception of a short-lived experience with Parliament in 1877–1878, the Ottoman State remained strictly authoritarian until 1908. There were, however, several groups that sought to introduce a parliamentary system and curb the powers of Sultan Abdulhamit. Some of these

---

36.   Ilber Ortayli, "Greeks in the Ottoman Administration During the Tanzimat Period," in Dimitri Gondicas and Charles Issawi, eds., *Ottoman Greeks in the Age of Nationalism* (Princeton, N.J.: Darwin Press, 1999).

37.   Gerasimos Augustinos, *The Greeks of Asia Minor: Confession, Community, and Ethnicity in the Nineteenth Century* (Kent, Ohio: Kent State University Press, 1992).

38.   Ibid., pp. 20, 21.

39.   Ibid., p. 23.

"Young Turks" were located in Western European capitals. This émigré group was divided between those who preferred a more centralized political system and those who envisioned an economically and politically decentralized one. A second part of the Young Turk movement was a group of young officers, who formed a secret organization—the Committee of Union and Progress (CUP). In 1908, this organization started a rebellion in Macedonia, which the Sultan could not crush. In July 1908 of that year, Abdulhamit was forced to sanction elections for a new Parliament.

As a result of the transition to a more democratic system, the fault lines in Ottoman politics became more visible. On one side was the CUP, which favored a centralized political system and sought to curtail the privileges of religious institutions, whether Muslim or Christian. The CUP's view on the Christian minorities, such as Greeks, was an extension of its more general ideology: it wanted to achieve a system in which the minorities would enjoy equal rights with the Muslims and, in return, it expected the Christian minorities to adopt an Ottoman identity that would trump their communal identities.[40]

With the benefit of hindsight, such an expectation on the part of the CUP leaders appears naïve and doomed to failure. Yet in 1908, there was some euphoria among Turks and Christian minorities about the new political system and its promises. After all, Greek and Bulgarian Christians had supported and welcomed the rebellion in Macedonia.[41] There were also some signs that the new constitution might lead to a decrease in the Greek and Bulgarian nationalist activity that had afflicted Macedonia in the last decade. For example, both the Bulgarian and Greek bands that were operating in Macedonia halted their activities after 1908.[42] The optimism at the time is well-illustrated by the words of a Greek observer in Macedonia, Athanasios Souliotes, who played an important role in Ottoman Greek politics: "the fact that a promise that was not particularly sincere could cause people of different nations that used to look at each other with suspicion to fill the streets holding hands convinced me that nations with so much in common could always find ways to cooperate, join forces, and live in amity."[43]

The second faction in Ottoman politics was an odd coalition of liberals and the religious elite that assembled to counter the CUP. What bound these forces together was a dislike for the centralist paradigm espoused by the CUP and a preference for a more decentralized system allowing for religious and communal autonomy. By implication, this faction favored

40.   Feroz Ahmad, *The Young Turks: The Committee of Union and Progress in Turkish Politics, 1908–1914* (Oxford: Clarendon Press, 1969); and Bernard Lewis, *The Emergence of Modern Turkey* (New York: Oxford University Press, 1961).

41.   Ahmad, *The Young Turks*; and Douglas Dakin, *The Greek Struggle in Macedonia, 1897–1913* (Salonica, Greece: Institute for Balkan Studies, 1996).

42.   Dakin, *The Greek Struggle in Macedonia*, p. 382.

43.   Thanos Veremis, "The Hellenic Kingdom and the Ottoman Greeks: The Experiment of the Society of Constantinople," in Dimitri Gondicas and Charles Issawi, eds., *Ottoman Greeks in the Age of Nationalism* (Princeton, N.J.: Darwin Press, 1999), p. 184.

retaining the communal privileges of Christian minorities, rather than pursuing policies that sought to "Ottomanize" and secularize them along with their Muslim counterparts.

This faction formed two political parties. The first one, Ahrar Firkasi (Liberal Party) was formed in September 1908. This party, however, proved to be short-lived, because it got involved in an attempted coup that was organized by a combination of religious officers and elite on April 13, 1909. The attempted coup was crushed by military units who arrived from the CUP stronghold of Macedonia and were sympathetic to this party. In the aftermath of the coup, the CUP used its regained strength to force the Liberal Party to dissolve itself. In 1911, the "liberal group," most of whom were already in the Parliament, formed yet another political party, named the Freedom and Unity Party (FU). The FU had some initial success in the intermediary elections of 1911, but its performance in the general elections of 1912 was mixed, not least due to CUP's violent tactics during the elections.[44] The FU's importance, however, lay not in its electoral success but in the fact that there were a lot of individuals in the cabinet, as well as in the Parliament, who were not officially members but were nevertheless sympathetic to its political agenda.[45]

Both the CUP and the FU were willing to cooperate with minorities for ideological reasons and to increase their political support against each other. The FU was widely supported by several Muslim minority groups such as the Arabs and Albanians, and it also succeeded in acquiring the support of the Greek leadership. When the FU was being established in 1911, the members of the Greek Party in the Parliament (MPs), which included sixteen of the twenty-six Greek MPs, were actually invited to join the FU.[46] The Greek parliamentarians did not want to officially join the FU, but they agreed to work closely with it against the CUP, and to this effect they assigned two MPs who were responsible for regulating the relations between the Greek Party and the FU. The FU members, the members of the Greek Party, and representatives of other nationalities met regularly in order to coordinate their activities against the CUP.[47] In addition to these regular meetings, there were election coalitions between the Liberal Party and the Patriarchate in 1908 and the FU and the Greek Party in 1912.[48]

---

44. This election is known as the "big stick" election in Ottoman History.

45. Kemal Pasa, who was sympathetic to the Liberals, twice served as the prime minister.

46. Ali Birinci, *Hürriyet ve İtilâf fırkasi: II. Meşrutiyet Devrinde İttihat ve Terrakki'ye Karsi Cıkanlar* (Istanbul, Turkey: Dergâh Yayınları, 1990). The "Greek Party" was not an official political party, but a parliamentary group of Greek deputies.

47. Ibid, p. 114.

48. Feroz Ahmad, "Unionist Relations with the Greek, Armenian, and Jewish Communities of the Ottoman Empire, 1908–1914," in Benjamin Braude and Bernard Lewis, eds., *Christians and Jews in the Ottoman Empire: The Functioning of a Plural Society* (New York: Holmes & Meier, 1982).

For its part, the CUP also made attempts to cooperate with the Greeks but, due to its centralizing tendencies, its relations with Greek leaders proved to be more difficult. The first potential conflict arose right after the 1908 revolution, when the Greek Patriarch, fearful of CUP's impact on the Patriarchy and the Greek community, asked the Ottoman Court (Sublime Porte) to guarantee the traditional millet privileges.[49] In order to allay the Patriarch's fears, the CUP sent a representative known for his liberal views to reiterate that the CUP did not intend to encroach on the Patriarchy's privileges. The second problem emerged on the eve of the first parliamentary elections in 1908, when some of the Greek residents of the empire were not given the right to vote in the elections. Some of these people were actually foreign subjects; others had avoided registering as citizens because doing so would have obliged them to pay high taxes or serve in the army. On this occasion, the CUP decided to act as the intermediary between the Porte and the Patriarch and sent a delegation to the Patriarch composed of two Muslims and one Greek. In the negotiations, the Patriarch was offered representation in the Parliament proportional to the share of Greeks in the population.[50] Though the Patriarch initially responded positively toward this offer, the conflict over voting rights and Greek representation in the Parliament was not totally resolved.

The relations between the Greek leaders and the CUP got considerably worse after the Greek Party allied itself first with the Liberal Union and then with the organizers of the coup attempt in April 1909. After the CUP regained power, it passed several resolutions that severely restricted the privileges of the Greek and other Christian communities. These resolutions included an educational reform that restricted communal rights, as well as the conscription of the Christians to the Ottoman Army without the option of paying to get out of service. These laws, however, were quickly rescinded in 1911. Part of the reason for CUP's change of heart was the formation of the FU and the potential threat that it posed to CUP's supremacy. To counter the FU threat, the CUP once again switched to a policy of conciliation with the Greek leaders. Prior to the elections in 1912, it sent a delegation to the Greek Patriarch and proposed to form an election coalition in return for several concessions, such as increasing the number of Greek MPs in the Parliament and giving the Minister of Justice position to a Greek politician.[51] This offer, however, was declined by the Patriarch under pressure from the Greek Party in the Parliament, which preferred to enter into an agreement with the FU. However, this decision was not unchallenged, and several Greek parliamentarians preferred to enter the elections on the CUP list.

---

49. Ibid, p. 407.

50. Ibid, p. 408.

51. Alexis Alexandris, *The Greek Minority of Istanbul and Greek-Turkish Relations, 1918–1974* (Athens: Center for Asia Minor Studies, 1992); Birinci, "Hurriyet ve Itilâf fırkasi," p. 138; and Tarik Zafer Tunaya, *Turkiye'de Siyasal Partiler* (Istanbul: Hurriyet Vakfı Yayınları, 1934).

The Greek community of the Ottoman Empire had its own political factions that evolved over time. In the 1850s, there were two main blocs. One, promoted by the Patriarchy, civil servants, and wealthy merchants, favored the existing status quo within the Empire. Another, supported by middle-class professionals, looked to the Greek state for guidance.[52] After the Greek defeat in the 1897 Greco-Turkish War, the attitude of the second faction started to change for two reasons. The first was the general disappointment in Greece's performance in the 1897 war; the second was the growing competition between the Orthodox Patriarchate and the Bulgarian Exarchate in Macedonia. As a result of these factors, a new outlook, which sought to endorse "Hellenism" within a multinational Ottoman Empire rather than joining the Greek state, took precedence.[53] This idea was promoted by two Greeks from mainland Greece, Ion Dragoumes, a diplomat, and Athanasios Souliotes. With support from the Foreign Ministry of Greece, Dragoumes and Souliotes also established the Society of Constantinople, which quickly gained a stronghold in the Greek population of Istanbul. The Society of Constantinople was actively involved in the formation of the Greek Party in Parliament and continued affecting its policies throughout its existence.[54] Initially, the relations between the Society of Constantinople and the Patriarchy were strained due to the secular nature of nationalism endorsed by the Society. However, the two institutions grew closer in the face of the CUP policies that challenged the political agenda of both groups, and they agreed on an election coalition with the FU.

In early twentieth century, another Greek faction, which preferred to cooperate with the CUP rather than the FU, also emerged. The members of this faction believed that the best way to further Greek interests was to form an alliance with the CUP. As a result, ten out of the twenty-six Greek deputies in the Ottoman Parliament did not join the Greek Party. These deputies and several other Greek leaders also parted with the Greek Party's common decision to enter an election coalition with the FU and, instead, entered the elections on the CUP list.[55] After the elections, the number of Greek delegates in the Parliament was reduced to sixteen, and most of these were on the CUP list. However, the success of the CUP supporters should not be taken as a strong indicator of the actual backing they enjoyed in the Greek community, because the CUP used extensive intimidation against the opposition parties in the 1912 elections. Nevertheless, it is noteworthy that a substantial number of Greek deputies were ready to collaborate with a party that openly challenged the traditional privileges of the Greek community.

---

52. Alexandris, *The Greek Minority*.

53. Veremis, "The Hellenic Kingdom," p. 185.

54. Ibid.; Catherine Boura, "The Greek Millet in Turkish Politics: Greeks in the Ottoman Parliament (1908–1918)," in Dimitri Gondicas and Charles Issawi, eds., *Ottoman Greeks in the Age of Nationalism* (Princeton, N.J.: Darwin Press, 1999).

55. Boura, "The Greek Millet in Turkish Politics."

The policies of Greece had an important impact on the Ottoman Greek population in general and their leadership in particular. Organizations from mainland Greece were highly influential in developing a standardized identity that united the Greeks of the Ottoman Empire.[56] The main tool for this type of influence was education. Starting in the second half of the nineteenth century, individuals and organizations from mainland Greece established schools in Anatolia with curricula similar to that of schools in Greece. These schools, as well as other organizations such as literary societies, were also actively supported and formed by the Greek consulates that existed in various cities of the Ottoman Empire.[57] Another important factor was the large number of Ottoman Greeks who went to mainland Greece for university education and then came back to the Ottoman Empire. These students typically received financial assistance from the University of Athens, various Greek banks, and the state itself.[58]

Another tool for promoting Greek identity was cross-border violence, specifically in Macedonia. In the first decade of the twentieth century, Greek and Bulgarian nationalists were in intense competition for the "identity" of the largely Slavic speaking population of Macedonia. The main criterion used to define "Greekness" or "Bulgarianness" in this context was membership in the Orthodox Patriarchy or the Bulgarian Exarchist Church. In order to sway the population of Macedonia toward "Greekness," the Greek State engaged in several policies. It aided the formation of bands by some Greek Army officers, who then crossed the border to Macedonia and organized the local population to counter similar formations by the Bulgarians. The activities of these bands, as well as the provision of arms, personnel, and espionage services, were organized by the Greek consular offices in major cities such as Monastir, Serres, Kavala, and Thessaloniki.[59] This network of institutions used several tactics to convert the local population to "Greekness." For example, they urged the population to boycott the shops of those individuals who adhered to the Exarchist church or they provided gifts and loans to those who willingly came back to the fold of the Patriarchy. When such "peaceful" strategies did not work, they also used strategic killings, beatings, and damage to private property.[60] The extensive campaign in Macedonia eventually succeeded in turning the tide of Bulgarian nationalism. But Greek-Bulgarian rivalry also divided Macedonia into "Bulgarian" and "Greek" areas and provided the setting for the mutual massacres and deportations that occurred during the Balkan Wars.

---

56.   Paschalis M. Kitromilides, "Imagined Communities and the Origins of the National Question in the Balkans," in Martin Blinkhorn and Thanos Veremis, eds., *Modern Greece: Nationalism and Nationality* (Athens: Sage-Eliamep, 1990).

57.   Ibid.; Augustinos, *The Greeks,* pp. 151; Richard Clogg; "A Millet within a Millet: The Karamanlides," in Dimitri Gondicas and Charles Issawi, eds., *Ottoman Greeks in the Age of Nationalism* (Princeton N.J.: Darwin Press, 1999), p. 129.

58.   Clogg, "A Millet within a Millet," p. 129.

59.   Dakin, *The Greek Struggle in Macedonia,* p. 197.

60.   Ibid., p. 206.

Greece also shaped the leadership and political alliances of the Ottoman Greek community. For example, prior to the elections in 1908, the Greek consular officials throughout the Ottoman Empire signaled their preferred candidates.[61] In addition, the Greek Foreign Ministry was involved in the establishment of the Society of Constantinople, as well as the Greek Party in the Ottoman Parliament. Politicians from mainland Greece also used their resources to affect the decisions of the Greek delegates in the Parliament by signaling that those candidates who did not enter the 1912 elections on the Greek Party ticket would not enjoy the backing of organizations financed from Greece.[62]

The Ottoman Empire faced two episodes of occupation by the Greek Army. The first, the Balkan Wars of 1912–1913, resulted in the loss of all territory in Europe except for Eastern Thrace; the second, the Greco-Turkish War of 1919–1922, resulted in the crumbling of the Empire and its replacement with the Turkish state. In each instance, the links between local Greeks and the occupying armies transformed the Ottoman Turkish elite's ideas about minorities. As already discussed, the fault lines between different communities in Macedonia had been drawn prior to 1912 due to the rivalry between Greece and Bulgaria. Once the war in the Balkans became imminent, the links that Greece and Bulgaria had formed with local Macedonian leaders throughout the 1900s became relevant again.

Such links were used for two purposes. First, before the war, some Greek volunteers who had already done work in Macedonia before 1908 were sent back to organize the local population. A good number of the local leaders responded to the call of these volunteers.[63] Second, these types of "unofficial" bands, which were formed not only by Greeks but also by Bulgarians and Turks, played a significant part during the war. They participated in the burning of villages and the killing of the civilian populations whom they considered to be on the "wrong" side of the war. Significantly, such activities were not the result of an age-old "ethnic hatred" that afflicted the populations of this area. They were a result of the fact that three states—the Ottomans on the defense, the Greek and Bulgarian states on the offense—had followed a conscious policy of dividing the population of Macedonia for decades in an effort to accord legitimacy to their territorial claims.

The Balkan Wars had a profound effect on the Young Turk movement, especially on the members of the CUP. To appreciate this effect, one has to recall that the birthplace as well as the initial stronghold of the CUP was Macedonia. Hence, after the Balkan Wars, the CUP began a deep search for the causes of the defeat that had led to the loss of Macedonia as well as Western Thrace. As a result, the CUP leaders made two important changes to their prior policies. First, they completely suppressed the opposition and took over the government through a coup. In fact, the CUP coup hap-

---

61. Clogg, "A Millet within a Millet."

62. Boura, "The Greek Millet."

63. Dakin, *The Greek Struggle in Macedonia*, p. 446.

pened as the Second Balkan War was ongoing, with the alleged reason that the current government, dominated by the opposition, could possibly cede the city of Edirne in Eastern Thrace to Bulgaria. To stop the government from surrendering Edirne, two leading CUP members went to the Parliament and forced the government to resign, shooting the Minister of War in the process. After this event, the main opposition party, the FU, dissolved itself, arguing that it did not wish to challenge the government during times of war.

The second important change to the CUP policy was that the party halted any efforts to collaborate with the Greek Party or the Patriarchy and adopted a policy of partial but forced deportation of Greeks in Thrace and the western regions of the Empire. This decision was guided by the emerging belief among the CUP leadership that "in order to end the trouble with the smaller Balkan states, they had to end the existence of populations that encouraged these states to seek territory from the Ottoman Empire."[64] Members of the CUP also expected that after the Balkan Wars, the Greeks would push toward the Aydin Province on the Aegean coast. In case of such an event, the CUP wanted to avoid the repetition of the events in the Balkans.[65] To implement its new policy, the CUP suggested an exchange agreement with the Greek government through which the Muslim population of Macedonia would be exchanged for the Greeks in the Aegean Islands, Aydin Province, and Eastern Thrace. The Greek government initially rejected this suggestion. But to force the hand of the Greek government, the CUP began to deport some Greeks in the western territories anyway, and the CUP turned a blind eye when Muslim refugees arriving from Macedonia and Western Thrace harassed Greeks on Ottoman territory.[66] Eventually, the Greek government agreed to the exchange in 1914, but the beginning of the World War I interfered and the agreement was not put into effect at the time. Nevertheless, in 1914, prior to World War I, about 100,000 Greeks from Eastern Thrace and Western Anatolia were deported to Greece or inner Anatolia.[67]

The second episode of Greek occupation started in May 1919, after the Ottoman defeat in World War I. The occupation was initially confined to the Izmir Sancak of Aydin Province, which was home to more Greeks than Muslims. But it soon extended to inner Anatolia as well as Eastern Thrace, where the majority of the population was Muslim. Soon after the invasion, several incidents increased the tension between the Turks and Greeks. In the first few days after the occupation of Izmir, several Turkish soldiers were apprehended and killed. In addition, the local Greek population, with the backing of the Greek Army, engaged in looting, beatings, and occasional killings of the local Muslim population. In other coastal

---

64. Cemal Pasa, *Hâtırât 1913–1922* (Istanbul, Turkey: Ahmet Ihsan ve Sürekâsı, 1922), p. 84.

65. Ibid.

66. Ibid.

67. A.A. Pallis, "Rational Migrations in the Balkans," n. 32.

towns, there were skirmishes between Turkish resistance groups and local Greek bands aiding the Greek Army. [68] During some of these clashes, Greek forces deported the population of Turkish villages and then burned the houses.[69] In Izmir and the surrounding area, such events stopped after the appointment of Aristidis Stergiadis as the Governor of Izmir.[70] Yet, similar events continued in Eastern Thrace, Bursa, and the area around Istanbul.[71]

The most important result of the occupation of Anatolia and the helplessness of the Istanbul regime against it was the emergence of a new leadership under the guidance of Mustafa Kemal. The goal of this leadership was to unite the various resistance movements in Anatolia and fight back against the occupying Greek, French, and Italian armies from a base in Ankara. The leaders of the movement were not entirely new to Ottoman politics; many of the leading figures, including Mustafa Kemal and Ismet Inonu, had been members of the Young Turk movement. What distinguished them from the previous leadership was that before 1919 they had not been involved in the political decision-making processes; instead, most of them had served as officers in the Ottoman Army. Since these individuals were not directly involved in politics prior to the occupation of Anatolia, it is difficult to correctly identify what policies they would have preferred on issues involving the Greek minority prior to 1919.

However, by 1922, the Ankara leadership, now quickly gaining ground against the Greek armies, sought to expel the Greek minority from the entire territory of Anatolia. As early as March 1922, the Ankara government told the British government that they were ready for an exchange of populations between the Greeks of Asia Minor and the Muslims of Greece.[72] The limits of the proposal were further clarified when, in October 1922, the envoy of the Ankara Government met with Fridtjof Nansen and reiterated that "the Ankara Government only permitted him to negotiate total and enforced exchange of populations."[73] This policy was put into effect after the Turkish Army won the war. In the regained areas, the Greek population was given a matter of weeks to leave, and young, able-bodied men were recruited for labor battalions; those who survived were then sent to Greece.[74] Apart from the forced expulsions, large numbers of Greeks fled

68.   Bilge Umar, *Yunanlıların ve Anadolu Rumlarının anlatımıyla İzmir savaşı.* (İstanbul, Turkey: İnkılâp, 2002).

69.   Ibid.; Stanford J. Shaw, *From Empire to Republic: The Turkish War of National Liberation, 1918–1923: A Documentary Study* (Ankara, Turkey: Turk Tarih Kurumu Basimevı, 2000), pp. 509–518.

70.   Michael Llewellyn Smith, *Ionian Vision; Greece in Asia Minor* (New York: St. Martin's Press, 1973).

71.   Ibid.

72.   Bruce Clark, *Twice a Stranger: The Mass Expulsions That Forged Modern Greece and Turkey* (Cambridge, Mass.: Harvard University Press, 2006).

73.   Ibid., p. 61.

74.   Ibid., p. 61; and Onur Yildirim, *Diplomacy and Displacement: Reconsidering the 0Turco-Greek Exchange of Populations* (New York: Routledge, 2006).

in anticipation of the approaching Turkish Army. Hence, by the opening of the Lausanne Conference in November 1922, which eventually stabilized the borders between Greece and Turkey, Greece had already received a large number of refugees from Anatolia.

An exchange agreement regarding the Greeks of Anatolia and the Muslims of Greece was one of the hotly debated issues in the Lausanne Conference. The Greek side favored an agreement that would leave the Orthodox Patriarchy, along with the Greek population of Istanbul, in Istanbul. The Turkish side favored a complete deportation of all the Greeks of Anatolia, including the Istanbul Greeks. Eventually, the Turkish side reluctantly agreed that the Istanbul Patriarchy and the Greeks of Istanbul would stay in Turkey in return for leaving the Muslims in Western Thrace in Greece. In the end, the Muslim population of Greece, except for those in Western Thrace, was exchanged for the entire Orthodox population of Anatolia, except for those in Istanbul.

Conclusion

This study started with the question of whether and how the depth of ethnic cleavages plays a role in the process that leads to ethnic cleansing. I argued that deep ethnic cleavages do not play a significant role in this process, as it is primarily the conflicts between states that cause interethnic relations to deteriorate prior to episodes of ethnic cleansing.

Broadly, the theory has three observable implications. First, in times of peace, both majority and minority groups are divided along political cleavages other than ethnicity. Second, during periods of peace, different ethnic groups cooperate along non-ethnic cleavages; this cooperation ceases to be an option once outside states form alliances with minority groups during times of war or occupation. Third, when faced with expansionist threats by states allied with minority groups, majority politicians that are friendly to such minorities either become hostile or are replaced by more radical leaders.

The two cases examined here generally fit the expectations of the theory. Throughout the interwar period, the Czech politicians on both the left and the right consistently cooperated with their German counterparts and provided the German community with extensive rights. Only after the German invasion and collaboration between local Germans and the occupiers did these politicians converge on forced deportation as a way to deal with the German minority. Similarly, the two major factions of the Young Turks (the Liberals and the CUP) tried to lure the Greeks into their fold and did not seriously consider using ethnic cleansing until after the Balkan Wars. Finally, the switch to forced expulsions came as a result of the two episodes of Greek invasions, first during the Balkan Wars and then after World War I, during which the potential of cooperation across ethnic groups disappeared as an option.

This study also focuses on the question of how minority groups form alliances with outside states. This question is theoretically important because it addresses the possible claim that the depth of ethnic cleavages determine whether or not minority groups ally with outside states. This chapter suggests two conclusions. First, the idea that deep ethnic cleavages on their own can push the minority to form an alliance with an outside state is empirically wrong. Minority groups such as the Germans in interwar Czechoslovakia and the Greeks in the Ottoman Empire were among those with the deepest differences from the majorities in the countries of their residence. The Sudeten Germans had been members of the dominant ethnic group within the Austrian Empire and had enjoyed access to all levels of education in German, as well as a host of other political and cultural organizations. The Greeks in the Ottoman Empire were officially defined as part of the Orthodox millet, which was legally separate from the Muslim majority and enjoyed several privileges.

Yet even in these contexts, the minority leadership was split between those who favored collaboration with the outside state and those who did not. What made the difference was intervention from Germany and Greece, which shaped the leadership of the minorities so that they became more open to forming an alliance with these countries. In Czechoslovakia, financial and organizational aid from the Reich gradually shifted the power from political parties which had a non-nationalist platform to the nationalist SHF-SdP. Policies of Greece played an important role in the organization of the Greek Party in the Ottoman Parliament, as well as in the generation of a network of organizations, especially in Macedonia, that could be mobilized in case of a war. Thus, even in these cases of deep ethnic cleavage, alliance formation with the minority required a good deal of work on the part of the expansionist state.

This chapter makes several important observations. First, during peacetime, ethnic groups have significant internal divisions, and they cooperate with the members of other ethnic groups against their co-ethnics. Second, ethnic cleavages trump other political divisions, and relations between ethnic groups deteriorate as a result of alliances between minority ethnic groups and territory-seeking states. Third, outside states initiate and sustain the formation of alliances by strengthening the factions within the minority ethnic groups who are open to alliance formation. More systematic analysis, including statistical tests and detailed studies of other cases, is needed to establish these points more conclusively.[75] However, the analysis here strongly suggests that focusing on interstate competition is a better way of explaining ethnic cleansing than focusing on age-old ethnic differences and their assumed impact on interethnic relations.

---

75. The author undertakes this task in her dissertation, "Territorial Conflict and Ethnic Cleansing," University of Chicago, 2009.

Chapter 4

Assimilation and Its Alternatives: Caveats in the Study of Nation-building Policies

Harris Mylonas

This chapter explains how states choose nation-building policies. Specifically, I focus on the strategic choice to use exclusionary state-planned nation-building policies toward non-core groups[1] instead of assimilating them or granting them minority rights. I define nation-building as the process whereby ruling political elites attempt to make the *political* and the *national* units overlap.[2] To achieve this overlap, these elites construct and impose a common national identity on the population of the state. Legitimacy in the modern state is connected to popular rule and thus majorities. Nation-building is the process through which these majorities are constructed.

Some countries are, or are at least thought of as, more homogeneous than others. For example, Japan is more homogeneous along ethnic and religious lines than Bosnia-Herzegovina or Nigeria. We know that countries that are considered homogeneous today were not necessarily so in the nineteenth century. For example, in Italy during the 1860s, "only 3 per

I would like to thank Kristin Fabbe, Erica Chenoweth, Keith Darden, Stathis Kalyvas, Jackie Kerr, Matthew Kocher, Adria Lawrence, George Th. Mavrogordatos, Karen Motley, Elpida Vogli, Elizabeth Saunders, Konstantinos Tsitselikis, and James Raymond Vreeland for their helpful comments. Previous versions of this paper have been presented at the Junior Faculty Workshop, George Washington University, Washington, D.C., October 22, 2009; the Georgetown University International Theory and Research Seminar, co-sponsored by the Department of Government and the Mortara Center for International Studies, Georgetown University, Washington, D.C., September 14, 2009. I would like to thank the participants at these events for their thoughtful comments.

1. Any aggregation of individuals that is perceived as an ethnic group (the relevant marker can be linguistic, religious, physical, ideological) by the ruling political elite of a country at the beginning of the period analyzed, I call a "non-core group." For a more detailed discussion of this definition, see Harris Mylonas, Assimilation and its Alternatives: The Making of Co-Nationals, Refugees, and Minorities, Ph.D. Dissertation, Yale University, 2008, pp. 50–52.

2. Ernest Gellner, *Nations and Nationalism* (Ithaca, N.Y.: Cornell University Press, 1983).

cent of the population spoke the north Italian version elevated to official status, and no more than 10 per cent understood it."[3] Things in Italy are quite different today. The consensus in the literature is that this homogeneity has been constructed.[4]

Within existing state borders, a wide range of possible strategies can lead to a more homogeneous country. Once a government of a modern nation-state decides who constitutes the core group and what the criteria of inclusion are, it pursues policies to construct a homogeneous nation-state. But how do ruling elites choose among these policies? What explains variation in nation-building policies across groups and over time? Many arguments, ranging from ethnic antipathy, racism, and ethnic dominance to strictly security considerations, have been proposed to explain aspects of this variation.[5] Many of the existing theories, however, focus on explaining the occurrence of the most violent state policies such as genocide, mass killing, or ethnic cleansing.[6] As a result, they end up over-aggregating the different "peaceful" outcomes under the residual category of "non-violent." As Stevan Pavlowitch notes, "There is a fascination with victims: the massacre of populations is more interesting than their daily

---

3.   Crawford Young, ed., *Ethnic Diversity and Public Policy: A Comparative Inquiry* (St. Martin's Press and the United Nations Research Institute for Social Development, 1998), p. 18.

4.   Benedict Anderson, *Imagined Communities: Reflections on the Origins and Spread of Nationalism* (New York: Verso, 1983); Eric Hobsbawm and Terence Ranger, *The Invention of Tradition* (Cambridge University Press, 2000); and James D. Fearon and David D. Laitin, "Violence and the Social Construction of Ethnic Identity," *International Organization*, Vol. 54, No. 4 (2000), pp. 845–877.

5.   Donald Horowitz, *Ethnic Groups in Conflict* (Berkeley: University of California Press, 1985); Roger Petersen, *Resistance and Rebellion: Lessons from Eastern Europe* (Cambridge: Cambridge University Press, 2001); Roger Petersen, *Understanding Ethnic Violence: Fear, Hatred, and Resentment in Twentieth-Century Eastern Europe* (Cambridge: Cambridge University Press, 2002); and Barry R. Posen, "The Security Dilemma and Ethnic Conflict," *Survival*, Vol. 35, No. 1 (Spring 1993), pp. 27–47.

6.   Barbara Harff, "No Lessons Learned from the Holocaust? Assessing Risks of Genocide and Political Mass Murder Since 1955," *American Political Science Review*, Vol. 97, No. 1 (February 2003), pp. 57–73; Scott Straus, *The Order of Genocide: Race, Power, and War in Rwanda* (Cornell University Press, 2006); Benjamin Valentino, *Final Solutions: Mass Killing and Genocide in the Twentieth Century* (Ithaca, N.Y.: Cornell University Press, 2004); H. Zeynep Bulutgil, "Territorial Conflict and Ethnic Cleansing," Ph.D. dissertation, University of Chicago, 2009; Michael Mann, *The Dark Side of Democracy: Explaining Ethnic Cleansing* (Cambridge: Cambridge University Press, 2005); Norman M. Naimark, *Fires of Hatred: Ethnic Cleansing in Twentieth Century Europe* (Cambridge, Mass.: Harvard University Press, 2001), Alexander B. Downes, "Desperate Times, Desperate Measures: The Causes of Civilian Victimization in War," *International Security*, Vol. 30, No. 4 (Spring 2006), pp. 152–195; Stathis N. Kalyvas, *The Logic of Violence in Civil War* (Cambridge University Press, 2006), Benjamin A. Valentino, Paul Huth, and Dylan Balch-Lindsay, "'Draining the Sea': Mass Killing and Guerrilla Warfare," *International Organization*, Vol. 58 (Spring 2004), pp. 375–407; Jack Snyder and Barbara Walter, *Civil Wars, Insecurity, and Intervention* (New York: Columbia University Press, 1999); and Monica Duffy Toft, *The Geography of Ethnic Violence* (Princeton, N.J.: Princeton University Press, 2003).

lives."[7] The argument I advance in this chapter accounts for both violent and non-violent policies toward non-core groups.

I propose a categorical conceptualization of nation-building which posits three possible state policies: assimilation, accommodation, or exclusion.[8] The ruling elites can pursue educational, cultural, occupational, marital, demographic, political, and other state policies aimed at getting the non-core group to adopt the core group's culture and way of life. This is assimilation. Alternatively, they can retain the non-core group in the state, but grant the group special minority rights. Certain "differences" of the non-core group are respected, and institutions that regulate and perpetuate these differences are put in place. This is accommodation. Finally, they can physically remove the non-core group through population exchange, deportation, or mass killing. This is exclusion. Exclusionary policies are the most violent. Assimilationist policies could be either violent or non-violent. Accommodation refers to non-violent policies. What distinguishes these policies is the different intention behind each. Despite the voluminous literatures on national integration, state-sponsored nationalism, and nationalist movements,[9] there is no theory that specifies the conditions under which a state is likely to assimilate, accommodate, or exclude a non-core group.

Following World War I, modernization theorists discussed national integration as a by-product of industrialization, urbanization, and political development. They emphasized the importance of economic transformations for identity change and suggested that national integration is a

---

7. Stevan K. Pavlowitch, "Europe and the Balkans in a Historical Perspective, 1804–1945," *Journal of Southern Europe and the Balkans*, Vol. 2, No. 2 (November 2000), pp. 141–148.

8. To be sure, these policies are not always terminal. For instance, a government that pursues a policy of assimilation in T_0 might choose deportation or genocide in T_1.

9. Karl Deutsch and William J. Foltz, eds., *Nation-Building* (New York: Atherton Press, 1966); S. N. Eisenstadt and Stein Rokkan, eds., *Building States and Nations: Analyses by Region*, Vol. II (Beverly Hills: Sage, 1973); Eugen Weber, *Peasants Into Frenchmen: The Modernization of Rural France, 1870–1914* (Stanford: Stanford University Press, 1976); Rogers Brubaker, "National Minorities, Nationalizing States, and External Homelands in the New Europe: Notes toward a Relational Analysis," *Reihe Politikwissenschaft*, No. 11 (December 1993); Rogers Brubaker, *Nationalism Reframed: Nationhood and the National Question in the New Europe* (New York: Cambridge University Press, 1996); Ronald Grigor Suny and Terry Martin, *A State of Nations: Empire and Nation-Making in the Age of Lenin and Stalin* (Oxford: Oxford University Press, 2001); Linda Colley, *Britons: Forging the Nation 1707–1837* (New Haven, Conn.: Yale University Press, 1992); Michael Hechter, *Internal Colonialism: The Celtic Fringe in British National Development, 1536–1966* (Berkeley: University of California Press, 1975); Miroslav Hroch, *Social Preconditions of National Revival in Europe: A Comparative Analysis of the Social Composition of Patriotic Groups Among the Smaller European Nations* (New York: Columbia University Press, 2000); Ronald Grigor Suny, *The Revenge of the Past: Nationalism, Revolution, and the Collapse of the Soviet Union* (Stanford: Stanford University Press, 1993); Konstantin Symmons-Symonolewicz, *Nationalist Movements: A Comparative View* (Meadville, Penn.: Maplewood Press, 1970); and Henry J. Tobias and Charles E. Woodhouse, *Minorities and Politics* (Albuquerque: University of New Mexico Press, 1969).

result of these processes.[10] But these theories never specify who pursues these policies and in what fashion. This set of theories gives little attention to direct state involvement in the process of nation-building. As Anthony Smith put it, "the role of the state is simply to act as a handmaid of history, whose goal is a world of large-scale nation-states or regions."[11]

Later generations of social scientists provided microfoundations for the various modernization theories.[12] These studies embraced the unplanned character of national integration posited by the modernization theorists. Their work, inspired by methodological individualism, focused on the calculations individuals make with respect to identity choices. However, individual-level decisions are always structured by the context of state policies. Without a theory that accounts for variation in state-planned policies toward non-core groups, we cannot have a complete theory of nation-building; the "supply side" of the phenomenon is under–theorized.

To address some of these shortcomings and enrich our understanding of the "supply side" of nation-building, my argument focuses on the importance of international, geostrategic concerns for nation-building policies. "Minorities" are often used as a pretext to fight expansionary wars or to destabilize neighboring countries, triggering specific—and predictable—policy responses by the targeted states. I argue that a state's choices of nation-building policies toward non-core groups are driven by its foreign policy goals and interstate relations. The foreign policy goals of a host state may be revisionist or status quo. For purposes of this chapter, revisionist states have lost territory in war and are unhappy with the international status quo; their foreign policy goals are focused on overturning it. Status-quo states have gained territory in war, are content with the international distribution of resources and want to preserve it. Interstate relations can take the form of rivalry or alliance; these in turn are influenced by—but independent from— international alliance blocs.[13]

I make four predictions. First, a host state is more likely to exclude a non-core group when the state has revisionist aims and the group is backed by a rival state. Second, a host state is more likely to assimilate a non-core group if the state favors the status quo and the non-core group is supported by a rival state. Third, a host state is more likely to accommodate a non-core group if that group is supported by an allied state. Fourth, assimilation is more likely if the non-core group has no external support. Figure 4.1 depicts these predictions.

---

10.   Karl Deutsch, *Nationalism and Social Communication* (Cambridge, Mass.: Technology Press, 1965).

11.   Anthony Smith, "State-Making and Nation-Building" in John Hall, ed., *States in History* (Oxford: Basil Blackwell, 1986), pp. 228–263, at p. 232.

12.   Hechter, *Internal Colonialism*; David Laitin, "Marginality: A Microperspective," *Rationality and Society*, Vol. 7, No. 1 (January 1995), pp. 31–57; and David Laitin, *Identity in Formation: The Russian-Speaking Populations in the Near Abroad* (Ithaca, N.Y.: Cornell University Press, 1998).

13.   For more details on the logic of the theory outlined here, see Mylonas, Assimilation and its Alternatives, chap. 1.

Figure 4.1. Theory Predictions.

External Power

		Yes: Interstate Relations		No
		Ally	**Enemy**	
Host State (Foreign Policy Goals)	**Lost Territory** (Revisionist)	Accommodation	Exclusion	Assimilation
	Gained Territory (Status Quo)	Accommodation	Assimilation	

My contribution to this volume is organized into three sections. In the first section, I discuss two prevalent problems that scholars of nation-building policies face: the politics of "counting people," and the tendency to conflate intentions and policy outcomes. In the second section, I use material from my research on the Balkans to test part of my argument and illustrate the ways in which I address these problems. Finally, I conclude by exploring the implications of my argument for nation-building policies today.

Methodological Problems in the Study of Nation-building Policies

Scholars who study state-planned nation-building policies and the reactions to these policies have been faced with two fundamental problems: the politics of "counting people" and distinguishing intentions from policy outcomes. The first issue refers to the difficulties and politics involved in three interrelated choices: identifying a group as an "ethnic group" or a "minority," deciding on an estimate of its population, and studying it as a relatively unitary and homogeneous entity. The most common methodological problems resulting are selection bias and over-aggregated actors. The second difficulty refers to the "revealed preferences problem" in the social sciences, namely the practice of inferring an actor's intentions by taking statements at face value or just observing the outcomes on the ground. Disentangling the relationship between intentions, policies, implementation, and outcomes is necessary to understand the process of nation-building. Both of these challenges hinder the study of state-planned nation-building policies. Not addressing them in our research can lead to wrongheaded theories. This chapter stands as a critique to studies in comparative politics and international relations which fail to address these problems.

The Politics of "Counting People"

The politics surrounding statistics on "ethnic minorities" is an extremely problematic aspect of the study of nation-building. First, whoever is doing the counting many times determines the results. Second, even if we assume that the existing statistics on ethnic composition are accurate, we can never be sure that the categories used in a census were the most salient ones for the people on the ground. For example, depending on which dimension the state census committee chooses to highlight—religious affiliation, mother tongue, regional identity, racial categories, or ethnic background—it can produce a very different "ethnic structure."

An aggregate approach to issues related to nation-building is precarious and cannot serve as the final word. Using census data to explain nation-building policies is, to an extent, confusing the outcome for the cause. Census data on "ethnicity" are part and parcel of nation-building policies and so are maps and atlases.[14] The obvious case is that of groups which are *not* represented in census categories and are thus muted.

Take the Ottoman Empire, for example, which granted official status only to religious communities (millets). The Ottoman censuses record Muslims, Orthodox Christians, Gregorian Christians, Jews, and later on Catholics and Protestants. Ottoman statistics provide no information about language, cultural difference, or national consciousness. In the Balkan Peninsula in particular, this meant that Muslim Albanian-speakers, Tatars, Turkish-speakers, Donmehs (Jewish converts to Islam), and other Muslim groups were all under the broad "Muslim" category. Similarly, all Christian Orthodox people—Slavic-speakers with various national affiliations, Albanian-speakers, Greek-speakers, Vlach-speakers, Sarakatsans, and so forth—were considered members of the "Rum" millet, represented by the Greek-dominated Patriarchate in Istanbul.

The transition from empire to nation-state occurred in the nineteenth and twentieth centuries, and with it a transition in the relevant recorded categories occurred. The same inhabitants of these territories were now aggregated with respect to language or a notion of national consciousness that was, at least initially, vague. This was the face of modernity in the region. Modern states in Western Europe recorded language use and national origin in their censuses, and the Balkan states followed suit in order to be on equal footing and to try to prove their historical rights to disputed territories. In the hands of the ruling political elites of the Balkan states, the census was part of a broader war for the hearts and minds of the newly incorporated rural populations.

Most studies rely either on census categories or on material produced by the elites of "oppressed" groups. Both sources are inadequate on their own if our research question has to do with state-planned nation-building policies. For example, when we use census data, we are likely to get de-

---

14.   Wilkinson, Henry R., *Maps and Politics: A Review of Ethnographic Cartography of Macedonia* (Liverpool, U.K.: Liverpool University, 1951).

flated population estimates of most non-core groups and no estimates for the ones that are targeted with assimilationist policies. Similarly, if we try to discern the ethnic makeup of a country or a region using material produced by the elites of non-core groups, we often encounter propaganda that inflates the numbers of non-core groups. In this latter case, however, what is more disconcerting is that we are not capturing any of the non-core groups whose elites have been successfully co-opted, or any non-core groups with no elites. Selection bias is therefore almost unavoidable.

How can we overcome this situation where available statistics are capturing host states' nation-building policies instead of realities on the ground? One way to avoid this bias is to shun data from conflict-ridden territories until a fair amount of time has passed. Biased estimates and census manipulation are much more likely in contested areas. Focusing on such cases only exacerbates the problem. Detached historical research can put things into perspective. For example, Yugoslavia and Austria both claimed Carinthia for the first half of the twentieth century. According to the Austrian census of 1951, there were only 7,000 Slovenes in the Klagenfurt area of Carinthia, while the Yugoslavs claimed that there were more than 35,000. What accounts for this discrepancy? The Austrian census grouped people by "language used daily" into nine identity categories: "German, Slovene, Windish (a Slovenian dialect), and six combinations of the three."[15] Scholars had no way to tell how many "Slovenes" were living there. Moreover, the population inhabiting Carinthia could be grouped in various different ways depending on the census question. Data from contested territories are unreliable; scholars studying such areas should be upfront about the various sources of bias.

Another solution involves looking at census data that were produced prior to significant political changes in a region. In the case of Southeastern Europe, I overcame several problems with the help of the Ottoman censuses from the nineteenth century, as well as confidential diplomatic reports prior to World War I.

The ideal solution, however, is to move our attention to state policymakers and take their perceptions seriously. The ruling political elites, who are central to the planning of nation-building policies, know that they cannot ignore non-core groups. These governmental officials, ministers, and governors write reports and confidential documents concerning groups of people that rarely come up in censuses. They are treasures for both building and testing hypotheses. In the empirical section of this chapter, I rely primarily on such sources.

---

15. Huey Louis Kostanick, "The Geopolitics of the Balkans," in Charles Jelavich and Barbara Jelavich, eds., *The Balkans in Transition: Essays on the Development of Balkan Life and Politics since the Eighteenth Century* (Hamden, Conn: Archon Books, 1974), pp. 1–55, 27.

Intentions vs. Outcomes

In the nation-building process, intentions, policy choices, and policy outcomes are definitely linked, yet intentions are not always translated into policy choices, nor do those choices always produce the desired outcome. Moreover, policy choices are sometimes a function of capabilities and not of intentions. For example, the latter are sometimes veiled because of external intervention by an international organization or a Great Power. Moreover, private interests and biases of state officials, especially at lower levels of the administration, interfere in the planning and implementation of state policies. As a result, many theories are developed and tested on "events" that were unintended consequences or "forced" outcomes rather than accurate reflections of the administration's intentions. The outcome often is deceptive empirical support for or incorrect falsification of theories.

An archival approach can help us address the revealed-preferences problem. Studying the decision-making process that led to nation-building policies helps differentiate between the intentions of the administration toward a particular non-core group and the actual policy plan that it eventually adopts. One might argue that this is not necessary because what actually matters in politics is the policy that is implemented. However, if we want to understand why state officials choose particular nation-building policies and not others, studying only the observed outcomes will not suffice.

For example, two different non-core groups might be granted the same minority rights, but with a different reasoning behind each case. In practical terms, the reasoning matters because it most likely will inform the policy implementation. In theoretical terms, understanding elites' reasons can help distinguish between rival explanations. For instance, a hypothesis might predict the granting of minority rights to a non-core group, but for completely different reasons than the ones that were behind the actual decision. In this case, although the hypothesis makes the "right" prediction, it does not capture the logic behind the policy.

In the next section I use empirical evidence from my archival research in the Balkans to test my argument against alternatives and address many of the methodological caveats I discussed above.

Nation-building in Western Macedonia, 1916–1920

What accounts for variation in nation-building policies toward different non-core groups within one state? I find that the Greek government chose its nation-building policies based not on objective measures of cultural distance or deep-rooted ethnic hatred, but rather on security and geostrategic concerns. The diplomatic relations between rival states and Greece largely determined both the perception of the non-core groups inside Greece and their consequent treatment.[16]

My analysis is based on archival research conducted in Greece in 2005 and 2006.[17] For the purposes of this chapter, I rely mostly on a compilation of reports written by Ioannis Eliakis between 1916 and 1920.[18] Prime Minister Eleftherios Venizelos sent Eliakis to be a representative of the "National Defense" revolutionary government in the region of Western Macedonia.[19] (See Map 4.1.) Eliakis later became the Governor-General of Western Macedonia. From 1916 to 1920, he was the ultimate authority in that region. His decisions overrode those of any other state official, including military officers. His reports had a wide range of recipients: the Prime Minister, the Ministries of the Interior, Foreign Affairs, and the Ministry of Military Affairs.[20]

Using both secondary sources and archival material, I focus on the national integration efforts in Western Macedonia. This nation-building effort took place during the turbulent context following the Balkan Wars[21] and during World War I, in a region that was under the same administrative system—the Ottoman Empire—for centuries and involved a linguistically, religiously, and culturally heterogeneous population.

Interstate alliances shifted in the region over this period, and a few shifts in territorial control occurred. During World War I, Greece was fighting for the restoration of its gains from the Balkan wars (revisionist). Following World War I, Greece was trying to secure its territorial gains (status quo). Moreover, some non-core groups had no external backing, some were backed by allied states, and some were backed by enemy states. The combination of the above characteristics and the important variation in my main independent variables render this region an ideal location to study the politics of nation-building and test my theory.

---

16. For a more detailed treatment of this case study and additional material on the geopolitical situation, see Mylonas, Assimilation and its Alternatives, chap. 2.

17. I conducted this research at the Museum of the Macedonian Struggle, Pavlos Kalligas Archive (PKA). All translations from the archival material are mine.

18. Ioannis Eliakis was a close friend of Prime Minister Venizelos from the island of Crete. He was born in 1878 and moved to Greek Macedonia in July of 1916. For more information on Eliakis and his life, see Ioannis Eliakis, *He Hestoria Exinta Hronon me eikones kai documenta* [The history of sixty years with pictures and documents], (Hania, 1940).

19. Western Macedonia is delimited by mountains: Pindos and Grammos in the west; Vitsi, Peristeri, and Kaimaktsalan in the north; Olympus, Kambounia, and Chassia in the south; and Bermion in the east. The largest cities at the time were Florina, Kastoria, Kozani, and Grevena. See Elisabeth Kontogiorgi, *Population Exchange in Greek Macedonia. The Rural Settlement of Refugees, 1922–1930* (Oxford, U.K.: Clarendon Press, 2006), p. 13.

20. PKA, Eliakis to Greek Ministry of Foreign Affairs, January 22, 1920.

21. The First Balkan War involved Serbia, Bulgaria, Greece, and Montenegro against the Ottoman Empire in 1912–1913. The Second Balkan War involved Bulgaria against Greece and Serbia in 1913.

Map 4.1. Western Macedonia, Greece.

Greek Macedonia   Western Macedonia

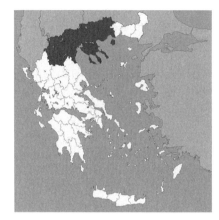

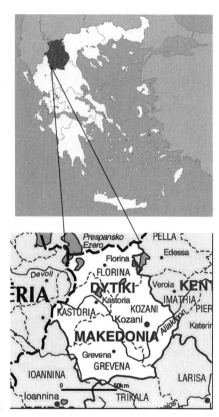

Detail of Western Macedonia

SOURCES: Greek Macedonia, http://commons.wikimedia.org/wiki/File:PosGreek
Macedonia.png; Western Macedonia, http://commons.wikimedia.org/wiki/File:
Periferia_Dytikis_Makedonias.png; Detail of Western Macedonia, http://europa.eu/
abc/maps/regions/greece/dytmak_en.htm.

Studying a specific region thoroughly allows me to trace the logic behind the nation-building policies proposed by the Greek administration.
We rarely have the opportunity to access the reasoning behind the planning of such measures. This type of evidence allows me to test the causal
mechanisms I have in mind. Additionally, by focusing on one region, I
can control for many state- and regional-level hypotheses such as levels of
economic development, regime type, elite understandings of nationhood,
and international norms, and test the plausibility of my argument against
three main alternative arguments: the cultural distance, status reversal,
and homeland arguments.

According to the *cultural distance* argument, the larger the cultural difference between the non-core group and the core group, the more likely exclusionary policies become. Only groups that fit the criteria of the core group should be targeted with assimilationist policies. The *status reversal* theory argues that the more intense the past conflict between the dominant group and the non-core group, the more likely exclusion becomes once the roles are reversed. Finally, according to the *homeland* argument, elites in a national homeland make credible commitments to co-ethnics in the near abroad; this in turn makes the non-core group assertive, and can lead to a secessionist war. The implicit prediction with respect to nation-building policies is that minorities with national homelands are likely to be mobilized along ethnic lines against the core group; and thus targeted with exclusionary policies by the host state rather than assimilation or accommodation.[22]

Integrating Western Macedonia: Intentions and Policies

The population residing in the "New Lands"[23] was far from being linguistically, ethnically, religiously, or culturally homogeneous. The inhabitants of the region were mostly peasants who lived in a world of corporate privileges for religious groups rather than individual rights. Industrial development was almost non-existent in Western Macedonia.[24] Moreover, the inhabitants were mostly illiterate, living in more or less homogeneous villages but overall mixed eparchies.

National categories such as "Greek," "Bulgarian," or "Turkish" did not signify the same thing to everybody, and nothing at all to many people. Sometimes people would call all Orthodox Christians "Greeks," regardless of their native languages or ethnic backgrounds. Christians would use the term "Turk" to refer to Muslims of all types of ethnic and linguistic background; thus they could mean an Albanian, Bosnian Muslim, Donmeh, or Muslim Vlach. The majority of the population still identified themselves in religious terms. When somebody was called "Bulgarian," it simply meant that person had joined the Bulgarian Exarchate, a church

---

22. For the cultural distance argument, see Clifford Geertz, "The Integrative Revolution: Primordial Sentiments and Politics in the New States," in Clifford Geertz, ed., *Old Societies and New States: The Quest for Modernity in Asia and Africa* (New York: Free Press of Glencoe, 1963); and Anthony D. Smith, *National Identity* (London: Penguin, 1991). For the status reversal argument, see Horowitz, *Ethnic Groups in Conflict*, pp. 17–18, 53; Stuart Kaufman, *Modern Hatreds: The Symbolic Politics of Ethnic War* (Ithaca, N.Y.: Cornell University Press, 2001); Petersen, *Resistance and Rebellion*; and Petersen, *Understanding Ethnic Violence*. For the homeland argument, see Brubaker, Nationalism Reframed, pp. 66–67; and Pieter Van Houten, "The Role of a Minority's Reference State in Ethnic Relations," *Archives européennes de sociologie*, Vol. 39, Issue 1 (May 1998), pp. 110–146.

23. This is the designation that the Greek government used for the territories annexed in the Balkans Wars and World War I until the late 1920s.

24. Kontogiorgi, *Population Exchange in Greek Macedonia*, p. 19.

organization established with Russian backing as recently as 1870.[25] Until the early twentieth century, most people collapsed religious and national categories in very counterintuitive ways, from a modern point of view.

Table 4.1 provides us with a categorization of non-core groups in the region, as discussed by the Greek administration in their confidential reports. Despite the fluidity of identities and the superficial character of some identifications, Greek policymakers were convinced that in the 1910s the "pure Greek element" was a minority in Western Macedonia. According to Eliakis, with the exception of the eparchies[26] of Servia and Anasselitsa, in all other eparchies Greeks were a minority. In Kozani, the Muslims were predominant and in Kailaria—today's Ptolemaida—Muslims and "Bulgarians" prevailed. In the eparchies of Kastoria and Florina, the majority were of the "Bulgarian" element together with a group of people with a fluid national consciousness. In the eparchy of Grevena, the influence of "Romanian-leaning" Vlachs was so great that Eliakis was not sure if there were any "pure Greeks" there.[27]

The Greek government had been thinking of nation-building policies for the population of these lands for over forty years before their actual incorporation; however, officials had to finalize and re-calibrate them after 1913.[28] As Mark Mazower put it, "Much time, money and effort was required by disciples of the new nationalist creeds to convert its inhabitants from their older, habitual ways of referring to themselves, and to turn nationalism itself from the obsession of a small, educated elite to a movement capable of galvanizing masses." [29]

In the early twentieth century, and especially during the Balkan Wars, we observe a drastic intensification of nation-building policies in the

---

25. Thomas A. Meininger, *Ignatiev and the Establishment of the Bulgarian Exarchate, 1864–1872: A Study in Personal Diplomacy* (New York: Arno Press, 1970).

26. An eparchy is a political subdivision of a province of Greece.

27. PKA, *Other Peoples*, Eliakis to the Provisional Government, Abstract of Report No. 5359, October 18, 1917. Also see PKA, *The State of Affairs of the Population in Western Macedonia*, Eliakis to the President of the Council of Ministers, Abstract of Report No. 7861, October 19, 1918). For detailed statistics of the regions, see Vemund Aarbakke, *Ethnic Rivalry and the Quest for Macedonia, 1870–1913* (Boulder, Colo.: East European Monographs, 2003).

28. Philip Carabott, "The Politics of Integration and Assimilation vis-à-vis the Slavo-Macedonian Minority of Inter-war Greece: From Parliamentary Inertia to Metaxist Repression," in Peter Mackridge and Eleni Yannakakis, eds., *Ourselves and Others. The Development of a Greek Macedonian Cultural Identity since 1912* (New York: Berg, 1997), pp. 59–78; Basil G. Gounaris, "Social Cleavages and National 'Awakening' in Ottoman Macedonia," *East European Quarterly*, Vol. 29, No. 4 (January 1996), pp. 409–425; Anastasia N. Karakasidou, *Fields of Wheat, Hills of Blood: Passages to Nationhood in Greek Macedonia, 1870–1990* (Chicago: University of Chicago Press, 1997); Iakovos Michailidis, "The War of Statistics: Traditional Recipes for the Preparation of the Macedonian Salad," *East European Quarterly*, Vol. 32, No. 1 (March 1998), pp. 9–21; Iakovos Michailidis, *Metakiniseis Slavofonon Plithysmon. O Polemos ton Statistikon* [Slavophone Population Movement. The War of Statistics] (Athens: Kritiki, 2003).

29. Mark Mazower, *Salonica, City of Ghosts: Christians, Muslims and Jews 1430–1950* (New York: Vintage, 2006), p. 256.

newly annexed territories by the three belligerents. Serbs pursued exclusionary policies against Albanians in Kosovo, Bulgarians against Greeks in Eastern Macedonia, and Greeks against Bulgarians in Central Macedonia.[30] (See Map 4.2.) After the Balkan Wars, the various national programs had already crystallized and internal nation-building intensified. The alliance pattern of the second Balkan War was preserved during World War I. This fact—which could have been otherwise—solidified the cleavages of the Second Balkan War.

Table 4.1. Non-core Groups in Greek Macedonia (circa 1916).

Non-core Groups	Religion	Language
Koniareoi	Muslim	Turkish
Valaades	Muslim	Greek
Albanians	Muslim and Christians	Albanian
Muslim Vlachs	*Muslim*	*Vlach*
Pomaks	*Muslim*	*Slavic*
Donmehs	*Muslim*	*Ladino/Turkish*
"Bulgarian-leaning" Slavs	Christian (Exarchate)	Slavic
"Greek-leaning" Slavs	Christian (Patriarchate)	Slavic
"Romanian-leaning" Vlachs	Christian (Romanian)	Vlach
"Greek-leaning" Vlachs	Christian (Patriarchate)	Vlach
Greeks	Christian (Patriarchate)	Greek
Sarakatsans	Christian (Patriarchate)	Greek
Armenian	*Christian (Gregorian)*	*Armenian*
Gypsies	*Christian (Patriarchate) and Muslim*	*Gypsy/Romany*
Jews	*Jewish*	*Ladino/French*

NOTE: Italicized non-core groups are not discussed in Eliakis's reports.

30.   George Frost Kennan, *The Other Balkan Wars* (Washington, D.C.: Carnegie Endowment for International Peace, 1993).

Map 4.2. Competing National Aspirations in the Balkans, 1912.

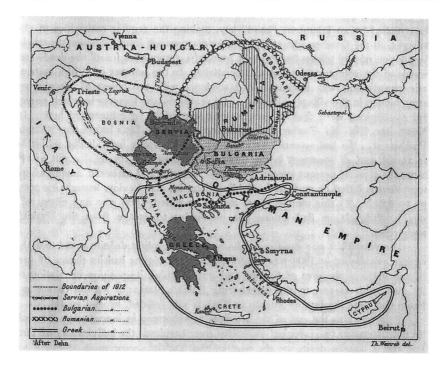

SOURCE: *Report of the International Commission To Inquire into the Causes and Conduct of the Balkan Wars*, Carnegie Endowment for International Peace, 1914.

When World War I broke out, historical Macedonia—the region corresponding roughly to the kingdom of ancient Macedonia—was once again at the center of controversy. (See Map 4.3.) Serbia and Bulgaria had entered World War I on the opposite sides of the war. Bulgaria allied with the Central Powers, and in 1915, Entente forces landed in Thessaloniki to assist Serbia.

In 1916, Bulgaria occupied Eastern and much of Western Greek Macedonia. This final blow to the territorial integrity of Greece led to the National Defense revolt in Thessaloniki and to the peculiar situation of two governments in Greece. This "national schism" in Greece was the culmination of an ongoing domestic conflict between the pro-German King Constantine and pro-Entente Venizelos. Venizelos' revolutionary government in Thessaloniki pushed for Greece to enter the war on the side of the Entente and create "Greater Greece"; King Constantine's plan was to keep out of World War I and sustain a "small but uncorrupted Greece."

Map 4.3. Boundary Changes after the Balkan Wars, 1912–1913.

SOURCE: *Report of the International Commission To Inquire into the Causes and Conduct of the Balkan Wars*, Carnegie Endowment for International Peace, 1914.

Ioannis Eliakis moved to the Western part of Greek Macedonia in July of 1916. In the rest of this section, I describe Eliakis's thoughts and policy recommendations about each non-core group under his jurisdiction. I structure the discussion based on the religious divide between Muslims and Christians, which was the oldest and most salient cleavage in the region.[31] Within each religious group, there were groups speaking different languages and having different national leanings (see Table 4.1). Moreover, some non-core groups had no external backing, some were backed by allied powers, such as Romania, and others were backed by enemy states, such as Bulgaria. During this four-year period, from 1916 to 1920, Greece moved from being a revisionist state to a status quo state, and in certain cases Eliakis's recommendations changed as well (see Tables 4.2 and 4.3).

Muslims in Western Macedonia

Approximately half of the inhabitants of Macedonia in the early twentieth century were Muslims.

After the incorporation of the so-called Aegean Macedonia into the Greek kingdom in 1913, Muslims could have chosen either the Ottoman or the Greek nationality. This was a policy clearly differentiating between the two religious communities and "encouraging" the Muslims that felt strong attachments to the Ottoman Empire to leave. There was variation in the effectiveness of this mechanism of "ethnic unmixing."

In Western Macedonia, fewer Muslims chose the Ottoman nationality than in other parts of northern Greece. Eliakis attributed this fact to the timely arrest of the Mufti[32] in Kailaria and of certain Beys[33] by the French Army in 1916, as well as to his personal efforts. He summoned all the Mukhtars[34] of the region and explained the program of the Greek authorities, asking them to accept Greek rule. These Mukhtars submitted to the new sovereign, and Eliakis promised to protect their human and community rights from both Greek and foreign authorities.[35]

---

31. Benjamin Braude and Bernard Lewis, *Christians and Jews in the Ottoman Empire: The Functioning of a Plural Society* (New York: Holmes and Meir, 2000); Konstantinos Tsitselikis, "The Pending Modernisation of Islam in Greece: From Millet to Minority Status," *Südosteuropa*, Vol. 55, Issue 4 (2007), pp. 354–372.

32. A Mufti is a Muslim cleric who gives opinions on Islamic law.

33. A Bey was a Provincial governor in the Ottoman Empire. By the end of nineteenth century, however, the term Bey is used for heads of ruling families, local notables, and military officials.

34. Mukhtar was the Turkish word for community leader, later mayor. They were appointed by the Ottomans in each community and were usually wealthy. The Mukhtar was responsible for enforcing law and order, collecting taxes, and calling the police when necessary. His house also functioned as the base for any visiting government officials.

35. PKA, *The Attitudes of Aliens toward the Movement: Voting Rights,* Eliakis to the Pro-

It is important to remember that Eliakis was from the island of Crete, where he had experienced the co-existence between Muslims and Christians. This experience informed Eliakis's attitude. More importantly, Prime Minister Venizelos, also from Crete, shared this experience and attitude. In a report to the Ministry of Military Affairs in 1917, Eliakis wrote:

With respect to the Muslims of my jurisdiction I am in the pleasant position to stress that because of my stance toward them, although they have been asked to satisfy many military needs, they understood that the State is protecting everyone irrespectively of race or religion, and this made them even more loyal subjects of our State. Holding the view that we should not grant political rights to the Muslims, since this would corrupt them, I have always argued we will not be able to sever their bonds with the Ottoman State unless we respect their human rights and their religious beliefs. Following this policy will allow us to use them as an important factor in every respect, but more importantly, it will prove that we are able to govern alien people, something necessary in order to enforce order in Macedonia. [36]

Not much later, Eliakis noted that the above policy produced amazing results. The Muslims had demonstrated their trust in the state by enthusiastically enlisting in the Greek Army. The benefits from this were clear, because the army needed these "obedient and healthy soldiers." Eliakis drew a parallel between them and the "Moroccan Spahis"[37] fighting for the French and suggested specific policies to ensure the success of this endeavor:

1. create Muslim battalions with their own flag, which should include the half moon in one of its corners; 2. allow each battalion to have an Imam[38] for prayer; 3. promote the best to non-commissioned officers; 4. allow them to wear the *fez*; 5. insert Greek soldiers fluent in Turkish to monitor the behavior of these battalions and spy on them if necessary. [39]

In general, Eliakis believed Muslims were easy to deal with *because* of their religion. It was enough to protect their life, honor, and property, respect their religion, and treat them equally. Having political rights was not a concern for them, he believed, as long as they could freely regulate their communal affairs. According to his analysis, if this policy were to be followed, the Muslims would gradually become "civilized" and understand themselves to be an indispensable part of the Greek nation. This would happen especially after the Muslims realized that the Turkish state would not be able to recapture these territories.

---

visional Government, Abstract of Report No. 564, November 11, 1916.

36. PKA, *Conscription of Muslims*, Eliakis to the Ministry of Military Affairs, August 25, 1917.

37. *Spahis* regiments were light cavalry regiments in the French Army recruited primarily from the indigenous populations of French Morocco. The name comes from *Sipahi*, an Ottoman cavalry man.

38. An Imam is a Muslim prayer leader.

39. PKA, *Conscription of Muslims*, Eliakis to the Ministry of Military Affairs, August 25, 1917.

The Muslims of Western Macedonia were not a homogeneous group. Eliakis distinguished between three main non-core groups: Koniareoi, Valaades, and Albanians. Koniareoi were the Turkish-speaking conquerors of Macedonia who came from Anatolia and, according to Eliakis, were still in an "animal state." The ones that felt closer to the Ottoman Empire would choose the Ottoman nationality and would be "encouraged" to leave. For the rest, he believed that they could be ruled easily through the Koran. The second group was Valaades, the Greek speakers of Vlach origin who had converted to Islam and lived in villages near Anasselitsa. According to Eliakis, many of them were aware of their Greek origin and most did not even speak Turkish. They would be easy to assimilate. As Eliakis put it: "Their assimilation will be complete once they are convinced that religion is not the attribute of Nations, but national consciousness and origin."[40]

After World War I, Eliakis's intentions with respect to these two groups were far from exclusionary. Valaades were perceived and treated as if they were Greek. Koniareoi were accommodated in the short term, but the ultimate goal was to assimilate them. Given that they were perceived as a group backed by an enemy power, the Ottoman Empire, and that Eliakis wanted to preserve the favorable status quo, my theory predicts assimilationist policies. Thus it correctly predicts Eliakis's long-term objectives, even though the actual policies initially looked more like accommodation than assimilation.

Finally, there was also the third group the Muslim Albanians.[41] According to Eliakis, religion did not matter to them and their Albanian consciousness prevailed.[42] The Albanians differed from the Koniareoi, who were looking toward Istanbul for protection. Many Albanians had economic interests in the Greek territories, emphasized the common origins of Greeks and Albanians, and worked for Greek-Albanian cooperation.

Two elements made Eliakis suggest a different treatment of Albanians: the desire to maintain friendly relations with the newly born state (Albania), and the distinct Albanian consciousness of this population, which disassociated them from other Muslims. He wrote:

If there is an Albanian State after the War it is to our benefit that this State is friendly to us. Thus, I think we should not take the same measures toward the Albanians ruled by our regime that we take against the other Muslims. We should not for example confiscate their land as if it was abandoned, even if it really is, as long as they do not emigrate to Turkey. The confiscated land of the Albanians who emigrated for a while but came back and declared their loyalty to our regime has to be returned to them even if their loyalty is not sincere.[43]

---

40.   PKA, Eliakis to the President of the Council of Ministers, Abstract of Report No. 7861, October 19, 1918.

41.   There were three other groups of Muslims that lived in Greek Macedonia at the time: the Muslim Vlachs (primarily from Meglen region); the Gypsies (Roma); and the Slavic-speaking Muslims (Pomaks). Eliakis, however, does not refer to them.

42.   He also noted there were few *Christian* Albanians sharing this Albanian consciousness.

43.   PKA, *Alvanistai*, Eliakis to the Provisional Government, Abstract of Report No.

Albania, which was established in 1913 but not yet a functional entity due to the outbreak of World War I, would be a new state that Greece had many reasons to befriend.[44] The Albanians in the Greek kingdom could operate as guarantors of friendly relations with Albania. The national interest would be better served by making this small material sacrifice of not confiscating Albanian land. Eliakis's proposal was implemented by the government a year and a half later. Thus the Albanians, members of a non-core group backed by a neutral power, were accommodated by the Greek administration, consistent with my theory.

The alternative hypotheses (see Tables 4.3 and 4.4) all incorrectly predict exclusionary policies toward the Albanians because they spoke a different language and had a different religion; they had a newly minted homeland; and they had been traditionally allied with the Turks within the dominant Muslim millet during Ottoman times. Similarly, all three alternative hypotheses predict that the Greek administration should have excluded the Koniareoi population because it was Muslim, spoke a different language and used to be the privileged group during the Ottoman times. While this was partially true during the Balkan Wars and World War I, it certainly does not appear to be in Eliakis's intentions and actions following World War I.

Christians in Western Macedonia

SLAVIC-SPEAKING CHRISTIANS

Having tested my theory on non-core groups with a different world religion from the core group, I now turn to non-core groups that shared the same religion (although not necessarily the same denomination) with the core group, but spoke a different language. The Slavic-speaking population of the region—especially the part loyal to the Bulgarian Exarchate—was considered a Bulgarian national minority by the Bulgarian state.

"BULGARIAN-LEANING" SLAVS. Although Eliakis was not worried about the loyalty of the various Muslim groups, he was less optimistic with respect to the Christian Orthodox, "Bulgarian-leaning" Slavs. These were people who sided with the Bulgarian Exarchate after its establishment in 1870. His reasoning, however, was not one of cultural differences or affinities but rather of diplomatic relations and war dynamics. He believed that if there had been no Second Balkan War in Macedonia, then:

389, January 27, 1917. Note: The date for Abstract of No. 389 report appears as 1918 in the original document but this must be a mistake. First, the report is addressed to the Provisional Government, which did not exist in1918; second, the report is between reports from 1916 and 1917.

44.   One of the reasons for this fact was that the Albanians could be Greece's allies in case of a pan-Slavic alliance in the Balkans.

the local Bulgarians would be so audacious that [Greek] Macedonia would be everything but Greek, since the 'Bulgarians' would be able to freely express their Bulgarian feelings. However, the second war followed and the local 'Bulgarians' were discouraged and converts to the schism [the Exarchate] presented themselves as orthodox [loyal to the Patriarchate] and Greeks, supposedly forced to convert religiously and consequently to change their nationality as well. In the midst of that terror, our state should have put aside everything else and focused its efforts on cementing in the hearts of the population these [national] ideas...It did almost nothing instead.[45]

Eliakis criticized the Greek government because it did not send its best civil servants and educators to Macedonia. He strongly believed that if there were schools in every village and if Greek priests took the place of those backing the Bulgarian Exarchate, then the population would have been assimilated quickly. However, the civil servants were below average, and many of them came in order to make a fortune; moreover, only a few schools started operating right away, and no priests were sent to the villages that returned to the jurisdiction of the Patriarchate. Despite all of these complaints, Eliakis was optimistic:

if we try to change the souls of the population, it should be easy to do, since they are used to being changed. They tell me that in one trial which took place in Florina during Turkish rule...a witness was asked by the President of the Court what his nationality was and he replied that eight years ago he was Bulgarian, two years later he became a Greek and remained such for three years, after which he became Bulgarian again....And he found this identity change unproblematic and really believed in each period that he was what [nationality] he thought he was. Thus if we work not spasmodically...but systematically, it would be possible to make the local population believe they have become Greeks and if they maintain this conviction for a long time it will be possible that they will really become such.[46]

The grave results from the government's inaction with respect to the assimilation of the local population were obvious during the Bulgarian attack in Western Macedonia, when many Slavic speakers welcomed Bulgarian soldiers as liberators. A further indicator of the pro-Bulgarian sentiment from a part of the local population was that even when the Entente (French and British) forces pushed out the Bulgarian troops, many believed they would come back. Some of them followed the defeated troops, hoping they would return as victors.

Following the Bulgarian defeat in the area, the Entente forces treated the people residing in Western Macedonia badly because they had demonstrated pro-Bulgarian feelings. The only refuge for these people was to adopt the Greek national identity and demonstrate their loyalty to the Greek state. According to Eliakis, this was an opportune moment for the Greek administration to achieve in two years what it would otherwise not be able to achieve in ten. The Slavic-speakers of Western Macedonia were trying to prove their "Greekness" by protesting the lack of schools. Once

45.   PKA, *The State of Affairs of the Population in Western Macedonia*, Eliakis to the President of the Council of Ministers, Abstract of Report No. 7861, October 19, 1918.

46.   Ibid.

again, the Greek government did not act upon this opportunity because of administrative failure. While Eliakis was writing his report in 1918, most schools remained closed and Athens did not provide schoolbooks.

Eliakis was not optimistic about assimilating the older Slavic-speaking population in the region, and he suggested that most policies should focus on the younger generation. He expected the best results to come from orphanages and girls' boarding schools. He also insisted that, based on experience, the assimilation of "Bulgarian-leaning" Slavs could not entail solely cultural and educational measures; it had to entail terror as well.

During World War I, methods such as deportations, arrests, and even killings were legitimized by the fact that Bulgaria was an enemy power fighting on the side of the Central Powers (the German, Austro-Hungarian, and Ottoman Empires). During peacetime—when Eliakis was writing this report—violent measures were harder to justify and pursue without attracting the attention of the international community. Furthermore, Greece was in favor of the international status quo. Nevertheless, Eliakis suggested that violent measures were essential even in peacetime in order to neutralize any obstruction to peaceful assimilation policies.

Indeed, the Greek government had passed a law during World War I that facilitated the deportation of individuals considered dangerous to the public order. Eliakis built on that law and suggested it had to be enforced when necessary. He thought that Greek authorities should deport not just the guilty party but his whole family. Moreover, the deportation and the reasons for it should be made known to the whole community.

The possibility of deporting all of the "Bulgarian-leaning" Slavs from Macedonia was suggested and described as a more "radical" measure of nationalizing the territory. However, Eliakis quickly dismissed this idea because "on the one hand, this would make a terrible impression to the liberal people of the civilized world, and, on the other, because we do not have those [Greeks], with whom we could replace them."[47]

In 1919, the repatriation of Greeks from Anatolia was unlikely, especially because the Greek kingdom needed to keep them where they were in order to justify its campaign to the East.[48] Under such circumstances, a mass deportation of all the Bulgarian-speakers would lead to a severe depopulation of Macedonia. This would make the kingdom look weak.

Moreover, the Greek government had to act as a civilized liberal polity in the eyes of the international community. This was the first concern of the Governor-General of Western Macedonia. In 1919, while considering a deportation proposal made by Konstantinos Mazarakis-Ainian,[49] Eliakis writes:

---

47.   Ibid.

48.   Eleutherios Venizelos, *Greece Before the Peace Congress of 1919. A Memorandum Dealing with the Rights of Greece*, published for the American-Hellenic Society by the U.S. branch of Oxford University Press, 1919.

49.   Konstantinos Mazarakis-Ainian (1869–1949) was the commander of the Xanthi division, which occupied Western Thrace for Greece.

In case of a deportation of 'Bulgarians' there will be a terrible manipulation of the affair. If we listen to the advice of the Greeks then there is a danger either of turning Northern Macedonia into a deserted land, which would call for the intervention of Europe and would damage our reputation in the eyes of the civilized world, or of providing the opportunity to these Greeks of all sorts of blackmail that would disturb human consciousness.[50]

For the above reasons, Eliakis concluded that the most sensible policy was assimilation. He argued that if the right measures were taken, only a few would not be assimilated:

We are obliged to follow the hard and rough way of proselytizing, through good and expensive administration, systematically in all sectors of the administration. I am certain that with such administration we will rapidly have results. And instead of transplanting the local population with the danger of not replacing them, through this kind of administration, we will implant in them our ideas and turn them into fanatic Greeks, more fanatic than the old Greeks.[51]

With respect to the "Bulgarian-leaning" Slavs, my theory correctly predicted Eliakis's preferred policies. During World War I, terror and intense assimilationist policies would have achieved the exclusion of the pro-Bulgarian population and successfully assimilated the rest of the Slavic-speaking population. "Bulgarian-leaning" Slavs were backed by a rival power while the Greek administration was fighting a war to recapture its lost territories. Following World War I, Greece wanted to preserve the international status quo in Macedonia, thus intense assimilationist policies were the preferred choice and exclusionary policies would only target specific families of agitators.

For the whole period under study, 1916–1920, external interference never stopped. Bulgarian agitators were present in all of Macedonia. Toward the end of the period under study, a voluntary population exchange between Greece and Bulgaria under the Treaty of Neuilly in 1919 was the middle road actually followed by the Greek government on this issue. As a result, about 56,000 "Bulgarian-leaning" Slavs left Greece for Bulgaria by the mid-1920s, "in many cases being forced to emigrate by the Greek authorities."[52] After 1919, a mix of assimilationist and selectively targeted exclusionary policies was the actual policy followed toward this group.

All but one of the alternative hypotheses predict exclusionary policies toward the "Bulgarian-leaning" Slavs because they spoke a different language; were organized under a different religion organization, the Exarchate; and had a national homeland. The status-reversal argument is the only one that predicts assimilationist policies, because the "Bulgarian-

---

50. PKA, *Deportation of Bulgarians*, Eliakis to the Ministry of Interior, Abstract of Report No. 4164, June 12, 1919.

51. PKA, *On the Ownership of the Fertile Lands*, Eliakis to the Ministry of Interior, Abstract of Report No. 4164, June 12, 1919.

52. Iakovos Michailidis, "National Identity versus Minority Language: The Greek and Bulgarian Experience in the 20th Century," in Ann Katherine Isaacs, ed., *Language and Identities in Historical Perspective* (Pisa, Italy: Edizioni Plus-Pisa University Press, 2005), p. 94.

leaning" Slavs were also disadvantaged during the Ottoman times, along with the rest of the Christians. Because of the mixed strategy followed toward the "Bulgarian-leaning" Slavs, all hypotheses find support. Significantly for my argument, however, the group was not accommodated.

"GRECOMANOI" OR "GREEK-LEANING" SLAVS. "Grecomanoi" was a term used to indicate Slavic speakers with Greek national consciousness. These people had sided with Greek guerrilla troops during the Macedonian Struggle (1903–1908) and had resisted the influence of the Exarchate.[53] They were not mobilized by a competing claim and were, as expected, targeted with assimilationist policies. Looking solely at the cultural differences of this non-core group from the core group could lead to a prediction of exclusion, because they spoke a different language and were of Slavic origins. The homeland argument likewise incorrectly predicts exclusion because Bulgaria could be understood as their homeland. The status-reversal argument accurately predicts this policy, because "Greek-leaning" Slavs were a politically disadvantaged group under Ottoman rule.

VLACH-SPEAKING CHRISTIANS

Many Vlachs were primarily herders living a nomadic life, while others were sedentary farmers. A few had settled in larger towns in the Balkans and become merchants or artisans. They spoke a Latin dialect close to modern Romanian. Most of them lived in the Pindus mountain range, but some also resided in the hills near trading centers such as Monastir, Grevena, Kastoria, Koritsa, Moskopol, Veroia, and Edessa.

"ROMANIAN-LEANING" VLACHS. The Romanian government began its efforts to "awaken" a Romanian identity in the Vlachs of Macedonia in the late 1860s. To gain Romania's support during the treaty conference in Bucharest in 1913, Prime Minister Venizelos declared that Greece was willing to provide autonomy to the Koutsovlach schools and churches in the newly acquired Greek possessions. The group was recognized as a national minority, and their schools and churches were funded by the Romanian state.[54] This was the first time that the minority provisions of a treaty signed by Greece referred to a *national* minority. Vlachs had to decide if they were "Romanian" or "Greek." The governments of the two countries had to compete for their allegiance.

In the eparchy of Grevena there were a few "Romanian-leaning" Vlachs, who during Ottoman times were under the protection of Romania. Their main incentive to identify with Romania was to facilitate herding

53.   Douglass Dakin, *The Greek Struggle in Macedonia 1897–1913* (Thessaloniki: Institute for Balkan Studies, 1966).

54.   See George Th. Mavrogordatos, "Oi Ethnikes Meionotites" [The National Minorities], in Christos Chatziiosif, ed., *Istoria tis Elladas tou 20ou aiona* [History of Greece of the Twentieth Century], Vol. II (Athens: Vivliorama, 2003), pp. 9–35, 16.

and commerce with Romania.[55] Romania had pursued a national agitation campaign in European Turkey during the late nineteenth century, and with the Treaty of Bucharest in 1913, Romania achieved the recognition of Romanian minorities in Serbia, Bulgaria, and Greece. The Romanian propaganda in Macedonia waned immediately after its occupation by the Greek Army, despite the treaty provisions; however, it was spurred during World War I under the temporary French military administration. The civil servant for finance at Grevena, Askarides, wrote to Eliakis:

If the French Administration lasts longer and if the National Defense does not incorporate the eparchy of Grevena soon, then they ["Romanian-leaning" Vlachs] will prevail over the Greek element since they are working systematically and intensely in order to establish a precedent which I hope will not be recognized as a permanent situation. [56]

During World War I, Eliakis was mostly worried about the spread of "Romanian propaganda." Unlike most Muslims and "Bulgarian-leaning" Slavs, who were perceived to be backed by enemy powers, Romania was an ally; therefore, the only reasonable policy toward the pro-Romanian Vlachs was to present Greece as a better and more prestigious protector of their rights. Eliakis firmly believed that as soon as the "Romanian-leaning" Vlachs realized that they no longer had a need for external protection, then with the help of school, military service, and church, they would become "pure Greeks."

In 1917, Eliakis warned Venizelos's government that the "Romanian-leaning" Vlachs in Grevena had been approached by the Italian authorities there in order to change them into "Italian-leaning" Vlachs. The Italians presented the idea of self-determination to the Vlachs living in the Pindus mountain range, and while the Italian troops were withdrawing, many locals expressed such desires. The Greek police arrested some of the rebels who were against Greek sovereignty. However, the ambassadors of both Italy and Romania protested to the Greek government over these arrests. Eliakis interfered and asked to meet with the prisoners before they were taken to the court-martial in Thessaloniki.

I asked them why they were arrested and they pretended that they had no clue or attributed their arrest to defamations by their enemies. I asked them if they are Greek, and they hesitated to deny the Greek national identity; some even said 'if only more were like us....' Following these questions, I talked to them for a long time in this manner: I told them, that since I hear that they speak Greek, I consider them Greek. And they should boast for being Greek since they have the most glorious history in the world.[57]

---

55.   PKA, "Romanian-leaning" Vlachs, Eliakis to Provisional Government, Abstract of Report No. 5359, October 18, 1917.

56.   PKA, "Romanian-leaning" Vlachs, Eliakis to the Provisional Government, Abstract of Report No. 389, January 27, 1917.

57.   PKA, "Romanian-leaning" Vlachs, Eliakis to Provisional Government, Abstract of Report No. 5359, October 18, 1917.

This is a typical example of Eliakis's cultivation of the local population. He would emphasize the superiority of Hellenism and Greek culture in general, while at the same time he would attempt to convince them of their Greekness. Sometimes he highlighted the linguistic attributes of the population he addressed, other times their religious affiliation, and sometimes even their dress, like in the following report:

The inhabitants of upper Grammatikovon, where the liturgy is in the Romanian language, are "Romanian-leaning" Vlachs and almost Romanians. The potential military recruits of this village are so fanatical that they did not enlist in the last draft; instead they went to work for the English service station. Because of this, the committee of grain storage in Kailaria did not want to supply grain to this village. So the head of this village came to complain. I asked him if he is a Greek and he replied "Don't you see what I am wearing?" pointing to his dress. I answered that I saw him wearing the Greek fustanella[58] and that I heard him speak Greek, which means that he is Greek, and one of the best for that matter, since the Evzones that also wear the fustanella are the best soldiers of the Greek Army. On this basis and with the above spirit I spoke to him and I could tell the powerful impression it produced. I made him wonder how he could have been unaware that he is Greek. [59]

More importantly for my argument, Eliakis moderated his assimilationist tendencies because of the geopolitical situation. Although he tried to instill Greek feelings in the "Romanian-leaning" Vlachs, he also told them:

If any of you has Romanian feelings, if he is Romanian, I respect his feelings, because Romania is a friend and allied power. We share both friends and enemies with her and we have no conflicting interests since Romania is not considering jumping over the Balkan Peninsula to come and conquer the territories you inhabit.[60]

Eliakis was willing to respect their Romanian leanings, both because he had to and because he considered them to be geopolitically harmless, since Romania was an ally. Accommodation was the policy toward the "Romanian-leaning" Vlachs. A population exchange between Greece and Romania was not considered at all. Greece needed Romania as an ally, and Bulgaria was the common enemy. Finally, the absence of a common border with Romania minimized the perception of threat for the Greek side.

"GREEK-LEANING" VLACHS. "Hellenovlachoi" was the term used by the Greek administration to refer to Vlach-speaking people who had Greek national consciousness; it stood for "Greek-leaning" Vlachs. These people had sided with the Greek guerrilla troops during the Macedonian Struggle (1903–1908) and had either resisted or escaped the influence of the

---

58.   A fustanella is a skirt-like garment worn by men in the Balkans up to the end of the nineteenth century. It was the uniform of the Evzones (light infantry) until World War II; today of the Greek Presidential (formerly Royal) Guard in Athens.

59.   PKA, *"Romanian-leaning" Vlachs*, Eliakis to Provisional Government, Abstract of Report No. 5359, October 18, 1917.

60.   Ibid.

Romanian and Italian propaganda. They were not mobilized by a competing claim and were thus a good prospect for assimilationist policies. This subgroup thus conforms to the expectations of my theory.

Looking at the Vlach-speaking population and its two sub-groups, we observe that focusing on cultural differences alone does not help us account for the variation in nation-building policies. Both groups spoke a Latin-based language and they should thus be excluded. Instead, the former non-core group, the "Romanian-leaning" Vlachs, was accommodated while the latter, the "Greek-leaning" Vlachs, was targeted with assimilationist policies.

Moreover, the homeland argument cannot help us distinguish between the two sub-groups of Vlach-speakers either, because Romania viewed both as potential co-ethnics. The status-reversal argument correctly predicts a policy of assimilation toward the "Greek-leaning" Vlachs, but is incorrect in the case of the "Romanian-leaning" ones, who were accommodated instead. Both groups were disadvantaged during the Ottoman times, and based on this fact we would expect the Greek administration to pursue assimilationist policies toward both of them. Finally, focusing on the religious affiliation of the two sub-groups leads to similar predictions. Because both groups were Christian Orthodox, they should be targeted with assimilationist policies; however, only the "Greek-leaning" Vlachs were targeted, while the "Romanian-leaning" ones were accommodated. To be sure, assimilationist tendencies were expressed by Eliakis, but the policy during that period was one of accommodation of their differences through Romanian schools and Romanian churches.

GREEK-SPEAKING CHRISTIANS

Within the "Greeks," the Greek-speaking or Greek dialect–speaking Christian Orthodox population, there was a group referred to by Eliakis as "Skenitai" or "Sarakatsans." They dressed like Vlachs and lived nomadic lives, but they were considered by everyone, including Eliakis, to be Greeks. There were approximately 40,000 in Greek Macedonia; they took their name, Skenitai (tent-people), from their way of life. In the winter they settled in the lowlands, especially Chalkidiki, while in the summer they tented up in the mountains. This group apparently made no claims to the communal property of the places it inhabited and did not interfere with their administration.[61] Eliakis suggested the settlement of this population among groups who had foreign national leanings and its conscription into the Greek Army.[62] Not surprisingly, all theories make the same prediction for the Sarakatsans: assimilation. They were indeed targeted with standard assimilationist policies such as schooling and military conscription.

---

61. According to Eliakis, the explanation behind the emergence of "Romanian-leaning" Vlachs was that they were people who immigrated to Romania, but when they came back they were in constant competition with the sedentary local population.

62. PKA, *Skenitai*, Eliakis to Provisional Government, Abstract of Report No. 5359, October 18, 1917.

Conclusion

WHAT ACCOUNTS FOR VARIATION IN NATION-BUILDING POLICIES?

My geostrategic argument is largely supported by the evidence provided here. Granted, a set of reports written by a particular administrator in a four-year period is not a representative sample of the Greek government as a whole—not to mention governments in general; however, this level of analysis is crucial if one wants to test the microfoundations of an argument. A theory might make the right predictions, but fail to identify the correct causal mechanisms at work. Historical contextualization coupled with rich archival material allows us to test both the predictions and the causal logic underlying a theory.

The different combinations of interstate relations with external powers and foreign policy goals lead to different predictions of my theory (see Figure 4.1). Looking at Tables 4.2 and 4.3 we see that, consistent with my argument, non-core groups without any external power backing them and claiming their allegiance were targeted with assimilationist policies, and were the least likely to get minority-rights protection. Allied-backed groups were accommodated (Albanians and "Romanian-leaning" Vlachs).

During World War I, we find that Eliakis's goal was securing the "New Lands" to the Greek kingdom through ironing out both internal and external enemies (See Table 4.2). Besides dealing with direct security concerns, he had to neutralize the propaganda of the various competitors in the region. Under these circumstances, exclusionary policies were pursued toward enemy-backed non-core groups (Koniareoi and "Bulgarian-leaning" Slavs). Toward the end of World War I, however, Eliakis becomes more optimistic about the assimilability of certain non-core groups.

Following the World War I, the Greek administration was in favor of the international status quo, and it adopted an assimilationist policy toward enemy-backed non-core groups with an emphasis on political equality and egalitarianism toward the population that it considered as assimilable *regardless* of cultural, religious, or linguistic differences (Koniareoi and "Bulgarian-leaning" Slavs). Consistent with my theory, the perception of these non-core groups was to a great extent endogenous to the external interference by competing states. The past political behavior of the various non-core groups *vis-à-vis* the Greek cause in the region prior to the annexation of the territories was also central in the planning of nation-building policies.

Another shortcut the Greek administration used in order to determine whether a non-core group was assimilable was not the particular marker that differentiated it from the core group, but rather the constraints put in place by international and bilateral treaties with neighboring states and Great Powers (France and Britain). To be sure, besides the constraints—which my theory emphasizes—there were also perceived opportunities, as in the case of the Albanians. Interstate alliances had an effect on the planning of nation-building policies in two ways: through a retrospective assessment based on existing alliances, and a prospective one based on future opportunities for useful alliances.

Table 4.2. Explaining Nation-building Policies in Western Macedonia, 1916–1918 (Greece Was Revisionist).

Non-core Groups	External Backing?	External Power: Rival or Ally?	Predictions	Intentions	Policy
"Greek-leaning" Slavs	No	·	Assimilation	Assimilation	Assimilation
"Greek-leaning" Vlachs	No	·	Assimilation	Assimilation	Assimilation
Sarakatsans	No	·	Assimilation	Assimilation	Assimilation
Valaades	No	·	Assimilation	Assimilation	Assimilation
Albanians	Yes	Neutral	Accommodation	Accommodation	Accommodation
"Romanian-leaning" Vlachs	Yes	Ally	Accommodation	Accommodation/ Assimilation	Accommodation
Koniareoi	Yes	Rival	Exclusion	Exclusion/ Assimilation	Exclusion/ Accommodation
"Bulgarian-leaning" Slavs	Yes	Rival	Exclusion	Exclusion/ Assimilation	Exclusion/ Assimilation

Table 4.3. Explaining Nation-building Policies in Western Macedonia, 1918–1920 (Greece Was Status Quo).

Non-core Groups	External Backing?	External Power: Rival or Ally?	Predictions	Intentions	Policy
"Greek-leaning" Slavs	No	.	Assimilation	Assimilation	Assimilation
"Greek-leaning" Vlachs	No	.	Assimilation	Assimilation	Assimilation
Sarakatsans	No	.	Assimilation	Assimilation	Assimilation
Valaades	No	.	Assimilation	Assimilation	Assimilation
Albanians	Yes	Future Ally	Accommodation	Accommodation	Accommodation
"Romanian-leaning" Vlachs	Yes	Ally	Accommodation	Accommodation/ Assimilation	Accommodation
Koniareoi	Yes	Rival	Assimilation	Assimilation	Accommodation/ Assimilation
"Bulgarian-leaning" Slavs	Yes	Rival	Assimilation	Assimilation	Assimilation/ Voluntary Exchange

Table 4.4. Evaluating Alternative Explanations in Western Macedonia, 1916–1918.

Non-core Groups	Language	Religion	Status Reversal	Homeland	Policy
"Greek-leaning" Slavs	Exclusion	Assimilation	Assimilation	Exclusion	Assimilation
"Greek-leaning" Vlachs	Exclusion	Assimilation	Assimilation	Exclusion	Assimilation
Sarakatsans	Assimilation	Assimilation	Assimilation	Assimilation	Assimilation
Valaades	Assimilation	Exclusion	Exclusion	Assimilation	Assimilation
Albanians	Exclusion	Exclusion	Exclusion	Exclusion	Accommodation
"Romanian-leaning" Vlachs	Exclusion	Assimilation	Assimilation	Exclusion	Accommodation
Koniareoi	Exclusion	Exclusion	Exclusion	Exclusion	Exclusion/Accommodation
"Bulgarian-leaning" Slavs	Exclusion	Exclusion	Assimilation	Exclusion	Exclusion/Assimilation

NOTE: Incorrect predictions in grayscale.

Table 4.5. Evaluating Alternative Explanations in Western Macedonia, 1918–1920.

Non-core Groups	Language	Religion	Status Reversal	Homeland	Policy
"Greek-leaning" Slavs	Exclusion	Assimilation	Assimilation	Exclusion	Assimilation
"Greek-leaning" Vlachs	Exclusion	Assimilation	Assimilation	Exclusion	Assimilation
Sarakatsans	Assimilation	Assimilation	Assimilation	Assimilation	Assimilation
Valaades	Assimilation	Exclusion	Exclusion	Assimilation	Assimilation
Albanians	Exclusion	Exclusion	Exclusion	Exclusion	Accommodation
"Romanian-leaning" Vlachs	Exclusion	Assimilation	Assimilation	Exclusion	Accommodation
Koniareoi	Exclusion	Exclusion	Exclusion	Exclusion	Accommodation/ Assimilation
"Bulgarian-leaning" Slavs	Exclusion	Exclusion	Assimilation	Exclusion	Assimilation/ Voluntary Exchange

NOTE: Incorrect predictions in grayscale.

How well do alternative arguments do in this context? State- and regional-level hypotheses such as levels of economic development, regime type, understandings of nationhood, international norms, and so forth are held constant by design. There is, however, group-level variation. Looking at Tables 4.4 and 4.5, we see that cultural-distance arguments cannot explain most of the variation. For example, with respect to the "Bulgarian-leaning Slavs" and "Romanian-leaning" Vlachs, Eliakis's reasoning was not one of cultural differences or affinities, but rather on diplomatic relations and war dynamics. The former group was backed by a rival power and was thus targeted with intense assimilationist and ultimately exclusionary measures, while the latter was backed by an ally and was accommodated. Even where they make correct predictions it is for the wrong reasons. Koniareoi were not targeted with exclusionary policies during World War I because of their cultural difference, but because of their links to the Ottoman Empire, which was fighting on the side of the Central Powers.

The status-reversal argument does better. This argument, however, can only differentiate between conflict and no conflict and thus has little to say about assimilation or accommodation. For example, although the Koniareoi were members of the dominant group before the Greek occupation, Eliakis pursued a policy of accommodation in terms of their culture and language. This policy directly contradicts the status-reversal argument. It also contradicts my argument, which predicts exclusion during and assimilation after World War I for this group, but the archival material helps us to understand this policy choice. As Eliakis stated, this phase of accommodation was just a step before assimilationist policies.[63]

The homeland argument does worse than the status-reversal one. Whether a non-core group has an external homeland or not is important, but it does not help us predict which nation-building policy the host state will pursue. My theory suggests that looking at the degree to which the homeland interferes with the fate of its "ethnic kin," as well as the interstate relations of the host state with the homeland, is crucial. Moreover, besides the degree of external interference, the foreign policy goals of the host state are an important factor in the planning of nation-building policies.

FUTURE RESEARCH ON NATION-BUILDING

On the methodological front, I have identified two fundamental problems in the study of nation-building policies: the politics of "counting people" and distinguishing intentions and policy choices from policy outcomes. Both of these challenges hinder the study of state-planned nation-building policies. Not addressing them in our research can lead to deceptive empirical support for theories. In this chapter, I demonstrate the centrality of archival research in the effort to overcome these important caveats in the study of nation-building.

---

63. For a discussion of the distinction between transitional vs. terminal policies, see Mylonas, Assimilation and its Alternatives, chap. 5.

Bridging the macro-level with the micro-level, i.e., understanding the structure of the international system within which nation-building takes place at the local level, is crucial. Studies that focus on specific regions or specific ethnic groups would benefit from a more explicit treatment of the international dimensions of the process they are analyzing. The international context affects the preference ordering of host states, external powers that contemplate interference, and non-core group elites alike. Scholars studying the politics of nation-building should focus more on the perceptions of state officials as well as the influential international players (Great Powers, international organizations, non-governmental organizations), and try to identify the new cleavage dimensions that are about to be politicized.

At the same time, studies that emphasize the importance of systemic effects but neglect the micro-level processes at work are also problematic. Such studies often fail to identify the right level of analysis for data collection and hypothesis testing. Moreover, they suffer from a "revealed preferences problem," because they frequently make inferences about the actor's motivations based exclusively on their public statements or observed behavior. Archival material coupled with historical contextualization is one way to mitigate this problem. A balanced study of nation-building should bridge the micro-level empirical work with the systemic effects of the structure of the international system by providing a theoretical argument at the meso-level, linking the macro- and the micro-level.

POLICY IMPLICATIONS

In this chapter, I have argued that external interference and support for specific non-core groups by competing states affects the nation-building policies the core-group elites pursue. When interstate relations change, policy changes follow suit. In the twenty-first century there are thousands of ethnic groups in over 190 countries, mostly concentrated in post-imperial and post-colonial territories similar to the ones I study. Understanding the logic of nation-building is therefore crucial. Such an understanding could help decision-makers in the international community devise incentives to prevent exclusionary policies, encourage accommodation, or foster national integration.

At least two policy implications follow from my argument: First, in order to improve core and non-core group relations, we should focus on improving interstate relations. The causes of interethnic conflict are often to be found outside the location in which they are taking place. External interference by interested powers politicizes differences that hadn't been as salient before and often triggers exclusionary policies by the host state; an example of this process occurring in 2008 was the war in Georgia.[64] To prevent exclusionary policies, we should uphold the principle of state sovereignty and minimize external interference as well as border chang-

---

64. For more on this, see Thomas Meaney and Harris Mylonas, "The Pandora's Box of Sovereignty," *Los Angeles Times*, August 13, 2008, p. A17.

es. The preservation of the international status quo is the best safeguard against exclusionary policies. As long as there are external powers that have an interest in destabilizing or partitioning other states, assimilationist and exclusionary policies will persist.

Second, if we want a world where non-core groups enjoy special minority rights, we should increase interstate alliances through regional integration initiatives and international institutions. There are two assumptions behind this prediction: that states participating in regional integration schemas such as the European Union are a) less likely to be revisionist; and b) more likely to be in an alliance with their neighboring states, and consequently more likely to accommodate their non-core groups. Countries in regions that have established stable security configurations are more likely to move toward non-aggressive multicultural arrangements.

Chapter 5 | Ethnic Partition Under the League of Nations: The Cases of Population Exchanges in the Interwar Balkans

Erin K. Jenne

I believe that an exchange of populations, however well it were carried out, must impose very considerable hardships, perhaps very considerable impoverishment, upon great numbers of individual citizens of the two countries who are exchanged. But I also believe that these hardships, great though they may be, will be less than the hardships which will result for these same populations if nothing is done.

—Lord George Nathaniel Curzon, Chairman of the Territorial and Military Commission under the Lausanne Convention, 1923

The rationale given for the postwar Greco-Turkish population exchange more than eighty years ago foreshadows the contemporary theory of ethnic partition. Partition theory is premised on the notion that societies destroyed by ethnic violence are so riven by hatreds and fears that they cannot be mended. Although the humanitarian costs of ethnic partition are immense and the ethical and moral implications deeply troubling, these disadvantages are far outweighed by the immense benefits of preventing future atrocities that are bound to take place in the absence of supervised partition. In this view, international arbiters are obliged to facilitate the inevitable ethnic unmixing after war in order to minimize the suffering of ordinary people on all sides.

The theory of ethnic partition holds that sectarian violence generates such intense security dilemmas on the ground that neither side will disarm because it cannot be certain that the other side will not utilize the resulting window of opportunity to gain a strategic advantage.[1] To the objection

The author would like to acknowledge the generous support of the Carnegie Corporation, which funded the research for this article.

1. See Stephen Van Evera,"Hypotheses on Nationalism and War," *International Security*, Vol. 18, No. 4 (Spring 1994), pp. 5–39; and Barry R. Posen, "Military Responses to Refugee Disasters," *International Security*, Vol. 21, No. 1 (Summer 1996), pp. 72–111. The term "security dilemma" refers to the paradoxical situation where one side arms

that it is impossible to devise territorial borders that will perfectly separate warring groups, partition theorists counter that border adjustments can be supplemented with population transfers to ensure that ethnic boundaries are aligned with political borders. Although scholars have assessed these claims by examining the consequences of postwar partition across a large number of cases,[2] this work has focused primarily on border adjustment and state creation. Partitioning through population transfers has received less attention as a technique for resolving entrenched conflicts—a curious omission considering the centrality of this tool for achieving *complete* separation.[3] This oversight is at least partly due to the fact that there are few cases of postwar population transfers after 1945, and this method is unlikely to enjoy a revival under current international norms. It is possible, however, that policymakers will revisit this technique in the future if it is believed necessary for consolidating peace following internecine conflict. For this reason, an exploration of the record of population transfers is highly opportune.

This chapter represents a first attempt to assess the effectiveness of partition through population transfers as a method of conflict management. To conduct a fair test, I have selected cases where population transfers were explicitly undertaken to resolve nationalist conflict. The post–World War I Balkan exchanges meet this criterion because they were justified as the best means of preventing the reemergence of ethnic violence—both within and among Bulgaria, Greece, and Turkey. International mediators believed that by aligning ethnic and political borders, the demographic security dilemmas might be resolved and the incentives for kin-state intervention eliminated. Also, consistent with the recommendations of partition advocates, the Balkan exchanges aimed to achieve *comprehensive* ethno-territorial partition. Although not perfect, the Greco-Bulgarian and Greco-Turkish exchanges produced as near to a complete partition as might reasonably be expected in the real world. The transfers were com-

---

to defend itself against external attacks, inducing others to arm in response. This leads the first side to arm still further, yielding an arms spiral that ultimately renders all sides less secure. I lay out the security dilemma logic in further detail below.

2.   Nicholas Sambanis,"Partition as a Solution to Ethnic War: An Empirical Critique of the Theoretical Literature," *World Politics*, Vol. 52 (July 2000), pp. 437–483; Thomas Chapman and Philip G. Roeder, "Partition as a Solution to Wars of Nationalism: The Importance of Institutions," *American Political Science Review*, Vol. 101 (November 2007), pp. 677–691; David D. Laitin,"Ethnic Unmixing and Civil War," *Security Studies*, Vol. 13 (2004), pp. 350–365; and Carter Johnson, "Partitioning to Peace: Sovereignty, Demography and Ethnic Civil Wars," *International Security*, Vol. 32, No. 4 (Spring 2008), pp. 140–170.

3.   Chaim Kaufmann, "Possible and Impossible Solutions to Ethnic Civil Wars," *International Security*, Vol. 20, No. 4 (Spring 1996), pp. 136–175; Chaim Kaufmann, "When All Else Fails: Ethnic Population Transfers and Partitions in the Twentieth Century," *International Security*, Vol. 23, No. 2 (Fall 1998), pp. 120–156. A notable exception is Stefan Wolff, "Can Forced Population Transfers Resolve Self-determination Conflicts? A European Perspective," *Journal of Contemporary European Studies*, Vol. 12, No. 1 (April 2004), pp. 11–29; he conducted a historical survey of population transfers and their effectiveness in resolving conflicts.

pulsory in the Greco-Turkish exchange under the Lausanne Convention, and de-facto compulsory in the Greco-Bulgarian exchange.[4] By the early 1930s, the three ethnic groups were effectively unmixed: almost no Bulgarians remained in Aegean Greece, while fewer than 10,000 Greeks resided in Bulgaria.[5] At the end of the Greco-Turkish exchange, a little over 100,000 Greeks remained in Turkey and vice versa. The remaining minorities were therefore too small to pose a security threat to their sizeable host states. Because the transfers affected a more-or-less complete ethnic partition between the warring groups and were intended to resolve sectarian violence and prevent its reemergence, they meet the central scope conditions of partition theory.

Another scope condition is that the conflicts in question be not strictly interstate but also intergroup. Such was the case in the Balkans at the close of World War I. Indeed, there had been discord between the Greeks and Turks on the Anatolian Peninsula for more than a decade leading up to the Greco-Turkish war.[6] According to partition theory, such conflicts are likely to attract kin-state intervention during times of political transition, because homeland states have incentives to "rescue" their co-ethnics when the enemy state is relatively weak. This prediction should hold for these cases. With the collapse of the Ottoman Empire, the successor states viewed their cross-border kin as marooned ethnic brethren in enemy states; in the context of regime change, incentives were therefore high for kin states to attempt to rescue their co-ethnics.

The Balkan exchanges have been cited as confirmatory evidence by partition theorists themselves, one of whom observed that the 1920s exchanges between Greece, Bulgaria, and Turkey (among other cases) showed that "where separation reduced the minority population to insignificant numbers, violence ended."[7] Chaim Kaufmann, while regretting the violence and humanitarian suffering that accompanied the transfers, noted that "the ethnic cleansing did substantially eliminate motives for further irredentism; Greece and Bulgaria have not fought for 85 years, nor Greece and Turkey for the last 80 years."[8] He further wrote that "the records of the two largest population transfers in twentieth-century Eu-

---

4.   The convention exempted certain persons from this compulsory exchange, but their numbers were relatively small.

5.   Joseph Rothschild, *East Central Europe between the Two World Wars* (Seattle: University of Washington Press, 1998), p. 328.

6.   Although the Anatolian Greeks and Turks had co-existed peacefully for hundreds of years, between 1908 and 1914 the Young Turk revolution and subsequent Balkan conflicts stimulated a wave of pogroms and persecution against the Anatolian Greeks. These were often initiated by local bands of Turks working in concert with Ottoman authorities. See Michael Llewellyn Smith, *Ionian Vision: Greece in Asia Minor 1919–1922* (Ann Arbor: University of Michigan Press, 1999), pp. 30–34.

7.   Alexander B. Downes, "The Problem with Negotiated Settlements to Ethnic Civil Wars," *Security Studies*, Vol. 13 (Summer 2004), p. 279.

8.   Chaim Kaufmann, "Michael Llewellyn Smith, Ionian Vision: Greece in Asia Minor 1919–1922/Isle of Discord: Nationalism, Imperialism, and the Making of the Cyprus Problem book review," *Nationalism & Ethnic Politics*, Vol. 8, No. 4 (Winter 2002), p. 109.

rope—the Greco-Bulgarian-Turkish population exchanges in the 1920s and the expulsion of ethnic Germans from Eastern Europe after World War II—suggest that [population exchanges reduce interstate violence]. Each of these exchanges was preceded by a series of wars that cost many times more lives than the population transfers did, and each has been followed by interstate peace."[9] The population exchanges have thus been credited with reducing internal as well as interstate warfare in the Balkans. Given that the interwar exchanges meet the scope conditions of partition theory, and on their surface appear to confirm the theory, these cases serve as important initial tests of the effectiveness of population transfers as a method of conflict resolution. If population transfers failed to resolve these conflicts—where they were applied most assiduously and where conditions were most optimal for their success—then there is little reason to believe that they would succeed in resolving conflicts elsewhere.

The following analysis suggests that partitioning the Greeks, Turks, and Bulgarians did little to prevent or resolve future conflicts between the groups and their kin states. Although the exchanges appear to have achieved their proximate aim of alleviating the suffering of victims of ethnic cleansing in the wake of the Greco-Bulgarian and Greco-Turkish wars, the transfers themselves cannot be credited with resolving nationalist conflict at either the substate or interstate level. The over-time sequence of conflict within each country-pair, and the patterns of conflict across the country-pairs, demonstrates that the perceived interests of the Bulgarian, Turkish, and Greek governments at any given time were better predictors of peace and conflict in the Balkans than the extent to which the population transfers resolved demographic security dilemmas on the ground. This implies that even where complete separation is achieved through population transfers, ethnic partition is unlikely to ensure peace following sectarian conflict so long as disputes remain between the relevant regional players. The fact that partition scholars have largely misinterpreted the lessons of the post–World War I population transfers probably owes more to general misconceptions concerning of the drivers of nationalist conflict in these cases. It is practically a truism that because Greece and Turkey have not engaged in direct warfare since the early 1920s, the postwar population transfers deserve at least partial credit for peace. Had these scholars examined the pattern and sequence of conflict within and between these states over time, however, they would be forced to question the proposition that the 1920 population transfers secured peace in the Balkans. The exchanges instead abetted government campaigns to consolidate control over territory without ensuring subsequent peace.

The following sections present the argument and findings of this analysis. I first provide an overview of the use of population transfers as a method of conflict resolution. Next, I lay out the theory of ethnic partition, paying particular attention to the role of population transfers in this strategy. I then outline the flaws in the premise of ethnic partition, arguing that the geostrategic interests of regional hegemons are a better predictor

---

9.   Kaufmann, "When All Else Fails," p. 125, n. 12.

of renewed conflict than whether the combatant groups were effectively separated after the previous conflict. This argument is illustrated with the Greco-Bulgarian and Greco-Turkish population exchanges, in which I first outline the conventional account of the two cases and then challenge this account by drawing on additional historical material to infer causal mechanisms underlying both conflicts. The final section of the chapter is devoted to developing the policy implications of this preliminary analysis.

Population Transfers as a Tool for Managing Conflict

Population transfers refer to the removal of a group of people from one territory to another by states or international bodies. This is typically done to achieve ethnically homogeneous polities. Population transfers have a long and storied history as a means of altering the ethnic makeup of state territory. Notable examples include the Roma and Jews, who were expelled from Spain in the late fifteenth century. The Huguenots, too, were driven out of France during the religious wars, and the Spanish Muslims, or Moriscos, were expelled from Spain in the early seventeenth century. In nineteenth-century United States, many Native American tribes were driven into "Indian territory" and onto reservations under a policy known as "Indian removal." The Ottoman authorities used population transfers as a means of consolidating control over the newly conquered Balkan territories—moving Muslims into these areas and simultaneously transferring Christian communities to Thrace and Anatolia.[10]

By the turn of the twentieth century, the principle of self-determination—which held that territorialized national minorities have the right to self-government—effectively strengthened the hand of ethnically homogeneous regions at the expense of ethnically heterogeneous states and empires. Population movements, where they occurred, were now undertaken in the name of resolving ethnic conflict, and to ensure that every nation had its own plot of land over which it could exercise sovereignty.[11] Beginning in the interwar period, "states began experimenting with the exchange of minority groups as a means of solving the ethnic problems so

---

10.   For more on the history of population transfers in Europe and elsewhere, see Norman M. Naimark, *Fires of Hatred: Ethnic Cleansing in Twentieth-Century Europe* (Harvard University Press, 2001); Andrew Bell-Fialkoff, *Ethnic Cleansing* (New York: St. Martin's Press, 1996); and Wolff, "Can Forced Population Transfers Resolve Self-determination Conflicts?"

11.   Despite their stated aim of reconfiguring post-imperial borders to approximate a one-to-one nation-state fit, the principle of self-determination was only implemented insofar as it furthered the interests of the victorious Allied powers. Czechoslovakia and Poland were established in part to give self-government to the Czechs, Slovaks, and Poles, but mainly to check the regional ambitions of Germany, Austria, and Hungary. Meanwhile, millions of ethnic Germans were forced to remain in Poland and Czechoslovakia; two-thirds of Hungary's territory was given to neighboring states; the Germans of Alsace-Lorraine were absorbed by France; and the German Tyrolians were handed over to Italy—all clear violations of the principle of national self-determination.

deeply interwoven into the changing patterns of political conflict in eastern Europe."[12] Paradoxically, the empowerment of territorialized minorities created perverse incentives for states to undertake minority expulsions in order to homogenize their populations. State governments began to view ethnic minorities as an implicit challenge to their claims of sovereignty over a given territory, in some cases leading to campaigns of ethnic cleansing. At the close of World War II, the interwar exchanges served as a blueprint for population transfers undertaken during and after the war, most notably in the case of German minorities.

Following the mass expulsions of Germans and Hungarians after World War II, international public opinion began to turn against the use of population transfers as a means of conflict resolution. Beginning with the Nuremberg judgment that Nazi population transfers constituted a war crime, the policy of involuntary resettlement gradually came to be seen as an anathema to the international community.[13] During the Yugoslav wars in the 1990s, mass expulsions were widely regarded as ethnic cleansing or even genocide. The 1993 UN Sub-Commission on Prevention of Discrimination and Protection of Minorities came out against the practice, and the subsequent Rome Statute of the International Criminal Court (Art. 7) designated population transfers a "crime against humanity."

Despite the taboo character of population exchanges today, a small group of security studies scholars began to reexamine the usefulness of this strategy in the mid-1990s, arguing that it was a potentially potent tool of conflict resolution.[14] These (mostly) hard-nosed realists have argued that, morally repugnant though they are, partition and population exchanges may be the only means of resolving an intransigent conflict in which two or more groups are locked in mortal combat. On the heels of internecine warfare, neither side can trust that the other will not take the opportunity to vanquish them if they disarm—thus, ethnic reintegration is a hopeless proposition. To the argument that such transfers violate human rights, partition advocates ask their critics to imagine the chaos that would occur in the absence of partition. Kaufmann urges policymakers to

---

12.   Office of Population Research, "Population Transfers: Facts and Reflections," *Population Index*, Vol. 13 (January 1947), p. 8.

13.   Population transfers are largely taboo under today's international norms and are widely viewed as illegitimate by contemporary scholars and policy analysts. Naimark deems population transfers only the most moderate form of ethnic cleansing, with genocide its most extreme form; see Naimark, *Fires of Hatred*, pp. 3–4. Others claim that these are simply different names for the same thing. Thus, "ethnic cleansing" is used to vilify expulsions by a hostile government, while "population transfers" is used to legitimize similar policies by a friendly government. See Robert Hayden, "Schindler's Fate," *Slavic Review*, Vol. 55, No. 4 (Winter 1996), p. 734.

14.   See Kaufmann, "Possible and Impossible Solutions"; Kaufmann, "When All Else Fails"; Downes, "The Problem with Negotiated Settlements"; Downes, "More Borders, Less Conflict: Partition as a Solution to Ethnic Civil War," *SAIS Review*, Vol. 26, No. 1 (Winter–Spring 2006), pp. 49–61; John J. Mearsheimer and Stephen Van Evera, "When Peace Means War," *New Republic*, December 18, 1995; and Barry R. Posen, "The Security Dilemma and Ethnic Conflict," *Survival*, Vol. 35, No. 1 (Spring 1993), pp. 27–47.

"endorse separation" in conflicts with significant sectarian violence, "otherwise, the processes of war will separate the groups anyway, at much higher human cost."[15]

The Flawed Premise of Partition Theory

The theory of ethnic partition is premised on security dilemma logic, which is based on deterrence theories of international relations.[16] Very generally, these theories hold that the absence of supranational authority creates a condition of anarchy at the systemic level, under which all states are forced to ensure their own security against external aggression. Security dilemmas emerge when one state defensively arms to make itself more secure, leading other states to arm in response. The resulting arms spiral paradoxically renders all states less secure. When the prevailing military technology is offensive, every state has an incentive to strike first in its conflicts with other states, making militarized conflict more likely. To deter external attacks, each state therefore has an incentive to signal that it has a significant defensive military capacity, indicating that it is unlikely to strike first but can retaliate against a first strike with overwhelming force. In this way, each state "deters" potential attackers, resulting in a peaceful equilibrium.

The ethnic security dilemma extends this logic to the substate level. In its classic formulation, a failed state produces the condition of anarchy at the domestic level, leading individuals to mobilize along ethnic lines as their most salient and therefore default identity, in order to ensure their security in the absence of state authority. Conflict occurs because the military technology in guerrilla warfare can be used either defensively or offensively, so combatant parties are unable to ascertain the motives of their opponents. This uncertainty leads to spirals of conflict as each side operates on worst-case assumptions concerning the other's motives.[17] Neither side will disarm until the costs of victimization are radically reduced, most likely through external security guarantees[18] or when one side achieves an outright military victory.[19]

The ethnic security dilemma also has implications for kin-state behavior. Perceiving that their co-ethnics are in a perilous position, the group's kin state may intervene, escalating an intergroup conflict into a conflict between the homeland state and the minority's host government. Eth-

---

15.   Kaufmann, "When All Else Fails," p. 123.

16.   Thomas Schelling, *The Strategy of Conflict* (Cambridge: Harvard University Press, 1960); and Robert Jervis, "Cooperation under the Security Dilemma," *World Politics*, Vol. 30, No. 2 (January 1978), pp. 167–214.

17.   Posen, "The Security Dilemma."

18.   Barbara F. Walter, "The Critical Barrier to Civil War Settlement," *International Organization*, Vol. 51 (Summer 1997), pp. 335–364.

19.   Roy Licklider, "The Consequences of Negotiated Settlements in Civil Wars, 1945–1993," *American Political Science Review*, Vol. 89, No. 3 (September 1995), pp. 681–690.

nically intermixed areas are magnets for kin-state interventions. Barry Posen writes that "where one territorially concentrated group has "islands" of settlement of its members distributed across the nominal territory of another group (irredenta)...[then] the brethren of the stranded group may come to believe that only rapid offensive military action can save their irredenta from a horrible fate."[20] Thus, "[local intermingling] will tempt potential rescuers [national homelands] to jump through any windows of opportunity that arise" in order to "rescue" diasporas that are marooned in enemy territory.[21] If the warring groups are not completely separated into defensible enclaves, the ethnic security dilemma will remain unresolved, perpetuating interethnic conflicts and provoking interstate conflicts by drawing the minority's kin state into the conflict.

The ethnic security dilemma is most effectively resolved by separating the warring groups into defensible enclaves. This removes incentives for violence at both the intra- and the interstate level. If the partition is incomplete, however, then any significant ethnic pockets that remain pose a security threat to their host state, because they tempt the kin state to intervene to rescue the group. Fearing this, the host government may seek to forestall kin-state interventions by eliminating any sizeable ethnic pockets through ethnic cleansing. Population transfers are therefore a necessary complement to border adjustments. This is because the one-to-one nation-state ideal is rarely achievable in practice, as mixed ethnic geography—a feature common to the vast majority of states today—rarely lends itself to neat demarcation. Recognizing this, Kaufmann calls for population transfers to complete the territorial division of warring groups so that ethnic enclaves are not isolated behind enemy territory.

Many have critiqued Kaufmann's proposal by pointing out that ethnic partition entails both practical and moral problems. Population transfers, for example, are associated with significant loss of life and property, as well as human rights violations. Moreover, partition through state creation risks transforming internal conflicts into even deadlier interstate wars. Territorial partition also encourages secessionist efforts elsewhere, while creating authoritarian statelets whose leaders are unaccountable to the people.[22] Finally, ethnic partition may not be able to deliver on its key

---

20.   Posen, "The Security Dilemma," p. 108.

21.   Van Evera, "Hypotheses on Nationalism," p. 20.

22.   Nicholas Sambanis, "Partition as a Solution to Ethnic War: An Empirical Critique of the Theoretical Literature," *World Politics*, Vol. 52 (July 2000), pp. 437–483. For these and other critiques of partition theory, see Horowitz, *Ethnic Groups in Conflict*. See also Radha Kumar, "The Troubled History of Partition," *Foreign Affairs*, Vol. 76 (1997), pp. 22–34; Robert Schaeffer, *Warpaths: The Politics of Partition* (New York: Hill and Wang, 1990); Amitai Etzioni, "The Evils of Self-Determination," *Foreign Policy*, Vol. 89 (Winter 1992–1993), pp. 21–35; Gidon Gottlieb, "Nations without States," *Foreign Affairs*, Vol. 73 (May/June 1994), pp. 100–112; David Carment and Dane Rowland, "Vengeance and Intervention: Can Third Parties Bring Peace without Separation?" *Security Studies*, Vol. 13, No. 4 (Summer 2004), pp. 366–393; and James D. Fearon, "Separatist Wars, Partition, and World Order," *Security Studies*, Vol. 13, No. 4 (Summer 2004), pp. 394–415. It is doubtful that population transfers will obtain the endorsement of the international

selling point—resolving conflict and forestalling the reemergence of violence. In his analysis of 125 civil wars, Nicholas Sambanis concludes that
wars terminated by partition are no less likely to recur than wars ended
through other means.[23] Despite the sizeable body of work critiquing the
morality of partition or the effectiveness of partitioning through border
adjustment or state creation, little attention has been devoted to assessing
whether partitioning through population transfers serves as an effective
means of resolving conflicts by achieving a more complete separation of
the warring groups.

The argument here is that partitioning through population transfers
is unlikely to resolve nationalist conflicts because it fails to address the
origins of such conflicts. Nationalist conflicts are more often driven by
the geopolitical interests of states or militant organizations than they are
by ethnic security dilemmas on the ground. In this view, the causal arrow
is top-down rather than bottom-up. Many, if not most, intractable ethnic
wars are the result of externally backed separatist movements staking
claims over a particular territory,[24] while the host state attempts to cleanse
the territory of "alien groups" to establish counterclaims of territorial sovereignty. Moreover, kin states rarely intervene to "rescue" co-ethnics in
the absence of geopolitical motives to do so. If sectarian conflict is largely
a top-down phenomenon, then the rationalization of national and political borders may not resolve conflicts at all, but merely assist one side in
establishing or consolidating control over a disputed territory. If this is
true, a more effective means of resolving such conflicts—including not
just ethnic, but also ideological or other types of civil violence—would be
to alter the incentives of the true principals of the conflict, in this case state
governments.

These two arguments make unique predictions that permit competitive testing through intensive case analysis. If the expectations of partition

community as a method of conflict resolution in the near future. The biggest concern is
that such programs create a dangerous precedent by legitimizing the actions of political
entities seeking to ethnically cleanse minorities from their territories. Second, there is
little reason to believe that the international community could supervise such transfers
in such a way as to prevent violent expulsions; the poor record of the international
community in halting genocidal violence in civil wars serves as a cautionary tale in this
regard. See Samantha Power, *A Problem from Hell: America and the Age of Genocide* (New
York: Basic Books, 2002).

23. Laitin corroborates Sambanis's findings in a more recent empirical analysis using the Minorities at Risk (MAR) dataset. See David D. Laitin, "Ethnic Unmixing and
Civil War," *Security Studies*, Vol. 13, No. 4 (Summer 2004), pp. 350–365. In "Partition as
a Solution," Chapman and Roeder reran Sambanis's statistical analysis using his own
data, after dropping all non-ethnic conflicts from the dataset. They find that *de jure* partition is less likely to result in reemergence of ethnic violence than all other solutions to
nationalist civil wars, with *de facto* separation the second-best solution and ethnic autonomy the worst. However, it should be noted that Chapman and Roeder ask a rather
specific question, which is which of the four solutions is most strongly associated with
peace in the wake of nationalist conflict.

24. Erin K. Jenne, *Ethnic Bargaining: The Paradox of Minority Empowerment* (Ithaca, NY:
Cornell University Press, 2007).

theorists hold, then ethnic violence should be generated from the bottom-up, beginning with a breakdown in security institutions and interethnic trust on the grassroots level. A spiral of hostilities should follow as both sides arm defensively and as kin states intervene to "rescue" their co-ethnics. Specifically, violent conflict should occur in and around stranded ethnic islands, which have incentives to break out of threatening enemy territory; they may be assisted in doing so by external kin states seeking to rescue them. In contrast, relative peace should prevail where demographic insecurities have been alleviated through partition and population transfers. Where the groups are incompletely partitioned, however, ethnic violence may reemerge as a result of demographic insecurities in these areas.

If violence is instead driven by the geostrategic interests of states or militant organizations, then ethnic violence is likely to (re)emerge as the result of top-down pressures. Here, powerful principals such as governments or military alliances intervene in the host state, ostensibly to protect their ethnic kin but in reality to pursue larger geostrategic aims such as destabilizing the host regime or annexing territory. Where the regional power balance has been restored—either through a peace pact between the major belligerents or because no hegemon has a clear interest in altering the status quo—then we should expect peace to prevail everywhere in the state, in ethnically intermixed and ethnically homogeneous areas alike. Moreover, if ethnic violence is driven more by geostrategic aims than by host state concerns about internal security, then large concentrated groups will be no more likely to suffer government repression than small, dispersed groups that constitute minimal threat to the state.

Finally, the flight of vulnerable minorities could occur under either theoretical framework—either because they are pushed out through government campaigns of ethnic cleansing or because they fear attacks by the majority group. However, the primordial group fears associated with the ethnic security dilemma suggest that vulnerable minorities in ethnically mixed areas will not choose to live with neighbors from the majority group after sectarian violence if they have the option of leaving. Each argument thus makes unique predictions concerning the patterns of ethnic peace and violence following political transition, allowing us to assess the relative explanatory value of the two competing models.

Case Evidence: Population Transfers in the Balkans

Among other things, World War I sounded the death knell for the Ottoman Empire and precipitated the "unmixing" of peoples in the Balkans. The conflicts that led to the 1920s population exchanges, however, predated the war. The first population exchange in the Balkans took place between Turkey and Bulgaria after the First Balkan War of 1912–1913. The Treaty of Constantinople ending the war mandated a reciprocal exchange of populations between the two countries, as well as the second partition of Bulgaria. The second and third exchanges following World War I—the cases dealt with in this chapter—were more substantial. The 1919 Treaty of Neuilly included an annex that provided for the voluntary reciprocal exchange of ethnic populations—Greeks in Bulgaria in return for Bulgarians in Greece. This exchange took thirteen years to complete and involved the simultaneous migration of 92,000 Bulgarians and 46,000 Greeks.[25] The second postwar exchange followed the Greco-Turkish War in the early 1920s. Under the 1923 Convention Concerning the Exchange of Greek and Turkish Populations, the signatory states agreed to an involuntary exchange of ethnic populations. Ultimately, between 350,000 and 500,000 Turks migrated to Turkey, and about 1.2 million Greeks from Turkey moved to Greece. To ensure adequate compensation and resettlement of refugees, Athens and Ankara agreed to a Mixed Commission under the League of Nations, which included Greek and Turkish representatives as well as delegates from neutral member states. The Commission was tasked with facilitating and monitoring the population exchanges to ensure an orderly and peaceable transfer of refugees. It also had the responsibility of liquidating property and possessions left behind by the refugees, compensating refugees for their lost property, and helping them to settle in their new homes.

International supervision of the Greco-Bulgarian and Greco-Turkish population exchanges was extensive. The League and other international organizations assisted the Greco-Bulgarian population transfers—offering the governments generous loans to resettle refugees upon their territory and adjudicating disputed property claims. The League took an even greater interest in the Greco-Turkish exchange. Along with providing compensation for lost property and assistance settling into their new homes, the agreement stipulated that the exchanged populations would automatically lose the citizenship of their old country and assume the citizenship of their putative homeland. It also established categories of non-exchangeable minorities in each country that were to be protected from property confiscation and any other diminution of their rights. The Mixed Commissions reported regularly to the Council of the League on the status of the exchanges throughout the 1920s, soliciting assistance when needed.

To protect the minorities who remained outside of their national homelands, in the Balkans and elsewhere in Europe, the victorious Allies—principally, the United States, Great Britain, France, and Italy—established a system of minority protections under the League of Nations. The regime consisted primarily of "minorities treaties" with the new states of East Central Europe and bilateral treaties with the defeated powers that committed them to give their minorities equal protection under the law and, in some cases, enact minority-friendly education and language poli-

---

25. Kalliopi K. Koufa and Constantinos Svolopoulos,"The Compulsory Exchange of Populations Between Greece and Turkey: The Settlement of Minority Questions at the Conference of Lausanne, 1923, and its Impact on Greco-Turkish Relations," in Paul Smith with Kalliopi Koufa and Arnold Suppan, eds., *Ethnic Groups in International Relations* (New York: New York University Press, 1991), p. 286.

cies. The treaties were to be taken as fundamental law by the signatory states and could not be contravened without the explicit consent of the League Council. If a government were suspected of violating its treaty, Council members could bring charges before the Permanent Court of International Justice, which had compulsory jurisdiction over such matters. Most importantly, the League provided a means by which nationalities could, for the first time, appeal for legal redress over the heads of their governments.[26] The minority protection system was to ensure the rights and protection of the non-exchangeable minorities in Greece and Turkey, as well as the minorities that did not avail themselves of the voluntary Greco-Bulgarian exchange.

THE CONVENTIONAL ACCOUNT—POPULATION EXCHANGES LED TO INTER-STATE PEACE

The received wisdom concerning the population exchanges in the Balkans is that they successfully resolved the conflicts between the three states and forestalled the reemergence of violence at every level. Their success is all the more remarkable, so the narrative goes, in view of the fact that the transfers took place against the backdrop of ethnic violence and mass expulsions, particularly in Asia Minor.

The Greco-Bulgarian exchange was established in an annex to the 1919 Treaty of Neuilly, which ended the war between the two states. The exchange was to be strictly voluntary, meaning that the Greeks in Bulgaria and Bulgarians in Greece could opt to resettle in their putative homelands or remain as national minorities on their land. The treaty, brokered by the Allied powers, reduced Bulgaria from 111,836 square kilometers at the end of the Balkan Wars to 103,146 square kilometers; Bulgaria was forced to cede its Aegean coastline to Greece and almost all of Macedonia to Serbia. The treaty also imposed punitive indemnity, restitutions, and war reparations on Sofia, leaving Bulgaria "an angrily revisionist state."[27] As much as 16 percent of its population now resided outside Bulgaria's shrunken borders.[28] The population exchange was instituted as a means of realigning national and political borders, thereby removing incentives for Bulgarian irredentism.

Like the Greco-Bulgarian exchange, the terms of the Greco-Turkish exchange were established in a protocol that was annexed to the treaty

---

26. The basic procedure for mediating minority disputes was laid out in the Tittoni Report of 1920, which provided that petitions, communications, and reports would be accepted from members of the Council, League members not in the Council, and from members of the minorities themselves. See Jacob Robinson, Oscar Karbach, Max M. Laserson, Nehemiah Robinson, and Marc Vichniak, *Were the Minorities Treaties a Failure?* (New York: Institute of Jewish Affairs of the American Jewish Congress and the World Jewish Congress, 1943), p. 87.

27. Rothschild, *East Central Europe,* pp. 123–125.

28. R.J. Crampton, *A Concise History of Bulgaria* (Cambridge: Cambridge University Press, 1997), p. 149, as cited in Wolff, "Can Forced Population Transfers Resolve Self-determination Conflicts?" p. 14.

ending the war between the two states. Unlike the previous exchange, however, the Greco-Turkish exchange was compulsory. This difference is directly attributable to Greece's failed military campaign to retake the Anatolian Peninsula and the flight to Greece of hundreds of thousands of ethnic Greeks from Asia Minor and Thrace on the heels of the retreating Greek Army. To accommodate the Anatolian Greek refugees in an already densely-populated country, Greek Prime Minister Eleftherios Venizelos insisted that the Muslim Turks of Thrace be simultaneously relocated to Turkey to make room for the Anatolian refugees, who would ultimately make up 20 percent of Greece's interwar population.[29] The two exchanges lasted through the 1920s and greatly assisted the leaders of Bulgaria, Turkey, and Greece in homogenizing their populations.

Unsurprisingly, the transfers created problems not just for the refugees, but also for the countries involved. Because the exchanges were highly asymmetrical, they created significant problems for the net receiving countries. Bulgaria, for example, had a net surplus of refugees and was faced with the daunting task of absorbing tens of thousands of Bulgarian refugees from Greece over a relatively short period. Although Greece was a net sender in the Greco-Bulgarian exchange, it was a net receiver in the Greco-Turkish exchange and was faced with the challenge of settling roughly 1,200,000 Greeks in the homes of 350,000–500,000 Muslims who were sent in the opposite direction. Net receiving countries were forced to provide additional housing for the surplus immigrants and help them settle, while their expellees were still in the process of leaving.[30] While international loans from the Red Cross and other organizations helped to defray the substantial costs of accommodating surplus populations, it placed a strenuous financial burden on states that were still recovering from the war and experiencing economic downturn as well as political upheaval. Indeed, there is some evidence that the massive influx of refugees in the interwar period contributed to Greece's eventual economic collapse in the 1930s.[31]

Although Turkey was a net sender of refugees, and therefore had plenty of land on which to settle the incoming Muslim Turkish refugees, its economy also suffered as a result of the exchange. With the out-migration of over one million ethnic Greeks, Turkey lost a significant proportion of its merchant and entrepreneurial classes, particularly those who worked in finance, industry, and commerce.[32] This significantly hampered Tur-

---

29.   See Stephen P. Ladas, *The Exchange of Minorities: Bulgaria, Greece and Turkey* (New York: Macmillan Company, 1932), chap. 17, for an in-depth discussion of the decision to make the Greco-Turkish exchange mandatory.

30.   In the beginning, the Greek government compelled Muslim homes in Thrace to take in Greek refugees, creating substantial resentment among Muslim Turks.

31.   Mark Mazower, *Greece and the Inter-war Economic Crisis* (Oxford: Clarendon Press, 1991).

32.   Renée Hirschon, "'Unmixing Peoples' in the Aegean Region," in Renée Hirschon, ed., *Crossing the Aegean: An Appraisal of the 1923 Compulsory Population Exchange between Greece and Turkey* (New York: Berghahn Books, 2003), p. 16.

key's efforts to develop its economy in the interwar period. With the loss of these citizens, the Anatolian Peninsula was now effectively depopulated, representing an important loss to the Turkish economy and state.

Another problem lay in the fact that the exchanged populations were not always able to take one another's place in their adopted countries. This was less a problem in the Greco-Bulgarian exchange, as the transferred populations were both largely rural. However, the incoming Greeks from Turkey were disproportionately urban with occupations to match, whereas the Muslims from Thrace tended to be rural. The predominantly urban Greek immigrants had difficulties adapting to the conditions of rural Thrace, while the rural Muslim Turks were spread thinly throughout the depopulated Anatolian countryside and failed to contribute significantly to the Turkish economy.[33]

There were also problems associated with the minorities who remained behind. Under the Lausanne Treaty, non-exchangeable minorities included Greeks in Istanbul, known as *Rums*, who could demonstrate residency in Turkey prior to 1918, and Greeks who lived on two Aegean islands, Imbros and Tenedos, which had been ceded to Turkey. In Greece, persons exempted from the exchange included the Muslim Turks in Western Thrace. In the end, about 130,000 Muslim Turks ("Moslems") in Thrace and about the same number of Rums in Istanbul remained in their homes.[34] Although the rights of these minorities were guaranteed under the terms of Lausanne, as well as the treaties that Greece and Turkey had signed with the League, their status was precarious at best. Both Turkey and Greece attempted to dilute the concentrations of their minorities. The Muslim Turks in Greece were reduced from a regional majority in Thrace to a minority, as Greek refugees helped themselves to Muslim land and livestock, forcing many to migrate to Turkey. At the same time, Turkey denied the right of self-administration to the Greek-inhabited islands, even though this had been guaranteed under the peace treaty; the Rums' right to education in their mother tongue was removed in 1927.[35] The reason for these problems, partition advocates would argue, is that the exchange achieved a less-than-perfect partition between Greece and Turkey; to prevent further violations, the remaining minorities would need to be exchanged. I return to this argument in the following section.

Conventional accounts agree that for most, the exchanges came too late to avert a humanitarian catastrophe in the midst of ethnic cleansing. Most ethnic Greeks had been expelled from Anatolia (tens of thousands

---

33. See Ladas, *The Exchange of Minorities*, pp. 721–723; and Ça lar Keyder, "Consequences of the Exchange for Turkey," in Renée Hirschon, ed., *Crossing the Aegean: An Appraisal of the 1923 Compulsory Population Exchange between Greece and Turkey* (New York: Berghahn Books, 2003), p. 43.

34. Baskin Oran, "The Story of Those Who Stayed: Lessons From Articles 1 and 2 of the 1923 Convention," in Renée Hirschon, ed., *Crossing the Aegean: An Appraisal of the 1923 Compulsory Population Exchange between Greece and Turkey* (New York: Berghahn Books, 2003), p. 100.

35. Oran, "The Story of Those Who Stayed," p. 102.

dying in the process) prior to the signing of the Lausanne Treaty in 1923. Of the 1.2 million refugees from Turkey to Greece, as much as 90 percent of them had been expelled before the treaty was signed. Even after the treaty came into effect, the reciprocal exchange between Greece and Turkey began too late to assist the beleaguered minorities it was designed to protect. Michael Barutciski writes that "the actual transfer of exchangeable persons began earlier than planned.... Both governments accelerated departures, which resulted in disorderly transfers."[36] The same was true for the Greco-Bulgarian exchange; by the time the Neuilly Treaty was ratified in 1920, 39,000 Bulgarians and 16,000 Greeks had already left their homes.[37] External supervision of the subsequent transfers was complicated by the fact that many refugees chose to migrate outside of officially sanctioned channels. One Mixed Commission report on Greek refugees noted that "waves of refugees have flooded [Greece] from time to time without passing through the hands of the official organizations, have dispersed to different parts of the country and since then have frequently moved from one place to another."[38]

Despite these numerous shortcomings, partition theorists point to the rapprochement between Greece and Turkey in 1930 and the joint initiatives between the Balkan countries in the early 1930s as evidence that the transfers had paved the way for ethnic peace. In this view, despite the tremendous hardships outlined above, the exchanges had the overriding virtue of resolving interstate conflict between the three Balkan countries. In 1930, Greece and Turkey signed the Ankara Agreement, which settled outstanding border disputes as well as disputed property rights of the refugees; relations between the two governments "normalized (and even became friendly) after this date."[39] In addition, Greece, Bulgaria, Romania, Turkey, and Yugoslavia held a series of trade conferences from 1930 to 1933 to explore potential areas of cooperation. By homogenizing their respective populations, the exchanges thus appear to have consolidated peaceful relations among the Balkan countries, which no longer had incentives to intervene in the domestic affairs of their neighbors.

In sum, the "exchange of populations was a drastic, but largely effective way of eliminating frictions that had been caused by the multi-ethnic character of certain regions."[40] According to Kalliopi Koufa and Constantinos Svolopoulos, the immense humanitarian costs of the exchange were at least partly justified by having "[removed...] the motives that had fed

36.   Michael Barutciski, "Lausanne Revisited: Population Exchanges in International Law and Policy," in Renée Hirschon, ed., *Crossing the Aegean: An Appraisal of the 1923 Compulsory Population Exchange between Greece and Turkey* (New York: Berghahn Books, 2003), p. 28.

37.   Koufa and Svolopoulos, "The Compulsory Exchange of Populations," p. 286.

38.   Eighth Quarterly Report of the Commission in League of Nations, *Official Journal,* February 1926, p. 324, as cited in Ladas, *The Exchange of Minorities,* p. 643.

39.   Oran, "The Story of Those Who Stayed," p. 101.

40.   Mark Mazower, *Greece and the Inter-War Economic Crisis,* p. 43, as cited in Wolff, "Can Forced Population Transfers Resolve Self-determination Conflicts?" p. 15.

the two peoples' long antagonism" so that "Greece and Turkey no longer had any justification for expansionist designs in each other's direction."[41] In so doing, it "helped to keep the presence of foreign ethnic elements in the interior of the two countries to an insignificant, or at least less important, level."[42] Another scholar writes that "the unmixing of populations in Asia Minor helped put an end to hostilities and secure pacification of the warring parties."[43] Because the pre-existing pockets of ethnic kin were virtually eliminated, and the ethnic security dilemma consequently resolved, Greece and Turkey no longer had any incentives to engage in revisionist campaigns against one another. This largely coincides with the judgment of Lord Curzon, whose statement began this chapter—that the Greco-Turkish exchange, although regrettable and even abhorrent in humanitarian terms, may have been the best solution to the conflict.

As noted earlier, the case for partition as a solution to sectarian conflict rests almost entirely on the argument that ethnic unmixing after war eliminates incentives by groups and their kin states to engage in conflict. The following section challenges this claim by examining the chain of events leading up to and following the Greco-Bulgarian and Greco-Turkish exchanges.

A REVISED ACCOUNT—POPULATION EXCHANGES UNRELATED TO INTER-STATE PEACE

REALPOLITIK CONSIDERATIONS UNDERLYING THE GRECO-BULGARIAN EXCHANGE (EARLY 1920S). Consolidating the new postwar borders and containing Bulgarian revisionism was the principal motive for establishing the Greco-Bulgarian exchange. After World War I, Venizelos was convinced that "no permanent peace between Greece and Bulgaria was possible, so long as a Bulgarian minority remained in that part of Greece which Bulgaria looked upon as an 'unredeemed' portion of the Bulgarian territory."[44] Having obtained western Thrace from Bulgaria, "the territory's new Greek masters wanted to get rid of the Bulgarians who lived there" in order to "make western Thrace a little more Greek."[45] Meanwhile, the Macedonian region of Greece (Aegean Macedonia) went from 119,000 Bulgarians (10 percent of the population) before the war to 77,000 Bulgarians (5 percent of the population) in 1926, making the region almost 90 percent Greek.[46] By the end of the exchange, the region was "virtually Slav-free."[47] The remaining Bulgarian minority was separated from the

---

41. Koufa and Svolopoulos, "The Compulsory Exchange of Populations," p. 301.

42. Ibid.

43. Barutciski, "Lausanne Revisited," p. 26.

44. Ladas, *The Exchange of Minorities*, p. 13.

45. Bruce Clark, *Twice a Stranger: How Mass Expulsion Forged Modern Greece and Turkey* (London: Granta Books, 2006), p. 53.

46. Ladas, *The Exchange of Minorities*, p. 700.

47. Hugh Poulton, *The Balkans: Minorities and States in Conflict* (London: Minority

Greco-Bulgarian border "by a solid Greek bloc, since Thrace and eastern Macedonia were cleared of Bulgars" and settled by Anatolian Greeks.[48]

Contrary to predictions that sectarian warfare produces ethnic insecurities so extreme that Greeks and Bulgarians would no longer choose to live together in a common state, relatively few minority members took advantage of the exchange program to relocate to their homelands. Rather than fleeing to their kin states in the wake of sectarian violence, the respective minorities overwhelmingly chose to remain in their mixed-ethnicity communities. Koufa and Svolopoulos note that for some time following the convention, "the prospect of emigration was attractive or desirable to neither ethnic minority," and that from November 1922 to July 1923 (when the Lausanne Convention was signed), only 166 Bulgarian families and 197 Greek families sought to emigrate to their respective kin states.[49] Following the Lausanne Convention, the number of applicants to the exchange program spiked on both sides. This was due, however, not to an increase in ethnic insecurities on the ground but to the logistics of ethnic cleansing by the three governments. The Greek government settled the Anatolian Greeks who had been expelled by the Turkish authorities in the homes of ethnic Bulgarians in Greece, who were simultaneously pressured to give up their homes and move to Bulgaria. The Bulgarian government settled these refugees in and around the homes of the minority Greeks, who were simultaneously pressured to relocate to Greece.

This is how the "voluntary" exchange between Greece and Bulgaria became de-facto compulsory. The first set of refugees was pushed out by Turkey, leading Greece to expel its minorities, who otherwise might have stayed, in order to make room for the net inflow of refugees. Venizelos himself acknowledged that the exchanges were more about the governments consolidating their territorial claims than about the inability of ethnic groups to co-exist due to the collapse of intergroup trust during the war. Indeed, far from seeking sanctuary in their mother countries, the minorities in each state actively *resisted* the partition. According to one account, "stirred by the instinctive feelings of attachment to the land and homes where their ancestors have lived for centuries, the Greek and Turkish populations involved... are protesting against the procedure...and display their dissatisfaction by all means at their disposal."[50] The exchange was thus a joint campaign by the governments not to resolve grassroots ethnic tensions and prevent their recurrence, but rather to ethnically cleanse their borderlands in order to strengthen their territorial claims.

BULGARIAN IRREDENTISM AND TERRITORIAL ASPIRATIONS (1920S AND 1930S). In the final reckoning, the rationalization of national and political boundaries under the Greco-Bulgarian exchange failed in its main pur-

---

Rights Publications, 1994), p. 176.

48.   C. A. Macartney, *National States and National Minorities* (London: Oxford University Press, 1934), pp. 530–531.

49.   Koufa and Svolopoulos, "The Compulsory Exchange of Populations," p. 286.

50.   Clark, *Twice a Stranger*, p. 43.

pose, which was to eliminate Bulgaria's irredentist ambitions toward its neighbors in the 1920s and 1930s. Rivalries between militarized factions of the Internal Macedonian Revolutionary Organization (IMRO), which sought to expand Bulgaria's territory into Macedonia and organized armed raids beyond Bulgaria's borders, was a major source of domestic instability throughout the interwar period.[51] In fact, it was in large part due to their fears of Bulgarian expansionism that Greece and Turkey finally normalized their relations in 1930. In 1934, the two states joined with Serbia and Romania to form the Balkan Entente as a means of countering the perceived military threat from Bulgaria.

Sofia's revisionist ambitions would ultimately make Bulgaria a natural ally to Nazi Germany; its passive alliance with the Axis Powers during World War II allowed Bulgaria to invade and occupy parts of Western Thrace and Eastern Macedonia with the aim of gaining an outlet to the Aegean Sea. The fact that these regions had been virtually emptied of their ethnic kin did not dissuade Sofia from this goal; Bulgarian officials actually set out to *reverse* the population exchange in the region. They thus began a campaign of "Bulgarizing" the population—closing Greek schools and other institutions and removing as many as 200,000 Greek nationals in preparation for repopulating the territory with Bulgarians.[52] In sum, Sofia's desire to annex these lands had not diminished with the transfer of ethnic Bulgarians from the region. In a very real sense, Bulgarian irredentism was not linked to the existence of Bulgarians outside its borders, but to aspirations for the lands it had briefly gained under the short-lived San Stefano Treaty of 1878 and then lost under the Treaty of Berlin later that year.

These patterns of conflict go against partition-theory expectations that the postwar separation of national groups reduces the likelihood of kin-state interventions because there are no longer isolated pockets of co-ethnics to "rescue." Although the Aegean region had been virtually emptied of ethnic Bulgarians through the exchange, Sofia retained its ambition to re-annex this territory and finally succeeded in occupying it through its alliance with the Axis Powers. Sofia's subsequent attempts to Bulgarize the land (and in effect reverse the population exchange) indicates that the government was interested in the region for its strategic value, not because it wanted to protect its co-ethnics, who no longer lived there.[53] Bul-

---

51.   See Duncan M. Perry, "Bulgarian Nationalism: Permutations of the Past," in Paul Latawski, ed., *Contemporary Nationalism in East Central Europe* (New York: St. Martin's Press, 1995), pp. 46–47; and Barbara Jelavich, *History of the Balkans: Twentieth Century* (Cambridge: Cambridge University Press, 1983), pp. 169–171.

52.   Jelavich, *History of the Balkans*, p. 256.

53.   It is significant in this respect that the three governments largely failed to tend to the needs of their in-migrating co-ethnics; the refugees often lived for years without adequate shelter or sustenance and were largely regarded as an unwelcome burden by their homeland governments. If the states were so concerned for the welfare of their co-ethnics across the border that they were prepared to intervene militarily to protect them, it begs the question why the exchanged minorities received such poor treatment upon arrival in their respective homelands.

garia thus viewed its ethnic kin as an instrument with which it could stake a claim to coveted territory. In sum, the exchange itself appears to have done little to temper Bulgaria's expansionism. This is because Bulgaria's geostrategic interests in regaining lost territories, especially an outlet to the Aegean Sea, explains Bulgaria's conflictual relationship with its neighbors in the interwar period far better than demographic security dilemmas on the ground, which by then were practically non-existent.

GRECO-TURKISH EXCHANGES

THE GEOPOLITICAL ORIGINS OF THE GRECO-TURKISH EXCHANGE (EARLY 1920s). It is widely known that the 1922 Greco-Turkish War gave way to a decade-long population exchange between the two countries. What is perhaps less well-known is that as a reward for joining the Allied Powers in 1917, the 1920 Treaty of Sèvres conferred the Anatolian Peninsula upon Greece. Prior to the conclusion of the treaty and in the midst of a Great Power dispute, the Greek Army was encouraged by Britain and France to invade and occupy the Peninsula in order to realize major territorial gains and weaken the new Turkish state. Due to shifting global alliances and the emergence of a more acceptable secular Turkish government, however, Allied support for Greece's military adventure began to weaken. In the end, the Western powers stood aside as Turkish forces routed the invading Greek Army.[54] Having reclaimed Anatolia from the Greek Army, Turkish troops proceeded to expel its entire Greek population in order to consolidate Turkey's claim to the land. Allied machinations had thus played a central role in Greece's decision to undertake the invasion, which led to a crushing defeat, minority reprisals, and hundreds of thousands of Greek refugees fleeing their homes.

It is clear that this fratricidal conflict was triggered by high-level state policy rather than ethnic security dilemmas on the ground. This does not mean, though, that ethnic partition was inappropriate for solving the conflict. According to Kaufmann, ethnic partition can help resolve any nationalist conflict because "solutions to ethnic wars do not depend on their causes."[55] This is because, regardless of their origins, internecine conflicts inevitably generate memories of interethnic bloodletting so intense that the warring groups are unable to reintegrate due to their mutual hatreds and fears of continuing depredations by the other side.[56] Separating the combatant groups into defensible enclaves sets these mutual fears to rest and reduces the potential for future conflict generated by ethnically intermixed communities.

Nonetheless, the Greco-Turkish population exchange had less to do with securing the postwar peace than it did with consolidating the states' territorial claims. Many Greeks who had been driven out of the Anatolian

---

54. Hirschon, "'Unmixing Peoples' in the Aegean Region," pp. 4–5.

55. Kaufmann, "Possible and Impossible Solutions," p. 137.

56. Ibid.; Kaufmann, "When All Else Fails."

Peninsula desired to return to their homes after the war, which one would not expect if they were fearful of living with Turks who had assisted in the ethnic cleansing. They were denied the option of returning, however, due to a clause in the Lausanne Treaty that forbade returns—a clause that had been inserted at the behest of the Turkish government. Thus, the apparently inexorable "unmixing of peoples" was instead a government-led enterprise that did more to further the territorial aspirations of state leaders than resolve intercommunal ethnic fears. The Muslim Turks, too, migrated to Turkey not out of fears of depredations by their Orthodox neighbors, but because Greek authorities had expropriated their property in order to house hundreds of thousands of Anatolian Greeks who had fled Turkey's scorched earth campaign.[57] Indeed, Greece's insistence that the Greco-Turkish exchange be compulsory—and the fact that the Greco-Bulgarian voluntary exchange *became* de-facto compulsory—are implicit acknowledgements that the exchanged populations did not want to relocate permanently and that many would have returned had they been permitted to do so.[58] The fact that vulnerable minorities sought to return to their homes so soon after sectarian warfare suggests that demographic insecurities did not preclude peaceful co-existence, contrary to the expectations of partition theory.

RAPPROCHEMENT BETWEEN GREECE AND TURKEY (1930S TO EARLY 1950S). Greco-Turkish relations normalized with the Ankara Treaty of 1930. This treaty was largely due to the efforts of newly reelected Greek Prime Minister Venizelos to establish peace with Greece's neighbors. Less than a decade after the war, Venizelos and Turkish President Mustafa Kemal Atatürk had managed to resolve the two countries' outstanding disputes and form a bilateral alliance. The impetus for this was the changing geopolitical context in which both countries found themselves. Both Ankara and Athens perceived a growing foreign threat from Bulgarian irredentism and sought to form a defensive alliance to deter external aggression. To pave the way for such an alliance, the Ankara Treaty affirmed their common borders, settled outstanding property claims by refugees, and established a balance of naval power between Greece and Turkey. In 1934, the two countries joined with Yugoslavia and Romania to form the Balkan Pact, under which they resolved outstanding disputes and pledged mutual assistance. From the 1930s to the early 1950s, relations between Ankara and Athens remained cordial; in 1954, Yugoslavia, Greece, and Turkey again formed a mutual defense pact to counter the perceived threat of the Stalinist Soviet Union.

The status of the reciprocal minorities in both countries changed dramatically as a result of Greco-Turkish rapprochement. Almost immediately, ethnic Greeks were allowed to migrate to Turkey with work and residence permits. In the 1930s, educational exchanges for minority schools in each country were established between Greece and Turkey, and textbooks

---

57. Koufa and Svolopoulos, "The Compulsory Exchange of Populations," p. 286.

58. Ladas, *The Exchange of Minorities*, p. 721.

were revised to reflect the progressive turn in Greco-Turkish relations. In the early 1950s, the Turkish government permitted minority Greeks on Imbros and Tenedos to be educated in their mother tongue. The 1930s also saw the emergence of a Greek union and ethnocultural society in Istanbul. For its part, the Greek government allowed Turkish Kemalist associations to operate openly in Thrace, and in 1954 permitted minority schools to be called "Turkish" rather than "Muslim." The two countries became the closest allies in the region.[59] Minority institutions in both countries were tolerated "so long as [bilateral] Greco-Turkish relations remained friendly."[60]

RENEWED CONFLICT BETWEEN GREECE AND TURKEY (MID-1950S). The treatment of minorities took a turn for the worse in the 1950s, as tensions re-emerged between the two countries over the status of Cyprus. As Alexis Alexandris states, "intercommunal disturbances in Cyprus and the deterioration of Greco-Turkish relations during the 1960s had a direct impact on the Greek [minority] in Turkey."[61] As diplomatic relations deteriorated, the Turkish government renounced the 1930 Ankara Convention, revoking the rights of the Hellenic minority to remain in Istanbul. By the late 1960s, almost all of the Rums had been expelled from Istanbul and their assets frozen. The Turkish government reinstated the ban against Greek language instruction on Imbros and Tenedos.[62] Around the same time, expropriations and cultural and educational restrictions targeting the Greek inhabitants of Imbros and Tenedos led all but a few Greeks to leave the two islands and seek new homes in Greece and other Western countries.[63] Altogether, these policies radically reduced the Rum population in Turkey; from a population of 125,000 in 1935, they numbered only a few thousand by the late 1990s.[64]

The treatment of the Turkish minority in Greece also worsened during this time, as the government passed a new citizenship law making it harder for ethnic Turks to gain citizenship, and thus easier for the state to deny re-entrance to ethnic Turks who travelled outside Greece. This led to the statelessness of as many as 10,000 people from the mid-1950s to the late 1990s. In the early 1960s, the government banned the word "Turkish" from the names of minority schools and associations, and the Turkish mi-

---

59.   Oran, "The Story of Those Who Stayed," p. 103. The improvement in minority treatment during this period should not be exaggerated. In the 1930s, for example, the Rum minority in Istanbul was still barred from forming ethnic associations.

60.   Alexis Alexandris, "Religion or Ethnicity: The Identity Issue of the Minorities in Greece and Turkey," in Renée Hirschon, ed., Crossing the Aegean: An Appraisal of the 1923 Compulsory Population Exchange between Greece and Turkey (New York: Berghahn Books, 2003), p. 118.

61.   Ibid., p. 119.

62.   Oran, "The Story of Those Who Stayed," p. 104.

63.   In 1970, Imbros was officially renamed Gökçeada to reflect its new Turkish character.

64.   Alexandris, "Religion or Ethnicity," pp. 119–120.

nority was no longer allowed to run its own schools.[65] Ethnic Turks faced disproportionate obstacles in setting up their own businesses, and the Greek government intervened heavily in the selection of Muslim muftis; there was no comparable intervention in the selection of Greek Orthodox clerics.

In sum, the treatment of reciprocal minorities by both governments went from very bad following the Greek invasion of Asia Minor in 1919 to much improved following the Greece-Turkey rapprochement in 1930 to bad again in the mid-1950s as bilateral relations worsened with the emergence of a right-wing government in Greece and escalating tensions over Cyprus. Rather than determining the degree of bilateral conflict, these "minorities could genuinely prosper only as long as Greco-Turkish relations were good, as in the 1930s and early 1950s."[66] The sequence of conflict between Greeks and Turks over time indicates that, contrary to the expectations of partition theory, threats to cross-border ethnic kin do not themselves provoke interstate conflict. Changes in the treatment of reciprocal minorities instead appear to be driven by exogenous changes in interstate relations or government policies. In other words, it was not the poor treatment of reciprocal minorities that worsened bilateral relations between Greece and Turkey, but the degraded relations between Athens and Ankara that led to poorer treatment of their respective minorities.

Conclusion

This chapter examines two competing accounts of the link between population exchanges and conflict in the Balkans after World War I. The conventional account, which accords with partition theory, is that the population transfers—though immensely costly and perhaps even repugnant from a moral and ethical point of view—were necessary for resolving the nationalist conflicts in interwar Balkans. It is true that the refugees suffered tremendously in attempting to rebuild their lives under difficult circumstances in societies that were often hostile to their presence. The asymmetry of the exchanges also created economic and societal pressures for both net-receiving and net-sending countries, while the occupational mismatch between the exchanged populations often meant that the refugees adapted poorly to their new communities. Property compensation was generally inadequate and housing insufficient. Most importantly, the internationally supervised exchanges came too late for hundreds of thousands of civilians who were summarily expelled from their countries; those who remained behind were poorly protected by the League minorities system. Advocates of ethnic partition argue that these are the tragic, but sometimes necessary, costs of preventing a much worse set of atrocities associated with a prolonged war in which minorities face expulsions

---

65. Oran, "The Story of Those Who Stayed," pp. 104–107.

66. Alexandris, "Religion or Ethnicity," p. 117.

with neither personal security nor legal safeguards. Better to facilitate the inevitable process of ethnic "unmixing," they would say, than try to force ethnic groups to live together under intolerable conditions.

The alternative account above challenges this interpretation of two of the most extensive population exchanges in modern history. Contrary to the predictions of partition theory, these population transfers failed to prevent the reemergence of state-led irredentism and interstate conflict in the Balkans. Although both interstate conflicts appeared to have been resolved by the time the exchanges came to a close in the early 1930s, the Greco-Bulgarian conflict reemerged when Bulgaria's passive alliance with Nazi Germany allowed the government to occupy territories in Greece and elsewhere. Although the Greco-Bulgarian exchange had virtually emptied these territories of ethnic Bulgarians, Sofia retained its expansionist ambitions toward Western Thrace and the Aegean, and proceeded to reverse the Greco-Bulgarian population exchange during its occupation in order to consolidate these new territorial gains. Ethnic partition through population exchanges thus did little to dampen Bulgaria's irredentist designs on Greek territory.

In the case of Greece and Turkey, bilateral conflicts were driven by state policy rather than ethnic security dilemmas on the ground. After the exchange, the Greek population in Turkey (scattered throughout Istanbul and two isolated islands in the Aegean Sea) was too small to constitute a genuine security threat to the Turkish majority. In contrast, the remaining Muslim Turks of Greece were largely concentrated near the state border in Western Thrace and could feasibly have launched an irredentist campaign that would challenge Greece's territorial integrity. Despite this, Turkey's treatment of the Rum minority was generally *worse* than Greece's treatment of the Turkish minority. As Alexandris pointed out, "Athens did not resort to such extreme measures as massive deportation of minorities or the instigation of destructive anti-minority riots."[67] This differential treatment is significant, because according to ethnic security logic, we should expect to see *more* government repression against minorities that are perceived to be a threat to the state's territorial integrity than against minorities that pose no credible threat to the state.

Not only did the exchange of minorities between Greece and Turkey fail to prevent the recurrence of bilateral conflict, but changes in the treatment of minorities nearly always followed a change in bilateral relations between the two countries. The status of the reciprocal minorities improved only after the rapprochement of Greece and Turkey in the 1930s, a honeymoon that would last until the early 1950s. With the emergence of a right-wing leader in Greece and escalating tensions over Cyprus, these historic minorities once again occupied center-stage in Greco-Turkish relations. Despite the fact that the post–World War II Greco-Turkish dispute had very different origins than its earlier incarnation, the conflict led to the maltreatment of minorities that were associated with an earlier episode of conflict. Thus, the repression of minorities on the "wrong" side of the

---

67. Ibid., p. 128.

border was not the *cause*, but rather the *effect*, of bilateral tensions between Greece and Turkey. These tensions, in turn, were a function of government policies driven by geopolitical considerations. In sum, demographic insecurities on the ground had little to do with the rise and fall of nationalist conflict in the Balkans, which was instead driven by geostrategic interests of the state governments.

What are the implications of this analysis for policy? First, it bears repeating that the events leading up to the expulsions in the Anatolian Peninsula were based on the calculations of Greece and Turkey in the context of Great Power intrigue. Although nothing is certain, the Allies might have significantly altered the preferences of Athens and Ankara so as to avert this chain reaction, without which population transfers are unlikely to have occurred. In any event, the fact that the exchanges merely legitimized accomplished facts on the ground calls into question whether the terms of the Conventions made any real difference to those involved. Given that the Balkan population exchanges were the most extensively supervised and regulated partitions in recent memory, one should not expect a better outcome for the vast majority of population exchanges where extensive international supervision is not a realistic possibility.

The most important conclusion of this analysis is that the actions of regional or global hegemonic players, and the relations between them, largely determine the level of ethnic conflict on the ground. Thus, the causal arrow in sectarian conflict generally runs top-down rather than bottom-up, as partition theorists would have it. As Stefan Wolff noted, "it would be wrong to argue that a more complete population exchange would have prevented tensions between the two countries. The situation of the reciprocal minorities is not deplorable because they were excluded from the population transfer, but because both Greece and Turkey have persistently denied basic minority rights…to [the] minority communities."[68] The minorities effectively "became hostages to the vicissitudes in Greco-Turkish state relations," where "treatment by the host states over the decades depended on larger geopolitical issues, on international relations, as well as on internal political interests."[69] This conclusion puts the onus of responsibility for minority protection on state governments, rather than on ethnic insecurities borne of a mismatch between political and national borders. The proper lesson to be drawn from these exchanges was best put by C. A. Macartney, an interwar scholar of minorities and nationalism: "Such experience as we possess of the exchange of populations as a means of solving the minorities problem is not… calculated to encourage a repetition of the experiment."[70]

---

68. Wolff, "Can Forced Population Transfers Resolve Self-determination Conflicts?" p. 16.

69. Hirschon, "'Unmixing Peoples' in the Aegean Region," p. 18.

70. Macartney, *National States and National Minorities*, p. 448.

Part II
Rethinking Non-state Violence

Chapter 6

Driven to Arms?
The Escalation to Violence in
Nationalist Conflicts

Adria Lawrence

On the morning of August 20, 1955, residents of Oued Zem, a small town in Morocco southeast of Casablanca, took to the streets armed with rifles, knives, and pistols, demanding the return of the exiled sultan Mohammed V and an end to French colonialism in Morocco.[1] Armed tribesmen from the countryside rode down from the hills and joined the rioting towns-people, who had severed telegraph and telephone lines connecting Oued Zem to the rest of Morocco. Accompanied by a single gendarme, the assistant civil controller, Paul Carayol, went out to calm the crowd; both were lynched. Mobs proceeded to sack and destroy European houses and enterprises. Moroccans accused of collaborating with the French were beaten and killed. At 10:30 am, a crowd entered the André Mallet hospital and killed all of the European patients. The hospital chief was also killed and his body was mutilated. For hours, rioters were able to act as if there was no French authority in Morocco. The French had foreseen little trouble in this normally peaceful town, and their troops were stationed elsewhere. By the time French forces arrived, an estimated 60–100 Europeans had died, along with many more pro-French Moroccans.[2]

The explosion of nationalist violence in the previously quiet town points to a general question for scholars of violence: what would incite

The author wishes to thank Younes Amehraye, Matthew Kocher, and Lisa Wedeen.

1.   The sultan had been sent into exile on August 20, 1953, for supporting nationalist demands. These events occurred on the second anniversary of his deposition.

2.   The events of Oued Zem have not been widely studied. This description relies on participant interviews and the following sources: Dr. René Pech-Gourg, *Oued-Zem, août 1955*, Ministry of Foreign Affairs Report 1955, Paris, France; Dale F. Eickelman, *Knowledge and Power in Morocco: The Education of a Twentieth Century Notable* (Princeton, N.J.: Princeton University Press,1985); Guy Delanoë, *Le retour du roi et l'indépendance retrouvée* (Paris: Éditions l'Harmattan, 1991); Khalid Bin Seghir, "Intifada 20 ghust 1955 bi waadi zem: al jidhour wa al waqaa'" [The August Twentieth Uprising in Oued Zem: Causes and Effects,] in *Nadwa al mouqaawama al maghrib did al Isti'maar, 1904–1955* (Rabat: undated), pp. 337–372; as well as archives at the *Service Historique de l'Armee de la Terre* (SHAT) in Paris and the *Ministère des Affaires Étrangères, Centre des Archives Diplomatiques de Nantes* (MAE).

normally peaceful townspeople to take up arms, destroy public buildings, lynch officials, and execute their neighbors? For some, the answer appears obvious: in the context of an ongoing nationalist struggle, the eruption of violence makes considerable sense, particularly when non-violent means have made little headway in achieving nationalist aims. By the time violence erupted in Oued Zem, Morocco had endured over forty years of French rule; a nationalist movement had been engaging in appeals and demonstrations in favor of independence for over ten years; and in major cities, an anti-colonial terrorist campaign had been operating for two years. Given the existence of an ongoing nationalist struggle, the actions of Oued Zem residents are comprehensible. One participant in the uprising thought the motivations were obvious to everyone involved: they were angry at continued French rule and tired of colonial oppression. "We rose up for our honor and our freedom," he remembered.[3] Faced with the continued French presence, the residents of Oued Zem were ultimately driven to take up arms to forcefully demand Moroccan independence.

In the context of nationalist struggles, in which multiple parties claim the right to rule the same piece of territory, the adoption of violence suggests a failure to resolve the conflict through other means. In this view, nationalists turn to violence when confronted by a state that refuses to cede its claim to the territory. Scholars of the French empire, for instance, have suggested that France's refusal to decolonize after World War II prompted nationalist violence, making French decolonization a bloodier process than it needed to be.[4] For Algeria, Frantz Fanon wrote that "the violence of the occupier, his ferocity, his delirious attachment to the national territory, induced the leaders no longer to exclude certain forms of combat."[5] The war of national liberation in Indochina has likewise been associated with France's determination to stay in Indochina despite nationalist demands.[6] Writing about ethnic conflicts more generally, Monica Duffy Toft argues that when an ethnic group demands independence and the state refuses, "ethnic war is almost certain to occur."[7] Violence, by this account, escalates from an unresolved national struggle.

Understanding violence as the outcome of escalating conflict is fairly common; violence is often conceptualized as a *degree* of conflict, rather

---

3. El Hajj Mohammed Naji, Moroccan insurgent, interviewed by author, Oued Zem, Morocco, March 6, 2006.

4. See Raymond F. Betts, *France and Decolonisation 1900–1960* (London: Palgrave Macmillan, 1991), p. 6; Anthony Clayton, *The Wars of French Decolonization* (London: Longman Group, 1994), p. 1; Hendrik Spruyt, *Ending Empire: Contested Sovereignty and Territorial Partition* (Ithaca, N.Y.: Cornell University Press, 2005).

5. Frantz Fanon, "Algeria Unveiled," in Prasenjit Duara, ed., *Decolonization: Perspectives from Then and Now* (London: Routledge, 2004), p. 51.

6. Stein Tønnesson, "National Divisions in Indochina's Decolonization," in Prasenjit Duara, ed., *Decolonization: Perspectives from Then and Now*, p. 253.

7. Monica Duffy Toft, *The Geography of Ethnic Violence* (Princeton, N.J.: Princeton University Press, 2003), p. 32.

than a *form*.[8] Violence, according to this logic, exists at the upper end of a continuum of conflict. The adoption of violence typically suggests that the conflict has grown worse, and reached a new level of contention. Violence thus tends to be treated as the "unproblematic extension of ordinary social movement processes."[9] Doug McAdam et al. see violent collective action as a subset of the larger phenomenon of contentious politics, and argue that both violent and non-violent acts result from similar mechanisms and processes.[10] The eruption of violence may reflect the existence of extreme grievances or strong commitment to a cause.

Yet others point to problems with understanding violence as a product of ongoing conflict. Rogers Brubaker and David D. Laitin assert:

We lack strong evidence showing that higher levels of conflict (measured independently of violence) lead to higher levels of violence. Even where violence is clearly rooted in preexisting conflict, it should not be treated as a natural, self-explanatory outgrowth of such conflict, something that occurs automatically when the conflict reaches a certain intensity, a certain "temperature." Violence is not a quantitative degree of conflict but a qualitative form of conflict, with its own dynamics.[11]

They advocate disentangling violence from conflict and theorizing violence as a distinct object of study. Stathis N. Kalyvas likewise critiques the tendency to treat violence as a synonym for conflict, such that terms like "ethnic conflict," "ethnic violence," or "ethnic war" take on the same meaning.[12] Conflict need not be violent; violence need not reach the level of war; and the causes of violence may differ from the causes of other forms of conflict. Several chapters in this volume suggest that the adoption of violence is a choice; actors in conflict adopt violence only in specific contexts.[13] Conflict does not eventually and inevitably produce violence if unresolved. The turn to violence may have little to do with the duration of the conflict, its intensity, or the level of antagonism between the parties to the conflict. Additionally, violence may not begin only after other options have been tried and rejected. Violence, according to this logic, is not a "stage" of conflict, but a separate kind of conflict, different from non-violent conflict.

The question of whether violence should be theorized as a stage of conflict or as a distinctive form of conflict is an empirical one, and cannot be settled solely by thinking through the problem theoretically. Both

---

8. Rogers Brubaker and David D. Laitin, "Ethnic and Nationalist Violence," *Annual Reviews of Sociology*, Vol. 24 (1998), p. 425.

9. See Stathis N. Kalyvas, *The Logic of Violence in Civil War* (Cambridge: Cambridge University Press, 2006), p. 22.

10. Doug McAdam, Sidney Tarrow, and Charles Tilly, *Dynamics of Contention* (Cambridge: Cambridge University Press, 2001), p. 4. See also Charles Tilly, *The Politics of Collective Violence* (Cambridge: Cambridge University Press, 2003).

11. Brubaker and Laitin, "Ethnic and Nationalist Violence," p. 426.

12. Kalyvas, *The Logic of Violence*.

13. See the chapters by Bakke, Bulutgil, Cunningham and Beaulieu, and Downes in this volume.

views are plausible. The idea that violence escalates from ongoing, intractable conflict remains appealing, and is widespread in both scholarly and journalistic accounts of violence. Treating violence as an autonomous phenomenon goes against the intuition that prior conflict must somehow be related to subsequent violence. Yet the critique that violence is qualitatively different from other kinds of political opposition also resonates with what is known about the vast number of differences between violent and non-violent contexts. Violence hardly seems to be an extension of ordinary politics, but is instead an abrupt rupture of the existing political process. To understand whether uprisings like the one in Oued Zem result from exasperation with ongoing conflict or from other factors, we need to consider the ways that violence emerges from conflicts theoretically *and* empirically.[14]

This chapter investigates the relationship between ongoing conflict and the eruption of nationalist violence, asking whether we should treat violence as a degree of conflict or a different form of conflict. The objective is not to address all potential explanations for nationalist violence, but instead to evaluate those arguments that conceptualize violence as the outgrowth of conflict.[15] I begin by considering the ways that conflict may escalate and produce violence theoretically, pointing to both possibilities and problems with accounts that see violence growing out of contexts characterized by political conflict. Second, I turn to empirics, drawing on cases from the French colonial empire. These cases should favor an account that associates escalating conflict with violence. The most common explanations for violence in the French empire see it emerging from the growing conflict between colonized populations and the French over France's refusal to relinquish its colonies. Yet while opposition to French rule exists in all of the cases under discussion, violence erupts in only some. This variation provides an opportunity to consider why an existing political conflict might or might not lead to violence.

Analyzing cases from this one empire is advantageous not only because of the degree of variation, but also because this research design controls for differences between occupying powers, holds imperial policies and attitudes common throughout the empire constant, and restricts the time frame of the analysis, thereby introducing fewer confounding factors. In addition, a medium-N analysis permits a better grasp of the case material than a large-N analysis would; data quality is higher. In section three, I provide additional empirical analysis in the form of a systematic subnational study of violence in colonial Morocco.

---

14. Brubaker and Laitin are correct in asserting that we lack evidence linking high levels of conflict to high levels of violence, but empirical evidence can be brought to bear in favor of or against this hypothesis.

15. I therefore bracket explanations for violence that do not fit into a violence-as-escalation framework. For example, one potential explanation for violence is based on diffusion: violence in one place may influence violence elsewhere. This alternative argument is not one I evaluate here; the objective is instead to consider one influential group of theories of violence.

I demonstrate that the eruption of violence cannot be explained by arguments that see violence resulting from intransigent French rule. France's refusal to cede to nationalist demands did not inexorably produce violent resistance. Surprisingly, violence did not erupt where French rule was most long-standing, stubborn, or cruel. Nationalist violence in the French empire does not fit an account that sees violence as the self-explanatory outgrowth of an ongoing, intractable conflict. These findings suggest that violence may indeed be a different form of conflict, rather than a higher degree of it. Violent conflict, I argue, is qualitatively different from non-violent conflict. I conclude by considering the wider implications of the argument for the study of violence.

Conflict Escalation and Violence

Nationalist conflicts are characterized by competing claims to the same territory, but not all conflicts become violent. Why might some nationalist conflicts lead to violence, while others do not? One obvious answer is that some conflicts may be resolved before violence erupts if one side withdraws its claim. If one side cedes the disputed territory to the other and the basis for conflict evaporates, it is hard to see why further conflict, violent or otherwise, would ensue. This point is entirely obvious: there needs to be some conflict for the conflict to be either violent or non-violent. Of course, this simple scenario could be complicated by a number of factors. For instance, if all the parties on the ceding side are not in agreement, the conflict cannot be said to have been resolved and may persist. Alternatively, even if the ceding side fully withdraws, conflict and violence could occur among the victors as they establish control over the territory, but this conflict would be not be the same as the initial one; it would oppose actors who had previously been on the same side, and might not be coded as nationalist.

But setting aside the possibility that one side gives up and the conflict ends, what are the consequences of intransigence? If both the existing ruler and the nationalists opposing the existing ruler persist in claiming the same territory, why might violence follow? Violence does not erupt in all unresolved nationalist conflicts; other options exist. Nationalists can negotiate, seek assistance from outside actors, organize non-violent demonstrations, and appeal in international arenas. We need mechanisms that link an existing conflict to the very specific outcome of violence. Below I discuss four reasons why ongoing conflict could prompt nationalists to take up arms.

First, ongoing conflict may turn violent if violence is believed to be more effective than non-violent tactics. Continued non-violent pressure may come to seem increasingly futile over time, and persistent conflict may point to the potential utility of violence for settling the question. One interviewee, El Hajj Mohammed Naji, claimed that the Oued Zem uprising was more effective than other forms of nationalist action because the French announced their withdrawal from Morocco just three months after it took place. "In one day, we achieved what it took eight years to achieve in Vietnam," he stated.

However, the potential effectiveness of violence is difficult to know in advance. The problem with Naji's statement is that the effectiveness of the Oued Zem uprising only became apparent after the French announcement; prior to the uprising, its potential efficacy might have seemed questionable.[16] When non-violent strategies have not yet achieved results, nationalists must make estimates about whether those strategies will pay off in the future or whether violent strategies will work better. Such calculations are exceedingly difficult to make; embracing violence might shift the balance of power in favor of the nationalists, but it might also fail spectacularly, leading to the destruction of nationalist actors and visiting brutal reprisals on the population. Violence by a non-state actor is risky, particularly when used against a well-armed foe.[17]

Moreover, evidence suggests that violence may be a suboptimal strategy for non-state actors. A number of scholars have argued that social movements turn violent at moments of weakness. Marsha Crenshaw suggests that elites embrace terrorism when they cannot get mass support for peaceful mobilization.[18] Sidney Tarrow and Donatella Della Porta argue that violence erupts on the downside of a mobilization cycle.[19] Della Porta, for instance, suggests that violence begins when resources for mobilization become scarce. V.P. Gagnon argues that elites in Serbia provoked ethnic violence to divert attention from the ongoing economic crisis and strong demands for democratic reforms.[20] These accounts see violence as a strategy seized out of weakness, not one chosen out of a belief in its efficacy. Using large-N data, Maria J. Stephan and Erica Chenoweth find that non-violent strategies are more effective than violent strategies at helping non-state actors achieve their goals.[21] The existing empirical evidence

---

16. Furthermore, attributing the French withdrawal to this particular uprising is problematic, given that both peaceful and non-violent tactics had been used elsewhere in Morocco and also affected the French decision.

17. Scholars also have difficulty assessing the effectiveness of violence, and sometimes assume that violence is chosen for its effectiveness without investigating the relative effectiveness of violent and non-violent strategies. For examples, see Edward N. Muller and Erich Weede, "Cross-National Variation in Political Violence," *Journal of Conflict Resolution*, Vol. 34, No. 4 (1990), pp. 624–651; and Andrew Kydd and Barbara F. Walter, "Sabotaging the Peace: The Politics of Extremist Violence," *International Organization*, Vol. 56, No. 2 (Spring 2002), p. 278.

18. Martha Crenshaw, "The Causes of Terrorism," in Catherine Besteman, ed., *Violence: A Reader* (New York: New York University Press, 2002), pp. 99–117.

19. Sidney Tarrow, *Power in Movement: Social Movements, Collective Action, and Politics* (Cambridge: Cambridge University Press, 1994); and Donatella Della Porta, *Social Movements, Political Violence, and the State: A Comparative Analysis of Italy and Germany* (Cambridge: Cambridge University Press, 1995).

20. V.P. Gagnon, "Ethnic Nationalism and International Conflict: The Case of Serbia," *International Security*, Vol. 19, No. 3 (Winter 1994/1995), pp. 130–166.

21. Maria J. Stephan and Erica Chenoweth, "Why Civil Resistance Works: The Strategic Logic of Nonviolent Conflict," *International Security*, Vol. 33, No. 1 (Summer 2008), pp. 7–44.

undermines the claim that non-state actors adopt violence because of its proven effectiveness.

A second way that violence may result from an ongoing conflict is via state repression. If non-violent mobilization is growing and demands on the state are mounting, the conflict may appear increasingly threatening. The state may therefore decide to respond to nationalist demands with violence. Nationalist violence may then erupt in response to state violence. Charles Tilly has suggested that the state is often the initiator of violence, starting off a violent conflict with its own use of violence.[22] Jeff Goodwin has argued that revolutions begin when the state represses non-violent political action, leaving non-state actors with no other option besides violence.[23] This argument implies that violence erupts when the non-state actor is in a position of strength; the logic is that a popular non-violent movement provokes state repression which then leads to the adoption of violence.

Evaluating the relationship between state repression and nationalist violence is tricky. The effects of repression on regime opposition have been widely discussed in the literature on opposition in authoritarian regimes. Yet repression seems to have contradictory effects. On the one hand, it is thought to be a critical authoritarian tool capable of silencing opposition.[24] But on the other hand, repression has also been said to spur opposition.[25] For example, one historian wrote that repression stifled Tunisian nationalists in 1938, but fueled Tunisian nationalism in 1952.[26] Repression apparently produces different results at different times. Even if repression does provoke opposition, it may do so by prompting further peaceful op-

---

22. Charles Tilly, *From Mobilization to Revolution* (New York: McGraw-Hill, 1978), p. 177.

23. Jeff Goodwin, *No Other Way Out: States and Revolutionary Moments, 1945–1991* (Cambridge: Cambridge University Press, 2001).

24. See, for example, Timur Kuran, "Now out of Never: the Element of Surprise in the East European Revolution of 1989," *World Politics*, Vol. 44 (October 1991), pp. 7–48; and Ronald Wintrobe, *The Political Economy of Dictatorship* (Cambridge: Cambridge University Press, 1998).

25. See Steven Heydemann, *Authoritarianism in Syria: Institutions and Social Conflict, 1946–1970* (Ithaca, N.Y.: Cornell University Press, 1999). Like Goodwin in *No Other Way Out*, he argues against the view that repression helps regime longevity, pointing out that authoritarian regimes have collapsed even with high levels of repression.

26. Jamil M. Abun-Nasr, *A History of the Maghrib* (Cambridge: Cambridge University Press, 1975), p. 349. This is but one example of the tendency to attribute contradictory outcomes to the use of repression. To take another, in *The Islamic Threat: Myth or Reality?* (New York: Oxford University Press, 1999), John L. Esposito argues that "Black Friday" was a turning point in the Iranian Revolution. On that day, repressive measures became intolerable; "white- and blue-collar workers, traditional and modern middle classes, city dwellers and rural peasants swelled the ranks of the opposition…in Tehran almost two million people called for the death of the Shah." Just two pages later, however, Esposito credits the excessive use of repression as the reason for Khomeini's success in implementing his revolution. His analysis thus suggests that repressive tactics can have unpredictable outcomes. Ellen Lust-Okar points to the failure of repression to explain divergent outcomes in *Structuring Conflict in the Arab World: Incumbents, Opponents, and Institutions* (Cambridge: Cambridge University Press, 2006), p. 15.

position or generating more popular support for the cause rather than by specifically causing violence. Repression can therefore have several different logical outcomes: it may silence opposition, provoke further peaceful mobilization, or lead to violence.[27]

Another difficulty with evaluating the impact of repression on violence is the potential for endogeneity. It can be hard to discern whether violence is initiated by the state or state violence is carried out in response to nationalist violence; there are often conflicting claims about which party first used violence.[28] One way to address this problem is by looking not at repression, but at its antecedent. If strong nationalist movements are more likely to appear threatening and therefore to invite repression, and repression leads to nationalist violence, then a strong nationalist movement may be a good predictor of violence.

A third way that an ongoing conflict may push people to embrace violence is by altering perceptions that violence is immoral. As conflict continues, and the state refuses to recognize the legitimacy of nationalist aspirations, the sense that violence is an inappropriate way to resolve conflict may erode. Ongoing conflict may serve to make the enemy appear unjust, even demonic.[29] The very intransigence of the foe may invite violence. For instance, one scholar writes: "the violence and cultural hubris of European colonialism called forth its violent negation in the national liberation movements of the 1950s."[30] The injustices of colonialism, in this view, merited a violent response; violence was an appropriate and equivalent answer to imperialism.

Violence may not just become appealing for cognitive, ethical reasons. A fourth and related way that enduring conflict may produce violence is via emotions. An unresolved conflict is likely to generate anger and frustration, which may spark violence.[31] A number of scholars have suggested

27.   Studies have also looked at the impact of repression on the use of violence in the context of ongoing civil wars, asking whether particular types of repression, either discriminate or indiscriminate, are effective against insurgencies. These studies do not posit, however, that such repression explains the initial adoption of violence, since in these contexts, state repression is used when violent conflict has already begun. For examples, see Kalyvas, *The Logic of Violence*, particularly chaps. 6 and 7; Matthew Adam Kocher, Thomas B. Pepinskiy, and Stathis N. Kalyvas, "Aerial Bombardment, Indiscriminate Violence, and Territorial Control in Unconventional Wars," unpublished manuscript; Jason Lyall, "Does Indiscriminate Violence Incite Insurgent Attacks? Evidence from Chechnya." *Journal of Conflict Resolution*, Vol. 53, No. 3 (2009), pp. 331–362.

28.   See Mark R. Beissinger, *Nationalist Mobilization and the Collapse of the Soviet State* (Cambridge: Cambridge University Press, 2002), p. 273.

29.   See Kalyvas, *The Logic of Violence*, p. 65, for a discussion of works that link violence to the demonization of the enemy.

30.   Edmund Burke III, "Theorizing the Histories of Colonialism and Nationalism in the Arab Maghrib," in Ali Abdullatif Ahmida, ed., *Beyond Colonialism and Nationalism in the Maghrib: History, Culture, and Politics* (London: Palgrave Macmillan, 2000), p. 21.

31.   See Roger D. Petersen, *Understanding Ethnic Violence: Fear, Hatred, and Resentment in Twentieth-Century Eastern Europe* (Cambridge: Cambridge University Press, 2002); and Ted R. Gurr, *Why Men Rebel* (Princeton, N.J.: Princeton University Press, 1971).

that ethnic and nationalist conflict in particular involves intense hatred and the desire for vengeance.[32] These emotions may then contribute to the sense that violence in morally warranted.

But the problem with basing a theory of violence on anger, frustration, or a sense of the justness of violence is one of incompleteness. These explanations assume an unproblematic leap from emotions to violence or from support for violence to its use. Beliefs about the appropriateness of violence and emotions about the enemy do not constitute an explanation for violence without an account of how such beliefs and emotions produce violent acts in particular. Anger, frustration, and a sense of injustice rarely generate violence. As Randall Collins put it:

such explanations assume violence is easy once the motivation exists. Micro-situational evidence, to the contrary, shows that violence is hard. No matter how motivated someone may be, if the situation does not unfold so that confrontational tension/fear is overcome, violence will not proceed. Conflict, even quite overtly expressed conflict, is not the same as violence, and taking the last step is not at all automatic.[33]

Collins finds that people are generally not good at violence; he shows that while humans certainly have the capacity to be angry and aggressive, the most frequent tendency is to stop short of violence. The typical response to confrontational situations is to swallow one's anger and frustration and back down, or to let emotions go with bluster and bluff.[34] In Jon Elster's terms, frustration can merely lead to "sour grapes," and induce preference change, whereby actors adjust to circumstances they find distasteful.[35]

If emotions and beliefs are consistent with a variety of actions, and violence only rarely results, it is difficult to base an explanation for violence on such factors. Ongoing nationalist conflict may indeed produce anger, frustration, and support for violent actions, but further consideration is required to specify the conditions under which these feelings lead to violence. Still, while these factors do not provide a complete account of violence, they may be useful as a partial account. Anger, frustration, and support for violence may raise the probability that violence erupts. They may be necessary for nationalist violence. The key challenge empirically

---

32. For examples, see Donald L. Horowitz, *Ethnic Groups in Conflict* (Berkeley: University of California Press, 1985); Robert E. Harkavy and Stephanie G. Neuman, *Warfare and the Third World* (New York: Palgrave, 2001); and Stuart J. Kaufman, *Modern Hatreds: The Symbolic Politics of Ethnic War* (Ithaca, N.Y.: Cornell University Press, 2001).

33. Randall Collins, *Violence: A Micro-sociological Theory* (Princeton, N.J.: Princeton University Press, 2008), p. 20.

34. Collins, *Violence*, pp. 10, 21, 27. On p. 22, he specifically addresses the eruption of violence in situations akin to nationalist conflicts when he discusses resistance theories that see violence as a response to subordination in large-scale social structure. He likewise argues that while such theories assume violence is easy and requires only a motive, resistance violence is just as difficult as other kinds of violence.

35. Jon Elster, *Sour Grapes: Studies in the Subversion of Rationality* (Cambridge: Cambridge University Press, 1985).

is measurement; it is difficult to measure emotions and beliefs, and even more difficult to compare relative levels of emotions and beliefs across places. Moreover, emotions and beliefs may be endogenous to violence once it begins.[36] In the next section, I consider whether places where the population had more reason to be angry and frustrated at the injustices and persistence of French rule were those where violence erupted. Before turning to an empirical evaluation of the proposed mechanisms that link conflict escalation to violence, two further issues are worth keeping in mind. First, accounts of violence often reason back from the violence to identify triggers of violence. For instance, the very presence of violence itself is sometimes seen as evidence that actors must have thought violence would be effective, or that participants were motivated by anger, frustration, or a sense of righteousness. It is likewise easy to identify an outburst of violence and fix on a preceding instance of repression as the reason for the violence. This practice of "doing history backward"[37] biases analysis of the causes of violence, both because the outcome is used as evidence of the causes of that outcome and because individual motivations are extrapolated from macro outcomes even when individual-level data are lacking.[38] The challenge is to measure the potential factors linking conflict to violence independently of any subsequent violence.

A second issue to consider is the relative rarity of violence. Violence could potentially be effective at attaining all sorts of ends, yet it is used only rarely. Anger, frustration, and moral indignation are common human emotions that generally do not prompt violence. Even in situations of persistent ethnic and nationalist difference, violence seldom erupts.[39] Most nationalist conflicts do not produce widespread violence.[40] Any useful theory of nationalist violence needs to address why conflict so often fails to produce violence. Using a dataset of cases from the former Soviet Union, Mark R. Beissinger finds it difficult to identify structural determinants of violence that differentiate violent conflicts from non-violent conflicts and concludes that "mobilized nationalist violence is generally a less structured and less predictable phenomenon than nonviolent nationalist mobilization."[41] While Lars-Erik Cederman and Luc Girardin find that violence is more likely to erupt where one ethnic minority dominates other ethnic groups, they too note that violence does not always erupt in such situations, and point to the need to analyze cases that actually feature

---

36. See Kalyvas, *The Logic of Violence*, p. 78; he suggests that while deep group rivalry and resentment is often seen as a cause of war, polarization between different parties may be endogenous to the war itself.

37. Frederick Cooper, *Colonialism in Question. Theory, Knowledge, History* (Berkeley: University of California Press, 2005), p. 26.

38. Kalyvas, *The Logic of Violence*, p. 76.

39. James D. Fearon and David D. Laitin, "Explaining Interethnic Cooperation," *American Political Science Review*, Vol. 90, No. 4 (December 1996), pp. 715–735.

40. Beissinger, *Nationalist Mobilization*, p. 273.

41. Ibid., p. 283.

ethno-nationalist violence from those that have similar structural features, but no violence.[42]

In the next section, I look at cases from the French empire. In these cases, the French dominated ethnically, linguistically, and racially different populations, ruling in a way that was widely acknowledged as unjust and exploitive, yet violence erupted in only a portion of these cases. These cases facilitate consideration of both the occurrence and the non-occurrence of violence in nationalist conflicts.

Violent and Non-violent Nationalist Conflict in the French Empire

The dominant explanations for the onset of nationalist violence in the colonial world focus on the intransigence of colonial rulers. For the French empire, the accepted wisdom is that exasperation with continuing colonial rule and the failure to achieve aims through other means prompted violence.[43] This explanation reflects the view that violence escalates from existing nationalist conflict in the ways suggested in the previous section: ongoing French rule has been linked to anger, frustration, and a growing sense of the justness and efficacy of violence, particularly given that the French often repressed peaceful nationalist activity. These cases therefore provide a difficult test for the argument that violence constitutes a separate form of conflict, and is not an outgrowth of a worsening, intractable conflict.

The French confronted numerous nationalist movements demanding independence in the mid-twentieth century, yet while nationalist opposition was widespread, violent opposition was rarer. Nationalists' use of violence varied across the empire, with lengthy wars in Algeria and Vietnam, terrorism and insurgency in Morocco, Tunisia, Syria, Cameroon, and Madagascar, and peaceful mobilization elsewhere (see Table 6.1).[44] If intransigence is to account for the distribution of violence across the empire, it needs to vary. Violence may have erupted only where the French were particularly stubborn about maintaining colonial rule. France wanted to retain control over Vietnam and Algeria, for instance, and fought long wars to do so. The problem with explanations based on intransigence is that intransigence itself is often measured by whether or not there is a

---

42.   Lars-Erik Cederman and Luc Girardin, "Beyond Fractionalization: Mapping Ethnicity onto Nationalist Insurgencies," *American Political Science Review*, Vol. 101, No. 1 (February 2007), p. 182.

43.   For examples that link violence to France's refusal to relinquish its territories, see Betts, *France and Decolonisation*; Clayton, *The Wars of French Decolonization*; and Spruyt, *Ending Empire*.

44.   Since this article is concerned with analyzing why conflict sometimes leads to violence, the table excludes French colonies with no significant nationalist movement in the mid-twentieth century (and therefore no ongoing nationalist conflict): French Polynesia, Guadeloupe, Martinique, St Pierre and Miquelon, Réunion, French India, Wallis and Futuna, French Guiana, and New Caledonia.

violent conflict, rather than through prior indicators of France's commitment to specific colonies. I posit instead a number of potential indicators of French intransigence, and evaluate their ability to account for patterns of violence across the empire.

Table 6.1. Twentieth-century French Colonies with Non-violent and Violent Nationalist Movement.

Non-violent Mobilization	Violent Mobilization
Cambodia	Algeria
Chad	Cameroon
Comoros	Madagascar
Dahomey	Morocco
Djibouti	Syria
French Sudan	Tunisia
Gabon	Vietnam
Guinea	
Ivory Coast	
Laos	
Lebanon	
Mauritania	
Middle Congo	
Niger	
Oubangui-Chari	
Senegal	
Togo	
Upper Volta	

ENDURING FRENCH RULE: TIME AND THE LIKELIHOOD OF VIOLENCE

The first indicator concerns the impact of time. If violence is more likely to occur when a conflict has dragged on, the passage of time should increase the likelihood of violence. This hypothesis reflects a number of the mechanisms linking escalating conflict to violence. Opponents of French rule may be willing to be patient for a time before using violence to attain their ends, but the passage of time may make the conflict seem more intractable and may lead actors to estimate that violence might be more effective. The passage of time may also anger and frustrate colonized populations and lead them to support the use of violence.

One indicator that captures these arguments could be the length of time that the French controlled a territory. Where the colonial power ruled for a longer period of time, we might reasonably expect people to be more exasperated with ongoing colonial rule and more willing to take up arms. Yet this distinction does not appear to correlate with the occurrence of nationalist violence across the empire. In addition to Vietnam and Algeria, which were long-standing French possessions, violence also occurred in Morocco and Syria, places the French had not controlled for long. Moreover, the French were adamant about maintaining their control over French Africa, yet there was little anti-colonial violence there, even in places like Senegal, which had been a French possession since the mid-nineteenth century. Instead, there was violent conflict in Cameroon, which had only been in French hands since World War I. Table 6.2 shows the territories with nationalist movements by century of French colonization. Only a quarter of the territories that were colonized in the nineteenth century had violent nationalist movements, while over a third of later acquisitions experienced violence. Enduring a longer period of colonialism is not associated with a higher incidence of nationalist violence.

Table 6.2. French Territories with Nationalist Movements, by Century of French Conquest.

Violence?	19th	20th	Total
No	13 (76%)	5 (63%)	18 (72%)
Yes	4 (24%)	3 (37%)	7 (28%)
Total	17 (100%)	8 (100%)	25 (100%)

Fisher's exact test: p=.6

This indicator does not specifically capture the duration of conflict between the colonizing power and the population, however. The relevant amount of time to consider may not be the overall length of the colonial period, but the amount of time that local peaceful organizers have been challenging French rule. According to this argument, the time-bomb starts ticking not when colonial rule begins, but when opposition to colonial rule begins; people will wait only so long before they turn to violence to solve the conflict. The duration of the conflict may also be a good indicator of the strength of the nationalist movement. Stronger nationalist movements may invite more repression and therefore may be more likely to become violent.

Identifying the onset of nationalist conflict in each territory is not easy. Evidence of resistance to French rule can often be documented from the early days of conquest, meaning that the duration of the colonial period may in fact be a good measure of the duration of conflict between the French and the occupied.[45] Alternatively, the conflict could be said to have

---

45.   Even where resistance was not overt, colonized populations relied on "weapons

begun with the first instances of organized political action objecting to French colonial rule, or the first calls for independence (which often came from those who were working or studying overseas in Europe, not inhabitants of the colonies), or the first instances of mass nationalist protest against French rule.

Regardless of how the start of the conflict is dated, its duration is unlikely to explain the distribution of violence across the empire. Nationalist conflict in three of the seven violent cases had a very limited history. In Madagascar, violence erupted only a year after the founding of the first nationalist party.[46] In French Cameroon, the *Union des Populations du Cameroun* (UPC) turned violent within five years of its founding.[47] Likewise, armed revolt broke out in Syria within five years of the establishment of the French Mandate.[48] The other violent cases occurred in places with varying histories of nationalist resistance. In Morocco and Tunisia, nationalist claims had been made for about a decade before violence began. In Vietnam, nationalist organizing had been sporadically occurring since the 1930s before violence erupted during World War II. Depending on how it is calculated, nationalist conflict in Algeria lasted between eight and seventeen years before violence erupted.[49] The wide variation in the time it took for violence to begin in these seven cases undermines the claim that long, intransigent conflict produces violence.

A look at the peaceful parts of the empire likewise fails to show a relationship between the duration of conflict and nationalist violence. Nationalist mobilization began at about the same time in Lebanon and Syria, yet violence erupted only in Syria. Senegal had a much longer history of political organization than Madagascar and Cameroon, where violence erupted despite the weakness of nationalist mobilization in both places.

---

of the weak" to resist throughout the colonial era. On this type of resistance, see James C. Scott, *Weapons of the Weak: Everyday Forms of Peasant Resistance* (New Haven, Conn.: Yale University Press, 1987).

46.   For more on nationalist violence in Madagascar, see Jacques Tronchon, *L'insurrection malgache de 1947* (Paris: Librairie François Maspero, 1974) ; and Jennifer Cole, *Forget Colonialism? Sacrifice and the Art of Memory in Madagascar* (Berkeley: University of California Press, 2001).

47.   See Richard A. Joseph, *Radical Nationalism in Cameroun: Social Origins of the U.P.C. Rebellion* (Oxford: Oxford University Press, 1977).

48.   See Philip S. Khoury, *Syria and the French Mandate: The Politics of Arab Nationalism, 1920–1945* (Princeton, N.J.: Princeton University Press, 1987).

49.   Nationalist demands were first heard from a small group in France, but it may be more reasonable to date the onset of nationalist conflict in Algeria to the founding of the *Parti du Peuple Algérian* (P.P.A.) in 1937, although nationalist mobilization was neither popular nor widespread in Algeria until the mid-1950s. Violence erupted briefly in 1945, but an organized, sustained violent campaign did not begin until 1954. For more on nationalism in Algeria, see Alistair Horne, *A Savage War of Peace: Algeria 1954–1962* (New York: Viking Press, 1977); John P. Entelis, *Comparative Politics of North Africa: Algeria, Morocco, and Tunisia* (Syracuse, N.Y.: Syracuse University Press, 1980); Benjamin Stora, *Algeria 1830–2000: A Short History* (Ithaca, N.Y.: Cornell University Press, 2001); and James M. McDougall, *History and the Culture of Nationalism in Algeria* (Cambridge: Cambridge University Press, 2006).

Although violence did not occur in most of French Africa, political conflict was not absent. Opposition to the French occurred across French territories in Africa, but it often took a different form; most opposition to the French focused on demanding equality and citizenship, not national independence.[50] Nationalist claims in much of Africa did not become widespread until 1956, but violence was not adopted before independence arrived, not even in places like Djibouti and the Comoros, which did not become independent until the mid-1970s.[51] It is thus difficult to sustain the argument that longer conflict leads to violent nationalism. Nationalist movements with a long history of opposition to colonial rule appear neither necessary nor sufficient for nationalist violence.

TYPE OF COLONIAL RULE AND THE LIKELIHOOD OF VIOLENCE

Another indicator of France's intention to maintain its rule is the status of the territory. France's imperial possessions were divided into several categories. Algeria was composed of three French departments, and thus was considered an integral part of the French republic itself. Other territories were designated as colonies, protectorates, or mandates. Protectorates and mandates were explicitly created as temporary arrangements, while colonies and departments were integral territories of France overseas. Mandates were supposed to be moving toward independence, and protectorates were understood to have distinctive national personalities that the French promised to protect. We might thus expect that because France saw its colonies and departments as integral possessions, it would be more reluctant to decolonize those than its protectorates and mandates. This reluctance might prove frustrating to opponents of the French living in colonies and departments. If frustration with seemingly permanent colonial rule produces violence, we should see more violence in colonies and departments than in protectorates or mandates.

Additionally, the status of the territory may be correlated with patterns of repression and injustice; the French may have had a freer hand to mistreat populations in their colonies and departments than they did in protectorates and mandates. The French had to answer to the League of Nations for their actions in the mandates; in protectorates, the French typically ruled in collaboration with a local leader who may likewise have been able to restrict French actions to some degree. If repression is cor-

---

50.   Frederick Cooper, *Africa Since 1940, the Past of the Present* (Cambridge: Cambridge University Press, 2002), p. 39. As in Algeria, demands for African independence were largely articulated by African student and activist groups in France, not in the African territories themselves, where political leaders advocated reform.

51.   For more on the peaceful parts of the empire, see Yves Person, "French West Africa and Decolonization," in Prosser Gifford and W.M. Roger Louis, eds., *The Transfer of Power in Africa: Decolonization 1940–1960* (New Haven, Conn.: Yale University Press, 1982), pp. 141–172; Patrick Manning, *Francophone Sub-Saharan Africa, 1880–1985* (Cambridge: Cambridge University Press, 1998); Tony Chafer, *The End of Empire in French West Africa: France's Successful Decolonization?* (Oxford: Berg, 2002); Cooper, *Africa Since 1940*; and Adria Lawrence, "Imperial Rule and the Politics of Nationalism," Ph.D. Dissertation, University of Chicago, 2007.

related with territorial status and increases the risk of violence, we would expect to see more violence in colonies and departments.

The data, however, do not suggest a relationship between territorial status and violence. Five of the seven territories with violent nationalist movements were protectorates or mandates (Syria, Cameroon, Morocco, Tunisia, and Vietnam). Table 6.3 suggests that colonies and departments were *less* likely to experience nationalist violence than mandates and protectorates, although the difference was not statistically significant. This indicator of intransigence does not appear to explain the pattern of violence.

Table 6.3. French Territories with Nationalist Movements, by Territorial Status.

Violence?	Colony/Department	Mandate/Protectorate	Total
No	14 (87.5%)	4 (44%)	18 (72%)
Yes	2 (12.5%)	5 (56%)	7 (28%)
Total	16 (100%)	9 (100%)	25 (100%)

Fisher's exact test: $p=.06$

SETTLERS AND THE LIKELIHOOD OF VIOLENCE

Another important indicator of French intransigence is the presence of settlers. Settlers could prompt nationalist violence for a number of reasons.[52] First, French settlers were consistent advocates of maintaining French rule; where large numbers of them lived, we might expect serious resistance to decolonization. Settler pressure to maintain colonial rule might then incite violence, since nationalists may see peaceful tactics as ineffective where settlers were blocking negotiations.

Second, settlers are an observable indicator of colonial injustice. Settlers enjoyed privileges that natives were denied; they had a voice in government, favorable land-settlement policies, and a better standard of living. French settlers were often cruel to indigenous populations, whom they saw as uncivilized and inferior.[53] Settler behavior may have exac-

---

52.   On settlers and conflict, see Ian S. Lustick, *Unsettled States, Disputed Lands* (Ithaca, N.Y.: Cornell University Press, 1993).

53.   For example, settlers in Algeria commonly referred to Algerians as *"sales Arabs"* (dirty Arabs). Even educated Algerians were often treated with condescension and contempt; settlers tended to address all Algerians not by name, but by an all-purpose name, usually "Ahmed." See Charles-André Julien, *L'Afrique du Nord en marche. Nationalismes musulmans et souveraineté française* (Tunis: Cérès Editions, 1972), p. 58 ; and David Prochaska, *Making Algeria French. Colonialism in Bône, 1870–1920* (Cambridge: Cambridge University Press, 1990), p. 208. The situation was no different in other parts

erbated grievances, produced anger and resentment, worsened the conflict between the colonizer and the nationalists, and ultimately provoked violence. If violence happened where colonial rule was most unjust, we should observe a correlation between settlers and violence.

Third, settlers often had a disproportionate say in colonial policy and typically advocated a hard line against nationalist agitators. It is reasonable to suppose that repression was more widespread in settler territories than in other places, because settlers influenced local policing. If repression provokes violent nationalist responses, settler colonies should be more violent.

Table 6.4 uses data from the post-war period to show the presence of European settlers across the French empire in the mid-1940s.[54] The territories are listed by increasing percentage of settlers, and are somewhat suggestive of a relationship between settlers and violence. The three territories with the largest percentage of settlers experienced violence, and eleven of the sixteen territories without violence had populations with less than a quarter-percent of settlers. Yet the correlation is imperfect: Senegal and Djibouti had a relatively large percentage of settlers, but no violence, and the populations of Cameroon and Vietnam were less than 1 percent settler, yet violence occurred.

In addition, sub-national population data do not support the view that the presence of settlers encouraged violence. The places where settlers were most numerous were often not the most violent places. In Vietnam, only 18 percent of French settlers lived in the north of the country, where the majority of violence occurred. The rest lived in the south and the center of the country. In Algeria, violence primarily occurred in the countryside, while settlers were concentrated in towns.[55] In Syria, the Great Revolt began as a local affair in a remote, mountainous region with almost no French presence.[56] In the third section of this chapter, I systematically consider the impact of settlers on violence in Morocco.

---

of the empire; French settlers used the more familiar "*tu*" rather than the more formal "*vous*" when addressing natives in Africa.

54.   Data are drawn from the *Annuaire Statistique de l'Union Française Outre-mer, 1939–1949, Tome Premier*, Ministère de la France d'Outre-mer, Service des Statistiques, Paris, 1951. Since the data concern the post-war empire, Syria and Lebanon, which had become independent, were excluded. Excluding them strengthens the relationship between settlers and violence, since Syria was violent yet had few settlers. Data on the French population were missing for Upper Volta, but can be assumed to be less than 1,000, since there were under 2,000 people in the European and assimilated natives category. The data come from censuses taken in individual territories from 1946–1950.

55.   In Algeria, violence most often took the form of insurgency in the rural areas, while the FLN employed terrorism in the cities. This conforms with Matthew Kocher, "Human Ecology and Civil War," Ph.D. Dissertation, University of Chicago, 2004. He argues that insurgency flourishes in less densely populated areas, while terrorism is the strategy of choice for cities, where state forces are concentrated.

56.   Khoury, *Syria and the French Mandate*, p. 152.

Table 6.4. French Settlers and Violence.

Territories	% Settler	Violence
Chad	0.03	No
Upper Volta	0.03	No
Togo	0.04	No
Niger	0.06	No
Mauritania	0.07	No
Oubangui-Chari	0.1	No
Laos	0.11	No
Dahomey	0.15	No
Comoros	0.17	No
Guinea	0.19	No
French Sudan	0.19	No
Cameroon	0.25	Yes
Vietnam	0.27	Yes
Gabon	0.3	No
Ivory Coast	0.34	No
Middle Congo	0.4	No
Madagascar	1.06	Yes
Senegal	1.09	No
Djibouti	2.14	No
Morocco	3.09	Yes
Tunisia	4.46	Yes
Algeria	10.1	Yes

Table 6.4 does not control for other demographic factors. Table 6.5 provides another list of French territories, this time ordered by total population size. The table shows that five of the six territories with nationalist violence were also those with the largest overall populations. One of the most robust findings in the literature on civil war is that places with larger populations are more prone to civil war.[57] Of the most populous territories, Algeria, Morocco, Madagascar, and Tunisia also had a relatively large percentage of settlers. The evidence is thus inconclusive; settlers and violence may not be causally related; instead they could both be artifacts of the overall population size.[58] Given the limits of existing data, it is dif-

---

57.   Paul Collier and Anke Hoeffler, "Greed and Grievance in Civil War," World Bank Report, 2001; and James D. Fearon and David D. Laitin, "Ethnicity, Insurgency, and Civil War," *American Political Science Review*, Vol. 97, No. 1 (February 2003), pp. 75–90.

58.   I also considered the impact of the absolute number of settlers on violence, although the percentage of settlers better captures the visibility of settlers in the population. Places with the largest number of settlers tended to be violent, although again this may be an artifact of overall population size. Elsewhere, I suggest that settlers indirectly affected violence via their impact on colonial government. See Adria Lawrence, "The

ficult to fully ascertain the importance of settlers for violence. A large-N dataset that could test alternative theories while controlling for factors such as population size would be helpful, but reliable cross-national data on colonial territories is currently unavailable.[59]

Table 6.5. Total Population and Violence.

Territories	Population 1,000s	Violence
Djibouti	56	No
Comoros	142	No
Gabon	409	No
Mauritania	518	No
Middle Congo	684	No
Togo	982	No
Oubangui-Chari	1072	No
Laos	1169	No
Dahomey	1505	No
Senegal	1992	No
Niger	2029	No
Ivory Coast	2066	No
Guinea	2180	No
Chad	2241	No
Cameroon	3006	Yes
Upper Volta	3070	No
French Sudan	3164	No
Tunisia	3231	Yes
Madagascar	4207	Yes
Morocco	8617	Yes
Algeria	8682	Yes
Vietnam	22663	Yes

Competitive Origins of Nationalist Violence," *International Security*, forthcoming.

59. A large-N dataset would also create new problems for analysis because it would include territories from other empires, yet settler populations may not have affected colonial decision-making in the same way in each empire. French settlers had an unusual amount of leverage in the central government in Paris and may thus have had more control over policy than settlers in other empires. See Spruyt, *Ending Empire*.

REPRESSION AND THE LIKELIHOOD OF VIOLENCE

Thus far, I have discussed the potential of state repression to explain the distribution of nationalist violence across the empire indirectly, via the strength of the movement, the type of settlement, and the presence of settlers. These factors may be associated with increased reliance on repression. But good direct comparative measurements of repression in the French Empire are difficult to assemble, in part because repression was fairly ubiquitous. The French were not bound by democratic principles outside mainland France, and ruled their colonial territories using authoritarian means. They frequently used repression against those seen as potential agitators; colonial administrators often jailed, exiled, and even killed those suspected of harboring ill feeling toward the French regime. Those targeted had no recourse to French courts of justice. My suspicion is that French repression was far too widespread to explain why some territories turned violence, while others did not.[60] Certainly, secondary sources suggest that repressive measures were used in many of the territories that never exploded with nationalist violence. But direct cross-colony testing awaits betters measures of state repression. In section three of this chapter, I make use of sub-national data on French repression in Morocco to consider the ability of state repression to account for the use of violence.

OTHER MEASURES OF INJUSTICE AND THE LIKELIHOOD OF VIOLENCE

The presence of settlers and the use of repression are both indicators of the injustices that accompanied colonial rule, but there are other indicators. Other forms of colonial injustice, such as forced labor, mandatory service in the French Army during times of war, and economic exploitation are also potential triggers of violence, if colonial injustice exacerbates nationalist conflict and raises the probability of violence. Secondary works on the colonial period, however, suggest that these factors were far more prevalent in the peaceful parts of the empire than the violent cases, with the notable exception of Algeria. In Syria, Tunisia, and Morocco, colonial rule was exploitive, but some native institutions were preserved and conditions were often better than they were in other parts of the empire.[61] In the territories of French West Africa and French Equatorial Africa, along with Algeria, indigenous populations were subject to the Native Code, which laid out penalties for the most minor infractions or perceived slights to French rule. Indigenous populations were required to fulfill *la corvée*—

---

60. See Lawrence, "Competitive Origins." This article disaggregates state repression and argues that only particular kinds of repression matter for violence. Specifically, it finds that decapitation of the nationalist leadership prompted actors to turn to violence to compete for leadership of the remaining movement. Leadership repression was only effective in silencing opposition if it was carried out when the movement was small and largely made up of elites.

61. Native leaders were preserved in Morocco and Tunisia, and the French often ruled through traditional elites. Syria had an elected parliament, which was limited by French authority but nonetheless was a form of representation absent in other French possessions.

forced labor on public works. Africans also served in both world wars, and were sometimes forcibly conscripted.[62] These types of exploitation are therefore unlikely to differentiate violent and non-violent territories. It is doubtful that Africans failed to violently rebel against French rule because they were more satisfied with it than those in other territories, given the persistent injustices of colonial rule in Africa. Indeed, Africans in Madagascar and Cameroon did employ violence, suggesting that there is nothing particular about Africa that made African subjects unwilling or unable to use violence.

Sub-national Evidence: Violence in Colonial Morocco

The Moroccan nationalist movement began in January 1944 with the creation of the *Istiqlal* (Independence) Party, the first organization in French Morocco to begin openly advocating independence. From 1944–1952, the *Istiqlal* Party was the dominant voice of Moroccan nationalism, advocating independence using peaceful means of protest and diplomacy. Nationalist violence began in 1952 and lasted through independence in 1956. The use of violence varied: an urban terrorist campaign opposed the French in a number of towns and cities, and a rural insurgency began in 1955 in remote mountain regions. Variation in the use and prevalence of violence across Morocco provides an opportunity to consider some of the hypotheses linking conflict escalation to violence at the sub-national level. In this section, I draw upon a dataset of violent events in urban Morocco to test competing explanations.[63] The data concern the campaign of urban terror, which entailed 4,520 armed attacks from August 20, 1953 to April 6, 1956, including assassination attempts, bomb attacks, arson, and sabotage.[64]

The most prominent explanation for nationalist violence in Morocco is the French decision to exile the Moroccan sultan. The sultan had worked with the French for many years, but in the post-war era, he began to show signs that he supported nationalist aspirations. The French administration

---

62.   During World War I, several episodes of resistance occurred in Africa in response to the efforts of French administrators to conscript soldiers, sometimes forcibly. On West Africa during World War I, see Alice L. Conklin, *A Mission to Civilize: The Republican Idea of Empire in France and West Africa, 1895–1930* (Stanford: Stanford University Press, 1997), chap. 5.

63.   My thanks to historian Mohammed Zade at *Le Haut Commissariat aux Anciens Résistants et Anciens Membres de l'Armée de Libération* in Rabat for providing me with data on the urban terror campaign. The data are drawn from two French newspapers: *le Petit Marocain* and *Maroc-Presse*, and two Arabic ones: *As-sa`âda* and *Al-`umma*. Arabic newspapers were severely censored by the French, but these papers were published in the Spanish zone. On the nationalist press, see Amina Aouchar, *La Presse Marocaine dans la lutte pour l'indépendance (1933–1956)* (Casablanca: Wallada, 1990).

64.   Acts of sabotage include the destruction of harvests and farm equipment owned by settlers and Moroccan sympathizers, attacks on telephone and electrical grids, and a spectacular sabotage of the rail line, which derailed the Casablanca-Algiers train on November 7, 1953.

decided it would be easier to maintain French rule without their increasingly recalcitrant partner and deposed him in August 1953. The majority of violent events followed his deposition, and violent resistance has been widely portrayed as an expression of outrage and loyalty to him.[65] The dominant story therefore fits an account that sees violence resulting from the worsening conflict between the French and the nationalists. French intransigence was manifested through the decision to exile the Moroccan leader, an action that exacerbated anger and frustration, and drove the nationalists to arms.

Another factor besides the sultan's dethronement may also have affected the eruption of violence: the presence of French settlers. Morocco had the second largest settler population in the empire. The 1952 census of French Morocco lists 7,442,000 Muslims, 363,000 non-Muslims (largely Europeans), and 199,000 Jews living in the French zone of Morocco. Table 6.6 lists the twenty-five most violent towns in Morocco, and gives the percentage of the town's population that was made up of settlers. Many of the most violent towns do indeed have a large proportion of Europeans, well above the national average of 4.4 percent European.

Variation in settler populations across Moroccan towns facilitates further disentanglement of the relationship between settlers and nationalist violence; settlers may matter for patterns of violence within states. The presence of settlers may suggest the potential permanence of the colonial system. A town with a high proportion of settlers may serve as a continual reminder to the population of the injustices of the political system and the inequality of colonial society. Settlers in Morocco also behaved in ways that may have provoked violence, displaying racism and superiority in their interactions with the population.[66] Indeed, one Moroccan likened the settler presence to the apartheid system in South Africa.[67] The presence of settlers also provides obvious targets for militant groups, so we might expect settler towns to experience more violence.

---

65. Those who attribute violence to the deposition include: Stéphane Bernard, *Le conflit Franco-Marocain 1943–1956* (Brussels: Editions de l'Institut de Sociologie de l'Université Libre de Bruxelles, 1963), p. 192; Abdelmajid Benjelloun, "Contribution à l'étude du mouvement nationaliste marocain dans l'ancienne zone nord du Maroc," Thèse, Université Hassan II, Casablanca, Faculté des Sciences Juridique Economiques et Sociales, 1983, p. 420; Selma Lazraq, *La France et le retour de Mohammed V* (Paris: l'Harmattan, 2003); Bernard Lugan, *Histoire du Maroc des origines à nos jours* (Paris: Perrin, 2000); Wilfred Knapp, *North West Africa: A Political and Economic Survey* (Oxford: Oxford University Press, 1977), p. 280; David Montgomery Hart, *The Aith Waryaghar of the Moroccan Rif: An Ethnography and History* (Tucson: University of Arizona Press, 1976), p. 423.

66. On the settler community in Morocco, see Daniel Rivet, *Le Maroc de Lyautey à Mohammed V: le double visage du protectorat* (Paris: Editions Denoel, 1999), p. 363–365. He compares them to the white community in South Africa, and suggests that tensions multiplied in the post–war era.

67. Leila Abouzeid, author and daughter of nationalists, interviewed by author, Rabat, Morocco, February 15, 2006. Abouzeid remembered watching settlers board first-class train compartments, while Moroccans had to board lower-class cars at the rear of the train from a separate platform.

I test the two main explanations for nationalist violence in Morocco using data from the urban terror campaign. The unit of analysis is towns with a population greater than 1,000 (see Map 6.1).

I test the relationship between settlers and violence by positing that towns where Europeans make up a larger proportion of the population are more likely to experience violence than towns where they constitute only a small portion of the population.

Table 6.6. Morocco's Most Violent Towns, 1953–1955.

Town	% European	# Violent events
Casablanca	19.7	1945
Rabat	26.1	273
Meknes	15.2	271
Fez	8.8	142
Marrakech	5.7	124
Oujda	33.8	110
Fedala	15.5	97
Settat	3.5	75
Kenitra	15.9	65
Safi	6.8	57
Khemisset	5.5	51
Sale	4.8	41
El Jadida	7.4	34
Berrechid	11.8	32
Berkane	18.7	30
Benahmed	5.4	27
El-Kelaa des Srarhna	3.6	25
Azrou	6.9	21
Beni-Mellal	2.8	19
Khenifra	4.7	19
Khouribga	17.8	17
Oued Zem	9.0	14
Agadir	20.1	13
Taza	18.5	10

Map 6.1. Towns in French Colonial Morocco.[68]

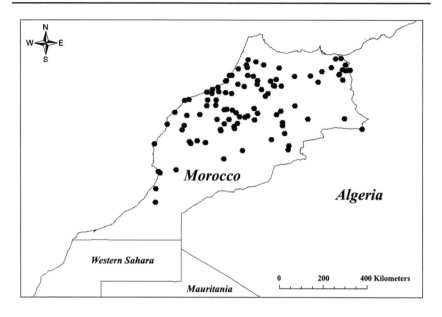

I also constructed a variable to test the hypothesis that loyalty to the sultan prompted violence. Moroccan towns were not equally likely to be outraged by the sultan's deposition; some had a longer history of rule by the sultanate and were more likely to be loyal to him. I coded towns in the south that were not historically controlled by the sultan, but spent most of the colonial rule under the thumb of the "Grand *Caids*" like the infamous al-Glawi. Such an instrument is imperfect, but it does attempt to differentiate between places in Morocco that were more likely to be loyal to the sultan from those that had fewer historical ties to the sultanate. The variable is a dummy variable which is coded 1 if the town fell in Tuhami al-Glawi's portion of the country, and 0 if it fell in the area of the country traditionally ruled by the sultan.

I also included several control variables: the logged population of each town, the percentage of the population that is Jewish, [69] and proximity to rail lines. The dependent variable is coded for each location with the total number of violent events from August 1953 to December 1955. I use a negative binomial model because the pattern of violent events, like many event count data, presents the problem of overdispersion. Table 6.7 summarizes the results.

---

68.   Map generated by author.

69.   French officials in Morocco suggested that anti-Semitism drove violence. I include the percentage Jewish even though I doubted the validity of this claim; the excluded population group is therefore Moroccan Muslims.

Table 6.7. Negative Binomial Regression Estimates of Violent Events in Moroccan Towns.

Independent Variables	Model 1 Coefficient	Model 2 Coefficient	Model 3 Coefficient
% European	.054 (.042)	-0.06* (.024)	-0.06* .(.024)
Glawi Territory	1.2 (1.273)	.056 (.681)	.052 (.695)
Log Population		1.60** (.190)	1.64** (.211)
% Jewish	4.980 (7.035)	-3.77 (2.85)	-3.70 (2.90)
Distance to rail	-2.269** (.727)	-0.463 (.480)	-.462 (.489)
Constant	2.725** (.792)	-11.63** (1.67)	-12.00** (1.87)
N	97	97	96

*p < 0.05 level   **p < 0.01

NOTES: Standard errors in parentheses. Model 3 drops Casablanca.[70] A likelihood-ratio test permits rejection of the null hypothesis of equidispersion.

The results do not support the hypothesis that towns with a higher proportion of settlers experienced more violence. In Model 1, the presence of settlers has a positive coefficient, although the result is insignificant. However, when logged population is added (Models 2 and 3), the settler variable becomes significant, but in the opposite direction from what we might expect. Controlling for population, a higher proportion of settlers actually had a *negative* effect on the incidence of violence. For every one-unit increase in the percentage of settlers, the expected number of violent events decreases by about six percent.[71] Places with a high percentage of settlers may have better policing, which may deter organizations from

70.   The city of Casablanca accounted for nearly 55 percent of violent events in Morocco, and thus is a major outlier. Casablanca was a hub of the urban violence campaign. While urban attacks were not coordinated by a central actor, many resistance groups in other towns began as offshoots of organizations in Casablanca or were made up of migrants to Casablanca who had witnessed the tactics of violent organizations, and returned to their home towns to organize terrorist cells. In Model 3, I dropped the city in case it was skewing the results, but a larger percentage of settlers continued to be associated with a lower number of violent events.

71.   I carried out two other tests that are not reported here. A test using absolute number of settlers rather than percentage of the population produced similar findings. I also tested to see whether the presence of settlers had a non-linear effect on violence, hypothesizing that areas with either very few settlers or a very high percentage of settlers would be less violent. I found no support for this hypothesis.

carrying out armed attacks. I also found no evidence that areas ruled by al-Glawi rather than the sultan were less susceptible to violence; towns with a long-standing connection to the sultan were not more violent in the wake of his deposition. The findings fail to demonstrate that French intransigence, measured by the presence of settlers or the affront to those loyal to the sultan, accounts for the distribution of violence across Morocco. The only consistently significant variable is population size. Larger towns experienced more violent events than smaller towns. These results support the view advanced in the previous section that violence is associated with large population centers, not with settler colonies.

Sub-national data can also illustrate some of the problems with associating state repression and violence. I compiled data on repression from *bulletins de renseignement* (information reports) issued by the political bureau of the French Residency in Morocco on a monthly, bi-weekly, or weekly basis for the entire colonial period. These reports summarize the main events in the protectorate for the specified time period and include information from civil controllers in the different administrative regions of Morocco. Each description of a nationalist event describes the response of the administration, detailing the actions of the police and the numbers of arrests, if repression occurred. If there were casualties, the reports typically list any available figures. Drawing on the reports, I coded whether or not the French employed repression for each month of the entire colonial period. Specifically, I coded a month as repressive if the French carried out political arrests or violently attacked those leading or participating in nationalist events.

These reports provide a unique opportunity to investigate the effects of repression. This kind of data is typically difficult to come by; most authoritarian regimes do not provide information on their use of repression. We might expect that the French would underreport their use of repression, but in fact, there is little evidence that they were reluctant to discuss their use of repression, perhaps because the reports were initially classified as secret. Indeed, in some places the reports betray a certain pride in the use of repression; one report described repression in 1937 as "swift and just."[72]

The overall picture of repression in Morocco does not support the hypothesis that nationalist violence follows state repression. Repression was simply too ubiquitous to explain why violence happened in particular times and places. Out of the 263 total months of colonial rule, the French repressed political activists during 71 months, nearly a third of the colonial period. Violent events mainly occurred in the last 33 months of the period. Figure 6.1 shows the pattern of repression for the colonial period.

---

72. *Bulletin de Renseignements Politiques et Economiques*, Novembre 1936, SHAT 3H1413.

Figure 6.1. French Repression in Morocco, 1934–1956.

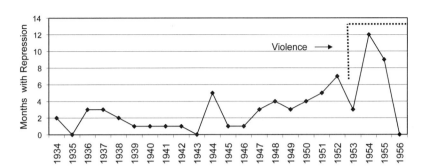

Repression occurs throughout the period; 1936 and 1937 saw three months of repression, while 1944 had five months of repression, and 1952 had seven months of repression, yet nationalist violence did not follow repression at any of these times. Moreover, we might expect repression to be highest in the period just prior to the eruption of violence if it is a trigger of violence, yet repression takes a downward turn in 1953, just before violent events really started to take off with the deposition of the sultan in August. Repression jumps to its highest point in 1954, after the campaign of nationalist violence has already begun. Every single month in 1954 saw some repressive action by the French, suggesting that repression was a response to the eruption of violence in 1953, not a cause of it.

Repression may be associated with nationalist action more broadly, rather than violence in particular.[73] Once again, a potential explanation for violence is confounded by the relative rarity of the phenomenon. Repression in Morocco cannot account for the non-occurrence of violence for much of the colonial period: it happened too often.

Conclusion

I began this chapter by asking whether we should conceptualize violence as the outcome of escalating conflict, a higher degree of conflict, or as a different and distinctive form of conflict. In both the theoretical and empirical discussions, I attempted to find ways to link unresolved conflict to the eruption of violence, but with little success. Both theoretical and empirical considerations suggest that violence cannot be treated as the unproblematic outgrowth of non-violent conflict. Non-violent conflict does not appear to escalate to violence when conflict reaches a particular duration or level of intensity.

73.   Elsewhere, I have found an association between the use of repression and the occurrence of non-violent nationalist events in Morocco, but this association does not imply causality. It is unclear whether repression causes mobilization or results from it. See Lawrence, "Imperial Rule," chap. 3.

I have drawn upon cases from the French empire to evaluate the connection between intransigent conflict and the eruption of nationalist violence. The problem with seeing colonial intransigence as the cause of nationalist violence in the French empire is that measures of colonial intransigence fail to differentiate the non-violent cases from the violent cases. At best, colonial intransigence is a necessary condition for nationalist violence, but only in the most trivial sense. Colonial intransigence is necessary for there to be any sort of conflict between nationalists and the colonial power, because if the colonial power were to immediately give up its claim and depart at the first call for national independence, we would not expect to observe peaceful or violent nationalist opposition. But colonial intransigence cannot answer the most important questions about nationalist violence: it cannot tell us which conflicts will turn violent, or when violence will erupt.

The French empire is only one context, and the results may not generalize to all instances of nationalist conflict. Yet the results are surprising. The selection of these cases should, if anything, be biased in favor of an account that sees violence as the outgrowth of an unresolved, deeply entrenched conflict. These cases are perhaps the archetype of the kind of places where we would expect to see violence escalating from an ongoing nationalist struggle. After all, the dominant explanations for violence in the French empire suggest that colonial intransigence was the key factor that led to violence, and case histories confirm that colonial subjects were angry and frustrated with the indignities and inequality of French rule and actively opposed it. If intractable, escalating conflict cannot explain the turn to violence in these cases, there are good reasons to expect that it likewise cannot explain the use of violence in other cases of nationalist conflict.

Decoupling conflict from violence is highly counterintuitive. Skeptics of this approach will surely state that in the end, violence is about the conflict, so clearly the conflict must play a causal role in the violence. Violence seems intrinsically linked to the underlying conflict, and indeed it is. Ongoing nationalist conflict provides a language and justification for violence; violent actors invoke the conflict and may be motivated by their desire to see the conflict resolved. But violence is a very specific outcome that only happens in a fraction of conflicts. Often, actors in conflict rely on non-violent strategies, which may either be disruptive (such as protest or other non-violent contentious action), or involve working through existing political channels to advocate change. Persistent conflict occurs far too often to serve as the basis for an explanation for the rare outcome of violence.

The explanations I have evaluated in this chapter do not exhaust the possible causes of nationalist violence; my goal has been to test only those that come from conceptualizing violence as the natural outgrowth of intractable conflict. To investigate nationalist violence as a distinct form of conflict and develop theories to explain why nationalist violence erupts in particular times and places, we need to turn away from explanations that point to conditions that are common in both violent and non-violent settings, and consider those that can account for the rarity of violence. This requires thinking of violence as a dynamic process that evolves over time, rather than looking only at stable factors designed to distinguish violent and non-violent places. The factors I considered here largely operate at the macro-level: the duration of the conflict, the type of regime, the presence of settlers, and the existence of institutionalized injustice. These variables are suitable for comparing different places, but have little to say about the timing of violence. We need to tie macro factors that raise the probability of violence in a particular place to mechanisms that lead to the specific outcome of violence at particular points in time.

Scholars of violence are beginning to meet this challenge. In this volume, Kathleen Gallagher Cunningham and Emily Beaulieu consider the conditions that prompt non-state actors to embrace violent strategies. H. Zeynep Bulutgil shows that timing and context are crucial for explaining the phenomenon of ethnic cleansing. Elsewhere, I have posited an explanation for nationalist violence in the French empire by looking not at the *longue-durée* consequences of colonial rule, but at specific colonial policies that fragmented certain nationalist movements and produced violence. I argue that competition among nationalist groups, rather than the conflict between the nationalists and the imperial power, creates incentives to use violence.[74] These kinds of explanations consider not only the kinds of places where violence might occur, but also the dynamics that produce incentives for violence at particular moments in time. More research and better data can help unravel the question of when and where nationalist violence is likely to erupt.

---

74. Lawrence, "Competitive Origins."

Chapter 7

Dissent, Repression, and Inconsistency

Kathleen Gallagher Cunningham and
Emily Beaulieu

States of all kinds repress dissent—both violent and non-violent protest. What are the effects of such repression? Much attention has been devoted to understanding whether repression increases or decreases dissent in general and whether repression of specific protest strategies, violent or non-violent, can induce dissidents to change tactics. Findings have been mixed, with support found for both the ideas that repression quells dissent and encourages it, and that when targeted at a specific kind of dissent, repression can make dissidents change tactics.[1] Although these existing works all focus on the importance of repression by the state, none look systematically at *how* this repression takes place. To date, studies of the effect of repression largely ignore the extreme variation in consistency with which states repress dissenters. States frequently respond in what appears to be an erratic fashion to dissidents, sometimes ignoring their activities and other times repressing the same activities ruthlessly.

In this chapter, we enter the debate about the effects of repression, looking specifically at the "substitution hypothesis," which is that repression of violent or non-violent dissent can induce dissidents to switch tactics. We argue that the effects of repression in this context will be conditional on the consistency with which states employ repression. We test this empirically on event data from dissent and repression in Europe. The nov-

The authors would like to thank David Cunningham and Irfan Nooruddin. Comments from Erik Gartzke and Will Moore on earlier drafts of this project were also helpful. Of course, any errors or omissions are the responsibility of the authors.

1.   See Douglas A. Hibbs, *Mass Political Violence: A Cross-National Causal Analysis* (New York: Wiley, 1973); Mark Irving Lichbach and Ted Robert Gurr, "The Conflict Process: A Formal Model," *Journal of Conflict Resolution*, Vol. 25, No. 1 (March 1981), pp. 3–29; Eduard A. Ziegenhagen, *The Regulation of Political Conflict* (Westport, Conn.: Praeger, 1968); Ronald A. Francisco, "Coercion and Protest: An Empirical Test in Two Democratic States," *American Journal of Political Science,* Vol. 40, No. 4 (November 1996), pp. 1179–1204; Christian Davenport, "State Repression and Political Order," *Annual Review of Political Science,* Vol.10, No.1 (June 2007), pp.1–23; and Adam Przeworski, *Democracy and the Market: Political and Economic Reforms in Eastern Europe and Latin America* (Cambridge: Cambridge University Press 1991).

elty of this approach is twofold. First, the role of consistency has largely been ignored in studies of dissent behavior, and we will fill a critical gap by examining it here.[2] Second, most of the literature on dissent examines the choice to use violence as dichotomous—dissidents are violent or not. We focus on the related choices to use violent and non-violent tactics by dissidents, allowing for the possibility of a mixed strategy of dissent. There is no reason to think that dissidents will not use both violent and non-violent tactics at the same time. Thus we frame our research question to ask: How does the use of repression affect dissident choices to use more or less violent or non-violent dissent? By allowing for dissidents to mix types of dissent in their overall strategy, we gain a more accurate understanding of how repression affects dissent behavior.

The chapter proceeds as follows. We present the theory in three steps. First, we introduce a basic Rational Actor (RA) model which lays out how dissidents make strategic decisions about how to challenge the state.[3] In this model, dissidents weigh the costs and benefits of dissent as they determine how much effort to put into violent and non-violent tactics. The state is assumed to be the main source of the costs and benefits that inform dissident choices. Second, we introduce the concept of consistency of repression, explaining why states are likely to be inconsistent and how this will affect dissident choices about protest behavior. We then argue that the effect of repression on dissent will be conditional on the consistency with which it is used, and we specify hypotheses that follow from our theory. Following this, we provide empirical evidence through a quantitative study of minority dissent in Europe and a qualitative examination of dissent in Northern Ireland. The final section offers concluding thoughts.

A Theory of Dissent Choice

Disaffected citizens protest in a number of ways—for example, lobbing bombs into buildings, hunger strikes, marches, or sit-ins. Some protest tactics entail purposeful violence against the state, while others are expressly non-violent. For example, Basque separatists have engaged in bombing campaigns and hostage-taking, but also use non-violent mass demonstrations to press their demands on the Spanish state. How do dissidents choose which tactics to use, and to what extent so they mix violent and non-violent protest?

In order to make that decision, they consider both the potential costs and benefits of specific dissent tactics (i.e., the expected utility) and compare these costs and benefits across available tactics. Following Mark

2. An important exception to this is Karen Rasler's study of repression in Iran. See Karen Rasler, "Concessions, Repression, and Political Protest in the Iranian Revolution," *American Sociological Review,* Vol. 61, No. 1 (February 1996), pp. 132–152.

3. This follows on Mark Irving Lichbach, "Deterrence or Escalation? The Puzzle of Aggregate Studies of Repression and Dissent," *Journal of Conflict Resolution,* Vol. 31, No. 2 (June 1987), pp. 266–297.

Lichbach, we assume that both the absolute and relative costs and benefits associated with each type of dissent are determined by the state.[4] The cost of dissent is incurred via state repression and some fixed costs of resources and time.[5] Benefits also emanate from the state in the form of accommodation, and while we believe accommodation is important for groups to consider when determining strategies of dissent, we assume that the effects of accommodation on strategy are independent of the effects of repression; therefore we focus solely on repression in this chapter.

ACTORS, TACTICS, AND GOALS

Dissidents are a subset of the population who have chosen to protest a grievance against the state. We conceive of dissident grievance in terms of some preferred policy outcome that differs from the state's preference. The particular policy may vary across cases, but all dissidents seek some policy change. Again following on Lichbach, we assume that dissidents act in a cohesive and coordinated manner. Lichbach uses the notion of a "team" to think about choices made by the group.[6] Dissident elites determine the overall strategy of the group, and the activities are then carried out by individuals in the group.

Once the decision to protest has been made, dissident elites must decide what kinds of tactics to use. We classify dissident tactics as either violent or non-violent.[7] The chosen mix of dissent tactics will be based on the tactics' expected costs and benefits, with dissidents attempting to minimize costs and maximize benefits. Because part of the cost of dissent is paid when the state responds to dissident activity with repression, dissidents must make an informed guess about the likely costs of dissent tactics. Previous treatments of this basic Rational Actor model of dissent choice have assumed that the costs associated with dissent are known, but we raise the question of how dissidents might actually make this estimation of the costs of their actions.

Here, we propose that tactical choices about dissent are made through a dynamic process in which dissidents estimate both the amount of re-

---

4. Ibid.

5. There is some possibility that certain challenging groups might perceive state repression to be a benefit to their cause, but such a benefit is clearly a means to some other desired policy end. This may be the case if, for example, it makes domestic audiences or outside supporters more sympathetic to the group's cause. In such cases, the cost of state repression might be mitigated to some degree by the perceived short-term benefit. It is unlikely, however, that even groups who view state repression as beneficial to their cause in the short term also see that repression as totally costless. In other words, we do not believe that any dissident group finds repression to be purely beneficial.

6. Mark Irving Lichbach, "Deterrence or Escalation?"

7. We can think about the mix of violent and non-violent dissent that a challenging group ultimately chooses in various ways: the number of different activities being undertaken, the number of individuals involved in these activities, or the number of days in which dissent occurs. In our analysis, we examine dissent activities as the relative number of dissent activities (violent and non-violent), counted as distinct protest events, and the number of days each protest takes place.

pression the state will employ and the likelihood that repression will be incurred for any particular instance of dissent. Thus, dissidents use a process of updating to adjust their expectations about the costs of violent and non-violent dissent tactics. To do this, dissidents look at two factors related to the past behavior of the state—how strong the repressive responses have been to a particular dissent tactic, and how consistently the state has employed this response.

The state is also assumed to act in a somewhat cohesive manner and seeks to maintain the status quo against which dissidents protest. State elites make decisions about the level of repression that will be used in response to a particular instance of dissent, and agents of the state execute the determined level of repression. As we elaborate in the next section, slippage between the principal (the state) and its agent (security forces employing repression) is a key source of inconsistency in states' repressive policies.

State elites must decide how much repression to employ in response to violent and non-violent tactics. We look at the responses to violence and non-violence separately, because states will take the type of dissent into consideration when determining a repressive response, especially if they want to curtail one type of dissent. We assume states would like to minimize dissent, and violent dissent in particular, as it is costly to the state.[8] Beyond this preference, particular states can vary in their willingness to use repression, from those who readily employ repression to those who use repression with extreme reservation. Several factors are likely to play into elite preferences about repression of violent and non-violent dissent. In general, states appear to use repression more readily in response to violent dissent, no doubt because it is easier to justify to relevant audiences than repression of non-violent dissent, and perhaps because it poses a greater threat to the state. Certain aspects of the dissident group or dissent activity in question may also affect the state's repressive response.[9] The state may perceive some benefit from repression, for instance, if it limits the extent to which the challenging group uses violence to press its demands in the future. It may receive an additional benefit if its repression of one group discourages certain protest tactics on the part of other challenging groups.[10] Dissidents will generally know if their state favors repression or not, but state attitudes toward repression can also change

8. Though preserving the status quo and minimizing violent dissent are goals of the state, we know empirically that repression can also work to galvanize the challenging group and inspire more violence, as Karen Rasler suggests it did in Iran. Karen Rasler, "Concessions, Repression, and Political Protest in the Iranian Revolution."

9. Davenport finds that various aspects of dissent, including frequency, range of tactics, and deviance of dissent from culturally accepted norms, will all affect the state's decision to employ repression. Christian Davenport, "The Weight of the Past: Exploring Lagged Determinants of Political Repression," *Political Research Quarterly*, Vol. 49, No. 2 (June 1996), pp.377–403.

10. Barbara F. Walter, "Building Reputation: Why Governments Fight Some Separatists but Not Others," *American Journal of Political Science*, Vol. 50, No. 2 (April 2006), pp.313–330.

quickly, making it necessary that dissidents update their estimations of the repression-based costs of dissent.[11]

This Rational Actor framework is a commonly used model of dissent. One of the central findings from this model is the substitution hypothesis, which posits that repression of one dissent tactic will raise the costs of that tactic and induce dissidents to substitute another alternative. Put another way, states can make dissidents use more violence by increasing the costs of non-violence through repression and vice versa.[12]

Substitution hypotheses:

H_1: Controlling for state repression of non-violence, increasing state repression of violence will *decrease* the likelihood of violence relative to non-violence.

H_2: Controlling for state repression of violence, increasing state repression of non-violence will *decrease* the likelihood of non-violence relative to violence.

We do not disagree with these predictions, but studies of the substitution hypothesis do not take into account the consistency of repression, which should affect the costs-benefit analysis that lead dissidents to substitute tactics. The next section will explain how consistency of repression should affect dissent strategies and build on these original substitution hypotheses.

CONSISTENCY OF REPRESSION AND ITS EFFECTS

Consistency refers to the variation in how frequently repression is used for the same dissent tactic, distinct from the level of repression the state employs.[13] For example, if riots are met with force at some times but not others, the state is responding inconsistently, regardless of whether force is employed at high or low levels on the occasions when repression is used.[14]

---

11. Mark J. C. Crescenzi, "Violence and Uncertainty in Transitions," *Journal of Conflict Resolution*, Vol. 43, No. 2 (April 1999), pp. 192–212.

12. This was first articulated by Lichbach then tested by Moore. Lichbach, "Deterrence or Escalation?"; and Will H. Moore, "Repression and Dissent: Substitution, Context, and Timing," *American Journal of Political Science*, Vol. 42, No. 3 (July 1998), pp. 851–873.

13. We could also think about consistency as just a variable level of repression ranging from none to high levels. We have chosen to examine consistency distinct from a level of repression because it may have different effects at different levels of repression. An advantage of our approach is that the level of response may be dictated by the level of violence or by the scope of protest. In that case, different levels of repression could be understood to be inconsistent behavior, when in reality they are designed to respond to different levels of dissent behavior.

14. Lichbach also discusses inconsistency in his RA model, but his notion is somewhat different than ours in that it refers to the use of repression *and* accommodation in response to dissent. See Lichbach, "Deterrence or Escalation?"

State elites decide on a level of repression in response to dissent, but the consistency of such responses can be compromised for two reasons. First, the actual process of repressing involves a potential principal-agent problem. State elites—the principal—decide that some acts of dissent warrant a repressive response. They dispatch security forces (police or military) to carry out the repression. Security forces engage in repressive tactics with varying degrees of oversight, leadership, and self-restraint. The less clear the policy directing a repressive response is and the less oversight of the execution of the policy there is, the more room for discretion there will be among the security forces physically responding. This allows security forces—the agents—to enact state policy to varying degrees in different situations, creating inconsistency in the state's overall response to dissent activities.[15]

A second source of inconsistency in state responses to dissent is the multiple constraints states have on their behavior beyond their interaction with a particular group of dissidents. Scott Gartner and Patrick Regan argue that the decision to repress is constrained by both domestic and international factors.[16] Such factors might include domestic political considerations (elections, other dissident actors), external threats (war on terror, international war), or characteristics of the government (change in leadership, coalition governments), which can affect both the willingness and capacity of states to employ repression. The particular domestic and international factors confronting a state at any point in time may affect its ability and willingness to use or refrain from using repression, and may change quickly. Christian Davenport also identifies attributes of dissident behavior that may influence the likelihood of encountering repression.[17] Moreover, Bryan Borphy-Baermann and John A.C. Conybeare introduce the possibility that governments make discretionary, as opposed to rule-based, decisions about repression, which would likely lead to inconsistencies in state policy.[18] Both principal-agent problems and the complex nature of the state's decision calculus with respect to repression invite the possibility that some states will be more consistent than other states, or more consistent at varying points in time, in their use of repression.

Several questions emerge from thinking about states using repression inconsistently. If states repress one tactic—violence or non-violence, but do so inconsistently, will the dissidents substitute the other tactic as Mark

---

15. In particular, periods of occupation or peacekeeping leave a great deal of room for the inconsistent application of repression.

16. Scott Sigmund Gartner and Patrick M. Regan, "Threat and Repression: The Non-Linear Relationship between Government and Opposition Violence," *Journal of Peace Research*, Vol. 33, No. 3 (August 1996), pp. 273–287.

17. Davenport finds that various aspects of dissent, including frequency, range of tactics, and deviance of dissent from culturally accepted norms will all affect the state's decision to employ repression. Christian Davenport, "The Weight of the Past."

18. Bryan Brophy-Baermann and John A. C. Conybeare, "Retaliating against Terrorism: Rational Expectations and the Optimality of Rules versus Discretion," *American Journal of Political Science*, Vol. 38, No. 1 (February 1994), pp. 196–210.

Lichbach and Will H. Moore suggest?[19] Moreover, is the effect of inconsistency conditional on the type of dissent tactic to which it applies?

We argue that the primary effect of inconsistency on dissidents' tactical choices will be to mute the deterrent qualities of repression that lead dissidents to substitute tactics. The central proposition by Lichbach and Moore is that the state can induce dissidents to shift tactics (violent to non-violent or vice versa) by increasing the relative costs associated with each tactic. However, dissidents must estimate the costs they will incur by examining past interaction with the state. When that state behavior is erratic, it sends a noisy signal to dissidents, making it hard to assess the likely costs of their actions. As such, an inconsistent use of repression will not clearly signal that costs to dissent will be higher, nor will it signal that there is some chance of repression but not a certainty. This leads us to the following hypotheses about dissent strategy:

Conditional substitution hypotheses:
Hypotheses 1 and 2 argue that all else held constant, the repression of one dissent tactic will increase the dissidents' use of the other. This effect should vary depending on the degree of consistency with which repression is used.

H_3: Controlling for state repression of non-violence, as repression of violence becomes less consistent, the substitution effect of repression will *decrease*.

H_4: Controlling for state repression of violence, as repression of non-violence becomes less consistent, the substitution effect of repression will *decrease*.

Testing the Effects of Inconsistency on Dissent

To evaluate these hypotheses, we employ both a quantitative analysis of dissent behavior in a set of European cases and an illustrative case study of repression and dissent in Northern Ireland.

Our quantitative tests examine the effects of repression on dissident tactics conditional on the consistency of repression in a set of European countries from 1980–1995. We use a dataset of twenty-four protesting minority groups in sixteen countries. Our theory speaks to a subset of openly dissident populations, and we seek to understand why some groups use more violent or non-violent tactics, and how the consistency of state repression affects this choice. Although the theory could apply more broadly to any disaffected group in any state, we have selected a sample of somewhat comparable dissident groups by focusing on minority populations that all have grievances against the state. The sample represents any minority groups that engaged in protest during the time period in ques-

---

19. Lichbach, "Deterrence or Escalation?"; and Moore, "Repression and Dissent: Substitution, Context, and Timing."

tion, and are recognized as "at risk" minorities.[20] The decision to limit the scope of this analysis to European countries was a function of available data, but it has the advantage of providing some control for regime type. Essentially, then, we are testing our theory of dissent and repression on minority protest in European democracies.

RELATIVE USE OF VIOLENCE OR NON-VIOLENCE

Our dependent variable captures the relative use of violent or non-violent tactics in dissent behavior. Though many studies focus on when actors employ violence against the state and when they do not, this dichotomous characterization is neither empirically supported, nor does it follow from the theoretical model we have outlined here. Dissidents choose to employ some level of violent dissent, often in conjunction with some level of non-violent dissent. To capture the strategy choices that dissidents make, we have designed a dependent variable that measures the dissidents' relative use of non-violent or violent protest, which we call *dissent strategy*. This measure indicates the relative amount of effort (event days) being devoted to non-violent versus violent activities in a given month weighted by the total number of dissent events. The formula is

$$dissent\ strategy = ((nve - ve) \div te) \times 100$$
Where nve = Number of non-violent events,
ve = Number of violent events, and
te = Total number of events

Dissent strategy ranges from -100, totally violent, to 100, totally non-violent. A group that perfectly balances non-violent and violent activities in a given month has a score of zero for dissent strategy. Months with no protest activity are excluded from the analysis, because our focus here is on protest strategy choices, not the decision of whether or not to protest.

"Violent" protest activity includes a range of actions such as armed attacks, hostage-taking, vandalism, and riots. "Non-violent" protest activities include demonstrations, rallies, and symbolic acts, among others. A full list of actions and their coding are available from the authors. Some actions, such as vandalism, were more difficult to designate as violent or non-violent. Our general rule is that any action involving damage to property or bodily harm is considered violent. The raw data from which we constructed our strategy measure codes daily protest and coercion events. Ongoing events, such as hostage crises, are coded for each day they are ongoing.[21] The average dissent strategy score for all minorities in the data set is -34, indicating that as a whole, there is more violent protest activity than non-violent protest.

---

20. Protest data comes from Ron Francisco's European Protest and Coercion Data; the "at risk" characterization of minority groups comes from the Minorities at Risk data set.

21. See Ron Francisco's Codebook for European Protest and Coercion Data for a full description of the event data coding at http://web.ku.edu/ronfran/data/index.html.

LEVELS OF PREVIOUS STATE REPRESSION

In order to estimate the likely costs of dissent, we assume dissidents look at how repressive the state was to their various dissent tactics in the past. To construct a measure of repression costs that captures this process, we create a variable that indicates the average number of repressive actions undertaken by the state in response to each dissent tactic in the previous twelve months (this is a rolling average). Repressive actions include coercive activity directed toward the dissenting group, such as arrests and raids. In order to establish whether the state was responding to violent or non-violent dissent, we designate each month of dissent as a relatively violent or non-violent month. "Violent" months are those where the group's dissent strategy value is lower than its average for the overall timeframe. Likewise, "non-violent" months are those where the group's dissent strategy value is higher than its overall average. By using the group average to determine relative non-violent or violent protest, we can account for changes in strategy across groups that have very different dissent strategies on average. Having established a designation of violent or non-violent dissent activity and information about the repressive responses for that month, we construct the rolling averages of repression to violent and non-violent dissent in the previous twelve months (to create the variable of *repression*).

To capture consistency of repression, we construct a measure of the variance in the state's repressive responses to violent and non-violent dissent over the previous twelve months.[22] With the same data used to construct our rolling averages of repressive responses to violent or non-violent dissent, we calculate standard deviations of those rolling averages. We call this variable *inconsistency*.[23] The greater the value of inconsistency, the less consistent the state has been in its application of repression to dissent.

FINDINGS

To assess the conditional effects of repression and the consistency of its application on dissent tactics, we employ a series of ordinary least squared regressions on dissent strategy. Table 7.1 reports the results of these regressions. The models examine the effects of repression of violent and non-violent dissent conditional on the consistency of repression. Model 1 shows the conditional effect of repression of violent tactics on dissent strategy. This regression includes measures of the level of recent repression, the consistency of this repression, an interaction term of these two

---

22.   Wright and Goldberg discuss the use of variance to gauge uncertainty, asserting that "the greater the variance, the less confident one would be about another's likely behavior." We focus this idea specifically on the cost term in an expected utility calculation. John R. Wright and Arthur S. Goldberg, "Risk and Uncertainty as Factors in the Durability of Political Coalitions," *American Political Science Review*, Vol. 79, No. 3 (September 1985), pp. 704–718.

23.   In cases where there was only one instance of violent or non-violent dissent in the previous twelve months, the *inconsistency* variable is not calculated.

variables, and controls for repression of non-violent tactics and consistency of repression of non-violent activity. Model 2 is similar but examines the conditional effect of repression of non-violent dissent, controlling for the use and consistency of repression of violence. If, as hypotheses one and two suggest, the effect of repression of one tactic is to induce substitution of the other tactic, we should observe that the effect of repression of violence is to decrease the relative use of violence and the repression of non-violence is to decrease the relative use of non-violence. If hypotheses three and four are correct, we should find that the effect of repression differs at varying levels of consistency. Greater inconsistency in the repression should diminish the deterrent effect that leads dissidents to substitute tactics.

Table 7.1. Ordinary Least Squares Regression on Relative Use of Violence or Non-violence.

Regressor	Model 1	s.e.	Model 2	s.e.
Level of Repression of Violence	30.91**	3.06	37.89**	3.46
Inconsistency of Repression of Violence	-23.32	12.18	-33.28**	8.22
Inconsistency*Repression of Violence	-5.94	4.32		
Level of Repression of Non-violence	-6.10	9.24	-5.86	9.68
Inconsistency of Repression of Non-violence	-0.32	10.27	9.26	4.23
Inconsistency*Repression of Non-violence			-8.45	5.75
Constant	-57.76	6.89	-60.66	9.51
R-squared	0.04		0.05	
N	316		316	

**indicates p<.05, two-tailed z test
NOTE: Adjusted R-squared values are not reported for regressions with clustered standard errors.

To interpret the effects of repression of violent and non-violent dissent and consistency of repression on the use of these tactics, we need to examine the marginal effects of repression at different levels of inconsistency. Though the coefficient on the interaction term is not statistically significant, Thomas Brambor, William Roberts Clark, and Matt Golder remind us that "it is perfectly possible for the marginal effect of X on Y to be significant for substantively relevant values of the modifying variable Z even if the coefficient on the interaction term is insignificant."[24] In terms of our analysis, this means that it is possible for a statistically significant relationship to exist between varying levels of repression and dissent tactics, for relevant values of consistency of repression, even if the interaction and constituent terms are not statistically significant. Thus, we

---

24.   Thomas Brambor, William Roberts Clark, and Matt Golder, "Understanding Interaction Models: Improving Empirical Analyses," *Political Analysis*, Vol. 14, No. 1 (Winter 2006), p. 74.

use the Brambor, Clark, and Golder method for graphing the marginal effects of repression on dissent tactics over the range of values for level of inconsistency. Figures 7.1 and 7.2 show this graphically for Models 1 and 2. Both indicate a statistically significant conditional relationship between repression and dissent strategy where increased repression causes dissident groups to substitute tactics. The effects of repression are conditional on the consistency of repression, though in different ways for violent and non-violent tactics.

Figure 7.1. Marginal Effects of Repression of Violent Dissent on Dissident Strategy.

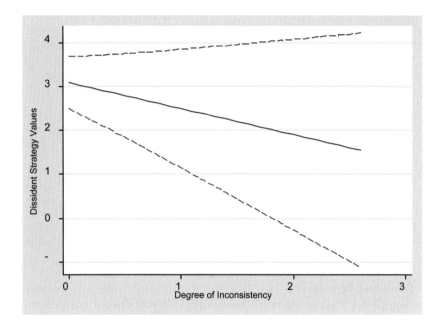

NOTES: ———————— = Marginal effects
– – – – – – – – = Boundaries of 95 percent confidence interval

---

Figure 7.1 depicts the marginal impact of repression of violence on the overall strategy chosen by dissidents. It reveals three important findings. First, portions of the graph where both the upper and lower bounds of the 95 percent confidence interval are above or below zero indicate that there is a statistically significant conditional relationship between repression of violence and dissent strategy. At these values of inconsistency, which include 92 percent of observations in the analysis, the conditional relationship between repression and dissent strategy is statistically significant. Second, because the marginal effects line is in the positive values, we know that repression does deter violence in the sense that dissidents are using more non-violent activities at higher levels of repression. Finally, the downward slope of the marginal effects line indicates that the marginal effects of repression become smaller as inconsistency of repression increases.

This means that repression of violence is less effective at encouraging substitution of non-violent for violent dissent as it is applied less consistently.

Figure 7.2. Marginal Effects of Repression of Non-violent Dissent on Dissident Strategy.

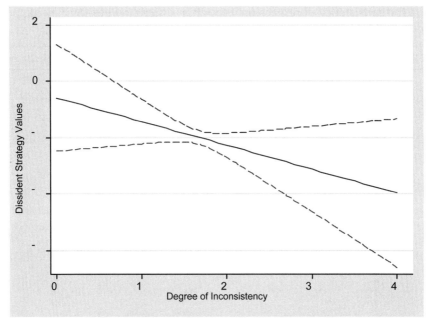

NOTES: ——————— = Marginal effects
------ = Boundaries of 95 percent confidence interval

Figure 7.2 depicts the marginal effects of repression of non-violence and shows that the effects of repression vary with the consistency of repression, but in a different way than repression of violence does. To interpret this graph, we look at the portions of the graph where both the upper and lower bounds of the 95 percent confidence interval are above or below zero. At these levels of inconsistency, there is a statistically significant conditional relationship between repression of non-violence and dissent strategy. Within this range of values, from about .07 onward (about 62 percent of the observations in the analysis), the conditional relationship between repression and dissent strategy is statistically significant. Because the marginal effects line is in the negative values, we know that repression of non-violent dissent leads to a relative increase in the use of violent dissent, which supports Hypothesis 2. However, the downward slope of the marginal effects line indicates that the marginal effects of a repression of non-violence become greater as inconsistency of repression of non-violence increases. This is in contrast to both our expectation in Hypothesis 4 and our findings about the conditional effects of repression on violent dissent, where increased inconsistency of repression mitigated the deterrent effects of repression. This leads us to reject Hypothesis 4. Moreover, the finding suggests that there are additional hazards to repressing non-violent dissent, which we discuss further in the conclusion, and raises the question of whether we should assume that repression will have consistent effects on violent and non-violent dissent.[25]

The Cycle of Dissent and Repression in Northern Ireland over Time

Our large-N study of dissent behavior in Europe demonstrates correlation between repression and dissent and shows that the consistency of repression affects this relationship. Yet there are a number of theoretical links in our story that the quantitative study cannot show. What are the sources of inconsistency? Are dissidents examining state repression and updating their beliefs about the costs of violent and non-violent dissent? Here, a closer examination on the cycle of dissent and repression in Northern Ireland over time can help to show that these mechanisms are at work, and that dissidents adjust their behavior based on the consistency of repression.

The history of Republican protest activity in Northern Ireland and the responses from the state provide further support for our theory that the effects of repression on dissident groups' strategies will be conditional, based on the consistency with which such repression is deployed, and supplements our finding that consistency affects tactical substitution differently, depending on whether the dissent being repressed is violent or non-violent. This case also helps to illustrate a number of the micro-processes that we assume to be at work in our theory.

The period from 1963 to 1976 is characterized as a movement for Catholic civil rights in Northern Ireland that degenerated into the Northern

---

25.   In addition to Models 1 and 2, we ran a series of sensitivity tests. Both models were run with an additional variable indicating whether any accommodation was made to dissidents in a given month. We also clustered the observations on the minority dissident group as opposed to country. Results were similar in both cases. In each of the sensitivity test models, we graphed the marginal effects of repression as we have done in Figures 7.1 and 7.2. For each, the relationship is statistically significant for approximately the same levels of inconsistency, the coefficients are similar in size and sign, and the direction of the marginal effects line is the same. Thus, we find the same conditional relationships between repression of the different dissent strategies and dissent choice hold across these models.

The trajectory of dissident behavior may also affect the dissent choices made in each month. Changing tactics may require additional resources that make the continuance of the same strategy more attractive (e.g., there are bullets left over). Thus, we re-ran the models including both three-month and six-month lags to account for a more general pattern of dissent behavior. The results remained similar. Different points in time may also affect dissent choices as global or regional trends in dissent tactics change. We included dummies for decades and then for years to control for the effect of time. Again the results were not substantially different from the original models. All results from the sensitivity analyses are available from the authors.

Irish "troubles."[26] The start of a civil rights movement marks a shift in the strategic orientation of Catholic activists from an emphasis on armed conflict with the British (1954–1962) toward a mixed strategy that emphasized non-violent dissent. This increased emphasis on non-violent dissent lasted into 1969, at which point violence began to escalate once again and continued to increase until 1973. The period from 1974 to 1976 witnessed another shift away from violent dissent back toward more non-violent protest. These shifts in dissent tactics followed changes in the consistency of state repression in response to Catholic protest activities.

As with every real-world case, the facts on the ground in Northern Ireland are far more complex than the simplified relationship we have isolated in our theory. In the stylized description that follows, we have largely excluded actors such as Unionist (British loyalist) paramilitary groups and the Irish state. This choice is not meant to suggest that such actors made no contribution to the dissent strategies of Northern Irish Republicans, but rather to isolate the impact of the consistency of state repression on Republican protest in Northern Ireland.

Before we can discuss the impact of repression consistency on Republican dissent in Northern Ireland, one important question must be addressed: who is the "state" in this story? For this analysis, we will consider responses from the governments of either Northern Ireland or England. This decision was made for both empirical and theoretical reasons. Empirically, both of these actors responded with repression to Republican dissent during the period we are examining, and had legal grounds for doing so. State responses primarily came from Northern Ireland, until they called in the British Army in 1969; repression then came from both England and Northern Ireland until England suspended Stormont, the Northern Irish Parliament, in May 1972. We believe it makes sense to examine both Northern Irish and English state repression because the Northern Irish state is arguably an extension of the English state, which is certainly how it was perceived by Republican dissidents at the time. Republicans saw their struggle as a dispute with England, whether they were interacting with Westminster directly, or its façade in Stormont.

THE CIVIL RIGHTS MOVEMENT, 1962–1969

The civil rights movement, which began to take shape in 1962, marked a period of increased non-violent protest among Catholic dissidents, such as the Irish Republican Army (IRA). Prior to the advent of the movement for civil rights, Republican dissidents had been involved in a prolonged "Border Campaign" of violence from 1956 to 1962, which had been met with consistent repression from the Northern Irish state, culminating in an extended period of dissident internment without trial, which lasted until April 1961.[27] Thus, the period from 1962 to 1969 was one of a strategic

---

26.   Richard English, *Armed Struggle: The History of the IRA* (New York: Oxford University Press, 2003).

27.   Ibid., p. 73.

shift toward non-violent protest, as consistent repression in response to violence had made violent dissent relatively more costly.

Those who favor a resource mobilization explanation for dissent strategy choices might attribute the lack of violence in this time period to a lack of resources on the part of the IRA.[28] After the violent border campaign, the IRA was typically understood to have limited funding, weapons, and volunteers.[29] Richard English argues, however, that throughout the period from 1962 to 1969, the IRA was rebuilding its forces, which should have been accompanied by an increase in violence, rather than non-violent protest, if resource mobilization explains Republican dissent strategy in this time period.[30]

Indications that a shift toward more non-violent dissent had occurred can be found in a 1966 Republican editorial in *Tuairisc*, a newsletter for the Wolfe Tone Society. This editorial noted that a key obstacle to the burgeoning civil rights movement was "the illusion still current in some pockets of the republican movement that a simple-minded armed struggle against the British occupation is alone sufficient...to complete the national revolution."[31] At the same time that this editorial emphasized the increased importance of non-violent Republican dissent, it also acknowledged that violent dissent might still be appropriate. This qualification suggests that even as non-violent Republican dissent was increasing, violent dissent had not been abandoned altogether as a protest strategy.[32] By mid-1968, however, the bulk of Catholic dissent activity was non-violent. The spring of 1968 witnessed a series of protest marches, and an August 1968 march is cited by some as the first "civil rights" march.[33] Marches continued throughout the fall of 1968, and near-constant protest marches are reported in Derry in November and December 1968, expanding to Newry in the first months of 1969.[34]

The state's use of repression in response to these new protest tactics was not consistent. Some of the earlier 1968 marches drew no repressive response from the state—the August 1968 Dungannon march, for example, was reportedly non-violent.[35] Other times, these marches were met with repression from the government, as in the October 5 March in Der-

28. For a summary of resource mobilization hypotheses, see J. Craig Jenkins, "Resource Mobilization Theory and the Study of Social Movements," *Annual Review of Sociology*, Vol. 9 (1983), pp. 527–553.

29. English, *Armed Struggle*, p. 83.

30. Ibid., p. 84.

31. Ibid., p. 89.

32. The same *Tuairisc* editorial, described in English, *Armed Struggle*, provides some indication that groups actually evaluate costs and benefits in the manner we have suggested. It cited "historical experience" as justification for their advocacy of increased non-violence with the option for future violent dissent to remain open.

33. Sabine Wichert, *Northern Ireland since 1945*, 2nd ed. (London: Longman, 1999), p. 108.

34. Ibid., p. 109–110.

35. English, *Armed Struggle*, p. 100.

ry.[36] By late 1968 and into 1969, however, the state was increasing repression of non-violent protests. A Republican march from Belfast to Derry on the first four days of 1969 encountered repression that Sabine Wichert describes as "police misconduct."[37] "Police misconduct" occurred in several more non-violent protests in 1969, and is a prime example of the sorts of principal-agent problems that can contribute to the inconsistent application of repression.[38] The notion of "misconduct" suggests that individuals with the capacity to implement repression are taking matters into their own hands, rather than following a specific policy set forth by the state.

Historical accounts provide some further insight into why state repression might have been inconsistent during this time period. English notes that "by 1966 unionism was in crisis, divided between reformist and hard-line instincts."[39] Terrence O'Neill assumed the office of North Irish Prime Minister in 1963 with a soft-line agenda.[40] His inclination toward greater inclusion of Catholics, however, was necessarily balanced against opposition opinions within his own Unionist political party and pressure from key constituent groups such as the Ulster Protestant Action.[41] In 1967, O'Neill faced an attempt by his Home Minister, William Craig, to bring down his government.[42] By early 1969, O'Neill was slowly losing his grip on power; Stormont was increasingly controlled by hard-line Unionists. O'Neill called elections in February in an attempt to consolidate power, and was returned as Prime Minister, but his position remained under attack until he ultimately resigned in May 1969.[43] Thus, from 1963 to 1969, the Northern Irish government was rife with tension between the preferences of the prime minister and other key political actors, which, in addition to the aforementioned principal-agent problems of "police misconduct," further contributed to inconsistent repressive responses to non-violent protest.

THE START OF THE TROUBLES, 1969–1970

Faced with inconsistent responses to non-violent protest in the previous period, Catholics increased their use of violent dissent in 1969 and 1970. A statement by the Provisional IRA, established on December 18, 1969, summarized the reasoning behind this strategic shift. "A civil rights movement, demanding justice and reforms, had been launched ten months

---

36. This particular instance of state repression resulted in two days of violent protest rioting—an example of how higher repression in response to non-violence might make violent dissent relatively more attractive.

37. Wichert, *Northern Ireland since 1945*, p. 110.

38. Ibid.

39. English, *Armed Struggle*, p. 90.

40. Wichert, *Northern Ireland since 1945*, p. 89.

41. Ibid., p. 94.

42. Ibid., p. 99.

43. Ibid., p. 111.

previously. The Unionist government and its supporters attacked the movement and in a number of confrontations 3 nationalists had died at the hands of the RUC [police]."[44] The acknowledgement that the non-violent civil rights movement had been greeted with repression, which we have argued was not consistently employed, suggests that Catholic dissidents were attuned to the changing costs of each tactic and re-evaluated the relative expected utilities for different dissent strategies.

August 1969 was a time of intense violence in Northern Ireland. England increased coercion against Republicans in response to this violence by deploying the British Army. Like the responses to non-violent protest in the previous period, however, this repressive response to increasingly violent protest was not applied consistently. Principal-agent problems continued to compromise the British state's ability to employ repression consistently, because British troops employed force against Republican dissenters unevenly and the continued army occupation of 1969–1970 promoted further inconsistency.

During these two years Republicans did not abandon non-violent dissent altogether, but the emphasis was clearly shifting toward violent dissent. By the spring of 1969, Republican dissidents were attacking public buildings and utilities.[45] Seasonal Protestant marches through Catholic neighborhoods were met with Republican rioting and petrol bombs.[46] August 2–3, 1969 witnessed "considerable violence in Belfast," and on August 4, more riots broke out in Catholic neighborhoods.[47] An August 12 Protestant march in Derry sparked violence between police and Catholics that spread to Belfast, ending in fires that left thousands of predominantly Catholic families homeless.[48] In December 1969, the Provisional IRA was founded, suggesting a further commitment to pursue violent dissent. By spring of 1970, the Provisionals were involved in attacks on Royal Ulster Constabulary (RUC) police stations and violent confrontations with the British Army.[49] By the fall of 1970, the Army reported that it felt the riots it was encountering were being carefully orchestrated.[50]

Repressive responses to this violent dissent were inconsistent during this time period. At times the state employed high levels of repression. On the morning of August 16, for example, the B-Specials (a police reserve force in Northern Ireland) were reported to have gone on a "rampage" in Catholic sections of Belfast in response to continued Republican violence.[51] But such episodes of repression occurred sporadically, and Brit-

---

44.   English, *Armed Struggle*, p. 126.

45.   Wichert, *Northern Ireland since 1945*, p. 111.

46.   Marc Mulholland, *The Longest War: Northern Ireland's Troubled History* (New York: Oxford University Press, 2002), p. 71.

47.   English, *Armed Struggle*, p. 101.

48.   Wichert, *Northern Ireland since 1945*, p. 112.

49.   Ibid., p. 134.

50.   Ibid., p. 137.

51.   Ibid., p. 103.

ish MPs described the army as having a "low key" attitude.[52] In April 1970, the state announced that petrol bombers risked being shot, and in July 1970 the state imposed "Falls Curfew," where violent house searches were performed in response to recent violent dissent. These examples of repression, however, represent punctuations in extended periods of a British military presence that was not consistently employing repression, but rather engaging in what English describes as harassment of Catholics.[53] Such harassment, again, represents not a consistent policy of repression on the part of the state, but rather agents of the state taking liberties with their repressive power to trouble Republicans.

Such inconsistent repression on the part of the army might actually be an inherent characteristic of military occupation when the military is not engaged in specific operations. As we have mentioned previously, principal-agent problems lead to inconsistent applications of repression. When a significant repressive presence under the control of multiple agents of the state is placed in close proximity to dissent activities, but not engaged in a specific military campaign beyond some vague notion of "peacekeeping," the probability that repression is applied inconsistently is likely to increase dramatically.

As multiple agents of the state have a repressive capacity, and no direct instructions about the extent to which they should employ repression, opportunities for discretionary decisions about repressive response abound. Military occupation is a tense situation, and as individual agents feel more or less threatened at any given time, they will respond with repression accordingly—either in a formal repressive capacity or with more informal repression, such as the harassment mentioned above. Furthermore, particular army units had distinct preferences regarding the use of repression. The paratroopers, for example, had a reputation for the excessive use of repression, which further contributed to the overall inconsistency in the application of repression during military occupation.[54]

THE TROUBLES CONTINUE AND BEGIN TO SUBSIDE, 1971–1976

By 1971, Republican violence had grown markedly, with an increasing amount of bombing activity directed at the British Army in particular.[55] Here we see a sequence of events where high state coercion in response to non-violence was not applied consistently, encouraging an increase in violent protest activity. The increased consistency of the state's repressive response in 1971–1973, and the subsequent decrease in Republican violence that followed in 1974–1976, illustrates how increased consistency in the application of repression can reduce violent dissent.

Republicans engaged in more violent dissent from 1971 to 1973. Early in 1971, the IRA began to shoot at British troops, and they killed their first

---

52. Ibid., p. 148.

53. English, *Armed Struggle*, pp. 122–123.

54. Ibid., p. 154.

55. Mulholland, *The Longest War*, p. 87.

English soldier on February 6.[56]   By spring of 1971, Republicans were described as bombing with "energy and intensity."[57] July 1971 saw increased
Republican violence in Derry, and in August 1971, lethal violence broke
out in response to the state's renewed policy of internment. Over twenty
people were killed, and thousands were left homeless by house fires. In
an August 13 press conference Republican dissidents stressed their commitment to violence, stating "we have plenty of guns and ammunition."[58]

In the last two weeks of January 1972, Republicans engaged in a number of shootings and planted several mail bombs. On January 27, two RUC
men were killed in Derry by Catholic dissidents. On February 22, 1972,
the Official IRA bombed a paratrooper barracks in response to Bloody
Sunday; seven were killed. On February 25, Republicans attempted the
assassination of a Unionist politician.[59] Two were killed and 136 injured
in a March 1972 bombing of a Belfast department store restaurant.[60] July
21, 1972, has been described as one of the North's "worst ever days of
violence"; Republicans planted over twenty bombs in the city center of
Belfast, killing nine people and injuring many more.[61]

This period also saw some non-violent protest, particularly as state repression of violence became more consistent with the use of house searches and internment. In September 5, 1971, Provisionals offered 'interim proposals' and made demands of the British government that, they claimed,
would bring "immediate" peace if the British publicly accepted them.[62] In
March 1972, the IRA once again issued a series of demands to the British
government, this time accompanied by a 72-hour ceasefire.[63] By mid-1972,
Republican dissidents were showing signs of beginning a strategic shift
away from violent dissent. On May 29, 1972, the Official IRA suspended
military action (though the Provisional IRA remained active).[64] June 13,
1972, marked a "significant" IRA press conference, where the IRA publicly
offered to meet the Northern Irish Secretary of State and to suspend all
violence for a week.[65] Then, on June 22, 1972, a Republican ceasefire was
announced, and on July 18, 1972, Republican leaders flew to London to
meet with British Labour politicians.[66]

While Republicans were continuing their campaign of violent dissent
in 1971 and 1972, the state grew more and more consistent in its use of

---

56.   English, *Armed Struggle*, p. 137.
57.   Ibid., p. 138.
58.   Ibid., p. 140.
59.   Ibid., p. 175.
60.   Ibid., p. 156.
61.   Ibid., p. 158.
62.   Ibid., p. 127.
63.   Ibid., p. 155.
64.   Ibid., p. 175.
65.   Ibid., p. 157.
66.   Ibid., p. 157–158.

repressive responses. From February to August 1971, the state attempted to engage in a sort of tit-for-tat repressive response to Republican violence.[67] House searches were another tactic of state repression in response to violence. They were performed by the army, and involved destruction of private property, including Catholic religious imagery. Approximately 250,000 house searches occurred, with increasing frequency, from 1971 to 1976.[68] In August 1971, internment was re-introduced.[69] Between August 1971 and December 1975, there were 1,874 Republicans detained without trial.[70] Here, then, is evidence that state repression toward the end of 1971 had increased in consistency, but was not entirely consistent. Repression would become more consistent as houses were searched and internment progressed in 1972 and 1973. On March 14, 1972, Army soldiers killed two IRA teenagers in Derry, and the leader of the Official IRA was killed by the British Army in April 1972.[71] Moreover, the state changed its policy regarding the non-patrolling of barricaded Catholic neighborhoods, which could previously have been seen as inconsistent with other repressive actions by the state. On July 31, 1972, in "Operation Motorman," the British Army reoccupied barricaded no-go areas of Derry and Belfast. All told, British soldiers killed 80 individuals in 1972.

The period of 1974–1976 saw increasing non-violent dissent on the part of Catholic dissidents, as state responses to violence in the previous period had grown more consistent. From 1971 to 1973, Republican dissidents killed 211 British soldiers. From 1974 to 1976, the number of British soldiers killed decreased to 73. The IRA engaged in a lengthy truce in 1975, and began to invest more in non-violent dissent, such as the *Republican News*, which became more professional and better-edited during this time period.[72]

This period illustrates how the consistency with which the state uses repression in response to both violent and non-violent actions will have consequences for the dissent strategies that groups choose to employ. When the state employed inconsistent repression in response to non-violent civil rights protests, Northern Irish Republicans began to employ more violent dissent. Although the state employed repression in response to violent dissent, the initially inconsistent application of that repression undermined its deterrent effect. Finally, as the state began to employ repression more consistently in response to violent dissent, Republicans began to shift their strategy back to a greater emphasis on non-violent dissent.

Some scholars have argued that increased consistency of the state repression did not reduce Republican violence. Many cite the reenactment

67. Ibid., p. 173.

68. Mulholland, *The Longest War*, p. 97.

69. English, *Armed Struggle*, p. 140.

70. Mulholland, *The Longest War*, p. 97.

71. Ibid., p. 160, 175.

72. Ibid., p. 173, 181.

of internment (which we identify as a factor in increasingly consistent repression) as being a "spur to more violence."[73] Before internment, in 1971, Republicans killed ten British soldiers; after internment thirty soldiers were killed. Similarly, Bloody Sunday was shown to have spawned several acts of violent retaliation.[74] Isolated instances of state repression, such as internment or Bloody Sunday, may have incited short-term violent responses from Republicans, but taken together, along with the other repressive activities employed by the British state during this time period, they contributed to eventual perceptions of an increased consistency in the state's use of repression. Though the major reduction in Republican violence did not occur until 1974–1976, it may have taken some period of time for dissidents in Northern Ireland to update their beliefs about how the state would respond to violence, given the high level of inconsistency it displayed in the past.

This interpretation of state repression and Republican dissent has shown how the effectiveness of repression in deterring violence depends on the consistency with which such repression is employed. When the state was able to repress violent dissent consistently—as in the period directly preceding 1963, and from 1972 to 1973—Republican protestors relied more on non-violent dissent. Furthermore, the consequences of the state's inability to repress non-violent protest consistently, and the subsequent increase in violent dissent, highlight how the effects of the consistency of repression will depend on the dissent tactics to which repression is applied.

A Cautionary Story about Repression

In this chapter, we have introduced a theory of dissent strategy and argued that the consistency with which a state employs repression in response to different dissent tactics should affect the choices that dissident groups make about violent and non-violent protest. In doing so, we have identified a significant determinant of dissent behavior that previous

---

73. Ibid., p. 141.

74. One major incident of repression and dissent during this time period has been excluded from this analysis because of the questions that surround it. The massive display of repression on "Bloody Sunday" could be understood as part of the increasingly consistent response to violent dissent, or as another inconsistent response to non-violent protest, depending on whether one believes that the events preceding soldiers opening fire and killing thirteen protestors were violent or non-violent. On Sunday, January 30, 1972, the army decided to arrest Catholic protestors following an anti-internment march that had degenerated into Republicans throwing stones at soldiers. The particular regiment charged with containing this protest was the paratroopers, who had the aforementioned reputation for excessive use of violence. While the high level of repression employed by the soldiers is not in doubt, questions still remain about the extent to which the soldiers were responding to violent or non-violent protest, which makes it difficult to say whether this particular incident is evidence of the consistent responses to violence during the period or more inconsistent responses to non-violence.

works on repression and dissent have ignored. The consistency of repression is a significant conditioning factor for the relationship of repression and dissent.

This study leads us to a number of conclusions about previous work on repression and about the real world use of repression. In line with Moore's finding, this work has provided further support for the substitution hypothesis.[75] States can cause dissidents to substitute violent and non-violent tactics by repressing one strategy (or by repressing it more than the other). The effect, however, is conditional on the consistency of this repression. Looking at the repression of violent and non-violent dissent in turn, we find that the effect of inconsistency is actually different, depending on which tactic the state represses. More inconsistency in state repression of violence reduces the effect that repression has in deterring the use of violence. Greater inconsistency in repression of non-violent tactics, however, appears to accentuate the effect of repression on inducing dissidents to use violence. Although the directional effects on tactical substitution are different if the state is inconsistently repressing violent or non-violent protest, the consequences of that inconsistency are actually the same: to encourage more violent dissent.

This finding on the different effects of inconsistency on violent and non-violent tactics raises some additional questions and has important implications for policy. The Rational Actor dissent model assumes that there is nothing inherently different about violent or non-violent tactics. Perhaps this is a problematic assumption. One idea about how tactics may differ is based on the general cost expectations associated with different dissent tactics. If the costs associated with violent dissent are routinely higher than those associated with non-violent tactics, dissidents will have different expectations about those costs (high for violence, low for non-violence). Given these prior expectations, dissidents may view inconsistency of repression in different ways. For example, if predominantly violent dissidents observe that some of their actions are not met with repression, they will see that the costs are potentially lower for further violent activities. If predominantly non-violent dissidents expect little repression, however, an occasional attack by the state may be seen as particularly unjust and can engender more radical tactics.[76]

There are several important implications of these findings about consistency of repression. First, even though consistent repression might seem desirable, the principal-agent problems inherent in the implementation of repression, as well as the numerous and changing constraints on the state's decision calculus, present the potential for inconsistency. This will be true even when consistency is a goal pursued by the state. Making a comparison between the consistent use of repression and an inconsistent use assumes that states can be totally consistent, which is incorrect. We offer two explanations for why states would be inconsistent—diverse aims

---

75. Moore, "Repression and Dissent: Substitution, Context, and Timing."

76. This is similar to the effect Rasler finds in Iran. See Karen Rasler, "Concessions, Repression, and Political Protest in the Iranian Revolution."

of state elites, and a principle-agent problem associated with how repression is carried out. To what degree these two factors affect the ability of states to consistently use repression will vary across states and across time or dispute within states. There is little reason, however, to believe that any state would be free of these constraints. All state elites have numerous issues to grapple with at the national level. All states must use security forces to employ repression. Thus, when we consider these findings that inconsistent repression causes more violence, we need to think beyond the extreme and simple conclusion that states should repress consistently all the time to deter violence.

Instead, a more nuanced reading of these findings presents us with a cautionary story about the use of repression and how it is employed. First, repression of non-violent dissent encourages violence, and repressing inconsistently does so even more. Though we expected inconsistency to diminish the effects of repression, a haphazard or intermittent response to non-violence encourages even more violence. Second, repression of violent dissent can deter violence, but the effect is substantially diminished when repression is used inconsistently. The question then becomes, how useful is it to repress dissent, given that consistency is virtually impossible? We should qualify this cautionary tale about repression. This dynamic is most likely to exist in already open political systems, where violent and non-violent dissent are both viable strategies for disaffected groups in society. Implicit in our model is the idea that accommodation *can* occur in response to either strategy, and thus dissident elites seriously consider both violent and non-violent tactics. That said, the increasing use of terrorism and violence in democracies means that state repression in these cases is a live and relevant concern in the twenty-first century.[77]

Finally, forward-looking state elites must be careful about repression decisions, because a consistent policy of repression today does not guarantee consistency into the future. The central message for states regarding repressive responses to dissent, therefore, is to proceed with caution. Any forward-thinking state elites concerned with violent dissent in the future must realize that the use of repression brings with it inherent potential for inconsistent application, which will only serve to encourage violent dissent.

---

77.   See Erica Chenoweth, "The Inadvertent Effects of Democracy on Terrorist Group Emergence," Belfer Center for Science and International Affairs, Harvard Kennedy School of Government, Discussion Paper, November 2006.

Chapter 8

A Composite-Actor Approach to Conflict Behavior

Wendy Pearlman

What brings an insurgent, protest, or self-determination movement to use violence as opposed to other strategies? This question is an important starting point for research on civil and asymmetric conflicts, increasingly dominant forms of conflict since the latter half of the twentieth century. With the aim of crafting generalizable theories of the circumstances under which political violence is likely or intense, scholars and analysts often treat movements as if they were unitary. There is thus a propensity to refer to the Tamils, Chechens, Tibetans, and other groups as coherent entities, and to explain their behavior as the outcome of that entity's pursuit of specific goals.

The assumption that movements are unitary actors is attractive because it simplifies the complex empirical world into identifiable decision-makers whose practices can be elegantly modeled. It invites scholars and commentators to equate the rational decision-making of a movement with that of a person, and thereby assert that the norm is for movements to act in ways that reasonably advance their objectives. This assumption, however, obscures dynamics *internal* to movements. This is a serious problem because some of the causes of civil violence stem from these dynamics; ignoring them can lead to mistaken explanations of conflict outcomes and misguided prescriptions for conflict resolution. Specifically, inattention to intra-movement processes can lead scholars and policymakers to exaggerate the degree to which movements carry out violence because they believe it to be strategically effective. It is difficult to account for suboptimal violence when one takes the agent of violence to be a coherent entity acting on the basis of coherent preferences.

In this chapter, I craft an approach that aims to produce better explanations of suboptimal violence and other puzzling conflict outcomes. To this end, I contrast understandings derived from the assumption that nonstate movements can be treated as unitary actors with what I call a "composite-actor" approach. The composite-actor approach departs from

The author would like to thank the Belfer Center for Science and International Affairs, the United States Institute of Peace, and the Palestinian-American Research Center for their support for the research on which this chapter is based.

theories that implicitly view social, political, and nationalist movements as single entities by explicitly bringing their amalgam and multifaceted character to the forefront of an analysis of their conflict behavior. Rather than directly asking why a movement chooses violent or non-violent methods, this approach asks precisely *who* within that movement does the choosing and how their choices influence those of others within their own community. My objective is to encourage investigation into the kinds of actors that make up movements and how their interactions affect the use of violence as opposed to other strategies. My analytical contention is that when we fail to take account of the interaction of those who constitute a movement, we are liable to misunderstand why and how violence takes place.

The composite-actor approach entails disaggregating political collectives into categories of individuals with similar kinds of objectives and resources. In this chapter, I operationalize this approach by identifying three general clusters of actors who shape politics in many movements: elites, aspirants, and masses. Other clusters of actors might also be specified, and future research can explore how different categorizations are relevant depending upon the political setting. I demonstrate this approach through analysis of the Palestinian national movement during the British Mandate (1920–1948), and specifically the Arab Rebellion (1936–1939). Some might argue that Palestinians' particularly acute divisions render them unique among self-determination struggles, and that the Arab Rebellion is hence an unrepresentative case with which to challenge unitary actor–based theories. Yet empirical evidence of fragmentation in nonstate groups is more widespread than mainstream theories of violence suggest. Comparative research shows that ethnic groups typically contain heterogeneous factions.[1] Recent works on insurgencies and civil wars similarly demonstrate the multiplicity of interests and identities within any given party to conflict.[2] Yet, while these and other studies cast doubt on the unitary view of a nonstate group, they have yet to provide an alternative conceptualization of the group's composite character. That is, they suggest that a movement is not a single actor, but do not necessarily tell us how to think about the multiple actors that it encompasses. In order to achieve the goal of "rethinking violence," we must also rethink the nature of the agents who we regard as driving violence. This chapter serves as an initial step toward that end.

Beyond its analytic value, an examination of the Arab Rebellion is worthwhile due to its historic importance. This uprising marked a turn-

---

1.   See Donald L. Horowitz, *Ethnic Groups in Conflict* (Berkeley: University of California Press, 1985), pp. 267–272.

2.   For an overview, see Stathis N. Kalyvas, *The Logic of Violence in Civil War* (Cambridge: Cambridge University Press, 2006); see also Macartan Humphreys and Jeremy M. Weinstein, "Handling and Manhandling Civilians in Civil War," *American Political Science Review*, Vol. 100, No. 3 (August 2006), pp. 429–447; and Jeremy Weinstein, *Inside Rebellion: The Politics of Insurgent Violence* (Cambridge: Cambridge University Press, 2007).

ing point in the history of the conflict between Palestinian Arab and Jewish nationalisms. One of the most protracted uprisings against the British in the Middle East, it drew world attention and profoundly shaped both national communities inhabiting Mandate Palestine. During these years of unrest, the Jewish community in Palestine consolidated its economic independence, strengthened its armed forces, and gained critical military experience through its cooperation with the British Army.[3] Palestinian Arabs, on the other hand, emerged from the rebellion fractured, economically devastated, and leaderless. It was under these circumstances that they faced a well-organized Zionist movement in the war of 1947–1949. The dissolution of the Palestinian national movement was all but a foregone conclusion.

This chapter proceeds in three sections. The first section critiques conventional explanations of civil conflict, which treat nonstate movements as unitary actors, and presents an alternative, composite-actor approach. The second section uses the case of the Arab Rebellion to illustrate the analytical fruitfulness of this approach and two arguments that extend it. The third section concludes and briefly demonstrates the relevance of these arguments for subsequent episodes in Palestinian history.

From a Unitary to a Composite-Actor Approach

Numerous studies of civil conflict have offered explanations of why nonstate groups use violence as a means of challenging an opponent. Many, however, build on an important assumption that scholars do not mention, no less scrutinize and defend: that movements behave as if they were unitary actors. This simplifying assumption underlies much mainstream research on the conceptual, methodological, and theoretical levels.

On the conceptual level, the unitary-actor assumption is implicit in many scholars' vision of civil conflict as consisting of a straightforward struggle between a movement and its external adversary. This conceptualization turns attention away from the struggles within either of these parties, which may play no less a role in driving violence. Stathis Kalyvas brings this conceptual problem to the fore when he critiques the conventional understanding that civil war is a "binary conflict" that is organized around a "master cleavage" rather than a host of overlapping local and private conflicts.[4]

On the methodological level, the unitary-actor assumption is the grounds on which scholars use nonstate groups as the unit of analysis in cross-national statistical tests of theories of political violence. Such is the case for many studies employing the Minorities at Risk (MAR) dataset.

3. Anita Shapira, *Land and Power: The Zionist Resort to Force, 1881–1948*, trans. William Templer (Stanford: Stanford University Press, 1999), chap. 6.

4. Stathis Kalyvas, "The Ontology of 'Political Violence': Action and Identity in Civil Wars" *Perspectives on Politics*, Vol. 1, No. 3 (September 2003), pp. 475–494.

It is likewise often the case for studies that critique MAR or use it as one of many sources in constructing new datasets. For example, Nicholas Sambanis and Annalisa Zinn consider why some self-determination conflicts evolve into civil war, and argue that denial of autonomy and other forms of repression bring minority groups to escalate their protest. They fault MAR for including only those ethnic groups prejudged to be "at risk," and develop a new dataset that avoids such selection bias. However, they accept MAR's view that the basic agent in civil conflict is a nonstate group. As they state explicitly, "We refer to [minority] groups and assume that they are coherent units with well-defined preferences."[5]

On the theoretical level, the assumption that nonstate movements behave as unitary actors is the bedrock of the dominant paradigm in security studies, which holds that violence is a strategy that a group employs purposefully to attain a given political objective.[6] On this premise, many scholars explore how a state's accommodative or repressive policies render some strategies more effective than others. Although a precise model of the nexus between repression and dissent remains elusive, many case studies find that regime repression escalates the type or rate of anti-regime activity.[7] Mark Lichbach predicts that groups rationally shift from non-violent to violent forms of rebellious activity when states use repression indiscriminately, while Karen Rasler argues that collective protest escalates when repression is inconsistent.[8] T. David Mason, and likewise Sambanis and Zinn, find that it is instead a regime's response to non-violent protest with coercion rather than concessions that leads to violence.[9] In these and other works, the assumption that movements act as

---

5.   Nicholas Sambanis and Annalisa Zinn, "From Protest to Violence: Conflict Escalation in Self-Determination Movements," unpublished manuscript: Yale University, 2006, p. 9.

6.   Anthony Oberschal, *Social Conflict and Social Movements* (Englewood Cliffs, N.J.: Prentice-Hall, 1973); William A. Gamson, *Strategy of Social Protest*, (Homewood, Ill.: Dorsey, 1975); James DeNardo, *Power in Numbers: The Political Strategy of Protest and Rebellion* (Princeton, N.J.: Princeton University Press, 1985); and Mark Irving Lichbach, *The Rebel's Dilemma* (Ann Arbor: University of Michigan Press, 1998).

7.   See the chapter by Cunningham and Beaulieu in this volume; Christian Davenport, Hank Johnston, and Carol Mueller, eds., *Repression and Mobilization* (Minneapolis: University of Minnesota Press, 2005); Robert W. White, "From Peaceful Protest to Guerilla War: Micromobilization of the Provisional Irish Republican Army," *American Journal of Sociology*, Vol. 94, No. 6 (May 1989), pp. 1277–1302; Marwan Khawaja, "Resource Mobilization, Hardship, and Popular Collective Action in the West Bank," *Social Forces*, Vol. 73, No. 1 (September 1993), pp. 191–220; and Donatella della Porta, *Social Movements, Political Violence, and the State: A Comparative Analysis of Italy and Germany* (Cambridge: Cambridge University Press, 1995).

8.   Mark Lichbach, "Deterrence or Escalation? The Puzzle of Aggregate Studies of Repression and Dissent," *Journal of Conflict Resolution*, Vol. 31, No. 2 (June 1987), pp. 266–297; Karen Rasler, "Concessions, Repression, and Political Protest in the Iranian Revolution," *American Sociological Review*, Vol. 6, No. 1 (February 1996), pp. 132–152.

9.   T. David Mason, *Caught in the Crossfire: Revolutions, Repression, and the Rational Peasant* (New York: Rowman and Littlefield, 2004); and Sambanis and Zinn, "From Protest to Violence," fn. 6.

if they were unitary entities is central to the explanation that movements carry out violence when external conditions render it rational to do so.

The twin assumptions of unitary actors and collective rational action are also increasingly commonplace in the literature on terrorism. The "instrumentalist" explanation of terrorism regards it as an efficient weapon of the weak against the strong.[10] Noteworthy in this regard is Robert Pape's research arguing that groups employ suicide bombing in a strategic bid to coerce liberal democracies to make territorial concessions.[11] Here, again, the internal coherence of a nonstate movement is fundamental to the theory of violence proposed. It is a requisite part of the argument that movements act, in Pape's words, to "achieve a specific political goal." It is also what gives movements the capacity to derive lessons from the past, and hence to "learn" that suicide terrorism "pays."[12]

That nonstate movements act strategically and adapt their behavior in response to state policies is evident in cases ranging from the U.S. civil rights movement to al-Qaida. Nevertheless, this emphasis on strategic rationality does not explain why movements sometimes take actions that are ineffective and even haphazard, or why they continue with a strategy after it fails to produce political results. It is not simply the case that theories assume that movements behave as unitary actors tend to overlook suboptimal violence. Rather, it is the very assumption of unitary actors that renders theories unable to explain such outcomes. After all, if a movement is a coherent unit, why would it ever carry out an incoherent strategy?

Faced with the conundrum of suboptimal violence, some theorists resort to attributing strategically inefficient choices to such factors as culture, religion, or ideological fanaticism. Even those who propose this line of explanation, however, do not necessarily relinquish the premise that movements are coherent entities acting purposefully. They simply suggest that the movement's goal is to fulfill a religious duty or extract revenge rather than achieve the more material objectives of land or political sovereignty. Hence, regardless of how a movement happens to define gains, it is believed that the movement acts in a unified way to increase those gains and decrease losses.

Is this assumption unproblematic? Even when a movement has an official leadership, a spectrum of persons beyond leaders plays a role in shaping the movement's course of action. Moreover, the context in which adherents of a movement make decisions that affect the movement is usually multidimensional.[13] They have opinions about issues relating to

10. See Martha Crenshaw, "The Causes of Terrorism," *Comparative Politics*, Vol. 13, No. 4 (July 1981), pp. 379–399; and Martha Crenshaw, "The Logic of Terrorism: Terrorist Behavior as a Product of Strategic Choice," in Walter Reich, ed., *Origins of Terrorism* (Washington, D.C.: Woodrow Wilson Center Press, 1990), pp. 54–66.

11. Robert A. Pape, "The Strategic Logic of Suicide Terrorism," *American Political Science Review*, Vol. 97, No. 3 (August 2003), pp. 343–361.

12. Ibid., p. 344.

13. See Richard McKelvey, "Intransitivities in Multidimensional Voting Models and

strategy, the proper procedures for reaching collective decisions, how decisions are implemented, and how the movement's resources are distributed. That is, when they negotiate strategy *vis-à-vis* an external opponent, they are likely also to be negotiating the classic "who gets what, when, and how" that defines politics within their nonstate group. Even when members of a nonstate group join forces in opposition to a common adversary or come together around the goal of national self-determination or regime overthrow, individuals' participation in collective action is often influenced by these other concerns. The implication of this multiplicity of preferences and objectives in any nonstate group is that the coherent status of a movement should be treated as a research question to be explored, not an assumption to be taken for granted.

It is to call attention to this question that I present the composite-actor approach to the study of violence. Operationalization of the composite-actor approach hinges on distinguishing the various kinds of actors that constitute what we commonly identify as a nonstate party to conflict. I identify three such categories of actors: elites, aspirants, and mass-level actors. "Elites" are leaders who, among other actors in society, wield the most political resources and enjoy greatest claims to represent the community. "Aspirants" are individuals who possess political skills and ambitions but lack institutional power. Looking toward leaders, aspirants actively seek greater recognition of their personal status or advancement of their preferred ends and means in the conflict. "Mass-level actors" refers to members of society who, like aspirants, possess preferences on matters of political process and policy, but unlike aspirants, are not actively pursuing a claim to direct the affairs of the collective.

The central claim of the composite-actor approach is that a movement's conflict behavior takes shape less as a choice on the part of a coherent entity than as an evolving social process in which these differently situated actors launch and sustain their participation for different reasons. Following this claim, I put forth two arguments. These arguments may be true or false regardless of whether scholars treat groups as composite or unitary; however, they can also be treated as analytic and empirical extensions of the composite-actor approach. The first argument is that the process by which people mobilize behind nationalist violence is not simply "top-down" or "bottom-up." That scholars have variably emphasized the roles of either elites or masses shows that many do look inside movements and explicitly take account of their composite character. In tending to emphasize only one kind of social actor rather than another, they underestimate the degree to which movement behavior is fundamentally the outcome of the interaction between them. This argument extends the composite-actor approach because it emphasizes the interactions among a movement's components, not the dominant role of any one component. The second argument I make is that the internal relationships and interactions driving conflict behavior change over time. More specifically, the factors responsible for an initial turn to violence differ from those that sustain

Some Implications for Agenda Control," *Journal of Economic Theory*, Vol. 12, No. 3 (June 1976), pp. 472–482.

it. This testable claim is an extension of the composite-actor approach because it derives from the idea that the interests of elites, aspirants, and masses shift as they interact with each other.

This central claim and the two arguments that extend it point to causes of violence derived specifically from exchanges and interactions internal to nonstate groups, rather than those resulting solely from the movement's interaction with its external adversary. The case of the Palestinian national movement under the British Mandate demonstrates these points. A unitary actor-based account of this case might straightforwardly posit the conditions under which violent or non-violent protest was rational for Palestinians in their effort to attain greater national sovereignty from the British authorities. Alternatively, it might attribute violence to Palestinians' collective despair or anger in its confrontation with Zionism or to some supposed aggression innate to Arab-Islamic culture. By contrast, a composite-actor approach traces conflict behavior to the interdependent decision-making of Palestinian elites, aspirants, and mass-level actors. I suggest that these actors' interests, as well as their resources and political opportunities, evolved endogenously in their interaction with each other. Iterative interaction shifted the calculations and relative power of these different actors during the years leading to the rebellion, and again over its course. These dynamics were not the only determinants of Palestinian behavior in the rebellion, but they were important ones. Ignoring them yields a mistaken understanding of why Palestinians did what they did. These are precisely the dynamics that go undetected by studies that conceptually, methodologically, or theoretically regard nonstate movements as unitary actors.

The Arab Rebellion

The Palestinian Arab society that emerged from the Ottoman Empire was overwhelmingly comprised of Muslim peasants, who tended to be illiterate, chronically indebted, and barely able to make livelihoods from the soil. Palestine's budding cities housed tiny working and middle classes, the latter of which was disproportionately Christian. Sitting atop this social pyramid was a handful of mostly Muslim, Jerusalem-based, elite families.[14] In the nineteenth century, these competing notable clans channeled their traditional prestige into political power. In making use of Ottoman tax, land, and other reforms to register large tracts of land in their names, they obtained both wealth and social control over the masses of sharecroppers and tenant farmers, whose livelihoods depended on absentee landlords. These elites obtained top posts in religious institutions,

---

14.   See Albert Hourani, "Ottoman Reform and the Politics of the Notables," in W. Polk and R. Chambers, eds., *Beginnings of Modernization in the Middle East* (Chicago: University of Chicago Press, 1968), pp. 41–68; Bayan al-Hut, "The Palestinian Political Elite during the Mandate Period," *Journal of Palestine Studies*, Vol. 9, No. 1 (Autumn 1979), pp. 85–111.

political bodies, and the Ottoman administration. They solidified their patron-client networks by virtue of their privileged status as intermediaries between state and society.

In the 1917 Balfour Declaration, the British government pledged to "favor the establishment in Palestine of a national home for the Jewish people." The 92 percent of the Palestinian population that was Muslim and Christian Arab adamantly protested that promise as a violation of their own rights to the land they viewed as their birthright. The traditional elite took the lead in voicing this opposition. Although these elites lost their political monopoly as the British established a League of Nations Mandate in Palestine, they remained the default leaders and spokesmen of the Arab population. In the early period of British rule, notable families were divided between those who called for Palestine's unity with Syria and those who favored national autonomy. By late 1920, however, elite opinion had largely coalesced around the latter. Members of the elite met and selected an "Arab Executive Committee" (AE) to represent Palestinian Arabs before the Mandatory authorities. They adopted a platform that called for the public recognition of Palestine as a distinct political entity, the rejection of the right of the Jewish people over Palestine, a ban on the transfer of Arab or state lands to Jewish control, and a halt to Jewish immigration. With this leadership and agenda in place, the Palestinian national movement took shape.[15]

Notable families assumed authority in what seemed an authentic extension of the religious, economic, and social prestige they had enjoyed for generations. In spite of their opposition to British policies, many accepted formal positions in the Mandate apparatus in municipalities, the religious establishment, or other institutions. These posts rendered them intermediaries with the government, thereby granting them recognition and resources that further solidified their political elite status. Thus, although elites had their own factional splits, they constituted a social-political class that went relatively unchallenged by other segments of society during this early phase of the national movement. Yehoshua Porath writes, "A leadership crystallized which was accepted, at least initially, by the entire political public as legitimate. There then followed a period of two or three years, in which almost the entire public was united around the Executive Committee."[16] At this point in the national struggle, aspirants outside this small circle of elites did not yet represent a political force in their own right. Mass-level actors were not politically active in a concerted way, as

---

15. Two important works on this era are Yehoshua Porath, *The Emergence of the Palestinian-Arab National Movement, 1918–1929* (London: Cass, 1974); and Ann Mosely Lesch, *Arab Politics in Palestine, 1917–1939: The Frustration of a Nationalist Movement* (Ithaca, N.Y.: Cornell University, 1977).

16. Yehoshua Porath, "The Political Organization of the Palestinian Arabs under the British Mandate" in Moshe Ma'oz, ed., *Palestinian Arab Politics* (Jerusalem: Jerusalem Academic Press, 1975), p. 10.

the overwhelming majority of the population was engaged in a struggle for subsistence.[17] Nationalist strategy was thus an elite affair.

Palestinian elites pledged to use constitutional and parliamentary strategies in the pursuit of national aims, and this strategy was generally dominant during the first years of the Mandate. The AE submitted memos, draft statutes, and petitions to the British authorities, met with the Colonial Secretary and High Commissioner for Palestine, and dispatched three consecutive delegations to meet with members of Parliament and other officials in London. It made the Palestinian case before the Turkish government, the Pope, and the League of Nations. It also organized demonstrations, delivered speeches, published articles, and distributed leaflets to mobilize and demonstrate its popular support.[18]

This non-violent and political work aside, outbursts of violence remained periodic. In Aaron Kleiman's words, the depth of emotions rendered Mandatory Palestine a "tinderbox" in which nearly any incident, rumor, or misunderstanding could spark violence.[19] As such, riots in 1920, 1921, and 1929 resulted in hundreds of Jewish and Arab deaths and injuries. British commissions of inquiry concluded that each violent episode was spontaneous and propelled by widespread Arab fear of the Balfour Declaration and disappointment with the failure to achieve independence.[20]

Elite influence over national strategy waned as other social-political actors came to have a larger impact within the national movement. The rural and urban poor increasingly moved from deference toward traditional elites to open dissatisfaction. The failure of elites' conservative tactics to stem the development of the Jewish national home led many to call for more radical strategies against the British. Jewish immigration and land purchases exacerbated the extreme economic duress among the Arab peasants, many of whom were forced to leave their lands and move to slums on the outskirts of the towns.[21] The misery of the poor put the political sensibilities of the base of the Palestinian social pyramid increasingly at odds with that of its top, given that most elites enjoyed privileged

---

17.   David Horowitz and Rita Hinden, *Economic Survey of Palestine, with special reference to the years 1936 and 1937* (Tel Aviv: Economic Research Institute of the Jewish Agency for Palestine, 1938), pp. 203–205; and J.C. Hurewitz, *The Struggle for Palestine* (New York: Schocken Books, 1976), pp. 32–33.

18.   Lesch, *Arab Politics in Palestine*, chap. 4.

19.   Aaron S. Klieman, "Introduction," in Aaron S. Klieman, ed., *The Rise of Israel*, Vol. 18: *The turn toward violence, 1920–1929* (New York: Garland Publishing, 1987), p. i.

20.   See, respectively, Great Britain, Cmd. 1540: *Palestine Disturbances in May 1921: Reports of the Commission of Inquiry … Haycraft, Chairman* (London: His Majesty's Stationery Office [HMSO], 1921); and Great Britain, Cmd 3530, *Report of the Commission on the Palestine Disturbances of August, 1929 …Shaw Report, Chairman* (London: HMSO, 1930).

21.   Yehoshua Porath, *The Palestinian-Arab National Movement, from Riots to Rebellion 1929–1939* (London: Cass, 1977), pp. 83–84; Ylana Miller, *Government and Society in Rural Palestine, 1920–1948* (Austin: University of Texas Press, 1985), p. 24; and Ilan Pappé, "Historical Features: Haj Amin and the Buraq Revolt," *Jerusalem Quarterly File*, Vol. 6, No. 18 (June 2003), pp. 6–16.

positions due to their comfortable relations with the British and were thus averse to antagonizing the government.[22] Caution and conservatism characterized the elites as a social-political class. The most popular Palestinian Arab leader, the Mufti of Jerusalem, Haj Amin al-Huseini, was no exception to this rule.

Palestinians were thus increasingly frustrated with their elites' failure to stem the tide of the Jewish national project. They also criticized intra-elite squabbles, particularly the rivalry between the Huseinis and Nashashibis, two elite Jerusalem families whose bitter competition intensified over the course of the 1920s. Understanding that aggrieved mass-level actors could be mobilized to radicalize nationalist strategy, a preacher named Izz al-Din al-Qassam rallied the urban poor behind the call for armed *jihad* against Zionism and Western imperialism. When al-Qassam was killed in his first battle against British troops, he became an emotive symbol for the longing of ordinary Palestinians for more bold and courageous leadership. His funeral inspired a mass outpouring that sent a warning to the traditional elite: Ghassan Kanafani wrote, "if they did not try to mount the great wave ... it would engulf them."[23] These developments represented a political awakening among mass-level actors and political aspirants in Palestinian society. Al-Qassam himself can be seen as an aspirant: lacking the formal post and aristocratic status of the Jerusalem notables, he both critiqued and circumvented them in his efforts to steer the Palestinian national struggle in a more militant direction.

Another aspirant challenge to Palestinian elites emerged with the crystallization of a cohort of middle-class activists. Urbanization and expanded access to literacy gave rise to a new class of Arab professionals with political, social, and economic ambitions that could not be satisfied under the customary distribution of power in society. Newly educated persons formed dozens of civil society organizations and political clubs through which they distanced themselves from the Jerusalem notables and criticized their factionalism and conciliatory politics.[24] These individuals became the producers and consumers of a budding Arabic press, using it to spread their call for more strident nationalist politics.[25] While this social sector was generally based in Palestinian towns, those who became teachers and civil servants in the countryside helped spread their politicized sensibilities to the rural hinterland.[26] In the terms of the composite-actor approach, these educated and politically engaged Palestinians can be seen

22.   Rashid Khalidi, *Iron Cage: The Story of the Palestinian Struggle for Statehood* (Boston: Beacon Press, 2006), p. 85.

23.   Ghassan Kanafani, *Thawrat 36–39 fi Filisteen* (Jerusalem: Abu Arifa Press Agency, n.d.), p. 70.

24.   Lesch, *Arab Politics*, pp. 61–64, 106–108; and Weldon C. Matthews, *Confronting an Empire, Constructing a Nation: Arab Nationalists and Popular Politics in Mandate Palestine* (London: I.B. Tauris, 2006), chaps. 3–4.

25.   Rashid Khalidi, *Palestinian Identity: The Construction of Modern National Consciousness* (New York: Columbia University Press, 1997), chap. 6.

26.   Miller, *Government and Society*, p. 69.

as an emergent group of aspirants. They were more literate and organized than the bulk of the population, and thus possessed more means of mobilizing collective action than it did. Yet they also lacked the supra-local influence and aristocratic stature of traditional elites, and hence had less power to implement their preferred strategy against the colonial authorities.

From the early 1920s to the mid-1930s, Palestinians thus witnessed something of a transition from a nationalist struggle that was almost solely directed by elites to one in which national action was influenced by elites, aspirants, and mass-level actors. In Ann Mosely Lesch's words, there was a switch in Palestinian politics from "mobilization from above" to "mobilization from below."[27] Nevertheless, national behavior was not strictly "top-down" or "bottom-up" as much as it was the product of the interaction of actors across social and political hierarchies. As aspirants and mass actors became more politically organized, their more radical leanings came to have a larger imprint on the national movement as a whole. These aspirants pushed elites to undertake some bolder actions, such as the AE's sponsorship of mass demonstrations against the British in 1933. Yet elites continued to resist doing more. As Nels Johnson summarizes their stance, "their class interests kept them from wavering seriously from a moderate and generally conciliatory position toward the Mandate, while their factional warfare kept them from dealing effectively with the pressure which choked the mass of people."[28]

Such was the composite character of the nationalist movement in April 1936, when Arab gunmen stopped a car and shot three of its Jewish travelers. In the days that followed, the Jewish paramilitary *Irgun* shot two Arabs in revenge, a Jewish funeral became an angry demonstration, false rumors spread about Jews' murder of Arabs, and Arab peasants and laborers rioted and indiscriminately attacked Jewish bystanders. These rapidly escalating events evolved into a three-year Palestinian campaign to force the British government to retreat from its support for the creation of a Jewish national home in Palestine, a revolt that became known as the "Grand Arab Rebellion." The course of the rebellion witnessed variation in Palestinian use of violence and other strategies of protest. What began as riots evolved into a general strike centered in the cities, spawned an armed uprising, and eventually descended into internecine warfare. These twists and turns are puzzling because they appear to have been strategically suboptimal, if not contradictory. It is difficult to account for these patterns when one views the Palestinian national movement as a single entity that calculated costs and benefits, learned from past experience, adapted to new information, and chose the course of action most likely to extract concessions from its opponent. When one appreciates the movement as the sum of differently situated individuals and groups, however, a new understanding of its conflict behavior comes to light. The composite-actor approach can facilitate this understanding.

---

27.   Lesch, *Arab Politics*, chap. 5.

28.   Nels Johnson, *Islam and the Politics of Meaning in Palestinian Nationalism* (London: Kegan Paul International, 1982), p. 57.

STRATEGY AS A RESULT OF COMPOSITE-ACTOR INTERACTION

The Arab Rebellion was not orchestrated by any one particular sector in Palestinian society. The initial riots were propelled by spontaneous action by mass-level actors. According to Britain's own commission of inquiry, the main driver of unrest was Palestinian Arabs' apprehension that they would become strangers in their own homeland if the British were not compelled to change their policies.[29]

As rumors and spontaneous rioting spread, however, other categories of social-political actors came to play a critical role in shaping Palestinian nationalist strategy. A crucial intervention came from the new cohort of educated, urban political aspirants. These activists stepped in as the "first-movers" of non-violent protest. In the first days of unrest, activists in two towns called public meetings and announced the commencement of a general strike. During the days that followed, activists in other towns followed suit. Calling their gatherings "National Committees," they appealed for mass participation in the strike, and pledged to sustain it until the British made concessions.[30] In calling on Palestinians to cease work, these aspirants sought to shore up the popular will to challenge the government. Yet they also sought to acquire a measure of discipline to prevent protest from spilling out of control. Lesch explains, "fearing intercommunal violence, middle-class Arab professionals and merchants hastily formed local committees which they hoped could organize a non-violent protest strike to channel the Arabs' explosive anger."[31]

National Committees emerged in nearly all Palestinian towns, and many established contact with neighboring villages to encourage and aid their participation, as well.[32] The press published calls for national unity and actively encouraged the entire public to contribute to the effort.[33] As communities across the country joined the general strike, different sectors of Palestinian society participated using the means at their disposal. The Arab Car Owners' and Drivers' Association halted transport facilities, merchants and city laborers stayed home, prisoners refused to perform penal labor, and schools and factories closed. Men, women, and children participated in public demonstrations and boycotted Jewish firms and products. Boy Scouts and young urban men enforced compliance at the neighborhood level. Although Arab civil servants did not go on strike, some donated a percentage of their salaries and submitted a memorandum to the government explaining Arab grievances and claims. Intellec-

---

29. Great Britain, Cmd. 5479: *Report of Palestine Royal Commission ... Peel, Chairman* (London: HMSO, 1937).

30. Akram Zu'aytir, *Al-haraka al-wataniyah al-filistiniyah, 1935–1939: yawmiyat Akram Zu'aytir* [The Palestinian National Movement, 1935–1939: The Diaries of Akram Zu'aytir] (Beirut: Institute of Palestine Studies, 1980), pp. 60–61.

31. Lesch, *Arab Politics*, p. 217.

32. Zu'aytir, *Al-haraka al-wataniyah*, p. 61.

33. Mustafa Kabha, "The Palestinian Press and the General Strike, April–October 1936: *Filastin* as a Case Study," *Middle Eastern Studies*, Vol. 39, No. 3 (July 2003), pp. 169–189.

tuals demanded "no taxation without representation," a call subsequently adopted by the National Committees.[34]

Aspirants appealed to traditional Palestinian elites to join the strike, but they remained averse to challenging the authorities. During the second week of unrest, National Committee representatives met and suggested electing their own country-wide coordinating body to lead the rebellion. Elites understood that aspirants' mobilization represented a threat to their monopoly claim to national-level leadership. If the Mufti and other elites did not join the rebellion, they risked being shunted aside by those who did.[35] It was thus the challenge of aspirants that drove elites to come together and assume leadership of the strike. Representatives of all major elite factions—including the Nashashibis and Huseinis, as well as Christians and Muslims—formed the Arab High Committee (AHC). The AHC chose Amin al-Huseini as its president. The AHC announced that the strike would continue until it achieved three goals: the establishment of a representative national government in Palestine, an end to Jewish immigration, and a ban on the transfer of Arab land to Jews.

Therefore, mass-level mobilization gave the protest campaign geographic scope and momentum. The intervention of political aspirants in various towns helped to steer and sustain it in a range of more organized and civic forms. The subsequent participation of elites with national stature gave the rebellion symbolic sanction, an official voice, and an interlocutor with the government. The revolt was not a choice on the part of a unitary entity acting on a well-defined strategic vision, because these sets of actors made decisions in response to each other. Spontaneous popular rioting and violence motivated aspirants to take the initiative in organizing a strike and other non-violent forms of protest. Aspirants' intervention in turn helped many urban mass-level actors to participate in rebellious activity that was less militant than armed attacks. At the same time, the combination of mass-level mobilization and aspirants' political organizing pressured elites to embrace greater militancy than they had previously endorsed. The start of the 1936 general strike thus demonstrates the key claim of the composite-actor approach: the strategy undertaken by this national movement was the outcome of a process that developed endogenously through the interaction of different sectors of society.

---

34. Porath, *Palestinian-Arab National Movement*, pp. 166–173; Mohammed Izzat Darwazah, *Mudhakkirat Mohammed Izzat Darwazah, 1305 H – 1404/1887 M – 1982: Sijil Hafil bi-Masirat al-Harakah al-Arabiyah wa al-Qadiyah al-Filastiniyah* [Memoirs of Mohammed Izzat Darwazah: Registrations on the Arab Movement and the Palestinians' Cause], Vol. 2 (Beirut: Dar al-Gharb al-Islami, 1993), pp. 20–22.

35. Subhi Yasin, *Al-thawrah al-arabiyah al-kubra fi Filastin, 1936–1939* [The Great Arab Revolt in Palestine, 1936–1939] (Damascus: Dar al Hind, 1961), p. 22; Porath, *Palestinian-Arab National Movement*, pp. 164–165; Yehuda Taggar, *The Mufti of Jerusalem and Palestine Arab Politics, 1930–1937* (New York: Garland, 1986), p. 391; Philip Mattar, *The Mufti of Jerusalem: Al-Hajj Amin al-Huseini and the Palestinian National Movement* (New York: Columbia University Press, 1988), pp. 121–125; and Darwazah, *Mudhakkirat*, p. 17.

COLLECTIVE ACTION AS THE OUTCOME OF A PROCESS THAT IS NEITHER
STRICTLY TOP-DOWN NOR BOTTOM-UP

The Arab Rebellion also illustrates the first argument that I propose as an extension of the composite-actor approach: violent and non-violent collective action is neither instigated solely by a movement's leaders nor driven exclusively by its grassroots. Rather, the form and intensity of a movement's insurgent activity is the product of a combination of top-down and bottom-up dynamics. This understanding of the composite character of strategy stands in contrast to many existing interpretations of the Arab Rebellion. On one end of the spectrum, echoing theories that self-interested leaders deliberately provoke ethnic violence, some critics have argued that the Mufti of Jerusalem incited the Arab masses in his pursuit of personal power and his uncompromising hatred of Zionism, if not Jews.[36] On the other end, echoing mass-level deprivation theories, others have argued that the rebellion was a spontaneous expression of ordinary Palestinians' pent-up grievances and feelings of injustice. In fact, some posit that the Arab masses who propelled the rebellion directed their outpouring at least in part against their own elites for not having done more to challenge the British.[37] George Antonius, a Palestinian historian who was a witness to the Arab Rebellion, wrote at the time: "Far from its being engineered by the leaders, the revolt is in a very marked way a challenge to their authority and an indictment of their methods."[38]

Process-tracing supports an interpretation that lies between and combines these two extremes. The bottom-up thrust of the rebellion came from the frustration of ordinary Palestinians. The top-down dimension took root as Palestinian leaders, at first loathe to confront the government, recognized that they could sit on the sidelines only at their political peril. Between elites and masses, political aspirants took the initiative to form committees and direct protest in their communities. Some of these aspirants explicitly invoked the example of Gandhi and called for civil disobedience and noncooperation with the British.[39] Yet, as in other cases of insurrections against colonial rule, sporadic violence was not uncommon, and Arabs carried out dozens of attacks on Jewish people and property.

36.   See John Marlowe, *Rebellion in Palestine* (London: Cresset Press, 1946); Maurice Pearlman, *Mufti of Jerusalem. The Story of Haj Amin el-Huseini* (London: Victor Gollancz, 1947); Joseph B. Schechtman, *The Mufti and the Fuehrer: The Rise and Fall of Haj Amin el-Huseini* (New York: Thomas Yoseloff, 1965); and Yehuda Bauer, "The Arab Revolt of 1936," Part I, *New Outlook* (July/August 1966), pp. 49–57, and Part II, *New Outlook* (September 1966), pp. 21–28.

37.   Kanafani, *Thawrat*; Kenneth W. Stein, "The Intifada and the 1936–39 Uprising: A Comparison," *Journal of Palestine Studies*, Vol. 19, No. 4 (July 1990), pp. 64–85; Ted Swedenburg, *Memories of Revolt: The 1936–39 Rebellion and the Palestinian National Past* (Minneapolis: University of Minnesota Press, 1995); and Baruch Kimmerling and Joel Migdal, *The Palestinian People: A History* (Cambridge, Mass.: Harvard University Press, 2003), pp. 107–114.

38.   George Antonius, *The Arab Awakening: The Story of the Arab National Movement* (New York: G.P. Putnam's Sons, 1946), pp. 405–407.

39.   Matthews, *Confronting an Empire*, pp. 69–71, 171–180.

Violence in the cities increased when the government refused to accommodate the strike's demands, and instead issued a schedule for new Jewish immigration.

The authorities moved to crush the violent rebellion through reprisals, including deporting and arresting participants, imposing curfew, and flattening rebellious neighborhoods *en masse*.[40] These military reprisals went far in suppressing armed activity in the towns; however, the armed rebellion continued to gain force in the countryside. The middle-class political aspirants who guided civic protest in the cities had minimal reach in rural areas, as did their civil society organizations and newspapers, which were key instruments for rallying the urban populations' participation in the strike and boycott. Thus, when the rebellion's center of gravity shifted to the countryside, its character was overwhelmingly violent. Peasants formed guerilla bands in the countryside to carry out shooting attacks and acts of sabotage against Jewish settlements and the British administration. The first bands were impromptu groups in which residents of a single village or members of an extended family came together to snipe at government or Jewish targets. The armed revolt spread, not only because of the Palestinians' fight against the British, but also because of competition among the mass-level actors constituting rural Palestine. Some clans formed rebel bands to avoid losing status to rival clans or as a way of defending themselves against potential attacks from other bands.[41] As more families and villages took up arms, bands developed into permanent units of some fifty to seventy regulars led by a local commander. From there they grew into networks in which a single commander directed both main and subsidiary bands.[42]

In the countryside as in the cities, bottom-up dynamics propelled by the grievances and interests of mass-level actors drove the diffusion of the rebellion. Given the family-based structure of society, the revolt spread as more peasant families took part. Nevertheless, it was not long before Palestinian elites became involved in the rural insurrection, and top-down dynamics also influenced the character and rate of rural bands' use of violence. The Nashashibi camp took the initiative and was the first to offer support to rebel bands. The Mufti and his faction soon followed by sponsoring other bands, so as not to lose influence.[43] Rival Jerusalem notables thus provided aid to the armed rebellion, doing so at least in part with the

---

40.   Robert John and Sami Hadawi, *The Palestine Diary*, Vol. 1 (Beirut: The Palestine Research Center, 1970), pp. 260–262.

41.   Porath, *Palestinian-Arab National Movement*, p. 182; Yuval Arnon–Ohanna, "The Bands in the Palestinian Arab Revolt, 1936–1939: Structure and Organization," *Asian and African Studies*, Vol. 15, No. 2 (July 1981), p. 233.

42.   Arnon-Ohana, "The Bands in the Palestinian Arab Revolt," pp. 230–233.

43.   See "Secret Despatch from the High Commissioner for Palestine, September 12, 1936," in Robert L. Jarman, ed., *Political Diaries of the Arab World: Palestine and Jordan*, Vol. 2 (Archive Editions, 2001), p. 671; Taggar, *Mufti of Jerusalem*, p. 391; and Darwazah, *Mudhakkirat*, Vol. 2, p. 246.

goal of competing with each other and solidifying their respective spheres of influence in the country.

Four months into the revolt, another top-down factor came to influence the character of rebel violence. A former Ottoman military officer named Fawzi Qawuqji led foreign Arab volunteers into Palestine and declared his own central command over the armed rebellion. Qawuqji developed good relations with the Nashashibi camp and voiced his disdain for the Mufti. Thereafter, the rural revolt proceeded on two uncoordinated tracks, which reflected the divide between rival Palestinian elite families. Qawuqji directed rebels in some parts of the countryside and the Huseinis managed bands in other parts.[44] With time, many Nashashibi leaders came to view the rebellion as futile and reduced their involvement. By contrast, Amin al-Huseini became more enmeshed in the rebellion's military component. In Yehuda Taggar's analysis, the Mufti calculated that assuming a leading role could help him preserve his preeminent standing within Palestinian society, which supported rebellion. He also reasoned that this would demonstrate to the British that he was irreplaceable. After all, if he controlled the rebellion, then the authorities would have trouble ending it unless they negotiated with him.[45]

The strike and rural revolt continued for six months. Its economic effects on the Arab community were dire. By fall, the AHC feared the strike would cause ruin if it continued into the citrus harvest season. In addition, the British were preparing to stiffen military repression of the rebellion, and the AHC feared what might ensue. Against this backdrop, Palestinian elites sought a way to end the rebellion without admitting defeat. The AHC asked leaders of several Arab countries to pen a public appeal for the strike's end, which it then published and endorsed. The strike came to a halt, and Palestine was calm for nine months.

In July 1937, the Royal (Peel) Commission charged with investigating the causes of the rebellion released its recommendations for resolving the conflict over Palestine: partition of the country into Jewish and Arab states. Most Arabs were horrified by this proposal, and rural bands regrouped in preparation for a renewal of the rebellion. In September 1937, Arab assassins killed the Governor of the Galilee and the rebellion began again in force. British authorities reacted to repress the rebellion more severely than they had during the first phase of the strike. This repression affected elites, aspirants, and mass-level actors, but in different ways. Targeting elites, the government declared the AHC illegal, and deported its members or prevented the return to Palestine of those members who were abroad. The Mufti went into hiding and then fled in secret to Lebanon. Stripped of his official position and rebuffed by the authorities whom he had sought to appease, he became increasingly bitter and uncompromising.[46] Whereas Huseini had once hesitated to endorse the strike for fear that it was too

44. Porath, *Palestinian-Arab National Movement*, pp. 191-292.

45. Taggar, *The Mufti of Jerusalem and Palestine Arab Politics, 1930–1937*, p. 391.

46. Mattar, *The Mufti of Jerusalem*, p. 122.

radical, he now became a leading proponent of armed violence. The Mufti established a new AHC headquarters in Beirut; other exiled AHC and political leaders opened a "Central Committee for the Jihad" in Damascus to guide, fund, and equip the Palestinian revolt. Nevertheless, the exiled leadership did not control the course of events in Palestine.

British repression also targeted aspirants. The government banned the National Committees and detained their members. In arresting hundreds of the mid-level activists who had spearheaded the strike, they also removed those who had guided the unarmed element of the 1936 uprising. In addition, British repression fell generally on mass-level actors. The government declared martial law and eventually poured extra troops into Palestine.[47] It also imposed various forms of collective punishment on the population.[48] This generalized repression, in addition to the enduring economic losses from the 1936 strike, left most Arab town-dwellers exhausted and wary of continued rebellion. Thus, although most people sympathized with the fight against the partition of Palestine, few were ready to participate in civic protest. Some aspirants who remained at large appealed for a return to the strike, but few mass-level actors answered that call.[49]

These changing conditions facing elites, aspirants, and masses influenced the strategies that came to be employed in the name of Palestinian Arab nationalism. The phase of the Arab Rebellion that began in 1937 saw the eclipse of non-violent protest and the escalation of Palestinians' pitched battles with British troops and sporadic attacks on government and Jewish targets. Rural bands' use of violence peaked in the summer of 1938, such that rebels took control of large stretches of the country and rendered government authority there practically non-existent.[50] As the rebellion came to center overwhelmingly in the countryside, over a dozen local commanders of rebel bands emerged as new kinds of political aspirants. The arrest or physical removal of traditional elites and urban middle-class aspirants opened new opportunities for those who enjoyed some freedom of maneuver in rural Palestine. Commanders of rebel bands had arms to act on their ambitions for political and social power. They came to compete with each other for power and turf, even as they took part in the same struggle against the British forces. The head of the Central Committee in

---

47.   See Yousuf Rad'ee, "Al-ijra'at al-Britaniyah al-mudaada lil-thawra 1936–1939 fi-Fitalstin" [British Measures against the 1936–39 Revolt in Palestine], Shu'un Filastiniyyah, Vol. 115 (June 1981), pp. 85–103; and Martin Kolinsky, "The Collapse and Restoration of Public Security," in Michael J. Cohen and Martin Kolinsky, eds., Britain and the Middle East in the 1930s: Security Problems, 1935–39 (London: Macmillan, 1992), pp. 147–168.

48.   Porath, Palestinian-Arab National Movement, pp. 238–241; and Tom Segev, One Palestine, Complete: Jews and Arabs under the British Mandate, trans. Haim Watzman (New York: Owl Books, 2001), pp. 416–417.

49.   "Officer Administering the Government, Jerusalem to Rt. Hon W. Ormsby-Gore, Secretary of State for the Colonies, October 14, 1937," in Robert L. Jarman, ed., Political Diaries of the Arab World: Palestine and Jordan, Vol. 3 (Archive Editions, 2001), p. 18.

50.   Lesch, Arab Politics in Palestine, p. 223.

Damascus lamented, "Each commander defined his area of his operations, which he saw as his own sphere of influence. He would become upset if a neighboring leadership encroached into his area in a way that he saw as a violation of his jurisdiction."[51]

Given the lack of central control, it was not long before the armed rural revolt took a chaotic turn. The rebellion became cover for those who used their weapons to engage in plunder, blood feuds, or acts of resentment against the urban well-to-do.[52] The fight against the British thus brought to the fore class, clan, regional, religious, and other social divisions in Palestinian Arab society. As the rebellion acquired the character of a class revolt, many middle and upper-class Palestinians fled the country.[53] At the same time, the mechanisms that had created some semblance of elite cooperation collapsed. Rivalries between those who vied to lead Arab Palestine thus came to play a more decisive role in determining the character of the violence. Sensing the population's fatigue by 1938, Fakhri Nashashibi, a leading member of the opposition camp, denounced the Mufti for the disastrous outcome of the rebellion. He also intervened to aid the British in ending it.[54] The rebellion descended into internecine violence as Huseini forces vilified the Nashashibis, Nashashibis supplied intelligence to the government, Huseini-allied bands assassinated Nashashibis, and Nashashibis organized their own "peace bands" to combat the rebels. By the time the rebellion died out in the spring of 1939, some 5,000 Palestinian Arabs had been killed and 15,000 wounded, out of a total population of 960,000. Approximately a quarter of these casualties were committed by Arabs.[55]

In the end, the contribution of elites and nonelites to rebellion violence evolved in their struggles for both national self-determination and individual advancement. In 1923, a British official had noted that, "in Palestine, a politician cannot hope to be successful unless he is an extremist." By the waning months of the Arab Rebellion, the Mufti was arguably more extreme in his opposition to the British than most of the population which he represented. Yet while his radicalism heightened the elite-driven aspect of violence, the revolt's popularly grounded dimension remained crucial. As Antonius wrote at the time, "Political incitement can do much to fan the flames of discontent, but it cannot keep a revolt active, month after

---

51. Darwazah, *Mudhakkirat*, Vol. 3, p. 115.

52. Ibid., pp. 114–116; Tom Bowden, "The Politics of the Arab Rebellion in Palestine 1936–39," *Middle Eastern Studies*, No. 2 (May 1975), pp. 147–174; and Swedenburg, *Memories of Revolt*.

53. "District Commissioner's Office, Southern District, Jaffa, Monthly Report for the month of September 1938, dated October 8, 1938," in *Political Diaries*, Vol. 3, p. 346; W. F. Abboushi, "The Road to Rebellion: Arab Palestine in the 1930s," *Journal of Palestine Studies*, Vol. 6, No. 3 (1977), pp. 23–46.

54. "Secret Despatch from the High Commissioner for Palestine, December 29, 1938," in *Political Diaries*, Vol. 3, p. 284.

55. Walid Khalidi, ed., *From Haven to Conquest: The Origins and the Development of the Palestine Problem* (Beirut: Institute for Palestine Studies, 1971), pp. 848–849.

month, in conditions of such violence and hardship."[56] In illustration of my first argument, the revolt's mix of violent and non-violent strategies was the outcome of neither strictly top-down nor bottom-up social processes. Rather, it was the interaction of both that gave the revolt its particular features. The distinct contributions of elites, aspirants, and masses remain obscure when one analyzes a national movement as a unitary entity. They come to light when one conceptualizes it as a phenomenon whose composite character has a causal effect on a movement's strategic behavior.

HOW INTERNAL RELATIONSHIPS AND INTERACTIONS SHAPING CONFLICT BEHAVIOR VARY OVER TIME

The discussion heretofore indicates how the motivations and capacities of different social-political actors constituting a nonstate entity evolve in interaction with each other, as well as in interaction with their external opponent. This provides a bridge to the second argument that I derive from the composite-actor approach: the factors responsible for the initial outbreak of a cycle of contestation differ from those that shape its mix of violent and non-violent activity over time. It can be said that the inter-Palestinian relations that helped launch the strike were relatively cooperative. Even as their interests diverged, elites, aspirants, and mass-level actors worked together. Their unique contributions complimented each other in propelling mobilization against British policy. But as economic losses took their toll and military reprisals suppressed the rebellion's mass character, inter-Palestinian relations became more antagonistic. These internal rivalries played a role in sustaining violence. Competition among elites and among aspirants, as well as the different preferences of the leaders in exile and the rebel commanders in Palestine, shaped the Palestinians' fight against the government. These internal influences on violence arguably helped to sustain the rebellion after much of the population longed for calm. They also generated an overlap between Palestinian violence against the British and Jewish community and Palestinian violence against other Palestinians.

Shifts among the changing set of actors within the Palestinian movement influenced the prospects for a peaceful settlement, as well as the character of the violence. As the rebellion petered out in 1939, the British put forward a White Paper that proposed independence for a unitary Palestinian state in ten years. It proposed restrictions on Jewish immigration and transfer of Arab land, and posited that the promise made in the Balfour Declaration could be considered to have been fulfilled. Most Palestinians regarded this as a victory, and a number of elite representatives welcomed it as a means of bringing the rebellion to a decisive end.[57] The White Paper did not grant the Mufti or his rebel commanders amnesty, however, and they were hence motivated to take a different stance.[58] Several command-

---

56. Antonius, *Arab Awakening*, pp. 405–406.

57. Yasin, *Al-Thawrah*, p. 226; and Kabha, *Thawrat*, pp. 97–98.

58. Mattar, *The Mufti of Jerusalemi*, p. 84; and Khalidi, *Iron Cage*, p. 117.

ers on the ground issued a statement that denounced the White Paper for falling short of nationalist aims. In it, they also sent a veiled threat to any political elites who considered signing an agreement with the government.[59] Given that rebels had already proven their readiness to assassinate compatriots, the Mufti understood that he would cross them at his own peril.[60] Against this backdrop, Amin al-Huseini announced that he too rejected the White Paper and vowed to continue the rebellion. As he was the most prestigious leader of Arab Palestine, few other elites dared to defy him once he made his stance known.

The 1939 White Paper granted Palestinian Arabs much of that for which they had been fighting. Their rejection of the proposal is thus difficult to explain from a strategic point of view. A unitary-actor approach cannot account for this outcome without resorting to the claim that Arabs were so intolerant of Jews that they refused any binational presence in Palestine. Yet this interpretation is inconsistent with the prior centuries of Arab-Jewish co-existence, as well as the declared positions of the Palestinian movement, which focused opposition against the political project of a Jewish state in Palestine. A better explanation for Palestinian conflict behavior is to be found in the composite-actor approach, which brings to light inter-movement struggles as an influence on strategy. Elites positioned themselves *vis-à-vis* the White Paper to serve not only their nationalist sensibilities, but also their private interests. The British refused to talk with Huseini, and thus he had no incentive to accept their proposal. For the same reason, Huseini's domestic elite rivals, who sought to establish themselves as interlocutors with the government, faced different incentives. Outside the small circle of elites, the rebel bands had become aspirants with a political power of their own. They were able to act as spoilers: those who use violence or other means to undermine negotiations in the expectation that a peace settlement will threaten their power or interests.[61] Pressure from rebel commanders played a role in convincing the Mufti to reject what most regarded as favorable terms for ending violence. As such, the lack of opportunity for a politically and physically safe exit served to sustain some Palestinians' advocacy of violence, even when others expected such violence to lead only to further losses.

Given this complex evolution of events, it is misleading to ask why *the* Palestinians chose a particular strategy in their struggle against Zionism during the 1920s and 1930s. The activity undertaken in the name of Palestinian nationalism was not the choice of a single entity as much as the aggregation of choices of differently situated individuals made on the basis of a variety of imperatives. Unitary-actor approaches miss these interactions, and can therefore lead to erroneous explanations of violence.

---

59.   Porath, *Palestinian-Arab National Movement*, p. 291.

60.   Khalidi, *Iron Cage*, pp. 116–117.

61.   Stephen John Stedman, "Spoiler Problems in Peace Processes," *International Security*, Vol. 22, No. 2 (Fall 1997), pp. 5–53; and Kelly M. Greenhill and Solomon Major, "The Perils of Profiling: Civil War Spoilers and the Collapse of Intrastate Peace Accords," *International Security*, Vol. 31, No. 3 (Winter 2006/07), pp. 7–40.

Conclusion

This essay has sought to offer a new angle on the question of why movements use violence rather than other means for contesting an opponent. It has done so by critiquing the assumption that movements can be seen as unitary actors that undertake coherent strategies. To treat a movement as a single entity is to ignore the real and analytically meaningful differences between the social-political actors that constitute such an entity. To pinpoint only one of these kinds of actors as single-handedly determining strategy on the part of the national collective is to ignore how their choices influence and are influenced by the choices of others within the community.

Based on this critique, I have advocated a composite-actor approach to the study of civil conflict. In examining political violence on the part of a nonstate movement, this approach does not ask why a movement uses violence. Rather, it asks who within that movement advocates what kind of strategy and how their actions affect those of others in the movement. For the sake of parsimony, I have concentrated on three clusters of actors internal to movements: elites, aspirants, and the mass-level actors that constitute the bulk of society. Analysis of the relations and interactions among these actors is useful for challenging the sometimes misleading idea that the norm is for movements to act in ways that are strategically rational. This idea disregards the fact that, even when people mobilize around shared objectives, they do not necessarily behave in a unified way. The composite-actor approach embraces this fact, and thereby provides tools for accounting for the seemingly suboptimal use of violence.

In my analysis of Palestinian nationalist mobilization during the British Mandate, I have demonstrated the central claim of the composite-actor approach: that collective violence takes shape less as a coherent choice on the part of a movement than as an evolving social process among the different kinds of actors within that movement. I have also advanced two arguments that I presented as extensions of this claim. First, the process by which people mobilize behind nationalist violence is not simply "top-down" or "bottom-up." Second, the factors and interactions that drive a movement's initial conflict strategy differ from those that shape it over time.

Subsequent junctures in Palestinian history, occurring in distinct political, social, and diplomatic contexts, illustrate similar patterns.[62] In December 1987, a roadside killing sparked riots among Palestinians in the Israeli-occupied West Bank and Gaza Strip. Unrest spread into a mass rebellion that was soon dubbed the *intifada*—literally, a "shaking off." As in the case of the Arab revolt, debates raged about the relative role of elite

---

62. See Wendy Pearlman, "Fragmentation and Violence: Internal Influences on Tactics in the Case of the Palestinian National Movement, 1918–2006," Ph.D. dissertation, Harvard University, 2007.

incitement and mass grievances in driving intifada activity.[63] A composite-actor approach reveals how both top-down and bottom-up dynamics came into play in different measure over time. The 1987 intifada gathered force due to the spontaneous participation of mass-level actors. Middle-ranking activists served as political aspirants who assumed field leadership. In leaflets distributed throughout Palestinian communities, they instructed people to contribute to the collective effort by partaking in specific protest actions on specific days. Official Palestinian leaders located in exile were initially taken by surprise by the grassroots outpouring in the occupied territories. Yet they gradually asserted control, and with time became more intensely involved in determining intifada strategy. These elites contributed to the increased use of violence in the intifada's later years.[64] The roles of different parts of the Palestinian community evolved over time in interaction with each other, and this shaped the character of strategy in the uprising.

A second intifada erupted some thirteen years later against the backdrop of disappointment with the Oslo peace process. The visit of Israeli leader Ariel Sharon to Jerusalem's Temple Mount/Noble Sanctuary in September 2000 triggered widespread protest. As mass-level actors joined demonstrations in large numbers and Israeli reprisals radicalized sentiments, unrest evolved from unarmed demonstrations to impromptu shootings to suicide bombings. Political aspirants gained presence as middle-strata activists in the Fatah movement who criticized the conservative strategy and undemocratic ways of the official Palestinian leadership. These aspirants took the lead in representing and advocating the continuation of the intifada. Palestinian Authority President Yasser Arafat was surprised by the scope of the initial outpouring, but thereafter his involvement deepened.[65] With time, new layers of competition within and between Palestinian factions emerged as prior political hierarchies became unsettled and aspirants advanced their preferred strategies against Israel, as well as their own claims to legitimate leadership of the Palestinian people. At the forefront of these aspirants was the Islamic Resistance Movement, Hamas. Multiple struggles among elites and aspirants thus shaped the kinds of action Palestinians took against their Israeli opponent.

Step-by-step analysis of these episodes demonstrates the value of the composite-actor approach to explaining violence in civil conflicts. Framing the debate as a question of how different Palestinian actors concurrently steer collective action, as opposed to why a single entity called "the Palestinians" chooses a given strategy, points to new questions for future research on other cases of ethnic or nationalist violence, insurgency, civil

---

63.   See Joost Hiltermann, *Behind the Intifada: Labor and Women's Movements in the Occupied Territories* (Princeton, N.J.: Princeton University Press, 1991), p. 173.

64.   Mary Elizabeth King, *A Quiet Revolution: The First Palestinian Intifada and Nonviolent Resistance* (New York: Nation Books, 2007), chaps. 9, 11.

65.   Yezid Sayigh, "Arafat and the Anatomy of a Revolt," *Survival*, Vol. 43, No. 3 (Autumn 2001), pp. 47–60; and Graham Usher, "Facing Defeat: The Intifada Two Years On," *Journal of Palestine Studies*, Vol. 32, No. 2 (Winter 2003), pp. 21–40.

wars, and social movement mobilization. For example, scholars can ask under what external circumstances, or in the presence of which internal political characteristics, nonstate groups behave more or less as if they were unitary. In addition, they can employ the composite-actor approach to the study of states and probe the degree to which they too should be conceptualized as composite actors. Furthermore, they can examine how different categories of social-political actors—beyond the categories of elites, aspirants, and mass-level actors discussed in this study—are salient in different kinds of nonstate movements.

Regardless of the precise research question or operationalization of the idea that movements are composite actors, scholars can push forward this research agenda insofar as they ask not why a movement carries out a strategy, but rather who leads an initial shift in conflict behavior, who follows, and how the roles of these leaders and followers affect patterns in contention over time. Such work will make a contribution to the rethinking of violence by uncovering the complex processes that shape which form, of many possible forms, a civil conflict will take.

Chapter 9

The Turn to Violence in Self-Determination Struggles in Chechnya and Punjab

Kristin M. Bakke

Why do some intrastate conflicts turn violent, while others do not? This is the question motivating this chapter. Focusing on Chechnya's path toward a violent conflict with Moscow in the early 1990s and Punjab's path to a violent struggle with Delhi a decade earlier, the study examines the turn to violence in self-determination struggles in decentralized states.

Each of these conflicts is notorious for a high death toll, a drawn-out counterinsurgency campaign, and a large number of "disappearances." Yet neither of these conflicts was bound to result in a *violent* center-region confrontation. Moscow's relationship to Chechnya grew tense when the Chechen government declared independence in 1991, but it did not turn into a civil war until December 1994, when the Russian Army entered Grozny, the Chechen capital. In the early 1980s, Delhi's relationship to militant groups in Punjab also appeared troublesome. In June 1984, the Indian Army attacked the Golden Temple in Amritsar, Sikhism's holiest temple, and by the late 1980s, Punjab found itself mired in a high-intensity insurgency and counterinsurgency campaign.

As in Chechnya and Punjab, in many of today's intrastate conflicts, the parties at odds with one another are central governments and ethnic groups in pursuit of greater autonomy or independence—self-determination or separatist struggles. Yet not all such conflicts turn violent. Some are fought through non-violent means or militant tactics, including protests

I would like to thank the scholars, journalists, and policymakers in Russia and India who took the time to discuss center-region relations with me in 2005 and 2006. I would also like to thank Joel Migdal, Erik Wibbels, Steve Hanson, and Paul Brass for their feedback on earlier versions of the argument presented here. Participants at the Paths to Violence workshop at Harvard University and the editors of this volume, Erica Chenoweth and Adria Lawrence, provided helpful comments, as did participants at the annual meeting of the Association for the Study of Nationalities annual meeting, New York, N.Y., April 10–12, 2008, and the American Political Science Association annual meeting, Boston, Mass., August 28–31, 2008, particularly Erin Jenne, Jason Lyall, and Lee Seymour. The research for this chapter was supported by grants from the National Science Foundation, the Chr. Michelsen Institute in Bergen, Norway, and the University of Washington. The Belfer Center for Science and International Affairs at Harvard University and the Peace Research Institute in Oslo, Norway provided support while writing. All errors and omissions are my own.

and boycotts.[1] This chapter aims to better understand some of the dynamics that precede the turn to violence.

In the Chechen case, idiosyncratic factors appear to explain the turn to violence. It is often pointed out that President Boris Yeltsin of the Russian Federation and President Dzhokhar Dudayev of the Chechen Republic never met one another face-to-face. Scholars of Indian politics have argued that, in the Punjab case, Prime Minister Indira Gandhi was more preoccupied with rescuing the falling fortunes of her Congress Party than addressing the concerns of the Punjabi Sikhs. I suggest that these case-specific arguments are part of a more general explanation of how the political ties between elites in the regions and the center affect the process of negotiation. Building on the federalism and intrastate conflict literatures, I argue that the *absence* of political ties between leaders at the center and in the separatist region, as well as the *presence* of political ties between the center and other regions of the state, can complicate intergovernmental negotiations by fueling divisions within the region, and, in turn, diminishing the chances of conflicts fought without bloodshed. While long-standing grievances and opportunities for collective action are important for explaining the emergence of a separatist conflict in the first place, they do not necessarily explain the paths to violent conflict. This chapter suggests that one path to violence, particularly in separatist conflicts in decentralized states, stems from the relationships among elites, both *between* the regions and the center, and *within* the regions.

The chapter traces the processes of the argument presented, focusing on how political ties, or the lack thereof, between central and regional leaders affected the turn to violence. It serves as a plausibility probe of the causal story.[2] Chechnya and Punjab share traits that make comparison fruitful.[3] They are regions of large multiethnic federal states, and the majority of both regions' populations are ethnic minorities in the state. The Chechens and the Sikhs are ethnic groups with long histories of resisting central control, and with historical ties to the territory they inhabit. These are factors often associated with separatist conflicts, yet their relative constancy over time means they cannot explain shifts from non-violent to

---

1.   Monty G. Marshall and Ted Robert Gurr, *Peace and Conflict 2005: A Global Survey of Armed Conflicts, Self-Determination Movements, and Democracy* (College Park: University of Maryland, 2005).

2.   On process tracing, see Alexander L. George and Andrew Bennett, *Case Studies and Theory Development in the Social Sciences* (Cambridge, Mass.: MIT Press, 2004). Kristin M. Bakke and Erik Wibbels, "Diversity, Disparity, and Civil Conflict in Federal States," *World Politics*, Vol. 59, No. 1 (October 2006), pp. 1-50, tests the argument in a statistical study across federal states.

3.   While the more common approach is to compare regions in one country (which has a number of advantages, such as holding "control" variables constant), region-level comparison across countries avoids a problem of the conventional research design. In in-country comparisons, the center's interaction with one region may influence its interactions with other regions. In Russia, for instance, Moscow's negotiations with Chechnya and other separatist regions, such as Tatarstan, were not independent of each other. The same cannot be said of Punjab and Chechnya.

violent struggles. The cases also differ in ways that allow consideration of how similar processes play out in diverse settings. While both Russia and India are considered democracies in the period under study, the Chechen conflict emerges shortly after the break-up of the former Soviet Union, in the early days of a democratic Russia. India, in contrast, has been a democracy since its independence in 1947.[4]

In addition, the two cases provide variation on the key variables of interest. In the Chechen case, I focus on the 1991–1994 time period, from the Chechen government's declaration of independence in November 1991 to the outbreak of full-fledged civil war in December 1994. Like almost all regions in the Soviet Union, Chechnya was ruled by a political ally of the center until 1991. From the fall of 1991, however, Chechnya was, unlike most regions in post-Soviet Russia, ruled by a non-ally of the center. In the Punjab case, I focus on the 1978–1987 time period, from the 1978 adoption of the Anandpur Sahib Resolution, which called for greater autonomy for Punjab, to 1986–1987, when the separatist conflict in Punjab turned into a spiral of insurgency and counterinsurgency campaigns. This case can be divided into three periods. From 1977 to 1980, while Punjab's chief minister was not of the same party as the country's prime minister, his party was, in Punjab, in a coalition government with the party of the prime minister. In this time period, most of the other major states in India were not political allies of the central government. From 1980 to late 1983, Punjab was ruled by the same party ruling at the center, which was the case for most other states in India as well. From late 1985 to 1987, Punjab was not governed by a copartisan of the center, but most other states were.[5] This variation allows me to explore each of the independent variables of interest separately, as well as different configurations of them.

Before presenting the argument, I briefly discuss lessons from the literature. The empirical part of the paper explores how political elites' ties shed light on the processes leading up to violence in Chechnya and Punjab. In the Chechen case, the absence of political ties between region and center helps to explain the inability of the parties to reach an agreement short of war, while in Punjab, the presence of political ties in neighboring regions made it difficult for the moderate separatists in Punjab to resolve their grievances with the center peacefully. The conclusion points to caveats and future research questions.

---

4.   The Punjab crisis emerged after India's Emergency (1975–1977), during which elections and civil liberties were suspended. While the Emergency is not equivalent to the period of authoritarian rule in the Soviet Union, both conflicts emerge following a switch from less to more democratic rule.

5.   From October 1983 to September 1985, Punjab is directly ruled by the center ("President's Rule").

Why Violence?

Scholars of political violence have investigated the underlying causes or reasons that help explain why conflicts—violent or not—emerge, how violence in conflicts unfolds, and the ways in which violent conflicts do, or do not, come to an end. Yet the transition from non-violent to violent conflict has been subject to less inquiry. What is it that happens at the point when a struggle moves from being fought through the means of pencils, pens, and protests to guns and grenades?

Several scholars have suggested that violence on the part of the state's challengers is a response to the state's use of repression.[6] Whereas discriminate repression can successfully eliminate challengers, indiscriminate or disproportionate repression can radicalize the more militant members of a movement while convincing the moderates that peaceful protest is no longer a fruitful option. In the Chechen case, the conflict between Moscow and Chechnya escalated and turned into a deadly civil war only after Moscow's invasion of Grozny in December 1994. It became an infamously bloody and gruesome war, characterized by a high civilian death toll, kidnappings, and extensive human rights abuses,[7] which in turn has fueled violence in the region.[8] This explanation, however, does not help us understand why Moscow used force in the first place. In June 1984, the government in Delhi ordered the Indian Army to attack the Golden Temple in Amritsar. Although the attack led to Prime Minister Indira Gandhi's assassination by Sikh members of her bodyguard troops—followed by deadly anti-Sikh riots in Delhi and a radicalized rhetoric among some of the Sikh militant groups[9]—violence in Punjab declined between 1984 and 1985. In fact, in 1985, it looked like the conflict would come to a peaceful end, which suggests that state repression is not bound to be followed by an escalation in violence.

Movements may also radicalize and turn violent in the absence of more routine channels for voicing demands.[10] In this view, whether the conflict can be fought without bloodshed depends on the process through

---

6. Mark Irving Lichbach, "Deterrence or Escalation? The Puzzle of Aggregate Studies of Repression and Dissent," *Journal of Conflict Resolution*, Vol. 31, No. 2 (June 1987), pp. 266–297; Donatella Della Porta, *Social Movements, Political Violence, and the State: A Comparative Analysis of Italy and Germany* (New York: Cambridge University Press, 1995); Karen Rasler, "Concessions, Repression, and Political Protest in the Iranian Revolution," *American Sociology Review*, Vol. 61, No. 1 (February 1996), pp. 132–152; and Jeff Goodwin, *No Other Way Out: States and Revolutionary Movements, 1945–1992* (New York: Cambridge University Press, 2001).

7. Anna Politkovskaya, *A Dirty War: A Russian Reporter in Chechnya* (London: Harvill Press, 2001).

8. Anne Speckhard and Khapta Ahkmedova, "The Making of a Martyr: Chechen Suicide Terrorism," *Studies in Conflict and Terrorism*, Vol. 29, No. 5 (June 2006), pp. 1–65.

9. Joyce Pettigrew, *The Sikhs of the Punjab: Unheard Voices of State and Guerilla Violence* (London: Zed Books, 1995).

10. Goodwin, *No Other Way Out.*

which the state and its challengers negotiate with one another. The federalism literature suggests a specific institutional channel for stable intergovernmental bargaining in decentralized states, namely political party ties between central and regional politicians.

Political Ties and Center-Region Negotiations

Beginning with William Riker, an influential branch of the federalism literature has focused on the role of political parties.[11] Political parties, argues Alfred Stepan, are the glue that holds multiethnic federations together.[12] According to Mikhail Filippov, Peter C. Ordeshook, and Olga Shvetsova, strong national or state-wide parties with regional branches, or "federal-friendly" parties, are likely to create incentives for both national and regional elites to cooperate with one another. Such parties constitute a self-reinforcing mechanism for federal stability, ensuring that highly divisive issues, such as the state's constitutional design or territorial integrity, are not challenged by political elites because "local and national parties and candidates rely on each other for their survival and success."[13] While the federalism literature's argument is specific to political parties, one can conceive of other factors that ease negotiations and make violence less attractive, including patronage networks.[14] The key is a certain degree of political dependence between central and regional elites.

This chapter focuses on the ways in which the *absence* of political ties among ruling elites or coalitions at the center and in a region affects the turn to violence in separatist conflicts, and how the *presence* of political ties between the center and other regions of the state affects the center's interactions with the separatist region. One can imagine the two independent variables at work separately, but also in conjunction with one another. The study's main contribution is specifying and tracing the steps that connect political elite ties to one of the most unstable forms of federal bargaining—violent separatist conflicts. Key to this story is how the negotiations between central and regional elites affect the relationships among elites and groups within the region.

---

11.   William Riker, *Federalism: Origin, Operation, Significance* (Boston: Little, Brown and Company, 1964).

12.   Alfred Stepan, *Arguing Comparative Politics* (Oxford University Press, 2001), pp. 315–362. On the flipside, Donald Horowitz, *Ethnic Groups in Conflict* (Berkeley: University of California Press, 1985) warns that local ethnic parties deepen ethnic cleavages, and Dawn Brancati, "Decentralization: Fueling the Fire or Dampening the Flames of Ethnic Conflict or Secessionism," *International Organization*, Vol. 60, No. 3 (July 2006), pp. 651–685, suggests that regional parties increase the chances of secessionist conflicts.

13.   Mikhail Filippov, Peter C. Ordeshook, and Olga Shvetsova, *Designing Federalism: A Theory of Self-Sustainable Federal Institutions* (New York: Cambridge University Press, 2004), p. 191.

14.   Julie A. George, "Separatism or Federalism? Ethnic Conflict and Resolution in Russia and Georgia," Ph.D. dissertation, University of Texas, Austin, 2005. See also Horowitz, *Ethnic Groups*, pp. 565–566.

The link between political elite ties across tiers of government and violent separatist conflict is the process of negotiation. Political ties between central and regional elites can affect the demands regional elites raise, the willingness of the central government to consider compromise solutions when faced with regional demands, and the credibility of promises given by both regional and central elites. Negotiations characterized by radical demands, few concessions, and non-credible commitments, which I refer to as stalled negotiations, are likely to foster a turn to violence by deepening opposition to the separatist challenger within the region, which further complicates the negotiation process between the center and the region. Below I elaborate on each of these steps.

First, if regional elites have a stake in keeping the state intact, they are less likely to voice radical demands. In particular, if the electoral fortunes or political careers of elites at the regional level depend on the party's success at the national level, or if funds or promotions come from the national level (that is, if regional elites owe their position to the elites at the center), they may think twice about pushing the central government for radical demands that challenge the integrity of the state.[15] Indivisible demands, such as independence, are harder to negotiate than more divisible ones, such as greater autonomy, because regional elites are less willing to accept a compromise and central elites less willing to accommodate.[16] It may also be the case that political ties across tiers of government provide regional elites with a sense of inclusion in the state. Political inclusion, argues Jeff Goodwin, "discourages the sense that the state is unreformable or an instrument of a narrow class or clique and, accordingly, needs to be fundamentally overhauled."[17] Thus, one would not expect to see radical demands, such as independence, from a regional government of the same party or coalition governing at the center.

Second, if national elites need the help of regional politicians to win elections or stay in power, they are likely to try to reach a compromise when faced with regional demands and, more generally, aim to strengthen the regional politicians' hold on power in the region. One would not expect the central government to oppose a compromise solution when the challenger is a regional government of the same political party affiliation.

Third, political ties among central and regional elites also ensure that concessions and promises, once given, are more credible, as defecting hurts both sides. Just like indivisible demands are considered obstacles to bargaining, so are non-credible commitments.[18] One would not expect a central government to easily break a promise given to a regional challenger of the same political party affiliation, and vice versa.

---

15. Filippov et al., *Designing Federalism*.

16. Monica Duffy Toft, *The Geography of Ethnic Violence* (Princeton, N.J.: Princeton University Press, 2003).

17. Goodwin, *No Other Way Out*, p. 46.

18. Barbara Walter, *Committing to Peace* (Princeton, N.J.: Princeton University Press, 2002).

The absence of any of these factors—regional elites owing their position to the center, central elites depending on regional elites, and credible commitments—is likely to result in a stalled negotiation process. Indeed, these three factors suggest a relationship of dependency between central and regional elites. If these actors do not depend upon each other, negotiations are more likely to stall than if they do rely on each other. In turn, stalled negotiations increase the likelihood that the conflict will turn violent.

It is important to note that the central government has political relationships to elites in not just one region, but in all regions of the state, and political elite ties to these other regions may affect the negotiation process. That is, center-region negotiations are not just about elites in the potentially separatist region and the center, but also about the relationship between the center and elites in regions elsewhere. The central elites' concern for their political allies in one region may come at the expense of other regions. Research on India and the United States, for example, suggests that parties at the center often target transfers to regional copartisans at the expense of regions governed by opposition parties.[19] Similarly, if concessions and commitments to a potentially separatist region hurt the center's political allies elsewhere in the state, the central elites' relationship to these other regions may trigger two of the characteristics of stalled negotiations described above—an unwillingness to provide concessions and to credibly commit to any promises made.

Once center-region negotiations stall, a deepening of divisions within the region makes the turn to violence more probable. Few, if any, separatists are unanimously supported by the population they claim to represent. If the regional elites involved in negotiations with the center fail in their efforts, opposition in the region may grow. Other groups may seek power, or even try to oust the regional elites, believing that they would be better able to represent the region's interests. Groups in fragmented movements may seek to "outbid" one another, propelling a radicalization of strategies and goals,[20] and the regional elites may adopt more radical positions to compete with their challengers. Fragmentation might also leave the movement without a disciplining leadership that can integrate its behavior, possibly leading to intra-movement violent conflict, which complicates the movement's bargaining with the central government because its leadership cannot credibly commit to peace.[21] Indeed, a fragmented separatist

19. Stuti Khemani, "Partisan Politics and Intergovernmental Transfers in India," Policy Research Working Paper 3016, World Bank Development Research Group, Washington, D.C., 2003; and Philip J. Grossman, "A Political Theory of Intergovernmental Grants," *Public Choice*, Vol. 78, No. 3/4 (1994), pp. 295–303.

20. Mia M. Bloom, "Palestinian Suicide Bombing: Public Support, Market Share, and Outbidding," *Political Science Quarterly*, Vol. 119, No. 1 (Spring 2004), pp. 61–88.

21. Kathleen Gallagher Cunningham, "Divided and Conquered," Ph.D. dissertation, University of California at San Diego, 2008; Adria Lawrence, "Imperial Rule and the Politics of Nationalism," Ph.D. dissertation, University of Chicago, 2007; Wendy Pearlman, "Fragmentation and Violence: Internal Influences on Tactics in the Case of the Palestinian National Movement, 1918–2006," Ph.D. dissertation, Harvard University, 2007.

movement or region is a particularly challenging negotiation partner for the center because there is no *one* movement there. Thus, growing regional opposition and fragmentation feed back into the process of stalled negotiations, making a peaceful resolution increasingly difficult.

Consider Table 9.1. The bottom boxes, which are scenarios where the potentially separatist region is not a copartisan of the center, indicate stalled negotiations, while the chances of stable negotiations are, in general, higher in the upper boxes, where the potentially separatist region is a copartisan of the center.

The most uncertain outcome is in the upper-left box; based on the potentially separatist region's copartisanship with the center, one would expect that negotiations would go smoothly, yet the expectation based on political ties to other regions of the state go in the opposite direction. Table 9.2 shows the placement of the Chechen and Punjab cases.

The Case of Chechnya

Several scholars have linked separatist tendencies in Russia in the early 1990s to the disintegration of the Communist Party, which severed institutional ties between tiers of government across Russia.[22] Special to the Chechen case was the Chechen Revolution of 1990–1991 and the ensuing power struggles within the republic, which made for an unstable regime.[23] This study maintains that the absence of political ties between the leadership in Moscow and in Grozny hampered negotiation efforts between 1991 and 1994, feeding into elite struggles within Chechnya. President Dudayev came to power in the Chechen republic as the leader of a nationalist organization, without owing his position to Moscow, and was consequently unafraid to raise radical demands. The Yeltsin administration, which had no political allegiance to Dudayev, offered few concessions and side-stepped the Chechen leadership in negotiations. The failure of this negotiation process was a deepening of divisions within Chechnya, which further complicated the negotiation process and helped pave the way for an armed conflict.

---

22.   Valerie Bunce, *Subversive Institutions: The Design and the Destruction of Socialism and the State* (New York: Cambridge University Press, 1999); Filippov et al., *Designing Federalism*.

23.   Gail Lapidus, "Contested Sovereignty: The Tragedy of Chechnya," *International Security*, Vol. 23, No. 1 (Summer 1998), pp. 5–49; Georgi M. Derluguian, "Ethnofederalism and Ethnonationalism in the Separatist Politics of Chechnya and Tatarstan: Sources or Resources?" *International Journal of Public Administration*, Vol. 22, No. 9–10 (1999), pp. 1387–1428; Tracey C. German, *Russia's Chechen War* (New York: Routledge, 2003), pp. 76–93.

Table 9.1. Expectations about Political Elite Ties, Negotiations, and Separatist Violence.

	Political center-region ties across most regions	Political center-region ties across few regions
Separatist region political ally of the center	Medium probability of violence: Possibility of negotiations and non-violence. However, negotiations can be jeopardized by political elite ties to other regions, paving the way for ensuing violence.	Low probability of violence: Possibility of negotiations and non-violence.
Separatist region not political ally of the center	High probability of violence: High possibility of stalled negotiations and ensuing violence.	Medium probability of violence: Possibility of stalled negotiations and ensuing violence.

Table 9.2. Punjab and Chechnya: Political Elite Ties, Negotiations, and Separatist Violence.

	Political center-region ties across most regions	Political center-region ties across few regions
Separatist region political ally of the center	Punjab: Stalled negotiations (1980–1983) and ensuing violence (1984).	Punjab: Negotiations and non-violence (1977–1980).
Separatist region not political ally of the center	Chechnya: Stalled negotiations (1991–1994) and ensuing violence (1994–1996). Punjab: Stalled negotiations (1985) and ensuing violence (1986–1987).	

NOTE: This table considers Chechnya between 1991 and 1996, and Punjab between 1977 and 1987. The violent conflict in Chechnya resumes in 1999 (and is still ongoing as of 2009). In Punjab, violence continued until 1993.

The Chechen Revolution refers to the events that brought Dudayev to power in Chechnya. As in the rest of the Soviet Union, the late 1980s saw the formation of new political organizations in what was then Chechnya-Ingushetia.[24] Chief among the activists was the nationalist writer Zelim-khan Yandarbiyev, who, along with other members of the Chechen intelligentsia, organized the first meeting of the National Congress of the Chechen People in November 1990. The National Congress adopted a nationalist, yet not separatist, resolution,[25] aiming to put pressure on the republic's Supreme Soviet. The strategy worked, and on November 27, 1990, the Supreme Soviet under Doku Zavgayev adopted a declaration of sovereignty for the Chechen-Ingush republic.[26]

By the end of summer 1991, demonstrations in the name of secession and the resignation of the republic's Supreme Soviet, which had long been considered corrupt, picked up. These demonstrations were organized by the National Congress, now under the leadership of Dudayev. On September 6, forces loyal to Dudayev stormed the Supreme Soviet building. A few days later, the Supreme Soviet agreed to dissolve, and a Provisional Council was to rule until elections that were scheduled to be held on November 17. In the meantime, on October 1, Dudayev's forces seized the republic's KGB headquarters, including weapons and secret files. These events took place with Yeltsin's blessing, as Dudayev—unlike the chairman of the Chechen Supreme Soviet, Zavgayev—had taken a clear stance against the coup-makers of August 19.[27] This gratitude was, however, soon replaced by concerns for Dudayev's undemocratic rule, and when the National Congress dissolved the Provisional Council, Moscow threatened to use force. Nonetheless, the Chechen Revolution carried on. On October 27, disregarding the previously scheduled date, Dudayev came to power in elections that can hardly be considered free and fair. On November 1, he declared Chechnya an independent state.

With the Chechen Revolution, all institutional and political ties linking the center and the region disappeared. In no other region of Russia did a similar development take place. Indeed, Chechnya was the only Russian region where the first immediate post-Soviet leader came to power as head of a nationalist movement,[28] allied neither with the Communists

---

24.   Timur Muzaev, *Novaia Checheno-Ingushetiia* [The New Chechnya-Ingushetia] (Moscow: Panorama, 1992).

25.   Valery Tishkov, *Ethnicity, Nationalism, and Conflict In and After the Soviet Union: The Mind Aflame* (London: Sage Publications, 1997), p. 199.

26.   This declaration was one among several such declarations from the Russian regions in the early 1990s.

27.   On August 19, hard-line Communists tried to oust Soviet President Mikhail Gorbachev. The Chechen Supreme Soviet did not condemn the failed coup, and there were rumors that Zavgayev had been involved. In September, representatives from Moscow helped persuade the Chechen Supreme Soviet to resign.

28.   Daniel Treisman, "Russia's 'Ethnic Revival': The Separatist Activism of Regional Leaders in a Postcommunist Order," *World Politics*, Vol. 49, No. 2 (January 1997), p. 238.

nor the emerging democratic movement at the center.[29] In the late 1980s and early 1990s, the Communist Party was disintegrating across Russia, and incentives for regional party officials to stay on the good side of the central party bosses mattered less and less. Yet into the mid-1990s, many regional leaders continued to be political allies of the center by virtue of being appointed by or in some way affiliated with the Russian president.[30] These ties provided media exposure, expertise, and financial aid that helped "glue" the regions to the center.[31] Not so in Chechnya. By November 1991, "all organs of federal authority in Chechnya had already been disbanded."[32]

This disbanding of ties with the federal level had several effects. First, it brought more radical demands to the table. While the Chechen Supreme Council issued a declaration of sovereignty in November 1990 that read like a rather radical declaration, it was meant to provoke "only" economic and political concessions from Moscow.[33] In an attempt to compete with the National Congress, Zavgayev's regime grew increasingly defiant of Moscow in 1991. Yet, observers have noted, Zavgayev's nationalist resolve only went so far; while he declared Chechnya sovereign, he did not want the republic to secede.[34] Unlike Dudayev, Zavgayev, as a Communist first

---

29.   Dudayev, who in 1990 was invited by the Chechen nationalist movement to become its chairman, had spent most of his life outside Chechnya. He was the first Chechen to rise to become major general in the Soviet air force. Although he had been a member of the Communist Party since 1966, he had no history as a politician in the party. In fact, because the Chechens' political participation in their own republic had been severely limited by the deportation in 1944, there hardly existed a Chechen political elite. Moshe Gammer, *The Lone Wolf and the Bear: Three Centuries of Chechen Defiance of Russian Rule* (Pittsburgh: University of Pittsburgh Press, 2006), p. 208.

30.   Only 9 of 89 regions held regional elections in 1991. Most of the 89 regions held their first regional elections in 1995–1996, which means that the center maintained control over the appointment of regional executives until then. Following the 1996 elections, less than half of the regional leaders were allied with the party in power, Our Home is Russia.

31.   Robert W. Orttung, ed., *The Republics and Regions of the Russian Federation* (Armonk, N.Y.: M.E. Sharpe, 2000). Treisman, "Russia's 'Ethnic Revival'," p. 237, finds that across the ethnic regions in Russia, leaders who had been appointed by Yeltsin were less separatist than leaders who were popularly elected, but he attributes this finding to the difference in administrative status of the regions.

32.   Russian analysts Pain and Popov, quoted in John B. Dunlop, *Russia Confronts Chechnya: Roots of a Separatist Conflict* (New York: Cambridge University Press, 1998), p. 116.

33.   Carlotta Gall and Thomas de Waal, *Chechnya: Calamity in the Caucasus* (New York: New York University Press, 1998), pp. 82–83.

34.   German, *Russia's Chechen War*, pp. 29–32. According to Mikhailov, "Had Zavgayev managed to stay in power, events in Chechnya would have followed a very different—peaceful—scenario." See Valentin Mikhailov, "Chechnya and Tatarstan: Differences in Search for an Explanation," in Richard Sakwa, ed., *Chechnya: From Past to Future* (London: Anthem Press), p. 56. Note that the Ingush did not want to join the Chechens in their quest for an independent state, and in 1992 Chechnya-Ingushetia formally became two republics of the Russian Federation.

secretary and chairman, to some extent owed his position to Moscow.[35] Dudayev, in contrast, came to power as head of the National Congress and owed little to Moscow. As a consequence, he was more outspoken in challenging the territorial integrity of the state.

The Chechen constitution adopted by Dudayev's regime in March 1992 begins by proclaiming the Chechen Republic "as an independent sovereign state and recognizing itself as equal in rights subject in the system of world commonwealth of nations."[36] Despite this rhetoric, Dudayev appeared willing to consider less radical demands. Observers have noted that Dudayev would likely have accepted Chechnya as a union republic within a revived Soviet Union or in an equal military and economic union with Russia.[37] Nonetheless, such a vision of an equal partnership implied a radical change in Chechnya's relationship to Moscow, which the center was unwilling to accept.

Second, the disbanding of political party and other elite ties between Chechnya and Moscow was followed by negotiations that never went anywhere. Moscow's talks of concessions alternated with attempts to remove Dudayev from power by force. It was already clear in November 1991 that Moscow was willing to use force against the new Chechen leadership: following the Chechen declaration of independence, Yeltsin issued a state of emergency decree and dispatched Interior Ministry troops to the republic. Although no violent clashes erupted, Moscow's show of force fueled the revolutionary movement in Chechnya.[38]

In 1992, more than ten meetings between members of the Russian Supreme Soviet and the Chechen Parliament and government occurred—although none took place between Dudayev and Yeltsin. Dudayev insisted on a face-to-face meeting, but Yeltsin was not willing to be seen negotiating with an "illegitimate" leader.[39] On March 14, 1992, a deputy chairman of the Russian Supreme Soviet, V. Zhigulin, and the Chechen vice-president, Yandarbiyev, signed a protocol that referred to "the recognition of the political independence and state sovereignty of the Chechen Republic." This was an agreement that Dudayev found acceptable, as it went a long way toward recognizing Chechnya's sovereignty. However, such negotiations

---

35.   When Vladimir Foteyev, an ethnic Russian, resigned as first secretary of the Chechen Communist Party in 1989, the Central Committee in Moscow backed down on its preferred Russian candidate and appointed Zavgayev, an ethnic Chechen. Zavgayev was the regional party committee's preferred candidate. Thus, unlike all previous first secretaries in Chechnya, Zavgayev did not owe his position only to Moscow.

36.   The constitution is available in Diane Curran, Fiona Hill, and Elena Kostritsyna, *The Search for Peace in Chechnya: A Sourcebook 1994–1996* (Cambridge: John F. Kennedy School of Government, Harvard University, 1997), pp. 101–118.

37.   Personal communication with one of Yeltsin's former advisors, Moscow, May 30, 2005. See also Dunlop, *Russia Confronts Chechnya*, pp. 195, 172; and German, *Russia's Chechen War*, p. 73.

38.   Dunlop, *Russia Confronts Chechnya*, p. 117; compare this with Lichbach, "Deterrence or Escalation?" on inconsistent use of repression and accommodation.

39.   German, *Russia's Chechen War*, p. 69.

alternated with less diplomatic strategies. On March 31, other Moscow officials supported an attempted coup against Dudayev. A few months later, a new Russian delegation claimed that the March protocol, known as the Sochi Agreement, constituted nothing but a preliminary, non-binding briefing.[40]

In November 1992, Russian troops again entered Chechnya, this time to halt a growing conflict between Ingushetia and North Ossetia, although an equally important motive could have been removing Dudayev from power.[41] Dudayev threatened retaliation. While violent conflict was averted, the stand-off was another indicator of the center's willingness to use force. Moreover, Moscow continued to arm, and even train, the growing internal opposition to Dudayev's regime in Chechnya. By 1994, Moscow had allegedly spent billions of rubles to fund the anti-Dudayev opposition.[42] In the summer of 1994, there were rumors that the central government was planning a military intervention in Chechnya.[43] Thus, not only was the disbanding of political elite ties followed by more radical demands from the regional government; it was followed by half-hearted concessions and non-credible commitments by the center.

The increasingly volatile situation in Chechnya reflected poorly on Yeltsin in the rest of Russia, who envisioned that a "small and victorious" war in Chechnya could help him win the 1996 presidential elections. In addition, leaders in some of Chechnya's neighboring regions—which felt the growing tension in Chechnya through migration flows, interrupted transportation routes, and regional instability—called on Moscow to "take all possible measures" to restore law and order in Chechnya.[44] Several of these leaders were Yeltsin appointees or were considered pro-Yeltsin. One of the pro-Yeltsin leaders in the North Caucasus was Nikolai Yegorov, governor of Krasnodar.[45] In May 1994, Yeltsin appointed Yegorov Minister of Nationalities. An eager proponent of a military solution in Chechnya, Yegorov was among the "hawks" in Yeltsin's administration. Indeed, after Yegorov's appointment, no meetings were held between the leadership in Grozny and Moscow,[46] and from July to December 1994,

---

40.   Dunlop, *Russia Confronts Chechnya*, pp. 169–171.

41.   Ibid., pp. 173–175.

42.   Nikolaj Gritchki, "Kakie dengi voyuyut v Chechne," *Izvestiya*, September 21, 1994.

43.   Personal communication, Moscow, June 3, 2005; and German, *Russia's Chechen War*, p. 102.

44.   "Chechnya: Reaction of Regions Bordering on Chechnya to Yeltsin's Address," *BBC Summary of World Broadcasts*, December 1, 1994. The North Caucasus includes the Russian-majority regions of Krasnodar, Stavropol', and Rostov, and the ethnically-defined regions of Chechnya, Dagestan, Ingushetia, Kabardino-Balkaria, Karachay-Cherkessia, North Ossetia, and Adygeya.

45.   Yegorov was considered a protégé of Vladimir Shumeiko, the speaker of the upper house of Parliament, who some considered to be Yeltsin's successor. Thomas de Waal, "Shumeiko Emerging as Yeltsin Heir Apparent," *Moscow News*, June 10, 1994.

46.   Vladimir Yemelyanenko, "New Vice-Premier Stakes His Position on the Use of Force in Chechnya," *Moscow News*, December 16, 1994.

the Yeltsin administration moved steadily toward a military invasion of Chechnya. While the negotiations between Chechnya and Moscow were already fraught with troubles—due to the demands raised, unwillingness to compromise, and commitments not met—Moscow's decision to use force was also influenced by concerns in Chechnya's neighboring regions, several headed by Yeltsin allies.

As negotiations were failing and the Chechen economy was deteriorating—due to corruption, the policies of Dudayev's regime, and Moscow's economic blockade of Chechnya—anti-Dudayev opposition within Chechnya grew. Indeed, while the Chechen Revolution's severing of political ties to Moscow complicated attempts at center-region negotiations, the difficulties that the new Chechen leadership faced locally, once in power, contributed to divisions within the region. While I suggest that an effect of stalled negotiations is increased divisions within the region, it is important to note that Dudayev's regime was early on confronted by an outspoken opposition within Chechnya. Policymakers in Moscow, with no political allegiance to Dudayev, used these internal divisions to undermine him.

While some consider the internal power struggles in Chechnya in the early 1990s a result of the region's clan-based social structure,[47] another source of division was divergent views of economic and social reforms, which were only reinforced as the economy deteriorated.[48] The failure of the negotiations between Chechnya and Moscow both fed into and followed from such divisions. Indeed, besides the failure of representatives of the Chechen executive and the Yeltsin administration to reach an agreement, the parties negotiating on behalf of the Chechens were not always allied with the Chechen executive.[49] Moscow's official line was to negotiate with all political forces in Chechnya, although in practice, it negotiated primarily with members of the opposition to Dudayev's regime,[50] thus deepening divisions within Chechnya and further impeding peaceful negotiations between the secessionist Chechen government and the center.

From summer of 1992, the Chechen Prime Minister, Yaragai Mamodayev, a Dudayev ally turned opponent, played a key role in negotiations with representatives of the Russian Parliament. In December 1992, he drafted an agreement with the Russian vice premier, Sergei Shakhrai, on the division of power between the Russian Federation and the Chechen Re-

---

47. Ekaterina Sokirianskaia, "Families and Clans in Chechnya and Ingushetia: A Fieldwork Report," *Central Asian Survey*, Vol. 24, No. 4 (December 2005), pp. 453–467.

48. Dunlop, *Russia Confronts Chechnya*, pp. 124–128; German, *Russia's Chechnya War*, pp. 80–83; Valery Tishkov, *Chechnya: Life in a War-Torn Society* (Berkeley: University of California Press, 2004), pp. 63–68.

49. The same can be said of the Russian side in 1992–1993. See Lapidus, "Contested Sovereignty." Note that divisions in Moscow may have complicated the negotiation process, but they cannot explain why negotiations with Chechnya failed at a time when the center was signing bilateral agreements with other regions, including separatist Tatarstan.

50. Dunlop, *Russia Confronts Chechnya*, pp. 154–156, 188–189, 197–198.

public. This attempt failed, however, because Dudayev, who was not part of the negotiations and did not approve of Mamodayev's initiative, saw the agreement as falling short of the sovereignty promised in the March 1992 accord brokered by his Vice-President, Yandarbiyev. The Chechen Parliament's negotiations on the draft treaty continued in January 1993, when Shakhrai headed a Russian delegation to Grozny. Again, though, Dudayev, who played no role in the negotiation process, dismissed the agreement.[51] Thus, the situation was one where the Chechen Parliament, increasingly opposed to the Chechen executive, and the federal center, with no political ties to Chechnya's executive (and eager to side-step his authority), reached an agreement that was unacceptable to the Chechen executive.[52] In the spring of 1993, the stand-off between Dudayev and the Chechen parliament peaked, and in June 1993, clashes broke out in the center of Grozny between Dudayev's supporters and opponents. In turn, Dudayev dissolved the Parliament.

While the dissolution of the Parliament ended the deadlock between the Chechen executive and legislature, several anti-Dudayev opposition movements developed in 1993, including Mamodayev's Government of Popular Trust, Yusup Soslambekov's Parliament of the Chechen Republic in Exile, Ruslan Khasbulatov's Peacemaking Group, and Umar Avturkhanov's Chechen Interim Council.[53] Moscow decided that the Interim Council was the only legitimate negotiating partner in the republic. Even prior to the declaration of Chechen independence in November 1991, there was internal opposition to Dudayev and the National Congress,[54] based on diverging views about the path to independence. But while the opposition prior to the spring of 1993 consisted primarily of civic or political organizations, the groups that emerged in 1993 and 1994 were more forceful in challenging Dudayev's regime, in part due to support from Moscow. By 1993–1994, Dudayev's regime faced two militias, which were loosely allied with one another: the armed forces of Beslan Gantemirov and of Ruslan Labazanov, both of whom were former Dudayev allies. Allegedly, Labazanov's group was supported by the Russian Secret Services, and in 1994 it briefly allied with Khasbulatov's Peacemaking Group. By August 1994, Gantemirov's forces had allied with Avturkhanov's Interim Council. Clashes between forces loyal to Dudayev and the opposition continued throughout 1994, giving Moscow the opportunity to claim that the situa-

---

51.   German, *Russia's Chechen War*, pp. 71–72.

52.   Märta-Lisa Magnusson, "The Negotiation Process between Russia and Chechenia—Strategies, Achievements and Future Problems," in Ole Høiris and Sefa Martin Yürükel, eds., *Contrasts and Solutions in the Caucasus* (Aarhus, Denmark: Aarhus University Press, 1998), pp. 407–434. In January 1993, Dudayev assembled a negotiation team that carried out talks with members of the Russian parliament, but these, too, failed. See Dunlop, *Russia Confronts Chechnya*, p. 183.

53.   Timur Muzaev, *Chechenskaia Respublika: organy vlasti i politicheskie sily* [The Chechen Republic: Organs of Power and Political Authority] (Moscow: Panorama, 1995); and German, *Russia's Chechnya War*, pp. 85–106.

54.   Muzaev, *Novaia Checheno-Ingushetiia*.

tion within Chechnya called for the army to step in and restore order.

The Chechen case is perhaps an extreme version of how federal bargaining is disrupted by the lack of intergovernmental political ties.[55] It further demonstrates how the "wrong" ties can be disruptive. The leader of the Interim Council, Avturkhanov, did have incentives to cooperate with the central government because he received both money and weapons that would help boost his local control. In return, he did not push for independence. Avturkhanov, however, controlled only some of Chechnya's districts and had limited popular support. Moscow's fostering of ties with a local leader in opposition to the region's executive alienated the Chechen leadership and further contributed to its weak hold on power. While such a weakening of the Chechen leadership was Moscow's very intention, the weakened local regime did not help avoid a violent center-region confrontation. Rather, internal power struggles due to a weak local regime appeared to further complicate intergovernmental bargaining.[56]

The Case of Punjab

While Punjab was the scene of violent communal confrontations between Sikhs and Hindus between 1978 and 1984, the conflict between the central government in Delhi and separatist forces in Punjab did not turn violent until the Indian Army stormed the Golden Temple in Amritsar in June 1984. Yet Operation Bluestar, as the attack was officially known, was not immediately followed by a rise in separatist violence. In 1985, it looked like the Akali Dal, the main party representing the Sikhs, and its leader, Sant Harchand Singh Longowal, would be able to steer the conflict to a peaceful end. From 1986, however, violence escalated in a spiral of insurgency and counterinsurgency campaigns. As Figure 9.1 shows, the years between 1989 and 1992 were particularly deadly. Among residents of Punjab, there was a sense that militants pursuing an independent Sikh state, Khalistan, were going to achieve their goal.[57]

The conflict between the central government and separatist forces in Punjab was not destined to turn violent. Political ties between central and regional elites affected the negotiation process and opposition within Pun-

---

55. While Tatarstan's president, Mintimer Shaimiev, was not a copartisan of President Yeltsin, Yeltsin was in the early 1990s willing to negotiate with Shaimiev, who used his control of the outcomes of the Russian federal elections in Tatarstan as a bargaining chip. The strategy worked because Yeltsin needed Shaimiev to "deliver" favorable electoral outcomes. See Kimitaka Matsuzato, "From Ethno-Bonapartism to Centralized *Caciquismo*: Characteristics and Origins of the Tatarstan Political Regime, 1990–2000,"*Journal of Communist Studies and Transition Politics*, Vol. 17, No. 4 (2001), pp. 43–77.

56. Lack of political center-region ties, stalled negotiations, and internal power struggles also contributed to the second Chechen war, which began in 1999. See David Hoffman, "Miscalculations Paved Path to Chechen War," *Washington Post*, March 20, 2000. Due to space considerations I do not address the second Chechen war here, but in terms of Table 1.2, it can be placed in the bottom right box.

57. Personal communication from Chandigarh and Amritsar, winter 2006.

jab. The case, which consists of three distinct phases, demonstrates how the presence of political ties with the central government dampened separatist demands (1977–1980), as well as how the center's political party ties to other states complicated negotiations with the separatist region (1980–1983, 1985–1987), even when the government in that region was a political ally of the center (1980–1983). Indeed, more so than in the Chechen case, the center's decisions with respect to Punjab were influenced by its political concerns in other Indian states.

Figure 9.1. Violence in Punjab, 1984–1993.

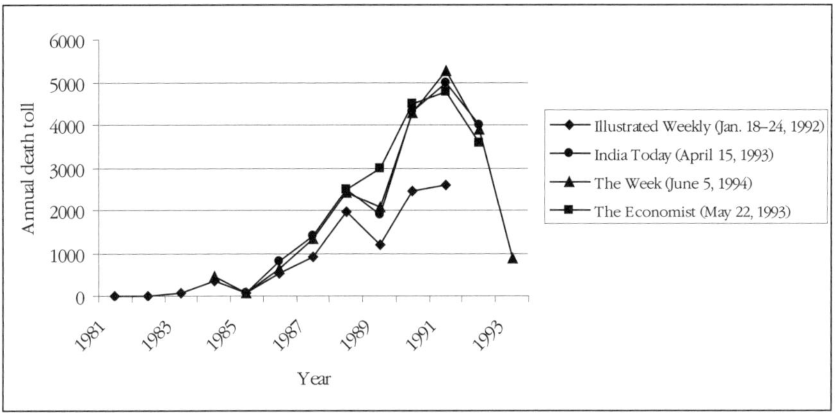

SOURCE: Adapted from Table 10.1 in Gurharpal Singh, *Ethnic Conflict in India: A Case Study of Punjab* (London: MacMillan, 2000), pp. 163–164.

HOW TROUBLE BEGAN

In 1977, Sant Jarnail Singh Bhindranwale was appointed head of the Damdami Taksal, a Sikh seminary near Amritsar. He quickly became a popular religious figure in Punjab's villages, and in the early 1980s, he became the unofficial leader of the emerging Sikh militant movement. The movement spoke of greater autonomy or a separate Sikh state, yet Bhindranwale never directly said he favored independence.[58] Most of his speeches addressed concerns about declining religious observance among young Sikhs and emphasized differences between Hindus and Sikhs, often referring to a history of a Hindu-ruled state discriminating against the Sikhs.[59] The emerging militant movement gained followers among Sikh farmers, especially those with small and middle-sized farms, and the All India Sikh Students Federation (AISSF). The recruits, mostly young men, were concerned with the protection of Sikh culture and religion and the plight of small farms in Punjab's modernizing economy. Bhindranwale's message

---

58.   Mark Tully and Satish Jacob, *Amritsar: Mrs. Gandhi's Last Battle* (London: J. Cape, 1986), p. 129.

59.   Paramjit Singh Judge, *Religion, Identity and Nationhood: The Sikh Militant Movement* (New Delhi: Rawat, 2005), pp. 128–157.

resonated with these concerns,[60] as did the "adventure" that the militant movement offered.[61] While the seeds of the militant movement were set in the late 1970s, it was not until late 1982 that Bhindranwale became a powerful force in Punjab.

Since 1920, the main political party representing the Sikhs in Punjab has been the Akali Dal. In the 1960s, the party spearheaded the Punjabi *Suba* agitation, which in 1966 led to the formation of present-day Punjab as a Sikh-majority state within India. In 1973, the party issued the Anandpur Sahib Resolution (ASR), which forms the basis for the political demands at the heart of Punjab's conflict with Delhi.[62] The ASR called for India to become a "real" federation, where the tasks of the center were limited to defense, foreign affairs, and communications. In 1978, the party adopted twelve resolutions, known as the Ludhiana resolutions, based on the 1973 document. These called for greater power for the states and a reconsideration of the sharing of Punjab's river waters, which had been institutionalized in 1966, when the central government decided to direct a portion of the water from Punjab's rivers to its neighboring states. The 1966 reorganization of Punjab had also made the capital of greater Punjab the *shared* capital of the two successor states, Punjab and Haryana, and made it centrally governed; the Ludhiana resolutions called for the capital, Chandigarh, to be transferred to Punjab only. These demands could all be met within the Indian federation, and the main faction of the Akali Dal never called for a separate Sikh state. In the early 1980s, however, the Akalis' inability to gain concessions from Delhi fueled dissatisfaction with the party within the state and boosted the militant movement, which was more inclined to use violent means.

PUNJAB, 1977–1980

The Akali Dal passed the Ludhiana resolutions while governing Punjab in a coalition with the Janata Party, which also ruled in Delhi. In June 1977, the long-dominant Congress Party lost elections both at the center and across a number of traditionally Congress-ruled states. At the center, Morarji Desai of the Janata Party, which was a coalition of anti-Congress parties and splinter groups, succeeded Indira Gandhi as prime minister. In Punjab, the Akalis joined forces with the Janata Party and formed a government with Prakash Singh Badal of the Akali Dal as chief minister.

While facing pressure to pursue an agenda of greater autonomy from within the party, Badal did not actively do so. In fact, the 1978 resolutions are often considered a watered-down version of the 1973 ASR. Particularly among its critics, the Akali Dal is known for turning to agitation and

---

60. Hamish Telford, "The Political Economy of Punjab: Creating Space for Sikh Separatism," *Asian Survey*, Vol. 32, No. 11 (November 1992), pp. 969–988; and Pettigrew, *Unheard Voices*.

61. Harish Puri, Paramjit Singh Judge, and Jagrup Singh Sekhon, *Terrorism in Punjab: Understanding Grassroots Reality* (New Delhi: Har Anand, 1999).

62. The ASR is reprinted in Verinder Grover, ed., *The Story of Punjab Yesterday and Today*, 2nd ed., Vol. 3 (New Delhi: Deep and Deep, 1999), pp. 307–321.

radical demands when out of power, while doing little to follow up on those demands while in power. Given the argument in this chapter, it is not surprising that the party's chief minister, when a political ally of the party ruling at the center, did not push an autonomy agenda; one of the effects of political elite ties across tiers of government is that regional elites may refrain from pursuing radical demands.

A Punjab scholar provided the following explanation for the Akalis' reluctance to pursue the goals of the ASR while in power: In an interview in 1978, an Akali leader was asked why the party, now in power, was not raising the demands of the ASR. He suggested that since the Akalis now had the responsibility for governing the country, the party did not have the time to talk about "small demands for small communities."[63] Similarly, according to an Akali politician who was somewhat disillusioned with the party's leadership, politics in Punjab is always about a certain dynasty whose only interest is to gain and hold on to power. Once in power, he suggested, no one has any interest in fighting for the ASR.[64] Thus, despite the adoption of the Ludhiana resolutions in 1978, the period from 1977 to 1980 was one where divisive issues were toned down and agitational tactics avoided. In March 1978, for instance, a religious Sikh leader began a fast-unto-death campaign, a frequent tactic of the Akalis, in the name of transferring Chandigarh to Punjab, but Akali leaders called for such issues to be dealt with through "peaceful negotiations" instead.[65] While the more radical aspects of the 1973 ASR were debated at Sikh gatherings, debates in the state's legislative assembly focused on greater autonomy for all states in India. The Akali Finance Minister in Punjab emphasized that the Akali Dal's autonomy demand was merely about restructuring center-state relations to secure more financial resources for the state.[66] Indeed, the coalition with the centrally governing Janata Party, which threatened to leave the coalition if Badal gave in to pressures from more extreme Akali factions, provided incentives for him to work out compromise solutions both among factions of the party and with Delhi.[67]

The Janata coalition at the center and the coalition between the Akali Dal and the Janata Party in Punjab were fraught with divisions, and in 1980, the Congress Party returned to power both in Delhi and in Punjab.

---

63. Personal communication with a Punjab scholar, Amritsar, February 23, 2006.

64. Personal communication with an Akali Dal politician, Amritsar, February 18, 2006.

65. Paul Wallace, "Religious and Secular Politics in Punjab: The Sikh Dilemma in Competing Systems," in Grover, *The Story of Punjab*, Vol. 2, p. 221.

66. Arun Mehra, "Akali-Janata Coalition—an Analysis," in Grover, *The Story of Punjab*, Vol. 2, pp. 227–238.

67. Ibid., pp. 242, 245. The Akalis are notorious for factionalism. In elections to the Shiromani Gurudwara Parbandhak Committee, which governs the Sikh temples, competition takes place only among Akali factions, thus pitting different Akali leaders against one another. See Paul Brass, *Language, Religion and Politics in North India* (New York: Cambridge University Press 1974), p. 313.

PUNJAB, 1980–1984

While Congress under Jawaharlal Nehru's leadership, from 1947 to 1964, was characterized by close ties between the national party and strong state-level party branches, the Congress Party of Indira Gandhi was one where the central party at times deliberately weakened the party's chief ministers to enhance central control.[68] The Congress governments in Punjab and Delhi in 1949 and 1956 negotiated agreements to meet Sikh demands (albeit none were implemented). In contrast, Punjab's Congress government under Sardar Darbara Singh, from June 1980 to October 1983, drew support from both the Hindu and Sikh populations; it was not similarly involved in negotiating the Sikhs' demands in the early 1980s. In fact, Indira Gandhi and her Home Minister (later President), Zail Singh, seemed to work against Darbara Singh. Zail Singh, a Sikh who had served as Punjab's chief minister from 1972 to 1977, initially backed Bhindranwale in order to split the Akali Dal and destabilize the government of Darbara Singh, a long-time political rival.[69] Ultimately, what seemed to matter for Delhi's decisions with respect to Punjab was Congress's electoral prospects elsewhere. Thus, the negotiations of Sikh demands took place between the Akalis and the Congress-ruled central government, in a process characterized by lack of compromise, non-credible commitments, and radicalization of the Akalis' demands and means. The consequence of this stalled negotiation process was a growing militant movement in Punjab, dissatisfied both with the state's Congress-led government and the Akali Dal.

The Akali Dal met with representatives of the central government more than twenty times between 1981 and 1984, yet none of these negotiations led anywhere. First, the parties could not reach a compromise. While Indira Gandhi and the Congress Party were willing to give in to relatively minor demands, they did not agree to grant concessions with respect to the Akalis' main demands, such as a reconsideration of the sharing of Punjab's river waters, the transfer of Chandigarh, and greater political autonomy for the states. After two days of negotiations in November 1981, one of the Akali leaders noted that Indira Gandhi seemed set on delaying discussions as a means to exhaust the Akalis. The last time Indira Gandhi was present at the negotiating table was in April 1982, and the Akali leaders left that meeting with the impression that the Prime Minister had decided not to concede to their demands even before she entered the room.[70]

68.   Paul Brass, *Ethnicity and Nationalism: Theory and Comparison* (New Delhi: Sage Publications, 1991); and Atul Kohli, *Democracy and Discontent: India's Growing Crisis of Governability* (New York: Cambridge University Press, 1991).

69.   Tully and Jacob, *Amritsar*, pp. 66–72, 105; Sucha Singh Gill and K. C. Singhal, "Genesis of Punjab Problem," in Abida Samiuddin, ed., *The Punjab Crisis: Challenge and Response* (Delhi: Mittal Publications, 1985), p. 48. See also the following editorials from India's *Economic and Political Weekly* in 1982: "Congress Party: Politics of Personal Loyalty," February 20, 1982; "Politics: Trouble in State," March 27, 1982; "Punjab: Congress (I)'s Dangerous Game," May 8, 1982; "Punjab: Willing to be Used," August 28, 1982; and "Punjab: More Opportunism," November 6, 1982.

70.   Kuldeep Nayar, "Towards Disaster," in Abida Samiuddin, ed., *The Punjab Crisis:*

Second, the talks were characterized by broken promises. In August 1982, the Akali leaders met with Swaran Singh, a Sikh Congress politician, and reached a settlement that addressed many of the Akalis' demands. After the meeting, Swaran Singh presented the settlement to the Prime Minister, who approved it. By the time the settlement was presented to Parliament for approval, however, the concessions had been watered down—and some of them were now dependent on the consent of the governments of Rajasthan and Haryana. Apparently, observes Kuldeep Nayar, the Prime Minister had changed her mind.[71] Subsequent talks broke down.

Third, while Chief Minister Badal had not actively pushed the party's autonomy agenda in 1977–1980, once the Akalis were out of power, it was back on the table. After the failure of negotiations in April 1982, the main faction of the Akali Dal under Sant Harchand Singh Longowal launched an agitational *morcha* (protest campaign), which represented a departure from the attempt to avoiding agitational tactics in 1977–1980 and is the closest the Akalis were to being associated with the separatists.[72] Over the next two years, agitation campaigns replaced negotiations as the dominant Akali tactic, which resulted in arrests of thousands of Sikh protestors—but to no avail.[73] The *morcha* made it easier for the center to conflate the Akalis' demands for greater autonomy with the militant movement, although after Operation Bluestar, the Indian Army's attack on the Golden Temple in June 1984, the official explanation was that the attack was not a response to the Akalis' demands, but a response to a growing secessionist movement. Notably, the secessionist movement grew and turned to violent means as it became clear that negotiations between Punjab's Akali-led government and the Congress government at the center were futile.

Why such a stalled negotiation process? Scholars and observers have noted that Indira Gandhi's concern for Congress's electoral fate elsewhere in India contributed to the failure of the Punjab negotiations between 1981 and 1984.[74] Indeed, when the negotiations between the center and

---

Challenge and Response (Delhi: Mittal Publications, 1985), pp. 124–125.

71. Ibid., pp. 132–134. The central government had similar views of the Akalis' changing their mind, due to in-party conflicts. See Government of India, "White Paper on Punjab Agitation," in Grover, *The Story of Punjab*, Vol. 3, p. 334.

72. Harish Puri, "Anandpur Sahib Resolution: What Do the Akalis Really Want?" *Interdiscipline*, Vol. 15, No. 2 (1983), p. 54.

73. According to the center, steps were taken toward meeting the Akalis' demands, notably the establishment of the Sarkaria Commission on Centre-State Relations. Government of India, "White Paper." The commission delivered its report in 1988. By 2005, most of the recommendations were at some stage of implementation. George Mathew, "Republic of India," in Akhtar Majeed, Ronald L. Watts, and Douglas M. Brown, eds., *Distribution of Powers and Responsibilities in Federal Countries* (Montreal and Kingston: McGill-Queen's University Press, 2006).

74. C.P. Bhambari, "The Failure to Accommodate," in Amrik Singh, ed., *Punjab in Indian Politics* (New Delhi: Ajanta Publications, 1985), pp. 207–208; L. Sheth and A. S. Narang, "The Electoral Angle," in Amrik Singh, ed., *Punjab in Indian Politics* (Delhi: Ajanta Publications, 1985), pp. 128–130; Brass, *Ethnicity and Nationalism*, p. 203, 207; and

the Akali Dal stalled in April 1982, state assembly elections in Haryana were only a month away, and Haryana's Congress chief minister, Bhajan Lal, had informed Indira Gandhi that he already faced enough troubles due to a decision she had made in December 1981 that modified the division of river waters between Punjab and Haryana. Similarly, in November 1982, the Akali Dal and the Prime Minister's team of negotiators reached a settlement, but Lal convinced Indira Gandhi not to agree to the deal before consulting his government, as well as the government in Rajasthan, another state benefiting from Punjab's river waters.[75] In 1983, Congress lost elections in the large states of Karnataka and Andhra Pradesh, making it even more apprehensive about acts that could cost it support in Haryana and Rajasthan.

The failure of negotiations discredited the Akalis among the more militant, extremist Sikhs, and the party was seen as both unable and unwilling to further the interests of the Sikh community, thus weakening its power in Punjab. An observer at the time noted that the failure of negotiations helped to make violence legitimate in Punjab.[76] According to Nayar, "The Akalis' main problem was how to maintain their credibility with the community; the government was not giving them any opportunity to show that by staying in the mainstream, they had won their demands."[77] Bhindranwale's claims that the path of peaceful and moderate resistance was a blind alley gained support, particularly among the youth. As a Sikh observer of Punjabi politics explained in 2006, people were frustrated because "the Akalis are notorious for saying one thing and doing another."[78] By 1982–1983, violence was spreading in Punjab's villages as young Sikh men, upon Bhindranwale's request, took up arms and rode around on motorcycles, killing both Sikhs and Hindus who were considered to be enemies, including police officials, people thought to be informers, and political figures.[79] In October 1983, Punjab was declared a "disturbed area" and placed under central control.

In 1982, Bhindranwale and his supporters had moved into the Golden Temple in Amritsar, which is the holiest of all Sikh shrines. The Akalis under Longowal wanted the militants out of the complex, but in late 1983, the militants instead moved into the Akal Takht, the primary seat of Sikh religious authority within the temple. This inability of anyone, particularly the Akalis, to control militant Sikh forces was central to the official justification for the Indian Army's attack on the Golden Temple. Again, however, the decision to employ the army in Punjab was informed by concerns for the Congress Party elsewhere. Aware that the precarious situation in Punjab reflected poorly on the Party, it sought to appear tough on

---

Kohli, *Democracy and Discontent*, p. 362.

75. Nayar, "Towards Disaster," p. 135.

76. Bhambhari, "The Failure to Accommodate," p. 206.

77. Nayar, "Towards Disaster," p. 138.

78. Personal communication, Chandigarh, February 6, 2006.

79. Tully and Jacob, *Amritsar*, pp. 130–131.

the Sikhs ahead of the coming elections. In May 1984, just a few weeks before Operation Bluestar, the Congress Party performed poorly in by-elections in twelve states across India. The losses in the northern states were attributed to Indira Gandhi's failure to stem Hindu anger at what was perceived to be Sikh secessionism.[80] In April 1984, a Hindu opposition leader even called for Indira Gandhi's resignation over the growing crisis in Punjab.[81] Yet rather than strengthen the position of her party, Indira Gandhi's decision to attack the Golden Temple in June 1984 cost her her life.

In sum, in the years between 1980 and 1984, the central government and Punjab's government were both ruled by the Congress Party. Yet due to the Congress Party's concern for its electoral fortunes elsewhere in India, particularly Haryana, it was a period characterized by a stalled negotiation process that nourished the militant movement. In this case, the center's concerns for political allies in other regions trumped its concern for the separatist region, even though the government in the separatist region was ruled by the party ruling at the center. In part, the Congress leadership's lack of concern with respect to the implications for its copartisan ally in Punjab—that it reflected poorly on Punjab's Congress Party to be unable to uphold law and order in the state—was a result of less generalizable factors, particularly the rivalry between the Home Minister, Zail Singh, and Punjab's Chief Minister, Darbara Singh. Yet in the counterfactual case, the central government would have been less concerned about its electoral fortunes in Haryana and more inclined to reach a compromise solution with the Sikhs, despite such personal competition.

PUNJAB, 1985–1987

Despite the Indian Army's attack on the Golden Temple in June 1984, the ensuing assassination of Indira Gandhi, and anti-Sikh riots in Delhi, the "Punjab crisis" looked like it was coming to a halt in 1985. While Punjab was still under central control, the Akali Dal, under Longowal, and Prime Minister Rajiv Gandhi reached an agreement.

The Rajiv-Longowal Accord, or the Punjab Accord, gave in to almost all of the demands rejected in 1981–1984, and included provisions for the transfer of Chandigarh and a promise that the water issue would be presented to a Supreme Court tribunal.[82] While the center did not concede to all of the Akalis' demands, it agreed to take them into consideration. On paper, the accord was promising. Although some Akali leaders and militants opposed the accord, it was well-received by Punjab's population. Indeed, it looked like Longowal was about to unite Punjab's population

---

80.   Ram Narayan Kumar, Amrik Singh, Ashok Agrwaal, and Jaskaran Kaur, *Reduced to Ashes: The Insurgency and Human Rights in Punjab* (Kathmandu: South Asia Forum for Human Rights, 2003), p. 32.

81.   Stewart Slavin, "Hindu Leader Calls for Gandhi's Resignation," *United Press International*, April 5, 1984.

82.   Reprinted in Grover, *The Story of Punjab*, Vol. 3, pp. 384–386.

and make peace with the center. However, some of the militants saw the accord as a sell-out by a power-hungry Akali leadership, and in July 1985, Longowal was assassinated. In the state assembly elections the following September, the Akalis won an unprecedented victory and for the first time were able to rule without a coalition partner. Observers have taken the election outcome to indicate popular support for the Rajiv-Longowal Accord.[83]

Upon Longowal's assassination, the Congress government at the center did not follow up on its promises in the accord. The first main provision of the accord was broken when Chandigarh was not transferred to Punjab by January 26, 1986. Similarly, in May 1987, the Supreme Court ruling on the sharing of Punjab's river waters reduced Punjab's share and doubled that of Haryana.[84] As of 2009, Chandigarh is still the shared capital of Punjab and Haryana, and the river water question remains unresolved. Both Atul Kohli and Paul Brass argue that the failure of the Rajiv-Longowal Accord rests with the Congress Party's concerns in other Indian states, particularly Haryana—and this undermined the Akali Dal.[85] In December 1985, Congress lost the state elections in Assam, fueling dissatisfaction with Rajiv Gandhi's leadership within the party. In June 1986, there were elections in Haryana, which had been ruled by Bhajan Lal, a Congress politician, since 1979.[86] In the Rajiv-Longowal Accord, neither the Chandigarh clause nor the river water clause was popular in Haryana. Indeed, after the signing of the accord, opposition parties in Haryana called for Lal's resignation if he accepted it,[87] and by January 1986, the proposed Chandigarh transfer had become such a contentious issue that violent demonstrations broke out in Haryana. The decision to delay the transfer of Chandigarh was based on disagreements about which areas of Punjab to give to Haryana in compensation.[88] In the end, Rajiv Gandhi backed out of the Punjab Accord. The accord's failure fueled the fires in Punjab, giving credence to those who had opposed it in the first place.

While Longowal's assassination was followed by a victory for the Akalis in the 1985 elections, the failed implementation of the Rajiv-

---

83.　Kohli, *Democracy and Discontent*, pp. 368–369.

84.　Singh, *Ethnic Conflict*, p. 133.

85.　Kohli, *Democracy and Discontent*, pp. 370–376; and Brass, *Ethnicity and Nationalism*, pp. 210–211.

86.　Since its creation in 1966, Haryana had only in 1977–1979 been ruled by a non-Congress Party. Notably, the chief minister in 1979 was Bhajan Lal, then of the Janata Party, who switched allegiance to Congress when it looked like the Janata Party would not remain in power. Lal stepped down in June 1986 but was succeeded by another Congress man, Bansi Lal. Congress lost the Haryana elections in June 1987.

87.　Richard Ford, "Haryana Opposition MPs Quit Over 'Sell-Out' to Sikhs: State Officials Criticise Agreement between Indian Government and Punjab Leaders," *The Times* (London), July 29, 1985.

88.　Jonathan Landay, "Tensions Rising over Transfer of State Capital," *United Press International*, January 20, 1986; and Eric Silver, "Extremists Hold the Keys to the Punjab Lock: Threats to Indian State's Sikh Accord," *Guardian*, January 8, 1986.

Longowal Accord undermined the party's ruling faction as a representative of the Sikh community. It also nourished factionalism and a growth in militant groups. As a result, it became difficult for Surjit Singh Barnala's Akali government to rule the state. In June 1987, the Congress government in Delhi placed the state under President's Rule, citing the Akalis' inability to curb the growing violence.

In February 1986, after the transfer of Chandigarh failed to take place, the Akali Dal faction under Prakash Singh Badal split from the ruling Longowal faction. By 1987–1988, another faction of the Akali Dal, under the still-active Simranjit Singh Mann, began calling for an independent Sikh state, Khalistan. The proliferation of Akali parties continued, and in 1991, ahead of the 1992 elections, there were as many as seven splinter groups of the party.[89] In addition, from 1986 to 1992, the number of militant groups in Punjab grew, among them the Babbar Khalsa, the AISSF, the Khalistan Commando Force (KCF), and the Bhindranwale Tiger Force for Khalistan (BTFK). Although these militant groups and their many splinter groups came under the umbrella of three coordinating "Panthic Committees," they operated relatively independently of one another, sometimes in pursuit of different goals.

There was growing conflict among the militant groups in Punjab in the late 1980s.[90] In January 1986, the first Panthic Committee was formed, and the KCF, which had emerged after Operation Bluestar, became its armed wing, under the command of Wassam Singh Zaffarwal in the late 1980s. By 1988, several of the field commanders of the KCF had formed their own armed groups, including the BTFK under Gurbachan Singh Manochahal. In November 1988, groups opposed to Zaffarwal's KCF—including two KCF splinter groups, the Babbar Khalsa, and a splinter group of the AISSF—came together under the leadership of the second Panthic Committee of Sohan Singh. In April 1990, a third Panthic Committee, led by Manochahal's BTFK, brought together militant groups—including the KCF splinter group under Gurjant Singh Rajasthani, the Dashmesh regiment, and an AISSF faction—that opposed members of the other committees. Almost twenty different militant groups, excluding the various Akali factions, were active in Punjab over the course of the 1980s.

From 1988 to 1991, violence in Punjab grew as spirals of insurgency and counterinsurgency campaigns intensified. Some of the violence was the result of militant groups fighting each other, not just police and security forces. In a fascinating study, Paramjit Singh Judge analyzes warnings that the militants placed in Punjabi newspapers.[91] The largest share of warnings, 34 percent, was directed at other militants, while the body that represented the counterinsurgents, the police, was targeted in only 17 percent of the warnings. The civilian population, too, was targeted in the warnings, which were directed particularly toward people breaking the

---

89. Based on Lakhwinder Singh Sidhu, *Party Politics in Punjab* (New Delhi: Harnam Publications, 1994).

90. Pettigrew, *Unheard Voices*.

91. Judge, *Religion, Identity and Nationhood*.

moral code of conduct issued by some militant groups. Thus, to a certain extent, the militants alienated the very population in whose name they were fighting, which contributed to the success of the counterinsurgency campaign under the command of Punjab's most infamous police chief, K. P. S. Gill.[92] Indeed, by 1993, most of the militant leaders had either been killed in the counterinsurgency campaign or had sought exile abroad. While violence in Punjab in the late 1980s took on a life of its own, pitting different groups against one another and the government, the failed implementation of the Rajiv-Longowal Accord played an important role in feeding these divisions in Punjab by discrediting the Akali Dal. In turn, the Akali Dal, plagued by intra-party factions, was opposed by a number of militant groups, and could neither rule the state nor negotiate with the center.

Conclusion

This chapter focuses on the turn toward violence in self-determination, or separatist, conflicts in decentralized states. It argues that the *absence* of political ties between leaders in the capital and in a separatist region and the *presence* of political ties between leaders in the capital and other regions of the state may complicate intergovernmental negotiations, enhancing the chances of the conflict being fought through violent means by feeding divisions among regional elites or groups. The study assesses this proposed process, linking the lack of political ties and violent conflict, but it does not contend that this is the only path through which separatist struggles turn violent.

In Chechnya, the revolution in 1990–1991 broke all political elite ties between the regional and central governments, complicating negotiations and deepening divisions within Chechnya, which further damaged the bargaining process. In Punjab, the center and the region were governed by the same political party, the Congress Party, during the early 1980s, but concerns for the party's fortunes in other regions, especially neighboring Haryana, were obstacles to a compromise in Punjab. In 1985, after the central government attacked the Golden Temple in Amritsar, the president of the Akali Dal, the main party representing Sikh interests, gained regional support for an agreement with the Congress government at the center. Again, the Congress Party's concern for its fortunes in other states proved to be an obstacle, and the negotiations failed, nourishing divisions within Punjab and contributing to a spiral of violence.

Central to the ways in which center-region political elite ties affect the turn to violence is how these ties influence the negotiation process between regional and central elites, and how that process, in turn, affects regional elites' ability to rule the state they are governing. In both Chechnya and Punjab, the central government's justification for military inter-

---

92. Kumar et al., *Reduced to Ashes,* argue that the success of this campaign came at a large cost in terms of extrajudicial killings and "disappearances."

vention (and also, in the Punjab case, direct central rule), was an increasingly violent situation *within* the region, with different groups fighting one another. A possible objection to the argument put forth in this chapter is the fact that Dudayev's National Congress and the Akali Dal faced local challengers *prior* to the stalled negotiation process, and, particularly in the Chechen case, these divisions contributed to the stalled negotiation process. The empirical narrative suggests that there is not a one-way, linear relationship from stalled negotiations to internal divisions. Yet while the stalled negotiation process did not *create* these divisions, it did feed into and deepen them. In both cases, negotiations characterized by radical demands, few compromises, or non-credible commitments were followed by a strengthening or growth of internal opposition movements, which made Dudayev and the Akali Dal even more problematic negotiation partners for the central government.

This chapter makes two contributions to the literature. While many studies of intrastate conflict assume that the presence of conflict means the presence of violent conflict, this chapter, along with the other chapters in this volume, does not consider violence to be a natural extension of conflict. Moreover, the study both draws from and builds on the growing body of research on intrastate conflict and decentralization, tracing the intervening steps that help to explain how political party relations, or lack thereof, affect one of the most unstable forms of intergovernmental bargaining—violent separatist conflicts.

The chapter also raises questions. First, the case of Punjab shows that political elite ties to other regions of the state may trump political elite ties to a separatist region. Future research can begin to systematically examine the conditions under which some copartisan regions are more important to the central government than others. Second, while this chapter focuses on how political ties between elites in the capital and in the region affect intergovernmental bargaining, it is worth exploring if other ties, such as economic ties, have similar effects. Finally, while this chapter focuses on dynamics between the capital and the regions and within the separatist region, it does not examine how struggles within the center affect bargaining with the regions; this is another potential area for future research.

Chapter 10

Mobilization and Resistance: A Framework for Analysis

Erica Chenoweth and Maria J. Stephan

Recent studies of unconventional warfare have attempted to evaluate the conditions under which "weak" actors defeat ostensibly "stronger" adversaries.[1] Some scholars have argued, for instance, that non-state armed groups are capable of defeating conventionally superior state adversaries when they employ indirect and opposite strategies.[2] Others have argued that we can make systematic predictions about outcomes of insurgencies based on the different gradations of violence used by belligerents.[3]

Such analyses often neglect systematic comparison of violent strategies with alternatives to violence, because many studies of civil war and conflict assume that the most forceful means of waging conflict entails

For helpful comments and suggestions, the authors would like to thank Peter Ackerman, Jack DuVall, Hardy Merriman, Kurt Schock, and Stephen Zunes.

1. Robert A. Pape, *Dying to Win: The Strategic Logic of Suicide Terror* (New York: Random House, 2005); Robert A. Pape, *Bombing to Win: Air Power and Coercion in War* (Ithaca, N.Y.: Cornell University Press, 1996); Daniel Byman and Matthew Waxman, "Kosovo and the Great Air Power Debate," *International Security*, Vol. 24, No. 4 (Summer 2000), pp. 5–38; Daniel Byman and Matthew Waxman, *Air Power as a Coercive Instrument* (Washington, D.C.: RAND, 1999); Daniel Byman and Matthew Waxman, *The Dynamics of Coercion: American Foreign Policy and the Limits of Military Might* (New York: Cambridge University Press, 2003); Michael Horowitz and Dan Reiter, "When Does Aerial Bombing Work? Quantitative Empirical Tests, 1917–1999," *Journal of Conflict Resolution*, Vol. 45, No. 2 (April 2001), pp. 147–173; Max Abrahms, "Why Terrorism Does Not Work," *International Security*, Vol. 31, No. 2 (Fall 2006), pp. 42–78; Ivan Arreguín-Toft, *How the Weak Win Wars: A Theory of Asymmetric Conflict* (New York: Cambridge University Press, 2005); Gil Merom, *How Democracies Lose Small Wars: State, Society, and the Failures of France in Algeria, Israel in Lebanon, and the United States in Vietnam* (New York: Cambridge University Press, 2003); Donald Stoker, "Insurgents Rarely Win—And Iraq Won't Be Any Different (Maybe)," *Foreign Policy Web Exclusive* (January 30, 2007), retrieved from http://www.foreignpolicy.com/story/cms.php?story_id=3689, October 14, 2009; and Maria J. Stephan and Erica Chenoweth, "Why Civil Resistance Works: The Strategic Logic of Nonviolent Conflict," *International Security*, Vol. 33, No. 1 (Summer 2008), pp. 7–44.

2. Arreguín-Toft, *How the Weak Win Wars*.

3. Jeremy Weinstein, *Inside Rebellion: The Politics of Insurgent Violence* (New York: Cambridge University Press, 2007).

violence. Civilian populations are often seen as victims of war or as potential recruits for armed combat, rather than as agents and instigators of a different form of resistance. As a consequence, scholars of conflict and civil war treat violence as a starting point, either examining the presence of violence compared to its absence, or comparing degrees of violent behavior once a conflict already exists.[4]

Little empirical analysis has been devoted to nonviolent resistance campaigns, in which organized civilian groups asymmetrically challenge adversaries using protests, demonstrations, boycotts, strikes, and other methods of civil disobedience and non-cooperation.[5] Yet recent evidence suggests that nonviolent resistance campaigns have often been more successful than campaigns that pursue comparable goals with violence.[6] If so, it is useful to consider both nonviolent and violent resistance in the same analysis, as functional alternatives, rather than ignoring nonviolent alternatives.[7]

---

4. For an example of how war onset is treated as dichotomous, see James D. Fearon and David Laitin, "Ethnicity, Insurgency, and Civil War," *American Political Science Review*, Vol. 97, No. 1 (February 2003), pp. 75–90. To see comparisons of degrees of violence once conflict has emerged, see Weinstein, *Inside Rebellion*; and Stathis Kalyvas, *The Logic of Violence in Civil War* (New York: Cambridge University Press, 2006).

5. Although nonviolent resistance campaigns may target non-state actors, such as corporations or paramilitary groups, for the purpose of this chapter we are concerned with state adversaries. Nonviolent resistance is the subject of numerous important works, and hundreds of tactics used during such campaigns are identified in Gene Sharp, ed., *Waging Nonviolent Struggle: 20th Century Practice and 21st Century Potential* (Boston: Porter Sargent, 2005); Gene Sharp, *The Politics of Nonviolent Action*, 3 Vols. (Boston: Porter Sargent, 1973); Peter Ackerman and Christopher Kruegler, *Strategic Nonviolent Conflict: The Dynamics of People Power in the Twentieth Century* (Westport, Conn.: Praeger, 1994); Peter Ackerman and Jack DuVall, *A Force More Powerful: A Century of Nonviolent Conflict* (New York: Macmillan, 2000); Adrian Karatnycky and Peter Ackerman, eds., *How Freedom is Won: From Civic Resistance to Durable Democracy* (Washington, D.C.: Freedom House, 2005); Kurt Schock, *Unarmed Insurrections: People Power Movements in Nondemocracies* (Minneapolis: University of Minnesota Press, 2005); Paul Wehr, Heidi Burgess, and Guy Burgess, eds., *Justice Without Violence* (Boulder, Colo.: Lynne Rienner, 1994); Stephen Zunes, "Unarmed Insurrections Against Authoritarian Governments in the Third World," *Third World Quarterly*, Vol. 15, No. 3 (September 1994), pp. 403–426; Stephen Zunes, Lester Kurtz, and Sarah Beth Asher, eds., *Nonviolent Social Movements: A Geographical Perspective* (Malden, Mass.: Blackwell Publishing, 1999); and Vincent Boudreau, *Resisting Dictatorship: Repression and Protest in Southeast Asia* (New York: Cambridge University Press, 2004).

6. For the purposes of this study, a resistance campaign is a series of observable, continuous tactics by a non-state actor toward a state actor in pursuit of a political objective. Campaigns have discernable leadership and often have names, distinguishing them from random riots or spontaneous acts. Usually campaigns have distinguishable beginning and end points, which are sometimes difficult to determine, as are events throughout the campaign. Although we recognize that campaign leadership is most often contested, we refer to campaigns in this chapter as unitary. For a more nuanced interpretation, see Wendy Pearlman's chapter in this volume. For more on data related to nonviolent campaigns, see Stephan and Chenoweth, "Why Civil Resistance Works."

7. We do not discuss actions and processes that occur within normal institutional channels, like negotiations, voting, or parliamentary action. Rather, we are interested in

Why might nonviolent resistance campaigns be more effective than violent resistance campaigns? We argue that in general, the former may be more likely to achieve mass, broad-based participation by civilian populations, which translates into leverage over the adversary through the collective withholding of consent and cooperation. The sustained and systematic application of a diverse repertoire of nonviolent sanctions by large numbers of oppositionists, as opposed to a relatively small vanguard of armed insurgents, may allow nonviolent resistance to wield greater power than armed struggle. Although violent campaigns may impose significant military, political, and economic costs and create major destruction in the process, such disruption does not necessarily lead to actual progress in strategic goals.[8] The risks involved in waging armed struggle, furthermore, are relatively higher than those involved in unarmed struggle.

In this chapter, we develop hypotheses based on the existing literature about how reliance on a particular set of resistance tactics—violent or nonviolent—might help to determine campaign success.[9] Our central purpose is to develop a framework for scholars to explore the factors that contribute to the success of one form of resistance over another. Here we are less focused on *why* groups embrace one form of resistance over another than on developing explanations for the relative *effectiveness* of violent and nonviolent resistance campaigns. Drawing on the current litera-

---

the collective application of nonviolent methods that take place outside of (but may be used coincident with) normal institutional channels. For an elaboration on this distinction, see Kurt Schock, "Nonviolent Action and Its Misconceptions: Insights for Social Scientists," *PS: Political Science and Politics*, Vol. 36, No 4 (October 2003), pp. 705–712. We define violence as that which inflicts or threatens to inflict bodily harm on another individual. While it goes beyond the scope of this study to elaborate on this debate, certain forms of property destruction—such as Gandhi's burning of identity cards in South Africa and Vietnam war protestors' burning of draft cards—are typically classified as nonviolent direct actions. In each of these examples, the acts of property damage were planned and conducted in the context of highly organized nonviolent campaigns, were limited in focus and specific in intent, and were explained by the activists, who were willing to face the legal consequences of their actions. These actions differ from acts of vandalism targeting shops and government buildings during demonstrations, often conducted by individuals who flee from the scene and are unwilling to face the legal consequences of their actions. Throwing rocks through shop windows during anti-globalization demonstrations are examples of actions that, while technically not violent, would not be classified by most as methods of nonviolent direct action.

8. For an empirical study, see Stephan and Chenoweth, "Why Civil Resistance Works."

9. A violent campaign is one in which the campaign relies primarily on violent tactics. A nonviolent campaign relies primarily on nonviolent tactics. As Cunningham and Beaulieu rightly point out, this distinction is often ambiguous, as most campaigns are varied. In this chapter, however, we deal with ideal types of campaigns. There are examples of such ideal types, which are campaigns that rely solely on nonviolent or violent tactics against the adversary (i.e., Gandhi's resistance against the British occupation of India, the Georgian Rose Revolution, etc). For the purposes of this chapter, we acknowledge that ideal types are rare, and refer to cases where the campaign relies primarily on violent or nonviolent resistance types while confronting the adversary. The effects of mixed campaigns can be the subject of further study elsewhere.

ture, we suggest that, in theory, a campaign's primary use of nonviolent or violent methods affects levels of mobilization against an ostensibly more powerful adversary. Different levels of mobilization and the type of force application may help to explain why there is systematic variation in the outcomes of these campaigns.[10]

The remainder of this chapter proceeds as follows. First, we develop our main contention—that nonviolent campaigns attract greater numbers of more diverse participants than violent campaigns—and provide evidence to support this argument. Second, we present testable hypotheses about how increased participation might help nonviolent campaigns achieve leverage over adversaries' regimes, compared to violent campaigns with limited participation. The purpose here is theory-building; we propose ways that nonviolent campaigns may be strategically advantageous, with the aim of directing future research. We conclude by discussing the implications of our arguments for the security studies literature, focusing on the need to consider alternative methods of asymmetrical warfare and to rethink the role of civilians in acute conflicts.

The Primacy of Mobilization in Nonviolent Resistance

All resistance campaigns—violent and nonviolent—seek to build the personnel bases of their campaigns. Scholars of conflict suggest that campaign participation may be paramount in determining the outcome of resistance struggles. In other words, numbers matter.[11] Furthermore, the more diverse the participation in the resistance—measured in terms of gender, age, religion, ethnicity, and socio-economic status—the more difficult it is for the adversary to isolate the participants and adopt a repressive strategy, short of maximal and undiscriminating repression. As such, diverse participation may afford a resistance campaign a strategic advantage, which, in turn, increases the pressure points and enhances the leverage that the resistance achieves *vis-à-vis* its state adversary.

---

10.   While we acknowledge the importance of structural conditions during nonviolent and violent conflicts, previous work has shown that both nonviolent and violent resistance campaigns have occurred, persisted, succeeded, and failed in multiple contexts. The outcomes of the campaigns—while certainly shaped by external constraints—have not been pre-determined by those constraints. The contentious politics research program accounts for the interaction between agent and structure in explaining outcomes. See, for instance, Doug McAdam, Charles Tilly, and Sidney Tarrow, *Dynamics of Contention* (New York: Cambridge University Press, 2001); Charles Tilly and Sidney Tarrow, *Contentious Politics* (Boulder, Colo.: Paradigm Publishers, 2006); and Kurt Schock, *Unarmed Insurrections*.

11.   James deNardo, *Power in Numbers* (Princeton, N.J.: Princeton University Press, 1985); Mark Lichbach, "Rethinking Rationality and Rebellion: Theories of Collective Action and Problems of Collective Dissent," *Rationality and Society*, Vol. 6, No. 1 (January 1994), pp. 8–39; Mia Bloom, *Dying to Kill: The Allure of Suicide Terror* (New York: Columbia University Press, 2005); and Weinstein, *Inside Rebellion*.

Skeptics may question this assertion on the grounds that potential recruits seeking immediate results from participation will find nonviolent resistance less appealing than violent resistance. Beyond the achievement of political objectives, loot obtained during operations, payoffs from resistance leaders, the seizing of territory or caches of weapons, or even feelings of power from harming people or exacting revenge could attract recruits to violent resistance. Frantz Fanon famously advocated armed resistance, on the grounds that it bestows feelings of actively fighting against injustice while being willing to die for a cause greater than one's self, thereby encouraging feelings of communal solidarity.[12] Violence may have its own attraction, especially for young people, for whom the allure may be further perpetuated by cultural references and religious defenses of martyrdom.[13]

Despite its supposed appeal, however, violence is rare, and therefore may not have the allure that some theorists ascribe to it.[14] On the whole, physical, informational, moral, and commitment considerations tend to give nonviolent campaigns an advantage when it comes to mobilizing participants, which we argue reinforces the strategic benefits to participation as well.[15] In the next section, we suggest why there are more incentives for individuals to actively participate in nonviolent resistance, compared to armed struggle, and the implications of this for strategic effectiveness.

PHYSICAL BARRIERS

Active participation in a resistance campaign requires variable levels of physical ability. The physical risks and costs of participation in a violent resistance campaign may be prohibitively high for many potential members. Actively participating in violent resistance may require physical skills such as agility and endurance, willingness to train, ability to handle and use weapons, and often isolation from society at large. While certain of these qualities, including endurance, willingness to sacrifice, and training, can also be applicable to participation in nonviolent resistance, the

---

12.   Frantz Fanon, *The Wretched of the Earth* (New York: Grove Press, 1961). Fanon, influenced by a Marxist paradigm that equates violence with power, probably did not consider that nonviolent resistance could engender similarly intense feelings of individual and collective empowerment and meaning. See Anders Boserup and Andrew Mack, *War Without Weapons* (London: Frances Pinter, 1974).

13.   Keith Breckenridge, "The Allure of Violence: Men, Race and Masculinity on the South African Goldmines, 1900–1950," *Journal of Southern African Studies*, Vol. 24, No. 4 (December 1998), pp. 669–693.

14.   See Adria Lawrence's chapter in this volume.

15.   While we recognize that there are a number of non-combat roles in armed resistance that do not entail violence (such as providing sanctuary, food, and supplies to guerrillas; raising funds; communicating messages; acting as an informant; or refusing to cooperate with government attempts to apprehend insurgents), here civilians act in a support role for armed combatants, who are responsible for planning and executing armed attacks against the adversary. This is quite different from the role played by civilians in nonviolent resistance, where they are responsible for planning and executing nonviolent campaigns targeting the adversary.

typical guerrilla regimen may appeal only to a small portion of any given population.

Physical barriers to participation may be lower for nonviolent resistance, because the menu of tactics available to nonviolent activists is broad and includes a wide spectrum ranging from high-risk confrontational tactics to low-risk discreet tactics.[16] Generally, participation in labor strikes, consumer boycotts, lock-downs, and sit-ins does not require strength, agility, or youth. Participation in a nonviolent campaign is open to female and elderly populations, where participation in a violent resistance campaign is often, though not always, physically prohibitive. Although female operatives—such as female suicide bombers and guerrillas—have sometimes been active in violent campaigns in Sri Lanka, Iraq, Pakistan, Palestine, El Salvador, and East Timor, they are nevertheless exceptions in most cases.

INFORMATIONAL DIFFICULTIES

Scholars have found that individuals are more likely to engage in protest activity when they expect large numbers of people to participate.[17] To successfully recruit members, campaigns must publicize their activities to demonstrate their goals, abilities, and existing numbers to potential recruits. Because of the high risks associated with violent activity, however, movement activists may be limited in how much information they can provide. They may need to remain underground, thereby exacerbating informational problems. Although violent acts, including assassinations, ambushes, bombings, and kidnappings, are public and often attract significant media attention providing signals of the campaign's abilities, the majority of the campaign's operational realities—including information about the numbers of active members—often remain unseen and un-

16. Sharp, *The Politics of Nonviolent Action*, identifies over 198 nonviolent tactics (including strikes, boycotts, sit-ins, and occupations), and scholars have since expanded the list to include many more due to advances in communications technology. See Brian Martin, *Technology for Nonviolent Struggle* (London: War Resisters' International, 2001).

17. See Mancur Olson, *The Logic of Collective Action* (Cambridge, Mass.: Harvard University Press, 1965); Gordon Tullock, "The Paradox of Revolution," *Public Choice*, Vol. 11, No. 1 (September 1971), pp. 89–99; Lichbach, "Rethinking Rationality and Rebellion"; Jack Goldstone, "Is Revolution Really Rational?" *Rationality and Society*, Vol. 6, No. 1 (January 1994), pp. 139–166; Mark Granovetter, "Threshold Models of Collective Behavior," *American Journal of Sociology*, Vol. 83, No. 6 (May 1978), pp. 1420–1443; Timur Kuran, "Sparks and Prairie Fires: A Theory of Unanticipated Political Revolution," *Public Choice*, Vol. 61, No. 1 (April 1989), pp. 41–74; Gerald Marwell and Pamela Oliver, *The Critical Mass in Collective Action: A Micro-Social Theory* (Cambridge: Cambridge University Press, 1993); Anthony Oberschall, "Rational Choice in Collective Protests," *Rationality and Society*, Vol, 6, No. 1 (January 1994), pp. 79–100; Thomas C. Schelling, *Micromotives and Macrobehavior* (New York: Norton, 1978); Karen Rasler, "Concessions, Repression, and Political Protest in the Iranian Revolution," *American Sociological Review*, Vol. 61, No. 1 (February 1996), pp. 132–152; Charles Kurzman, "Structural Opportunity and Perceived Opportunity in Social-Movement Theory: The Iranian Revolution of 1979," *American Sociological Review*, Vol. 61, No. 1 (February 1996), pp. 153–170; and Charles Kurzman, *The Unthinkable Revolution in Iran* (Cambridge, Mass.: Harvard University Press, 2004).

known.[18] The absence of visible signs of opposition strength is, therefore, problematic from the perspective of recruitment. Thus, violent resistance may be at a disadvantage in this regard, since the actual number of activists may not be clear.

On the other hand, nonviolent, public tactics have important demonstration effects, which help to address the informational problem. Nonviolent campaigns sometimes include clandestine activities (e.g., the use of *samizdat* underground publications during the Polish Solidarity struggle), particularly during the early stages when the resistance is most vulnerable to regime repression and decapitation. Typically, however, nonviolent campaigns rely less on underground activities than armed struggles.[19] When communities observe open, mass support and collective acts of defiance, their perceptions of risk may decline, reducing constraints on participation. This contention is supported by critical-mass theories of collective action, which contend that protestors base their perceptions of protest opportunities on existing patterns of opposition activity.[20]

As with violent campaigns, regime infiltration and the use of *agent provocateurs* to instigate opposition violence are also common elements of nonviolent resistance campaigns. Although these are significant obstacles, nonviolent campaigns have historically been able to use social ostracism, publicly declared dress codes, public statements, and explicit codes of conduct to counter these typical adversary infiltration tactics.[21] Armed campaigns have employed similar tactics, though they also employ the maiming and killing of collaborators, which often leads to opposition disunity and popular alienation.

MORAL BARRIERS

Moral barriers may constrain potential recruits to resistance campaigns, but are far less likely to inhibit participation in nonviolent resistance. Although an individual's decision to resist the status quo may follow a certain amount of moral introspection, taking up weapons and killing adds a new moral dimension. Unwillingness to commit violent acts or support armed groups necessarily disqualifies segments of the population that sympathize with the resistance but are reluctant to translate that sympathy into violence. For violent resistance campaigns, the leadership may need to rely on the proportion of the population that is willing to use violence against the adversary and its supporters, while settling for sympathy and passive support from the rest of the population.

---

18.   At the same time, satellite television and the Internet have made it easier for armed resistance groups to communicate their goals, attract recruits, and exaggerate their membership. This is also true for nonviolent resistance campaigns.

19.   See Boserup and Mack, *War Without Weapons*, on the advantages and disadvantages of underground and aboveground activity.

20.   Kurzman, "Structural Opportunity and Perceived Opportunity," p. 154.

21.   See, for instance, Srbja Popovic, Slobodan Djindric, Andrej Milivojevic, Hardy Merriman, and Ivan Marovic, *A Guide to Effective Nonviolent Struggle* (Belgrade: CANVAS, 2007), pp. 87–88.

Nonviolent resistance campaigns, however, can potentially mobilize the entire aggrieved population without facing moral barriers. Joining a nonviolent resistance campaign against a powerful adversary "requires less soul-searching than joining a violent one. Violent methods raise troublesome questions about whether the ends justify the means, and generally force the people who use them to take substantial risks."[22]

COMMITMENT PROBLEMS

Beyond physical, informational, and moral barriers, nonviolent resistance campaigns may offer people with varying levels of commitment and risk tolerance the opportunity to participate. Campaigns that rely primarily on violent resistance must depend on participants who have high levels of both commitment and risk tolerance. First, the new recruit to a violent campaign may require more training than a recruit to a nonviolent campaign, creating a lag between volunteering and participation. This lag—and the strenuous requirements for participation in a violent campaign—may reduce the number of people who join a violent campaign on a whim.[23]

Second, violent campaigns typically enforce higher levels of commitment at the outset. Screening potential participants is much more intense in violent movements. Often, new recruits to violent movements must undertake a violent act to demonstrate their commitment. This is a further inhibition to participation in armed struggles, because potential recruits may wish to eschew drastic screening processes, and movement leaders may find it hard to trust new recruits.

Third, during the prosecution of a conflict, participants in nonviolent campaigns can return to their day jobs, daily lives, and families with lower risk than a participant in a violent campaign. Compared to armed struggle, participants in nonviolent resistance can more easily retain anonymity, which means that they can often participate in acts of resistance without making major life sacrifices. This is particularly true when a campaign uses nonviolent methods of dispersion, such as a stay-at-home strike or a consumer boycott, in which cooperation is withdrawn without leaving the state with a tangible target for repression.[24] The commitment required by people who join violent campaigns often prevents them from resuming their lives during or after the conflict, and they are more likely to be on the run in order to evade state security.

Fourth, nonviolent resistance offers a greater repertoire of lower risk actions. Although nonviolent struggle is rarely casualty-free, the price of participating (and being caught) in armed struggle is often death. The likelihood of being killed while carrying out one's duties as an armed in-

---

22.   DeNardo, *Power in Numbers*, p. 58.

23.   Thanks to Hardy Merriman for this particular insight.

24.   We return to this concept later in the chapter. See Schock, *Unarmed Insurrections*, p. 52; and R. J. Burrowes, *The Strategy of Nonviolent Defense: A Gandhian Approach* (Albany: State University of New York Press, 1996), pp. 224–225.

surgent is high, whereas many lower-risk tactics are available to participants in a nonviolent resistance campaign.[25] The wearing of opposition insignia, the coordinated banging of pots and pans and honking of horns, the creation of underground schools, and the refusal to obey regime orders are a few examples of less risky nonviolent tactics that have been used by groups around the world.[26]

The aspects of participation discussed thus far point in one direction. They suggest that nonviolent campaigns will be more successful at generating large bases of participants.

Proposition₁: Nonviolent resistance campaigns are more likely to obtain mass, broad-based participation (including women, children, and elderly) than violent resistance.

The Iranian Revolution of 1978–1979 illustrates this point. Although violent insurgencies such as the Fedayeen and Mujahideen had resisted the Shah since the 1960s, they were only able to attract several thousand followers. Reza Pahlavi's regime crushed the armed groups before they produced meaningful change in the regime. The nonviolent revolution that emerged between 1977 and 1978, however, attracted several million participants who engaged in boycotts, protests, stay-aways, and sit-ins until the regime fell.

Notwithstanding the Shah's deep unpopularity *vis-à-vis* large numbers of Iranians, many Iranian citizens were unwilling to participate in protest activity until the revolution had attracted mass support—which occurred only after nonviolent popular struggle replaced guerrilla violence as the primary mode of resistance.[27] A similar dynamic could be seen in the 1988 popular ouster of General Augusto Pinochet in Chile, and the 1986 "people power" revolution against Ferdinand Marcos in the Philippines.[28]

If such mass participation is associated with campaign success, then nonviolent campaigns have an advantage over violent ones.[29] In the fol-

---

25. Stathis N. Kalyvas and Matthew A. Kocher dispute this point, arguing that the risks of participation in violent insurgencies are not as high as nonparticipation. "How Free is Free-riding in Civil Wars? Violence, Insurgency, and the Collective Action Problem," *World Politics*, Vol. 59, No. 2 (January 2007), pp. 177–216.

26. See Gene Sharp, *The Politics of Nonviolent Action, Vol. 2: The Methods of Nonviolent Action* (Boston: Porter Sargent, 1973).

27. Kurzman, "Structural Opportunity and Perceived Opportunity."

28. Ackerman and DuVall, *A Force More Powerful*; Schock, *Unarmed Insurrections*; and Boudreau, *Resisting Dictatorship*.

29. We recognize that numbers alone do not guarantee victory in resistance campaigns. Strategic factors, like the identification of realistic goals and the sequencing of a particular set of tactics, along with the navigation of structural constraints (including regime repression) are also crucial determinants of campaign outcomes. However, we do suggest that the execution of any resistance strategy—violent or nonviolent—and the ability to stay in the contest with the adversary depend on the availability of willing recruits. For this reason, insofar as participation influences these other variables, which have direct bearing on the outcome of campaigns, nonviolent campaigns have an advantage over violent campaigns.

lowing sections, we assume that Proposition 1 is empirically correct, and consider how mass, broad-based mobilization activates numerous mechanisms that offer advantages that violent campaigns lack.

The Effects of Mobilization on Mechanisms of Leverage

As Kurt Schock writes, leverage "refers to the ability of contentious actors to mobilize the withdrawal of support from opponents or invoke pressure against them through the networks upon which opponents depend for power."[30] In this section, we discuss the mechanisms through which broad-based mobilization allows nonviolent campaigns to maximize leverage over their adversaries, even when their adversaries outnumber them in size, capabilities, and resources.

The disruptive effects of violent and nonviolent resistance may result in significant political, economic, and military costs for an adversary.[31] The results of sustained disruption include the failure of the government to perform basic functions, a decline in GDP and investment, loss of power by government elites, and the breakdown of the normal order of society.[32] The sum total of the domestic and international costs of sustained disruption may cause members of the target regime to accommodate resistance campaigns—or force them to give up power completely.

COERCION

Violent campaigns physically coerce their adversaries, which may significantly disrupt the status quo and enhance the chances of victory.[33] Destroying or damaging infrastructure; killing or threatening officials, elites, and military personnel; and disrupting the flow of goods and commerce may raise perceptions of ungovernability and continued instability, while loosening the regime's grip on power. A sustained violent resistance campaign may produce significant disruption and serve an important communicative role. For example, the Palestine Liberation Organization's use of terrorism and guerrilla violence from the mid-1960s to the late 1980s is often credited with "keeping the Palestinian issue alive" internationally.[34] The armed wing of the East Timorese independence movement, the

---

30.   Schock, *Unarmed Insurrections*, p. 142.

31.   DeNardo, *Power in Numbers*.

32.   Elisabeth Jean Wood, *Forging Democracy from Below: Insurgent Transitions in El Salvador and South Africa* (New York: Cambridge University Press, 2000), p. 15.

33.   In *How the Weak Win Wars*, Arreguín-Toft argues that during strategic interactions between stronger and weaker conflict parties, the use of opposite tactics (indirect-direct) against a stronger adversary can translate into victory for the weaker power. Others have argued that continual and escalating disruption is the key variable determining success; see Wood, *Forging Democracy From Below*.

34.   As early as 1982, the PLO's offers of direct talks with Israel were rejected as long as the PLO used violence against Israel. It was not until the late 1980s and early 1990s,

FALANTIL, similarly used armed attacks against Indonesian military targets to attract media attention and to demonstrate that there was opposition to the Indonesian occupation. The Iranian guerrilla movement justified their use of armed attacks against the Shah's regime as a way of demonstrating that the reality was not as the Shah presented it, and that there was opposition to the monarchy.[35] The Maoist guerrillas in Nepal launched armed attacks against the monarchical regime for years, resulting in hundreds of fatalities and prolonged instability in the country.[36]

In the aforementioned cases, however, there is scant evidence of a causal relationship between the political violence and political victories, suggesting that disruption should not be confused with victory. Although the armed resistance may have had a symbolic function, many of the major changes that have occurred in each of these cases were precipitated by mass, nonviolent campaigns. In the case of Nepal, for instance, what directly preceded the restoration of democratic rule in Nepal was not armed resistance, but a brief mass civil-resistance campaign, where even the Maoists chose to put down their guns so that they could participate.

The coercive capacity of nonviolent resistance is not based on violent disruption to the social order. Rather, it is based on the removal of the adversary's key sources of power through sustained acts of protest and non-cooperation—a process that we describe below. Some may argue that nonviolent resistance is only powerful because regimes fear that they will become violent, thereby posing even greater threats. Social movement scholars refer to this dynamic as a "positive radical flank effect." This concept posits that violence may sometimes increase the leverage of challengers, which occurs when external actors offer selective rewards and opportunities to moderate competitor groups to isolate or thwart the more radical organizations. In other words, the presence of a radical element in the opposition may make the moderate oppositionists in the nonviolent campaign seem more palatable to the regime, thereby contributing to the success of the nonviolent campaign. In this way, some argue that violent and nonviolent campaigns can be symbiotic, in that the presence of both types improves their relative positions.[37]

---

when a new form of mass-based Palestinian nonviolent resistance emerged inside the Occupied Territories, that significant pressure was applied on Israel, resulting in talks with the PLO and a general acceptance of a two-state solution. The popular uprising (known as the first Intifada) inside the Occupied Territories increased the Palestinians' leverage over the exiled PLO leadership in Tunis, which was forced to moderate its views and accept negotiations with Israel or risk irrelevance. It also increased leverage over Israel, which paid a high political price for its violent response to the first Intifada and reconsidered permanent control over the territories.

35. Maziar Behrooz, "Iranian Revolution and the Legacy of the Guerrilla Movement," in Stephanie Cronin, ed., *Reformers and Revolutionaries in Modern Iran: New Perspectives on the Iranian Left* (London: Routledge Curzon, 2004).

36. For figures of attacks perpetrated by the Communist insurgency in Nepal, see the Global Terrorism Database, START/CETIS, accessed at http://www.start.umd.edu/data/gtd/.

37. For applications of the positive radical flank effect, see Herbert Haines, "Black

But opposition violence is just as likely—if not more likely—to have the opposite result. A "negative radical flank effect," or spoiler effect, occurs when another party's violence decreases the leverage of a challenge group. In this case, the presence of an armed challenge group causes the regime's supporters to unify against the threat.

There is no consensus among social scientists about the conditions under which radical flanks either harm or help a social movement.[38] In our estimation, however, many successful nonviolent campaigns have succeeded because they systematically stripped away the regime's sources of power, including those within the ranks of economic and military elites, who may have hesitated to defect if they suspected that the campaign would turn violent. As a general rule, the more a regime's supporters believe a campaign may become violent, the greater the extent to which those supporters and potential participants may perceive the conflict to be a zero-sum game.[39] As a response, regime supporters are likely to unite to counter the perceived existential threat, while potential participants may eschew participation for the reasons identified above. A unified adversary is much harder to defeat for both violent and nonviolent campaigns.

Therefore, rather than effectiveness being a result of a supposed threat of violence, nonviolent campaigns achieve success through the mechanism of nonviolent coercion as a result of sustained pressure derived from

Radicalization and the Funding of Civil Rights: 1957–1970," *Social Problems*, Vol. 32, No. 1 (October 1984), pp. 31–43; William A. Gamson, *The Strategy of Social Protest*, 2nd ed. (Belmont, Calif.: Wadsworth, 1990); Steven E. Barkan, "Strategies, Tactics, and Organizational Dilemmas of the Protest Movement Against Nuclear Power," *Social Problems*, Vol. 27, No. 1 (October 1979), pp. 19–37; Martin N. Marger, "Social Movement Organizations and Response to Environmental Change: The NAACP, 1960–1973," *Social Problems*, Vol. 32, No. 1 (October 1984), pp. 16–27; Doug McAdam, *Political Process and the Development of Black Insurgency, 1930–1970*, 2nd ed. (Chicago: University of Chicago Press, 1999); and J. Craig Jenkins and Craig M. Eckert, "Channeling Black Insurgency: Elite Patronage and Professional Social Movement Organizations in the Development of the Black Movement," *American Sociological Review*, Vol. 51, No. 6 (December 1986), pp. 812–829.

38. For different viewpoints on this topic, see Herbert Haines, *Black Radicals and the Civil Rights Mainstream* (Knoxville: University of Tennessee Press, 1988); McAdam, *Political Process and the Development of Black Insurgency*; Jenkins and Eckert, "Channeling Black Insurgency"; Frances Fox Piven and Richard A. Cloward, *Poor People's Movements: Why They Succeed, How They Fail* (New York: Vintage Books, 1979); Gamson, *The Strategy of Social Protest*; Carol McClug Mueller, "Riot Violence and Protest Outcomes," *Journal of Political and Military Sociology*, Vol. 6 (Spring 1978), pp. 58–60; David Colby, "Black Power, White Resistance, and Public Policy: Political Power and Poverty Program Grants in Mississippi," *Journal of Politics*, Vol. 47, No. 1 (June 1985), pp. 579–95; Paul Schumaker, "Policy Responsiveness to Protest Group Demands," *Journal of Politics*, Vol. 37, No. 2 (May 1975), pp. 488–521; Gene Sharp, *The Politics of Nonviolent Action*; James Button, *Blacks and Social Change* (Princeton, N.J.: Princeton University Press, 1989); and Kurt Schock, *Unarmed Insurrections*, pp. 47–49. While the concept of radical flank effects is interesting and important, we do not take on simultaneity of violent and nonviolent resistance campaigns as we are dealing primarily with ideal types. Empirical studies could help shed light on the different effects of radical flanks.

39. Stephan and Chenoweth, "Why Civil Resistance Works," pp. 9–13.

mass mobilization that withdraws the regime's economic, political, social, and even military support from domestic populations and third parties. Leverage is achieved when the adversary's most important supporting organizations and institutions are systematically pulled away through mass non-cooperation.

For example, sustained economic pressure targeting state-owned and private businesses and enterprises has been an important element in many successful popular movements.[40] As the anti-apartheid struggle in South Africa demonstrated, massive collective actions such as strikes and boycotts can impose significant economic costs on those benefiting from the status quo. International actions can compliment these domestic actions, such as when the international divestment campaign targeting the apartheid regime created significant economic pressure, which was an important factor in the regime's ultimate decision to negotiate with the African National Congress (ANC). In another example of complimentary internal and external action, the withholding of loans and economic assistance to the Suharto regime in Indonesia by international financial institutions (against the backdrop of the 1998 Asian financial crisis), combined with mass popular uprising in that country, led to Suharto's ouster. The withdrawal of external financial support to the Marcos regime in the Philippines similarly coincided with an economic crisis in the early 1980s, combined with a broadening anti-Marcos movement inside the country that enjoined the support of moderate reformers, church leaders, and businesspeople—a move toward the center by the opposition that would have been unlikely had the resistance been confined to Communist and Muslim guerrillas.

As in South Africa, the cumulative costs of continuous nonviolent resistance may limit the possible or desirable courses of action available to economic and political elites, often forcing them to negotiate on terms favorable to the nonviolent campaign. Sustained pressure through civic mobilization, combined with the belief that the opposition represents a burgeoning and viable governing alternative, can influence key regime adherents, causing them to reconsider their preferences and alternatives to the status quo.[41] This dynamic has marked a number of democratic transitions, including those in Chile, the Philippines, and Eastern Europe.[42]

40.   Ackerman and Kruegler, *Strategic Nonviolent Conflict*; Ackerman and DuVall, *A Force More Powerful*; Schock, *Unarmed Insurrections*; Zunes, Ascher, and Kurtz, *Nonviolent Social Movements*; and Sharp, *The Politics of Nonviolent Action*.

41.   Wood, *Forging Democracy from Below*, p. 21.

42.   See, for example, Jason Brownlee, *Authoritarianism in an Age of Democratization* (New York: Cambridge University Press, 2007); Ruth Berins Collier, *Paths to Democracy: The Working Class and Elites in Western Europe and South America* (Cambridge: Cambridge University Press, 1999); Michael Bernhard, *The Origins of Democratization in Poland* (New York: Columbia University Press, 1993); Susan Eckstein and Manuel Antonio Garretón Merino, *Power and Popular Protest: Latin American Social Movements* (Berkeley: University of California Press, 2001); Michael McFaul, "Ukraine Imports Democracy: External Influences on the Orange Revolution," *International Security*, Vol. 32, No. 2 (Fall 2007), pp. 45–83; Schock, *Unarmed Insurrections*; Ackerman and Kruegler, *Strategic*

In cases where there is an inverse economic dependency relationship (meaning the opposition is more dependent on the state than vice versa), it may be difficult for a nonviolent resistance campaign to achieve significant leverage without working through parties with closer political and economic ties to the state. Examples of nonviolent campaigns in this circumstance are the Palestinians in the Occupied Palestinian Territories, the Tibetans in occupied Tibet, and the West Papuans in Indonesian-controlled West Papua, all of whom are more economically dependent upon the state than vice versa. Although consumer boycotts and labor stoppages launched by populations living under foreign occupation can impose a certain level of economic costs on the occupying power (this occurred when Palestinians boycotted Israeli products and withheld labor during the first intifada), the impact is much less than when the regime is more economically dependent on the resisting population, as is the case with many nonviolent campaigns challenging regimes.[43] This may be especially true when a state is subsidized from the outside, so that it can survive internal economic disruption.[44] These so-called "rentier states," which rely on external sources, including export sales in natural resources, tourism, and economic aid, for a sizeable portion of net income, have proven to be especially resistant to domestic pressure.[45]

An inverse dependency relationship between a state and a nonviolent campaign does not doom the nonviolent campaign to failure. In a number of anti-authoritarian struggles, economic crises combined with organized mass nonviolent pressure have led to the ouster of regimes reliant on external rents, which were believed to be immune to such pressure (e.g., Iran, Indonesia). In certain cases of foreign occupation, working with or through third parties may help a nonviolent campaign to "extend the nonviolent battlefield" and gain increased leverage over its adversary.[46]

Nonviolent Conflict; Ackerman and DuVall, *A Force More Powerful;* and Sharp, *The Politics of Nonviolent Action.*

43.   Mary E. King, *A Quiet Revolution: The First Palestinian Intifada and Nonviolent Resistance* (New York: Nation Books, 2007); Souad Dajani, *Eyes Without Country: Searching for a Palestinian Strategy of Liberation* (Philadelphia, Penn.: Temple University Press, 1994); Maria J. Stephan, "Fighting for Statehood: The Role of Civilian-Based Resistance in the East Timorese, Palestinian, and Kosovo Albanian Self-Determination Struggles," *Fletcher Forum on World Affairs,* Vol. 30, No. 2 (Summer 2006), pp. 57–80; and Maria J. Stephan, "Nonviolent Insurgency: The Role of Civilian-Based Resistance in the East Timorese, Palestinian, and Kosovo Albanian Self-Determination Movements," Ph.D. thesis, Fletcher School of Law and Diplomacy, 2005.

44.   For example, the junta in El Salvador was able to survive a wave of strikes from 1979–1981 because of the junta's strong support from the United States. Thanks to Stephen Zunes for this point.

45.   Thomas Carothers, *Aiding Democracy Abroad: The Learning Curve* (New York: Carnegie, 1999); Thomas Carothers and Marina Ottoway, eds., *Unchartered Journey: Promoting Democracy in the Middle East* (New York: Carnegie, 2005); Larry Diamond, *The Spirit of Democracy: The Struggle to Build Free Societies Throughout the World* (New York: Times Books, 2008); and Hassanein Tawfiq Ibrahim, "Social and Political Change in the Wake of the Oil Boom," Arab Insight Report, Fall 2008.

46.   For an elaboration on the notion of "extending the nonviolent battlefield" to ad-

Violent campaigns, we suggest, are more likely to unify the adversary's main pillars of support and increase their loyalty and obedience to the regime, as opposed to fragmenting and reducing their loyalties to the regime.[47] The questioning of authority and loyalty shifts toward the opposition are less likely to occur when the regime is confronted with an armed challenger and can more easily justify a violent crackdown. A "rally around the flag" effect is more likely to occur when the adversary is confronted with violent resistance than with disciplined nonviolent resistance. Although small armed groups may be perceived as less threatening to a regime's survivability than mass nonviolent protests, states may be more susceptible to internal fissures in the face of massive action rather than limited, violent opposition.

Hypothesis₁: When it achieves mass participation, nonviolent resistance is more likely to succeed than armed struggle because it deprives the state of domestic and international political, social, economic, and military support.

LOYALTY SHIFTS, NEW INTERESTS, AND BACKFIRE

When a resistance campaign is able to influence the loyalties and interests of people working in society's dominant institutions, it increases its chances of success.[48] Campaigns can shift power relations within the adversary by accessing sympathizers, defectors within the elite, or ordinary people who work below the elite. When campaigns produce divisions among erstwhile stable elites about the proper course to take, power relations between the regime and the campaign shift, increasing the campaign's ability to extract concessions from the adversary. Regimes grant concessions when acts of protest or noncooperation lead to shifts in people's loyalties and interests—or perceptions thereof. Thus, measuring the impact of different forms of resistance on the loyalties and interests of a regime's key pillars of political and military support may help to predict campaign success and failure.

Among economic elites within the regime, perception of costly continued conflict may convince them to pressure the regime to adopt conciliatory policies toward the resistance. Elisabeth Jean Wood argues that the accumulating costs of insurgency and its attendant repression ultimately

---

dress the challenge of inverse dependency relationships in the context of civil resistance campaigns, see Stephan, "Fighting for Statehood"; Maria J. Stephan and Jacob Mundy, "Battlefield Transformed: From Guerilla Resistance to Mass Nonviolent Struggle in the Western Sahara," *Journal of Military and Strategic Studies*, Vol. 8, No. 3 (Spring 2006), pp. 1–32; Stephan, *Nonviolent Insurgency*; Johan Galtung, *Nonviolence in Israel/Palestine* (Honolulu: University of Hawaii Press, 1989), p. 19; and Schock, *Unarmed Insurrections*.

47.   Robert Helvey defines "pillars of support" as "the institutions and sections of society that supply the existing regime with the needed sources of power to maintain and expand its power capacity." See Robert L. Helvey, *On Strategic Nonviolent Conflict: Thinking About the Fundamentals* (Boston: Albert Einstein Institution, 2004), p.160.

48.   Greene, *Comparative Revolutionary Movements*, p. 57; and McAdam, et al., *Comparative Perspectives on Social Movements*, p. 306.

convince economic elites to press the regime to negotiate, changing the balance of power within the regime between those willing to consider compromise and those resolutely opposed.[49]

Beyond influencing workers, businesspeople, and economic elites, the sheer numbers of participants lend legitimacy to the campaign in the eyes of those in the regime. While their demands strain state budgets, nonviolent campaigns may also lead soldiers, policemen, and, often later, their commanding officers to question the viability, risks, and potential costs of military actions against the nonviolent campaign.[50] This occurred within the ranks of the Iranian armed forces during the anti-Shah resistance; to Filipino armed forces during the anti-Marcos uprising, within the Israeli military during the first Palestinian intifada; and over the course of the Indonesian military campaign in East Timor, to take but a few examples. Fighting an armed actor is likewise costly, but it is less likely to create as much introspection among the commanding officers, who might instead feel physically threatened by the violence and view the violent insurgents as minorities within the population, who are resorting to violence out of desperation.

Loyalty shifts may occur directly in response to opposition activities, or in response to regime actions that are perceived as unjust or excessive. One common scenario in which loyalties shift is when the regime violently cracks down on a popular nonviolent campaign with mass civilian participation. In this case, the regime's actions may cause backfire to occur, a process that occurs when an action is counterproductive for the perpetrator.[51] Backfire creates a situation in which the resistance leverages the miscalculations of the regime to its own advantage, as domestic and international actors that support the regime shift their support to the opposition because of specific actions taken by the regime.[52]

Repressing nonviolent campaigns may backfire if the campaigns have widespread sympathy among the civilian population by turning erstwhile passive supporters into active participants in the resistance.[53] Alternatively, repressing nonviolent activists may lead to loyalty shifts by increasing

---

49. Wood, *Forging Democracy from Below*, p. 6.

50. Jane Hathaway, ed. *Rebellion, Repression, Reinvention: Mutiny in Comparative Perspective* (Westport, Conn.: Praeger, 2001).

51. Martin, *Justice Ignited*, p. 3.

52. Ronald Francisco, "The Dictator's Dilemma," in *Repression and Mobilization*, eds. Christian Davenport, Hank Johnston and Carol Mueller (Minneapolis: University of Minnesota Press, 2005), pp. 58–83; Anika Locke Binnendijk and Ivan Marovic, "Power and Persuasion: Nonviolent Strategies to Influence State Security Forces in Serbia (2000) and Ukraine (2004)," *Communist and Post-Communist Studies*, Vol. 39, No. 3 (September 2006), p. 416. Brian Martin emphasizes the important role played by media coverage of contentious interaction involving unarmed protestors and security forces. Furthermore, regimes have developed their own strategies to inhibit the effects of backfire. See Brian Martin, *Justice Ignited*. Martin's concept of backfire is a more nuanced approach to what Gene Sharp first described as "political ju-jitsu" (Sharp, *The Politics of Nonviolent Action*).

53. deNardo, *Power in Numbers*, p. 217.

the internal solidarity of the resistance, increasing foreign support for it, or increasing dissent within the enemy ranks—provided violent counter-reprisals by the resistance do not occur. This effect may be catalyzed further if the repression is communicated to domestic and international audiences that are prepared to act.[54]

Resistance of any kind against a regime is often met with repression. However, it is easier for states to justify violent crackdowns against resistance campaigns and draconian measures, like the imposition of martial law or states of emergency, to domestic and international audiences when they are challenged by an armed insurgency.[55] On the other hand, converting, co-opting, or successfully appealing to the interests of those targeted with violence is more difficult. As we know from cognitive theories, when violent militants threaten the lives of regime members and security forces, the latter are less likely to think critically—and more likely to think defensively—about their own behavior.[56] Regime functionaries are therefore less likely to see violent protestors as potential bargaining partners than nonviolent groups.

Hypothesis$_2$: Repression against nonviolent campaigns should induce loyalty shifts within the regime and generate more acts of anti-regime mobilization than repression against violent campaigns.

This hypothesis is counterintuitive, because it is often assumed that violent repression always *weakens* nonviolent campaigns relative to violent campaigns—an assumption that requires empirical testing.

EXTERNAL SUPPORT

A resistance campaign may also achieve leverage over its adversary through diplomatic pressure or international sanctions against the adversary. International sanctions are certainly controversial; common arguments against them include the point that they often harm the civilian population more than the targeted regimes.[57] They may be useful, however, in some cases. Such sanctions had discernable effects in bringing about successful opposition campaigns in South Africa and East Timor,

---

54. Stephan and Chenoweth, "Why Civil Resistance Works"; and Boserup and Mack, *War without Weapons*, p. 84. A combination of sustained confrontation with the adversary, the maintenance of nonviolent discipline, and the existence of a sympathetic audience may be necessary conditions for triggering ju-jitsu. See Brian Martin and Wendy Varney, "Nonviolence and Communication," *Journal of Peace Research*, Vol. 40, No. 2 (March 2003), pp. 213–232; and Martin, *Justice Ignited*.

55. Martin, *Justice Ignited*, p. 163. This is not to suggest that it is necessarily strategically wise for nonviolent campaigns to purposefully evoke repression from their adversaries. On the contrary, many nonviolent campaigns have succeeded without relying on the backfire process.

56. Abrahms, "Why Terrorism Does Not Work."

57. See Donald M. Seekins, "Burma and U.S. Sanctions: Confronting an Authoritarian Regime," *Asian Survey*, Vol. 45, No. 3 (May/June 2005), pp. 437–452.

to take but two examples.[58] The ANC leadership demanded sanctions for decades, but they came about only after mass nonviolent resistance had spread.[59] Some argue that the international sanctions against the apartheid regime in South Africa were critical in creating a bargaining space for the resistance campaigns to finally come to the negotiating table.[60] International sanctions against Indonesia aided the successful ouster of Indonesian troops from East Timor.[61] Conversely, lack of sanctions or diplomatic pressure has often been cited as contributing to the failure of some opposition groups. Some have suggested, for example, that the application of sanctions by China or Russia would hasten the Burmese junta's downfall, or that pressure by South Africa would hasten the demise of the Robert Mugabe regime in Zimbabwe.[62]

External support may be more easily generated when outside actors see large numbers of resistance participants as a sign of the movement's legitimacy and viability. The international repercussions of a violent crackdown against civilians who have made their commitment to nonviolent action known may be more severe than against those that could be credibly labeled as terrorists. Nonviolent campaigns sometimes receive direct support from foreign governments, international organizations, nongovernmental organizations (NGOs), and global civil society. The aid often comes in the form of government financial assistance, sanctions targeting

---

58.   Martin, *Justice Ignited*, pp. 13, 15, 23.

59.   On the role of international sanctions in the South African anti-apartheid struggle, see Zunes, Kurtz, and Asher, *Nonviolent Social Movements*; Schock, *Unarmed Insurrections*; and Ackerman and DuVall, *A Force More Powerful*. On the role of democratic embassies in the anti-apartheid struggle, see the Community of Democracy's *Handbook for Diplomats in Democratic Development*, accessible at: www.diplomatshandbook.org.

60.   The relative importance of the armed and nonviolent resistance in the anti-apartheid struggle is controversial. Some have argued that the violent and nonviolent resistance were complementary; see Tom Lodge, "The Interplay of Non-violent and Violent Action in the Movement against Apartheid in South Africa, 1983–94," in Adam Roberts and Timothy Garton Ash, eds., *Civil Resistance and Power Politics: The Experience of Nonviolent Action from Gandhi to the Present* (Oxford University Press, 2009). Others have argued that these forms of resistance were not complementary, and that the ANC-led armed struggle played a far less important role than the mass nonviolent resistance in ending apartheid. See Janet Cherry, "The Intersection of Violent and Nonviolent Strategies in the South African Liberation Struggle," paper presented at "Liberation in Southern Africa: New Perspectives," Centre for African Studies, University of Cape Town, September 4–6, 2006; Howard Barrel, "Conscripts to Their Age: African National Congress Operational Strategy, 1976–1986," Ph.D. thesis, St. Antony's College, Oxford, 1993.

61.   Stephen Zunes, "Indigestible Lands? Comparing the Fates of Western Sahara and East Timor," in Brendan O'Leary, Ian Lustick, and Thomas Callaghy, eds., *Rightsizing the State: The Politics of Moving Borders* (New York: Oxford University Press, 2001), pp. 289–317.

62.   Seekins, "Burma and U.S. Sanctions"; U.S. State Department, "U.S. Report on Trade Sanctions Against Burma," 2004, retrieved from http://www.state.gov/p/eap/rls/rpt/32106.htm, March 30, 2008. On Zimbabwe, see BBC News, "G8 To Move Against Mugabe Allies," retrieved from http://news.bbc.co.uk/2/hi/africa/7495807.stm, October 14, 2009.

the adversary, or NGO funding.[63] The Serbian resistance movement Otpor, for example, received millions of dollars from funding agencies linked to the U.S. and European governments prior to the toppling of the Milošević regime.

At the same time, external support is unreliable, inconsistently applied to nonviolent opposition groups around the world, and sometimes ineffective in helping nonviolent campaigns. In fact, external support can at times delegitimize a movement in the eyes of the domestic population within a country by leading to accusations of corruption within the movement. Furthermore, even when external support could be helpful to a nonviolent campaign, as Clifford Bob notes, the decision to support resistance movements depends upon a variety of internal considerations, including the donor's mission, sponsors, and the political atmosphere.[64] Nonetheless, we believe that external actors are more likely to contribute diplomatic support to nonviolent campaigns than violent ones. The effects of these resources on campaign outcomes should be explored in subsequent studies.

Hypothesis$_3$: Nonviolent resistance campaigns are more likely than armed campaigns to win outside support in the form of diplomatic pressure, international sanctions, or support from global civil society.

Foreign governments may lend material support to violent resistance campaigns, giving them advantages against powerful adversaries.[65] Many would argue, for example, that Francisco Franco's revolutionary Fascists would have been defeated by the Spanish Republicans without the support of Nazi Germany and Fascist Italy. State sponsors may give direct aid to violent or nonviolent campaigns, depending on the political context and domestic conditions. However, in violent campaigns, external state support may undermine insurgents' incentives to treat civilian populations with restraint, because civilians are viewed as dispensable rather than as the main sources of support.

Hypothesis$_4$: Violent resistance campaigns are more likely than nonviolent campaigns to win outside support in the form of direct state support.

---

63.   On global civil society and NGO support, see Schock, *Unarmed Insurrections,* and Bob, *Marketing Rebellion,* respectively. On the role of transnational advocacy networks in supporting local nonviolent movements, see Margaret Keck and Kathryn Sikkink, *Activists Without Borders: Advocacy Networks in International Politics* (Ithaca, N.Y.: Cornell University Press, 1998).

64.   Bob, *Marketing Rebellion.*

65.   Jeffrey Record, "External Assistance: Enabler of Insurgent Success," *Parameters,* Vol. 36, No. 3 (Autumn 2006), pp. 36–49. State sponsorship of insurgencies and terrorist groups has been an ongoing foreign policy dilemma for decades; see Daniel Byman, *Deadly Connections: States that Sponsor Terrorism* (New York: Cambridge University Press, 2005).

TACTICAL DIVERSITY AND INNOVATION

Strategic innovation occurs with some regularity among both nonviolent and violent campaigns. However, the greater the number of participants from different societal sectors involved in the campaign, the more likely the campaign is to produce tactical innovations. Charles Tilly, Sidney Tarrow, and Kurt Schock have argued that tactical innovation occurs "on the margins of existing repertoires," and as such, "the more expansive the margins, the greater the likelihood of permutation and innovation."[66] We have pointed out earlier that nonviolent campaigns attract a larger number of more diverse participants than violent campaigns because the physical, moral, and informational barriers to mobilization are lower. The diversity of these campaigns therefore privileges them with regard to tactical innovation.[67]

A specific type of tactical diversity is shifting between methods of concentration and methods of dispersion. In methods of concentration, nonviolent campaigns gather large numbers of people in public spaces to engage in civil resistance.[68] Well-known applications of this method include the Chinese student protests in Tiananmen Square or the occupation of Red Square during the Russian Revolution. More recent examples of concentration methods include the mass sit-ins in Maidan Square in Kiev during the Orange Revolution and the creation of a tent city in downtown Beirut during the Lebanese Independence intifada. Methods of dispersion involve acts that are spread out over a wider area, such as consumer boycotts, stay-aways, and "go slow" actions at the workplace. Dispersion methods, like the consumer boycott in South Africa, intentional obstructionism at the workplace by Germans during the French occupation of the Ruhr, labor strikes by oil workers during the Iranian revolution, and the banging of pots and pans by Chileans during the anti-Pinochet movement, force an adversary to spread out its repressive apparatus over a wider area, afford greater protection and anonymity to participants, and allow participants to engage in less risky actions.

Among violent campaigns, tactical diversity could include alternating between concentrated attacks and ambushes in urban areas and more dispersed hit-and-run attacks, bombings, and assassinations in smaller towns and villages. For both violent and nonviolent campaigns, adopting diverse tactics reduces the effectiveness of the adversary's repression and helps the campaign maintain the initiative.[69] Tactical innovation enhances the campaign's adaptability and room for maneuvering when the state focuses its repression on a particular set of tactics. This is especially crucial when the repression makes some tactics, like street protests, highly risky and dangerous.[70]

---

66. Tilly and Tarrow, *Contentious Politics*; Schock, *Unarmed Insurrections*, p. 144.

67. Schock, *Unarmed Insurrections*, p. 144.

68. Schock, *Unarmed Insurrections*, p. 51.

69. Schock, *Unarmed Insurrections*, p. 144.

70. Ibid.

Because tactical innovation occurs on the fringes of a movement, campaigns with larger numbers of participants, and consequently wider margins, are more likely to produce tactical innovations. The relatively larger number of active participants expands the repertoire of sanctions available to nonviolent campaigns, allowing them to shift between methods of concentration and dispersion while maintaining pressure on the adversary.[71] Tactical diversity and innovation enhance the ability of nonviolent resistance to strategically outmaneuver the adversary compared to armed insurgencies. This leads us to the following hypothesis.

Hypothesis₅: Nonviolent resistance campaigns should feature greater tactical diversity and innovation than violent resistance.

Tactical innovation in turn affects the resilience of the campaigns over time, an issue we take up in the next section.

EVASION AND RESILIENCE

Another significant challenge of resistance is opposition resilience, which, writes Schock, "refers to the capacity of contentious actors to continue to mobilize collective action despite the actions of opponents aimed at constraining or inhibiting their activities."[72] Researchers can observe levels of resilience by determining a campaign's ability to maintain a significant number of participants, recruit new members, and continue to confront the adversary in the face of repression.

Many scholars consider resilience a crucial factor of campaign success, because it may determine the ability of the campaign to maintain its strategic advantage despite adversary oppression or attempts at co-optation.[73] Continual regime counterattacks against a resistance campaign can remove key members of the campaign and raise the costs of continued participation among remaining members. Decapitation is often used by states to undermine a campaign's organizational coherence over time.

A common assumption in security studies is that a necessary determinant of resilience is the ability to wage a successful war of attrition against a regime.[74] Seizing territory or enjoying sanctuary from a neighboring

---

71. Schock argues that the more broad-based participation is, the more likely tactical innovations will be. Ibid.

72. Schock, *Unarmed Insurrections,* p. 142

73. Clifford Bob and Sharon Erickson Nepstad, "Kill a Leader, Murder a Movement? Leadership and Assassination in Social Movements," *American Behavioral Scientist,* Vol. 50, No. 10 (June 2007), pp. 1370–1394; Schock, *Unarmed Insurrections;* Ronald A. Francisco, "The Dictator's Dilemma"; Will H. Moore, "Repression and Dissent: Substitution, Context, and Timing," *American Journal of Political Science,* Vol. 42, No. 3 (July 1998), pp. 851–873; Lichbach, "Rethinking Rationality and Rebellion"; Marwan Khawaja, "Repression and Popular Collective Action: Evidence from the West Bank," *Sociological Forum,* Vol. 8, No. 1 (March 1993), pp. 47–71; and Ruud Koopmans, "The Dynamics of Protest Waves: West Germany, 1965 to 1989," *American Sociological Review,* Vol. 58, No. 5 (October 1993), pp. 637–658; and Weinstein, *Inside Rebellion,* p. 45.

74. Weinstein, *Inside Rebellion,* p. 37.

state may allow violent insurgencies to meet two key challenges for resilience—maintaining their membership and recruitment operations in the face of state repression. Though their numbers may be smaller than mass nonviolent campaigns, violent insurgencies may be able to survive for decades, like the Karen insurgency in Burma, which has endured since 1949, and the Revolutionary Armed Forces of Colombia (FARC), which has waged guerrilla warfare against the Colombian state since 1964. Although durable violent campaigns boast impressive stubbornness in the face of repressive and powerful adversaries, longevity does not necessarily translate into strategic success. Isolation in the countryside, in the mountains, or in neighboring safe havens does not necessarily afford violent insurgencies leverage over their state adversaries. The only reason why some violent insurgencies have been able to survive is that they operate in remote areas not penetrated by the state.[75]

Persistence may be necessary to campaign success, but it is insufficient. To achieve success, a campaign must go beyond persistence and achieve a shift in power between the opposition and the adversary. Resilience involves increasing mobilization and action, maintaining key assets and resources, and bringing a diverse constellation of assets and tactics to bear against the adversary, regardless of whether the adversary is materially more powerful. Successful campaigns endure despite regime repression while making tangible progress toward stated goals, even if those goals change over time. Because of the tendency of nonviolent campaigns to involve mass numbers of diverse participants, they should be better suited than violent campaigns to maintain resilience and continue their operations regardless of the adversary's actions. Regime crackdowns arguably debilitate armed campaigns more than similar crackdowns against unarmed campaigns, because of the greater number of potential assets and "weapons" available to nonviolent resistance campaigns.

Hypothesis$_6$: In comparably repressive conditions, nonviolent resistance campaigns should be more resilient than armed campaigns.

This hypothesis clearly challenges the conventional wisdom, but again, we think that the conventional wisdom should withstand empirical tests before it is accepted.

When Violent Campaigns Succeed: Some Key Outliers

It is important to note that there are some important deviations from our assumption that violent campaigns only attract limited numbers of participants. The Russian revolution (1917), the Chinese revolution (1946–1950), the Algerian revolution (1954–1962), the Cuban revolution (1953–1959), and the Vietnamese revolution (1959–1975) come to mind as major examples of violent conflicts that generated mass support sufficient to bring about revolutionary change. Such cases are key outliers to the

---

75. Thanks to Kurt Schock for this point.

argument that nonviolent campaigns are likelier than violent campaigns to galvanize mass participation.

Upon examining the revolutions, however, it is clear that many of the features common to successful nonviolent campaigns occurred in these revolutions—especially diverse, mass mobilization, which led to loyalty shifts within the ruling regimes' economic and military elites, and external supporters. These and other successful armed campaigns typically succeed in building a strong base of popular support while creating parallel administrative, political, social, and economic structures.[76] The importance placed on mass mobilization and civilian non-cooperation by scholars and theorists of revolutionary warfare suggests that the nonviolent components of successful armed campaigns are as significant—possibly even more significant—than the military component.

One must consider, however, the consequences of such victories. Although violent insurgencies captured power in these cases, the human costs were very high, with millions of casualties across these cases. Moreover, the conditions in these countries after the conflict ended have been overwhelmingly more repressive than in transitions driven by nonviolent civic pressure. In all five cases, the new regimes featuring the victorious insurgents were quite harsh toward civilian populations after the dust settled. None of these countries could be classified today as democratic.

Such trends are not limited to these five cases alone. In a 2005 study of 67 regime transitions between 1973 and 2000, Adrian Karatnycky and Peter Ackerman find that among the twenty cases where opposition or state violence occurred, only 4 (20 percent) qualified as "free" (according to 2005 Freedom House criteria) at the time of the study.[77] On the other hand, among 40 cases where the major forces pushing the transition were nonviolent civic coalitions, 32 (80 percent) were classified as "free" at the time of the study.[78] There are some clear theoretical reasons why successful nonviolent resistance leads to fewer civilian casualties and higher levels of democracy after the conflict than successful violent resistance. Victorious violent insurgents often feel compelled to re-establish the monopoly on the use of force, and therefore seek to purge any remaining elements of the state. Although they may seek to establish a democratic order, doing so is difficult under circumstances of constant violent threat from regime leftovers. Even if the violent insurgency enjoyed mass support, the new state led by the former insurgents will quickly attempt to consolidate its

---

76. Mao Tse-tung's writings on revolutionary warfare emphasized the importance of building oppositional consciousness, winning broad-based support, and achieving mass mobilization. The creation of parallel structures and institutions—a form of nonviolent intervention—is another critical component of successful revolutionary warfare. See Gerard Chaliand, ed., *Guerrilla Strategies: An Historical Anthology from the Long March to Afghanistan* (Berkeley: University of California Press, 1982); Walter Lacqueur, *The Guerrilla Reader* (New York: Wildwood House, 1977); SunTzu, *The Art of War*, translated with an introduction by Samuel B. Griffith (London: Oxford University Press, 1963).

77. Karatnycky and Ackerman, *How Freedom is Won*, p. 19.

78. Ibid.

power and remove the ability of the masses to rise up against it. Because the insurgents used violent methods to succeed in gaining power, there are fewer inhibitions against the use of violent methods to maintain power. Indeed, the capacity to do so may only increase. Therefore, although violent insurgency sometimes works, the long-term consequences leave much to be desired.

As for nonviolent campaigns that succeed, it is likely that these successes will become reference points for those particular societies, and nonviolent resistance will be regarded as an effective method of transforming conflicts. This does not suggest that such states become "pacifist" states, but rather that the shift from non-institutional to institutional types of nonviolent means of dealing with dissent is easier, even when normal channels for resolving conflicts are blocked, ineffective, or in the hands of a hostile party. At the same time, the way in which nonviolent resistance tends to decentralize power in society leads to a greater ability of the population to hold elites accountable.[79] Opposition leaders that come to power via nonviolent resistance may feel the need to deliver public goods to the masses, given that failure to respond to their demands may result in yet another ouster. In these ways, mass participation and mobilization through nonviolent action may contribute to a greater sense of trust and accountability when the conflict is over.

Hypothesis₇: Successful nonviolent campaigns will have fewer post-transition casualties and higher levels of democracy than successful violent campaigns.

Summary and Pathways for Future Research

The primary reliance on nonviolent or violent campaign methods may influence the ways that resistance campaigns are able to approach major challenges faced by insurgencies. We explain the historical success of nonviolent resistance by its advantages in meaningful aspects of leverage and resilience relative to violent resistance. In Table 10.1, we identify summary expectations based upon our theoretical discussion.

The discussion above is largely theoretical, but it allows us to introduce a framework for further analysis. We suggest that future studies consider the hypotheses identified in Table 10.2, which provides observable and testable propositions based upon our discussion.

To test these propositions, researchers should collect and analyze cross-national data that distinguish carefully between violent and nonviolent events and campaigns. Existing datasets, such as those developed by Ronald Francisco and Philip Schrodt, provide beginnings by which to

---

79. Thanks to Hardy Merriman for this insight.

Table 10.1.: The Advantages and Disadvantages of Nonviolent and Violent Resistance.

	Where Nonviolent Campaigns Have the Advantage	Where Violent Campaigns Have the Advantage
Participation	Low moral barriers to participation Low physical barriers to participation Informational advantages	Immediate rewards for participation, including social status Presumed therapeutic value Cultural glorifications of violence
Coercion	Coercion based on legitimacy and withdrawal of consent and cooperation by economic, political, and military forces	Physical coercion Economic damage Publicity
Loyalty Shifts and Backfire	Regime loyalty shifts Withdrawal of cooperation and consent	
External Support	International sanctions, NGO assistance, and diplomatic support	State sponsorship
Tactical Diversity and Innovation	Shifts between methods of concentration and dispersion Large numbers lead to tactical diversity, which leads to innovation	
Evasion and Resilience	Shifts between methods of concentration and dispersion Over-extension of the adversary	Survivability and sanctuary Physical defense against adversary

NOTES: These conditions are obviously dependent on a variety of structural and agent-based factors that vary according to each case. Structural factors include regime type, regime repression, country GDP, literacy rates, degree of urbanization, and geopolitical factors. Agency-based or strategic variables include goal selection, leadership and organizational types, and selection and sequencing of tactics.

Table 10.2.: Testable Hypotheses.

Challenge	Hypothesis
Participation	P_1: Nonviolent resistance campaigns are more likely to obtain mass, broad-based participation (including women, children, and elderly) than violent resistance.
Coercion	H_1: When it achieves mass participation, nonviolent resistance is more likely to succeed than armed struggle because it deprives the state of domestic and international political, social, economic, and military support.
Loyalty Shifts and Backfire	H_2: Repression against nonviolent campaigns should induce loyalty shifts within the regime and generate more acts of anti-regime mobilization than repression against violent campaigns.
External Support	H_3: Nonviolent resistance campaigns are more likely than armed campaigns to win outside support in the form of diplomatic pressure, international sanctions, or support from global civil society. H_4: Violent resistance campaigns are more likely than nonviolent campaigns to win outside support in the form of direct state support.
Tactical Diversity and Innovation	H_5: Nonviolent resistance campaigns should feature greater tactical diversity and innovation than violent resistance.
Evasion and Resilience	H_6: In comparably repressive conditions, nonviolent resistance campaigns should be more resilient than armed campaigns.
Post-Conflict Stability	H_7: Successful nonviolent campaigns will have fewer post-transition casualties and higher levels of democracy than successful violent campaigns.

test these hypotheses.[80] Many of the hypotheses listed here, however, require greater detail than is available in country-year datasets. As such, researchers should seek out primary source material to assess the relative influence of nonviolent and violent campaigns on the decisions of policymakers. To obtain such information, researchers may require access to the policymakers themselves, or to their archives, such as those used by Harris Mylonas in this volume. Additionally, public opinion surveys that compare attitudes toward nonviolent and violent campaigns are scarce. To delve into problems of legitimacy and loyalty, which are at the heart

80. See, for example, Ronald A. Francisco, "European Protest and Coercion Data," available at http://web.ku.edu/ronfran/data/index.html; and Philip Schrodt, "Kansas Event Data System Project," http://web.ku.edu/keds/index.html. Many data sets focus on violent conflict or are ambiguous about whether events are violent or nonviolent.

of many of these hypotheses, extensive micro-level research is required.

In the meantime, this chapter emphasizes that nonviolent resistance is worthy of empirical examination as a functional alternative to armed insurgency. Scholars need not analyze violent or nonviolent forms of resistance in isolation of their strategic alternatives.

Conclusion

To the extent that a resistance campaign can separate the adversary from its main sources of economic, social, political, and military support through sustained pressure (domestically and through third parties) and remain resilient in the face of repression, it is likely to succeed. At the same time, we have argued that mass participation in the resistance is a critical factor in determining a movement's ability to achieve leverage. When a regime can no longer rely on the obedience and cooperation of its erstwhile domestic and international allies for its economic, political, diplomatic, or military sources of power, its ability to maintain control is seriously undermined, and this may lead to a regime's ouster or the withdrawal of a foreign occupier. A campaign's reliance on nonviolent methods—even extremely disruptive ones—may make the adversary's characterizations of the campaigns as extremist less credible, while also making the regime more introspective about yielding concessions.

If, as we argue, nonviolent resistance can be strategically superior to violent resistance, then why does violent resistance occur at all? What compels members of erstwhile nonviolent resistance movements to adopt violent resistance? The chapters in the second part of this volume have focused on these specific questions from the point of view of non-state opposition groups, but many fruitful avenues of research remain.

Contributors

Kristin M. Bakke is Lecturer in Political Science at University College London. She received her Ph.D. from the University of Washington in Seattle. She has published articles on the effects of decentralization on intrastate conflicts and on intergroup relations in post-conflict societies.

Emily Beaulieu is Assistant Professor at the University of Kentucky. She studies political protest strategies, particularly in electoral settings. Her work has appeared in *Comparative Political Studies,* and she is currently working on a book-length manuscript about the consequences of election-related protest for democracy in the developing world.

H. Zeynep Bulutgil is a Postdoctoral Research Associate at the Empirical Studies of Conflict Project at the Woodrow Wilson School of Public and International Affairs at Princeton University. Her dissertation, "Territorial Conflict and Ethnic Cleansing," focuses on the causes of ethnic cleansing in Europe.

Erica Chenoweth is Assistant Professor of Government at Wesleyan University, where she founded the Program on Terrorism and Insurgency Research in 2008. She earned an M.A. and Ph.D. in political science at the University of Colorado at Boulder. She has been an Associate (2008–2010) and Postdoctoral Research Fellow (2006–2008) at the Belfer Center for Science and International Affairs at the Harvard Kennedy School and has also held fellowships at the University of California at Berkeley and the University of Maryland.

Kathryn McNabb Cochran is a Ph.D. candidate in Political Science at Duke University with concentrations in international relations and political methodology. Her dissertation, "Strong Horse or Paper Tiger? Assessing the Reputational Effects of War Outcomes," investigates the conditions under which third parties are more or less likely to challenge the combatants in the aftermath of war. In 2008, her paper, "International Competition and the Spread of Democracy: The Effects of Selection, Emulation, and Socialization," won the Midwest Political Science Association award for the best paper in international relations.

Kathleen Gallagher Cunningham is Assistant Professor at Iowa State University and a Senior Researcher at the Center for the Study of Civil War at the International Peace Research Institute in Oslo, Norway. Her research is based primarily on the politics of self-determination and on ethnic and civil conflict, and has appeared in *International Studies Quarterly*. She is currently working on a book about self-determination politics and a project on leadership in rebellion.

Alexander B. Downes is Assistant Professor of Political Science at Duke University. He is the author of *Targeting Civilians in War* (Ithaca, N.Y.: Cornell University Press, 2008), winner of the 2008 Joseph Lepgold Book Prize from Georgetown University. He spent the 2007–2008 academic year as a Research Fellow at the Belfer Center for Science and International Affairs at the Harvard Kennedy School, and previously held fellowships at the Olin Institute for Strategic Studies at Harvard University and the Center for International Security and Cooperation at Stanford University.

Erin K. Jenne is Associate Professor in the International Relations and European Studies Department at Central European University in Budapest. She is currently in residence as a Fernand Braudel Fellow at the European University Institute in Florence, Italy. Her most recent book, *Ethnic Bargaining: The Paradox of Minority Empowerment* (Ithaca, N.Y.: Cornell University Press, 2007) is the winner of the 2007 Edgar S. Furniss Book Award from the Mershon Center for International Security Studies at The Ohio State University.

Stathis N. Kalyvas is Arnold Wolfers Professor in the Department of Political Science, Director of the Program on Order, Conflict, and Violence, and Co-Director of the Hellenic Studies Program at Yale University.

Adria Lawrence is Assistant Professor of Political Science at Yale University and a Research Fellow at the MacMillan Center for International and Area Studies. Her research considers how people come to mobilize in favor of ideologies such as ethnicity, nationalism, religion, and democracy. She is currently working on *Imperial Rule and the Politics of Nationalism*, a book about nationalist opposition in the French Empire. She was a Research Fellow at the Belfer Center for Science and International Affairs at the Harvard Kennedy School from 2007–2008, and has also held fellowships from the Olin Institute for Strategic Studies at Harvard University and the Harry Frank Guggenheim Foundation.

Harris Mylonas is Assistant Professor of Political Science and International Affairs at the Elliott School of International Affairs at George Washington University. His research focuses on nation- and state-building, as well as immigrant and refugee incorporation policies. For the 2008–2009 academic year, he was a Fellow at the Harvard Academy for International and Area Studies, where he worked on *Making Nations: The International Politics of Assimilation, Accommodation, and Exclusion*, a book manuscript on state policies toward minorities in the Balkans.

Wendy Pearlman is Assistant Professor of Political Science and the Crown Junior Chair in Middle East Studies at Northwestern University. She has held fellowships sponsored by Fulbright, the U.S. Institute of Peace, and the Belfer Center for Science and International Affairs at the Harvard Kennedy School.

Maria J. Stephan is a strategic planner at the U.S. Department of State. Previously, she served as the Director of Policy and Research at the International Center on Nonviolent Conflict (ICNC), a non-profit organization that develops and advocates the use of nonviolent strategies to defend rights and freedoms around the world. She has taught at the School of Foreign Service at Georgetown University and at the School of International Service at American University. She is the editor of *Civilian Jihad: Nonviolent Struggle, Democratization, and Governance in the Middle East* (New York: Palgrave Macmillan, 2010).

INDEX

Belfer Center Studies in International Security

Published by The MIT Press

Sean M. Lynn-Jones and Steven E. Miller, series editors
Karen Motley, executive editor
Belfer Center for Science and International Affairs
John F. Kennedy School of Government, Harvard University

Acharya, Amitav, and Evelyn Goh, eds., *Reassessing Security Cooperation in the Asia-Pacific* (2007)

Agha, Hussein, Shai Feldman, Ahmad Khalidi, and Zeev Schiff, *Track-II Diplomacy: Lessons from the Middle East* (2003)

Allison, Graham T., Owen R. Coté, Jr., Richard A. Falkenrath, and Steven E. Miller, *Avoiding Nuclear Anarchy: Containing the Threat of Loose Russian Nuclear Weapons and Fissile Material* (1996)

Allison, Graham T., and Kalypso Nicolaïdis, eds., *The Greek Paradox: Promise vs. Performance* (1996)

Arbatov, Alexei, Abram Chayes, Antonia Handler Chayes, and Lara Olson, eds., *Managing Conflict in the Former Soviet Union: Russian and American Perspectives* (1997)

Bennett, Andrew, Condemned to Repetition? *The Rise, Fall, and Reprise of Soviet-Russian Military Interventionism, 1973–1996* (1999)

Blackwill, Robert D., and Paul Dibb, eds., *America's Asian Alliances* (2000)

Blackwill, Robert D., and Michael Stürmer, eds., *Allies Divided: Transatlantic Policies for the Greater Middle East* (1997)

Blum, Gabriella, and Philip B. Heymann, *Laws, Outlaws, and Terrorists: Lessons from the War on Terrorism* (2010)

Brom, Shlomo, and Yiftah Shapir, eds., *The Middle East Military Balance 1999–2000* (1999)

Brom, Shlomo, and Yiftah Shapir, eds., *The Middle East Military Balance 2001–2002* (2002)

Brown, Michael E., ed., *The International Dimensions of Internal Conflict* (1996)

Brown, Michael E., and Šumit Ganguly, eds., *Fighting Words: Language Policy and Ethnic Relations in Asia* (2003)

Brown, Michael E., and Šumit Ganguly, eds., *Government Policies and Ethnic Relations in Asia and the Pacific* (1997)

Carter, Ashton B., and John P. White, eds., *Keeping the Edge: Managing Defense for the Future* (2001)

Chenoweth, Erica, and Adria Lawrence, eds., *Rethinking Violence: States and Non-state Actors in Conflict* (2010)

de Nevers, Renée, *Comrades No More: The Seeds of Political Change in Eastern Europe* (2003)

Elman, Colin, and Miriam Fendius Elman, eds., *Bridges and Boundaries: Historians, Political Scientists, and the Study of International Relations* (2001)

Elman, Colin, and Miriam Fendius Elman, eds., *Progress in International Relations Theory: Appraising the Field* (2003)

Elman, Miriam Fendius, ed., *Paths to Peace: Is Democracy the Answer?* (1997)

Falkenrath, Richard A., *Shaping Europe's Military Order: The Origins and Consequences of the CFE Treaty* (1994)

Falkenrath, Richard A., Robert D. Newman, and Bradley A. Thayer, *America's Achilles' Heel: Nuclear, Biological, and Chemical Terrorism and Covert Attack* (1998)

Feaver, Peter D., and Richard H. Kohn, eds., Soldiers and Civilians: *The Civil-Military Gap and American National Security* (2001)

Feldman, Shai, *Nuclear Weapons and Arms Control in the Middle East* (1996)

Feldman, Shai, and Yiftah Shapir, eds., *The Middle East Military Balance 2000–2001* (2001)

Forsberg, Randall, ed., *The Arms Production Dilemma: Contraction and Restraint in the World Combat Aircraft Industry* (1994)

George, Alexander L., and Andrew Bennett, *Case Studies and Theory Development in the Social Sciences* (2005)

Gilroy, Curtis, and Cindy Williams, eds., *Service to Country: Personnel Policy and the Transformation of Western Militaries* (2007)

Hagerty, Devin T., *The Consequences of Nuclear Proliferation: Lessons from South Asia* (1998)

Heymann, Philip B., *Terrorism and America: A Commonsense Strategy for a Democratic Society* (1998)

Heymann, Philip B., *Terrorism, Freedom, and Security: Winning without War* (2003)

Heymann, Philip B., and Juliette N. Kayyem, *Protecting Liberty in an Age of Terror* (2005)

Howitt, Arnold M., and Robyn L. Pangi, eds., *Countering Terrorism: Dimensions of Preparedness* (2003)

Hudson, Valerie M., and Andrea M. den Boer, *Bare Branches: The Security Implications of Asia's Surplus Male Population* (2004)

Kayyem, Juliette N., and Robyn L. Pangi, eds., *First to Arrive: State and Local Responses to Terrorism* (2003)

Kokoshin, Andrei A., *Soviet Strategic Thought, 1917–91* (1998)

Lederberg, Joshua, ed., *Biological Weapons: Limiting the Threat* (1999)

Mansfield, Edward D., and Jack Snyder, *Electing to Fight: Why Emerging Democracies Go to War* (2005)

Martin, Lenore G., and Dimitris Keridis, eds., *The Future of Turkish Foreign Policy* (2004)

May, Ernest R., and Philip D. Zelikow, eds., *Dealing with Dictators: Dilemmas of U.S. Diplomacy and Intelligence Analysis, 1945–1990* (2007)

Shaffer, Brenda, *Borders and Brethren: Iran and the Challenge of Azerbaijani Identity* (2002)

Shaffer, Brenda, ed., *The Limits of Culture: Islam and Foreign Policy* (2006)

Shields, John M., and William C. Potter, eds., *Dismantling the Cold War: U.S. and NIS Perspectives on the Nunn-Lugar Cooperative Threat Reduction Program* (1997)

Tucker, Jonathan B., ed., *Toxic Terror: Assessing Terrorist Use of Chemical and Biological Weapons* (2000)

Utgoff, Victor A., ed., *The Coming Crisis: Nuclear Proliferation, U.S. Interests, and World Order* (2000)

Williams, Cindy, ed., *Filling the Ranks: Transforming the U.S. Military Personnel System* (2004)

Williams, Cindy, ed., *Holding the Line: U.S. Defense Alternatives for the Early 21st Century* (2001)

Belfer Center for Science and International Affairs

Graham Allison, Director
John F. Kennedy School of Government
Harvard University
79 JFK Street, Cambridge, MA 02138
Tel: (617) 495-1400; Fax: (617) 495-8963
http://belfercenter.ksg.harvard.edu   belfer_center@hks.harvard.edu

The Belfer Center is the hub of the Harvard Kennedy School's research, teaching, and training in international security affairs, environmental and resource issues, and science and technology policy.

The Center has a dual mission: (1) to provide leadership in advancing policy-relevant knowledge about the most important challenges of international security and other critical issues where science, technology, environmental policy, and international affairs intersect; and (2) to prepare future generations of leaders for these arenas. Center researchers not only conduct scholarly research, but also develop prescriptions for policy reform. Faculty and fellows analyze global challenges from nuclear proliferation and terrorism to climate change and energy policy.

The Belfer Center's leadership begins with the recognition of science and technology as driving forces constantly transforming both the challenges we face and the opportunities for problem solving. Building on the vision of founder Paul Doty, the Center addresses serious global concerns by integrating insights and research of social scientists, natural scientists, technologists, and practitioners in government, diplomacy, the military, and business.

The heart of the Belfer Center is its resident research community of more than 150 scholars, including Harvard faculty, researchers, practitioners, and each year a new, international, interdisciplinary group of research fellows. Through publications and policy discussions, workshops, seminars, and conferences, the Center promotes innovative solutions to significant national and international challenges.

The Center's International Security Program, directed by Steven E. Miller, publishes the Belfer Center Studies in International Security, and sponsors and edits the quarterly journal *International Security*.

The Center is supported by an endowment established with funds from Robert and Renée Belfer, the Ford Foundation, and Harvard University, by foundation grants, by individual gifts, and by occasional government contracts.